Praise for Jules Feiffer's
Backing into Forward

"A thoughtful, introspective cartoonist who can also write beautifully? Yes, it is possible. *Backing into Forward* is vivid, buoyant, and even a little discomfiting in its candor. I couldn't put down."

CHRIS WARE

"*Backing into Forward* . . . succeeds in sounding like the best of Mr. Feiffer's cartoons: funny, acerbic, subversive, fiercely attuned to the absurdities in his own life and in the country at large."

MICHIKO KAKUTANI, *New York Times*

"*Backing into Forward* is dark and charming, touching and barbed and crackling with wit. An important book by a critical artist that sheds light on his fascinating life and the most vibrant period in the life of American culture."

MICHAEL CHABON

"Reading Feiffer, you know where the truth lies because it is there on every page—resonant, self-lacerating and frequently hilarious. . . . The voice in *Backing into Forward* is not spry, not pretty energetic for an old person, but youthful, full of insouciance, vanity and playfulness. While other accomplished men bronze their success or dip it in amber, Feiffer treats his own as one big, wonderful caper."

DAVID CARR, *New York Times Book Review*

"Jules Feiffer, prolific hand and eye behind so many brilliant comics, screenplays, novels, illustrations and now this fine, humane autobiography, remains one of the signature voices of a long era of American satire and dissent, the bridge from Lenny Bruce to *The Simpsons*."

JONATHAN LETHEM

"'Have you noticed my cartoon voice is more ambivalent than my writer's voice?' a cartooned Feiffer asks at the book's end. Maybe. Or you could say that his pictures and words work in complex harmony, yielding more layers of insight and pleasure. . . . *Backing into Forward* is a fine companion to his art. It's also an illuminating book about the creative process, an entertaining read, and a cautionary tale about an era that really doesn't deserve a memorial."

JULIE PHILLIPS, *Village Voice*

"Jules Feiffer's original and neurotic voice—expressing the whiny child in every adult and the world-weary sophisticate inside every kid—reinvented comics in the 1950s and made possible what's now called the 'graphic novel.' His engaging new memoir is told in that same witty and perceptive New York cadence, now mellowed and laced with wisdom. He's an inspiration."

ART SPIEGELMAN

"For those of us for whom *Sick Sick Sick* was the first glimmer of cool, who fled to the *Village Voice* for forty years to get Feiffer's take on our American disasters, and who learned the dark truth about men from *Carnal Knowledge*, this is the book that finally explains how one guy did all that. *Backing into Forward* is not only a hilarious memoir by the dazzling, discomfiting comet that is Jules Feiffer, but a rambunctious and vivid cultural history by an American master."

HONOR MOORE

"Can you smile and grit your teeth at the same time? That's what Jules Feiffer's hilarious, savage memoir makes you want to do. Don't miss it."

ANTHONY LEWIS

"Self-lacerating and hilarious, well written, smart—in short, unfailing Feiffer."

PETER MATTHIESSEN

BACKING INTO FORWARD

Jules Feiffer

BACKING INTO FORWARD

A MEMOIR

The University of Chicago Press

The University of Chicago Press, Chicago 60637
Copyright © 2010 by Jules Feiffer
All rights reserved
University of Chicago Press edition 2012
Printed in the United States of America

21 20 19 18 17 16 15 14 13 12   1 2 3 4 5

Published by arrangement with Nan A. Talese, an imprint of The Knopf
Doubleday Publishing Group, a division of Random House, Inc.

Portions of this work originally appeared in *Martha's Vineyard
Magazine*, *On Writing*, and *The South Hampton Review*.

Illustration credits can be found on page 447.

ISBN-13: 978-0-226-24035-0 (paper)
ISBN-10: 0-226-24035-5 (paper)

Library of Congress Cataloging-in-Publication Data
Feiffer, Jules.
Backing into forward : a memoir / Jules Feiffer. p. cm.
ISBN-13: 978-0-226-24035-0 (paperback : alkaline paper)
ISBN-10: 0-226-24035-5 (paperback : alkaline paper)
1. Feiffer, Jules. 2. Authors, American—20th century—Biography.
3. Cartoonists—United States—Biography.   I. Title.
PS3556.E42Z46 2012   818'.5409—dc22   [B]
2011035542

♾ This paper meets the requirements of
ANSI/NISO Z39.48-1992 (Permanence of Paper).

For my children, my grandchild, my future grandchildren—

Success is nothing to sneeze at but failure, too,
offers great possibilities.
And always remember, do not let your judges define you.

"Unlearn"

—LINCOLN STEFFENS

Contents

BACKING INTO FORWARD

Part One

GUNSLINGER

BOY CARTOONIST

Food was out to get me. Food devoured me with every mouthful I took. I chewed for minutes without being able to swallow. I gagged, spit up into a napkin, then secretly shook the remains into the garbage when my mother's back was turned. She didn't suspect.

Much in the manner of immigrant Jewish mothers of her time and circumstance, my mother placed all her hopes and dreams on me. She wanted me to be big and healthy. But I wouldn't cooperate. I was small for my age and underweight for any age. I could count my own ribs when I stripped down to my shorts.

"It's good for you," was her unpersuasive catch phrase as she tried to shovel noodle pudding down my throat. "It's your favorite," she insisted against the evidence of my tightly sealed lips. "I have no time for this," she pleaded.

She had anointed me, the only male child in the family, to succeed where she had not. But at the rate I was going, I had three months to live. Or so my mother worried. I knew I'd do fine if I could only get away from her noodle pudding. I despised her noodle pudding.

My mother had failed to live up to her early promise as a fashion designer. It was never clear why her career had gone flat, but what was clear, much too clear, was how she toiled, night and day, over her drawing table stationed in a corner of our living room, sandwiched between the piano no one knew how to play and the bookcase stacked with Russian, French, and English novels (read by my father) and uplifting essays by Emerson and others (studied by my mother). She drew her fashion sketches, cloaks and suits they were called, in pencil and lightly tinted watercolor. Three days a week she packed them up and subwayed down to the Garment District on Seventh Avenue, where she peddled them door-to-door to dress manufacturers. Each sketch earned her three dollars. Since my father perennially failed at business and his various other jobs didn't last that long, it was my mother's three-dollar sketches that brought us through hard times.

She performed dutifully the roles of breadwinner, wife, and mother, unsought obligations inflicted on her by a bad choice in husbands and the Great Depression. She was said to be good at design, but how was I to know? Except for superheroes in tights and capes, I was indifferent to fashion. But from an early age I was forced to observe how absent pleasure was from her work, how often she mentioned the strain, her headaches, her throbbing temples—

I was meant to grow up to right the wrong of her stalled career, undermined by my grandparents, who prodded her into marrying Dave Feiffer. So much had been taken from her, small wonder the anxiety she brought to raising me. Her offers of food felled me like a battering ram. She pushed, cajoled, browbeat, destroyed my appetite for the very things she offered. "Eat, it's delicious," "You'll love this, you know you'll love this." This is not the job she wanted. What she wanted was to get on with the day, get back to her drawing board, dive deep into the world of fashion, which, though it offered few rewards, remained her single escape from this marriage she was drafted into. Her aim was to stuff me at least to the extent that I wasn't a physical embarrassment to the neighbors, a reproach to her reputation as a mother, forty pounds at seven years, my reminder of her failure.

I had my appetites, not for food but for comics. I didn't see that food had anything in it to sustain me. I ate only because I wanted to be a good boy. I wanted to keep my mother happy. Not that I, or anyone else, could keep her happy. But more about not keeping my mother happy later.

Comics: I ate them, I breathed them, I thought about them day and night. I learned to read only so that I could read comics. Nothing else was worth the effort. Marginalized from every aspect of the Bronx world I inhabited, my only escape was a life of escapism: reading comics, going to movies, listening to radio serials and favored comedians—Jack Armstrong, *I Love a Mystery, Fibber McGee and Molly,* Charlie McCarthy, Jack Benny, Burns and Allen—each transporting me out of real life into a totally impossible fantasy reality that I bought as a metaphor for my future.

My alternate dream was to someday work myself into the ranks of the great cartoonists. Getting to the top, where I'd be invited to hang out with Milton Caniff of *Terry and the Pirates,* Will Eisner of *The Spirit,* Roy Crane of *Wash Tubbs and Captain Easy,* E. C. Segar of *Popeye,* Raeburn Van Buren of *Abbie an' Slats,* Alex Raymond of *Flash Gordon,* Al Capp of *Li'l Abner* . . .

These men were *heroes!* Brilliance in four-paneled daily strips and full-page gloriously colored Sunday extravaganzas that they routinely created. I loved the look, the dazzling interplay of words and pictures that leaped off the comics page at me, a preferred universe to the one I was mired in. But not for long. If I had anything to say about it. I lived in circumstances where I was poor (a drawback in real life, an incitement to high adventure and rags to riches in comics), where I was small and powerless, so inadequate that I couldn't bat, throw, or catch a ball (a disaster in real life, but in comics a self-imposed limitation that hid my superpowers from evildoers).

I could have used superpowers. If you grew up poor in the Bronx during the Great Depression, missing out on the joys of boyhood as others knew them—baseball, football, basketball (fun for others, failed challenges for me)—then what was your way out? A fantasy of fame and fortune as a cartoonist! So went my exit strategy.

The scenario begins with my own Bronx version of a movie Western shootout. It's Saturday. It's summer. It's Stratford Avenue in the Soundview area of the East Bronx. Five- and six-story dreary brick apartment houses line the streets. Brown, gray, and rust are the colors that dominate. On the corner of Stratford and Westchester, the Lexington Avenue El clatters by, noticeably noisiest in the middle of the night. Kaminkowitz's drugstore is on the corner of Stratford, next to Horowitz's vegetable store, next to a vacant lot. I worked at Kaminkowitz's as a delivery boy when I was eleven and twelve.

Pensky's candy store is across the street, the near corner. Pensky was important to my life because his store was where I scanned comic books before buying them. Pensky also had a soda fountain and gum ball machines and, in a booth at the back of the store, one of the few phones on the block. If my mother got a call, Pensky sent a kid (in the store for a candy or a soda) up Stratford to our house, 1235, to call my mother to the window. "Mrs. Feiffer, you're wanted on the phone!" the kid shouted from the street.

My mother walked three flights down, meandered to the store (she had two speeds: slow and slower), ambled into Pensky's, said, "I have a phone call, Mr. Pensky?" as if it had to be a mistake, thanked Pensky correctly but without feeling (he was a tradesman, she was a snob), and then, no matter how hot the day, closed herself off in the phone booth to take the call.

My mother minded her own business and wanted Pensky to mind his. And her children to mind ours. She kept secrets, who knew how many and of what gravity? Secrets about finances, about family, about family and finances, about disappointments, about betrayals, about debt and more debt, about so much that she couldn't let on, could only hint at: "You're not old enough. I'll tell you when you're old enough."

My mother's secrets gave depth to her rigidity. And God knows, for a woman who started out a blithe spirit, the abuses that broke but did not bend her succeeded in alienating all three of her children, who were incipient blithe spirits themselves.

S he was not affectionate. Not a hugger, a holder, a kisser, a squeezer, or a pincher. She didn't go in for bodily contact, certainly not with my father. I've suspected for a long time that mine was a virginal birth. I can't prove it. But in my life I've never been in much of a position to prove anything. My motto has been: Even if you have to make it up, move on. That's just one of my mottos. My other motto is: Duck!

So I'm back in the Bronx in the 1930s, which I'm told was a fine place to be if you were a different kind of poor Jewish boy than I was. I hear, now and again, from Bronx nostalgia associations and Web sites set up for expats who remember their Bronx childhoods fondly, romantically, a bit misty-eyed. That's not how I remember it: Walking down three flights of narrow stairs from Apartment 2-F at 1235 Stratford. I have a piece of chalk in my hand instead of a gun. But walking down those stairs and out the door into the sunlight is a little like walking down a lone Western street through the swinging doors of a saloon. Gunfighters everywhere—they know they can take me. I know they can take me. My three-year-old sister, Alice, who worships the ground I walk on, even *she* knows they can take me.

But of course it's not a saloon, it's the very block I live on. My enemies are armed not with guns but with balls and baseball gloves and broomsticks. And they know when they see me walking out my front door (if they do see me, which I doubt), that I am of absolutely no consequence. I can't hit, I can't throw, I can't catch.

I was missing a basic Bronx gene, the ball-playing gene. It seemed that every kid had it but me. Later, John F. Kennedy was to famously say, "Life is not fair." He was never to know that, a generation earlier, I had proved his point over and over again.

Anyhow, back to the scenario: I have chalk, that's my weapon. They have balls and sticks and gloves. They outsize, outweigh, and outgun me. I don't know what I'm doing out here. I wouldn't be here, but my mother made me. "You can't stay in the house and draw all day." "You need fresh air." "Go out and play."

Play? If she paid attention to anything but her own rules, she'd know that I *can't* play. I am physically at odds with sports. My body has been fitted with a hand that can draw but can't catch or field a ball. She is sending her only son out to die.

Hence the piece of chalk in my hand. At seven I have begun to strategize. If no one else, not my mother, not my father, is aware enough to look after my survival, then it's up to me. Chalk is my weapon, the sidewalk my battleground. While they, the other, the enemy, the kids with size and muscles and coordination, take over the street, a dozen or more, batting balls, fielding base hits in and around traffic, I establish my terrain, down on my knees on the sidewalk. I draw in large, brash strokes. I don't know

Popeye by Jules, age seven

what it is until I've laid down the first lines. It's . . . Popeye. Next I do
Wimpy. I do a better Popeye than a Wimpy, but it beats any Wimpy these
jocks can draw.

One or two of the athletes wander over. They trot off their turf, the
street, over to my gallery on the sidewalk.

"Hey, it's Popeye."

Duh.

"Can you draw Dick Tracy?"

I can and I do. And I am fast. They are startled by my speed.

"Can you draw Tom Mix?"

Tom Mix is a favorite cowboy star of the thirties. I draw a ten-gallon-
hatted gunslinger firing with both barrels. It doesn't matter that it doesn't
look like Tom Mix. The growing crowd is responding to me, the fastest
chalk in the West.

Of course, after five or ten minutes they are bored and go back to their game. Besides, I have a limited repertoire, only so many cowboys and cartoon characters that I know how to draw or fake draw. But it doesn't matter, I've made my point, I've taken my ground: the sidewalk. And on that sidewalk I've carved out a niche for myself in the neighborhood. I'm the *artist*.

I've won respect if not acceptance. Admiration if not friendship. I've drawn myself into the pecking order. It's an early use—perhaps my earliest—of a basic survivor's technique: backing into recognition.

I figured out what the jocks couldn't do that I could. I could draw. They couldn't. I used their lack of talent to prove that even though I wasn't a ball player I was visible, I existed! Inadvertently, I had stumbled onto the use of comics as judo. Talk about epiphanies.

Jules at nine

COMICS CARAVAN

I have before me a slightly soiled but amazingly intact copy of the *Comics Caravan,* dated July 1940. I was eleven when I wrote and drew it, dating my creations just as the real comic books in Pensky's candy store were dated, months ahead of their appearance. I did my best to imitate the pros, so my *Comics Caravan* dated for July was probably drawn in April. Comic books were sold at sixty-four pages for a dime. My comics, drawn in pencil, were also sixty-four pages but I notice the price on the cover is nine cents, so either I saw myself as a penny less competent than the pros or I was trying to undersell them.

A ribbon running under the title of the *Comics Caravan* reads, "Lightning, Fast Action, Adventure." And on the cover we see a masked superhero, the Dial Man, slugging a knife-wielding bad guy, while unbeknownst to him, a huge packing crate hurtles toward him from above, a millisecond away from smashing him to pieces.

In little boxes on the cover on the far left are featured four other characters who fill out the comic book: *The Streak* (stolen from *The Flash*), *The Flower Man, Stormy Craig,* and *Ruff Rawson,* all unabashed copies of admired comic book or newspaper strips.

And so went my after-school days and weekends at ages ten, eleven, and twelve. If I wasn't reading comics, I was making up my own. Sixty-four pages a week, stories and art by Jules Feiffer under a series of pseudonyms, so that the imaginary readers would be fooled into thinking that this outpouring of work (*Radio Comics, Star Comics, Streak Comics*) was turned out by a diverse staff. On page 48 of *Comics Caravan,* for example, I see that *Gunner Dixon* is credited to the writing-drawing team of Rogers and Craig, in imitation not only of Jerry Siegel and Joe Shuster's soldier-of-fortune hero, Slam Bradley, but of their joint authorship as well. *The Flower Man,* which follows, is by George Smith and, six pages on, *Ruff Rawson.*

Here's how Roger and Craig's *Gunner Dixon* begins:

Entering New York Gunner Dixon two-fisted adventurer gets into
a mess of trouble.
    "New York at last!"
    "Swell to be back!"
    "Step on it!"
    "Hey watch out you crazy fool!"
    "Who d'ya think ya are lug!"
    "I got a good minds to slug ya!"
    "Better luck next time!"
    "Get him!"
    "He hit the boss!"
    "Break it up!"
    "Don't hit me!"
    "Leggo!"
    "Who are they anyhow?"
    "Brother your playin' with dynamite! That's boss Kelly!"

I was passionate about these underwritten, speedily sketched enter-prises. They meant my life. My mother urged me to get out of the house, and I couldn't understand why. Hiding out in my room drawing comics was far more rewarding than anything I could possibly find in the alter-nately deadly dull and scary streets. Out in the street, I wasn't the best of anything. But in my bedroom I was the best cartoonist. And on my block I was the best cartoonist. In my school I was the best cartoonist! My dream and my scheme were to take over the world as best cartoonist. But that required practice, practice, practice.

I tried to draw in different styles to fool the reader. One style was bor-rowed from Milton Caniff, whose *Terry and the Pirates* had an increasingly

hypnotic effect on me. Caniff was a master of complex light and dark shading and contrast, of movie-angle shots, alternating long shots, medium shots, and close-ups.

If I couldn't design a page or draw as well as Caniff, at least I could steal from him. In comic book parlance, stealing was known as "swiping." Not only did I swipe from Caniff, but in my other comics I swiped from Alex Raymond, whose slick and elegantly illustrated Sunday-page *Flash Gordon* was an enormous influence on everyone, including, years later, George Lucas in *Star Wars*. I even swiped from the swipers, whom I could imitate better than the big boys because I found their level of proficiency less of a challenge.

There was no onus to swiping other cartoonists' art. Looking *not* like yourself was a goal to shoot for. Extraordinary work was out there for the taking, why restrict oneself? I preferred Caniff's look and Alex Raymond's and, not to be ignored, Hal Foster's *Prince Valiant* and Burne Hogarth's *Tarzan*. So many riches out there to be plundered. I plundered, proudly.

Caniff's movielike action sequences, strong on atmosphere and eloquent silences, inspired me, among others, to wholesale thievery of his art.

Above, but one of many "swipes" where I did my best to make the Caniff look my own.

THE BAR MITZVAH HOSTAGE

As far back as I can remember, religion was a puzzle to me that I had no interest in solving. I understood what it did for others, but I could never figure out what it could do for me. As a kid, I would see on my walks Jews on their way to shul, Catholics coming out of church, and I remember thinking: "They actually do this, I mean, outside of movies?"

I understood the role of God in movies. He was in place to be on our side. I was meant to admire and did admire the GIs that crossed themselves before going into battle. I understood that the enemy didn't do that. We did that. And in a way, it made sense in movies, the way everything else made sense, but it wasn't understood to work that way in the real world. From Fred and Ginger to the rewards of worship, it didn't work that way in the real world.

It wasn't that I lacked faith. I was an American boy: I believed, oh yes, I believed. In movies, in comics, in radio, in the New York Yankees . . . I believed in FDR and the New Deal, I believed in the perfectibility of man, I believed that all men were brothers (women had not yet been metaphored into the club), I believed that if I did unto others that they would do unto me, I believed in the rational, the idealistic, the essential goodness of man—and that I was an integral part of the American dream. I believed that I was destined to be a famous cartoonist and that would change my life—and I believed that my life very much needed changing. So I had more faith than I knew what to do with. It just didn't seem to have anything to do with Jews or God, who, I could see from the facts of my life, were almost never on my side.

Rhoda, Jules, and Dave Feiffer, 1940

Rhoda Feiffer, 1938

Mimi and Jules, 1932

Cousin Harriet Davis, Mimi (top), Jules, and Alice, 1938

Years before I lost my faith in God, my mother's sister Celia and her husband, Eugene, became Christian Scientists, less a conversion than an evasion. They slid from Jewishness to not-Jewishness, a halfway station of the cross on their way to Protestantism. In my youth Christian Science seemed to recruit Jews with a little money or a lot of money who left the Bronx and Brooklyn behind in order to walk the walk and talk the talk of Riverdale and Westchester.

The rest of us, without money, were left in the boroughs with our immigrant parents, who neither knew nor cared how they fit in. Their Jewishness made the Atlantic crossing, abandoning the old-time orthodoxy for an ad hoc mishmash of liberalism, socialism, Communism, and Trotskyism, all very secular except you went to shul on the High Holy Days. The Communists, Trotskyites, and Socialists worked very hard at not getting along with each other. The noise brought on in the neighborhood by the embattled factions of left-wing idealism could be deafening.

My parents took no part in the debate. They steered clear of anything that smacked of grown-up argument. My mother restricted her confrontations to her children, only one of whom (Mimi) argued back, while my father remained above the fray, passive and dismissive.

My block, Stratford, was, except for two or three Italian families, rigorously Jewish. A block over, Morrison, was Italian and Catholic. We got along by staying apart. Now and then there were block wars. Their kids invaded our block (or vice versa) and everyone threw stones, resulting occasionally in some kid getting a hole in the head, a term I've heard only in the Bronx, as in "Yussie got a hole in the head." I never saw an actual hole in the head. I don't know what it was, exactly. But it was epidemic in my childhood and not heard of again thereafter. Medical science must have done something about it when I wasn't paying attention.

Surrounded by Jews, I felt un-Jewish. In the company of my Christian Scientist relatives, I was so Jewish I hardly recognized myself. It took Gentiles or neo-Gentiles to make me a Jew; it took Jews to make me an anti-Semite. I defined myself by distancing myself. Others noticed it: "Do you always have to be different?"

Choice had nothing to do with it. I would have given anything to be more like everyone else. But, no getting away from it, I *was* different. Another accusation that often came my way: "Who do you think you are, a privileged character?" Who, me? Not me, no, never—well, actually, yes.

Underneath a formidable shyness and shoe-shuffling humility lived an arrogant, easily offended hanging judge. He and I regularly convened. We agreed that I was in the right and they were wrong, wrong, *wrong*. But power, for the time being, was in their hands. And the only way to pacify them was to pretend to share their thoughts and values. So I should act funny, sometimes servile, always nice.

Now I'm not sure my sister Alice, four years my junior, would recognize this portrait. I doubt if she ever saw me servile—more likely the opposite. I can't actually testify to how others might have described my behavior. But I recall clearly how I felt in those Bronx years. I felt helpless, scared, off-balance, and cowardly. My older sister, Mimi the Communist, dismissed me as an opportunist. If only. That would have been something to rise to.

Fear was the principal emotion of my childhood. I was never not afraid. I sidestepped arguments, fled confrontations, pedaled away from fistfights. What Fred Astaire did with Ginger Rogers, I practiced with bullies in the Bronx. I tap-danced offstage so skillfully that it might not have occurred to them that I was running away. I danced backwards, kidding, making jokes, laughing it up, pretending we were buddies. I confused them with my cowardice. Abject fear mixed with fancy footwork got me out of the Bronx alive.

Out of the Bronx was the main place I wanted to be. The Bronx symbolized my too apparent state of inadequacy. As I grew older, I grew smaller in my own eyes. Living my life with these people in these surroundings diminished me. And to speak of utter diminishment, now the time had come to prepare for my bar mitzvah. It was announced that I was to go to Hebrew school. I said I wasn't going. My mother and father said, "What are you talking about? Of course you're going." I said, "Why did you wait till I was twelve and a half? What am I going to learn in six months, especially when I have to learn it in Hebrew? Especially when I haven't been inside a shul in a year?" My mother said, "You'll do the best you can." My father left the room. "You don't believe this stuff any more than I do," I said. "You're doing this for the neighbors. It's all hypocrisy."

That was my best shot. My mother's response was, "You're being fresh, Sonny Boy. I don't like to see you this way. Don't break my heart."

I went to Hebrew school. Where I was to be groomed to become a man by a rabbi who barely knew my name, who was to guide me in learning a ritual that I didn't believe in, presented in a language that made no sense to me.

Rabbi Cohen looked at me as if he didn't know I was a privileged character. He looked at me as if I weren't there, as if nothing I did or would ever do could spark his interest. It took another seven years, until I was drafted into the army, for me to face an experience of equal anonymity.

Previously I had avoided Young Israel on every possible occasion, and now I was there five afternoons a week, taking a crash course in a ceremony I wanted no part of, learning by rote how to say *Baruch ata Adonai Eloheinu*, learning to apply as if a bandage the tallis and tefillin. Every minute of this six months' episode, right down to its final moments, was an agony to me.

I did not believe. And I did not believe that my parents believed. What did they believe? They believed—and this was the crux of it—that they should not be ashamed in front of the neighbors. None of whom were their friends. If they gave in to my wish to skip my bar mitzvah, they would owe an explanation to the Peterniks and the Moskowitzes. It would cause a fuss.

My parents were against fuss. If they had a passion, that passion had to do with being against fuss. Fuss got them noticed, got them attention, the wrong kind. They'd be singled out, their parenting called into question. The fuss I was trying to stir up was going to get *them* into trouble.

When their children got into trouble, my parents took the other side. They looked the other way, any which way that would save them from siding with Mimi, Jules, or Alice, whoever brought home a complaint that could be dealt with in only one way: by siding with the grown-up.

It didn't matter if we, their children, had a legitimate grievance—we had to apologize. Grown-ups could never be in the wrong in a dispute with their children. My mother, who was immovable and implacable in standing up to us, couldn't stand up to grown-ups.

I have no doubt that at least one part of my radical politics came out of those years when, time after time, I was herded by my mother down avenues and into positions that I thought were against my best interests. And I was forced to shut up about it. After a certain point I wasn't allowed to argue against her judgment. She worked too hard to be upset by a stubborn, willful son. She had an upside-down stomach that made her ill, and what contributed to her upside-down stomach? Sons who ignored her condition and refused to cooperate.

I lacked representation. Somebody should have been out there standing up for me and against the grown-ups. And no one was. I gave in and gave in some more. And gave in even more after that. And after giving in to a point where there was little left to surrender, even a coward like me dreamed of rebellion. If my mother had just once backed me up, I might have gone a little less extreme in my rage against injustice. I might have remained as indecisive as Mimi said I was. But thanks to my mother's desertion, I was forced back onto my inner resources. I dug scarily deep and found radicalism.

So it wasn't solely the sway of Cold War America that shaped my political sensibility. It was the politics of Rhoda Feiffer, instilled in her by God knows what: memories of the shtetl, the pogroms, the steerage, a frightened Jewish girl ridiculed by the goyim in grade school in Richmond, Virginia, a lifetime of humiliations that became so routine they lost the power to humiliate. All in the aggregate teaching her this lesson: you dare not stand up to them.

So she didn't. When push came to shove, she let her children be shoved. And the more shoved we became—Mimi, Jules, and Alice—the more the three of us realized that we were engaged in a high-wire act, youth, without a net.

Mimi's need for parenting led her to the Communist Party and the patriarch, Stalin. My need led to a more indigenous, romantic radicalism with shades of Big Bill Haywood and the Wobblies and Clarence Darrow and Mabel Dodge. The issues of the day, the suppression of the Left, the blacklist, Pat McCarran, and Karl Mundt certainly raised my ire, but in the end it wasn't the suppression of other Americans that fueled me, it was my own suppression. Civil liberties, schmivil liberties. If my mother had been there when I needed her, I might have stayed docile.

But I was no schmuck. I kept my emerging radical response to my mother to myself. The extremes of my rebellion were not yet well established enough to stand up to her upside-down stomach.

Mimi had no such problem. She cavalierly ignored my mother's condition. Once more employing judo skills to turn a weakness into a strength, I disguised my fear of my mother as principle rather than abject surrender. In my eyes I became the staunch defender of my mother and her upside-down stomach against my badly behaved sister. I was the good son, standing tall, acting righteous, making a moral argument on my mother's behalf. Mimi's lack of control agitated my mother's upside-down stomach. How unfair to a woman who sacrificed so much for me and my sisters! Better that I, her only son, back off from hurting her further. My conscience was too strong to add to her burden. I was blessed with a conscience that had a low threshold for confrontation and a high threshold for surrender.

I couldn't believe what my aunt Frances was telling me. She said that I couldn't invite more than one friend to my bar mitzvah party. Frances had taken charge. She was my father's older sister, beloved by everyone in the family—my sister Mimi liked her, for God's sake!—and I couldn't stand her. Frances was kind, I was told. A heart of gold, I was told, thought of everyone but herself, and so on. And I found her on her infrequent visits from Atlantic City, where she and her husband, Herman, owned a men's shop on Steel Pier, to be a pushy, nosy, overbearing, boorish, self-righteous—have I made myself clear?

She swooped down on 1235 Stratford like an avenging angel, her punishing benevolence welcomed by everyone in the family but me. She lay down the time for my party, the rules for my party, the number of guests at my party, which guests, and what they would eat and drink. And Rhoda, this mother who took no prisoners, smiled sweetly, acquiescently, and obeyed. To every request that Frances set forth, my mother said yes.

My mother's role in my bar mitzvah was to implement Frances's decisions. My father's role was to stay out of the way, something he was practiced at. My role was to be the excuse for a Feiffer family reunion. All the relatives and near relations who had made it in the Jewish migration to these shores were now to find out why they had come to America: to attend Frances's party of the half century in honor of Dave's son, whatzisface.

Hundreds accepted. So many that I was told, days before the event, how many of my friends I could invite to the party. The list had been scaled back to none. We had run out of room. "My friends can't come to my own bar mitzvah party?!"

"Don't be selfish," was my mother's response to my complaints. "This is a wonderful occasion, Sonny, don't spoil it."

What she dared not say to Frances, who was well on her way to spoiling it, she had no trouble saying to me.

Frances was, for reasons I still don't understand, a towering presence in my parents' lives. My mother's own three sisters—Celia, Selma, and Ida—had little or no influence on us. Selma lived across the river in Paterson with her once-wealthy husband, Sam, and their two grown children, Herbert, a lout, and Frances, a nervous wreck. Sam went broke at the start of the Depression and sat on his front porch in benign retirement for the rest of his life, spouting monologues of dreary advice that no one listened to.

My mother's eldest sister was Ida, pretty at one time, soft-spoken, and Southern accented. Ida lived as a single mother in Washington, abandoned by another failure, another Sam, who went out of business, then out of sight.

Celia, two years older than my mother (Rhoda was the youngest and cutest), was the one I knew best. She and her family lived in Riverdale, that part of the Bronx that liked to think of itself as Westchester, just as

Celia and her husband, Eugene, thought of themselves as not Jews but Christian Scientists. Celia had early dreams of becoming an opera singer but her father said no, and Jewish girls obeyed their fathers in those days. So she gave up opera for attitude and from then on lived under the pretense that she was a Gentile and a society lady, demonstrating her superiority by speaking in an affected contralto, sounding as if her end of the conversation were sung as recitative.

She did have her moment in the sun, however. It happened when I was thirty-two, and was marrying that day my longtime live-in girlfriend, Judy Sheftel. My strongest memory of the wedding party afterwards stars Celia. Among the party guests were Julie Andrews, at that time starring on Broadway in *Camelot,* and her then husband, the brilliant production designer Tony Walton. Celia was introduced and in the beginning managed to contain herself. But as the party bubbled on, I noticed that wherever Julie Andrews happened to be standing, there, a short distance away, stood Celia. Cordial and charismatic, Julie moved about the room, mixing and mingling, and Celia moved, not quite beside her but never more than two wedding guests away. Her shadowing act made me increasingly uncomfortable. Before Julie became aware of it, I moved in to shoo Celia. As I made my move, Celia made hers. She sidled up to Julie and, no more than an inch from her ear, crooned in a sotto voce contralto her famous solo from *My Fair Lady*: "I could have dahnced all night, I could have dahnced all night . . ." I wanted to kill her at the time. But almost fifty years later I look back on it as the one fond moment that my imperious aunt ever gave me.

As highfalutin as Celia was, her husband, Eugene, was straightforward, a regular guy, the only relative I went to for advice, although I don't think I ever took it. It didn't matter, I trusted him. He was short and stolid, a man of few words, fewer when Celia was around.

While I thought of my father as primarily gentle and not very significant in my life—or his own—I saw Eugene as made of sterner stuff, more a man to be reckoned with. I could talk to Eugene, discuss my ambitions, even go in for a touch of experimental grandiosity, knowing I wouldn't be laughed at. I was flattered by his attention. In my late teens, working for

---

the cartoonist Will Eisner, whose offices were down in the Financial District, I would make dates with my uncle. His business was close by, at 92 Liberty Street. He'd take me to lunch and listen, not unsympathetically, as I shot my mouth off. He'd respond with advice I found useless, like "Go to college, have a backup plan in case this cartooning thing doesn't work out. Don't put all your eggs in one basket."

Eugene was conservative, a Republican, practiced Christian Science, and never once proselytized. He listened, disagreed with everything I said, and made no judgments. He was the kind of grown-up I needed more of but just had one of.

On the other hand, my aunt Frances was an extreme example of what I had learned to expect from grown-ups. She didn't listen, she only proselytized, and she knew right from wrong: right was what she said, wrong was what I said.

I was used to it. I came from a family of Franceses, some less overbearing than others, some even benign, but every one of them, even my obliging father, judgmental and righteous when it came to discussions with children. And guilt-provoking. It was astonishing—something to marvel at, really—how adults of my parents' generation could instill guilt and reject blame. Among them, my aunt Frances was unrivaled.

"Don't spoil it," my mother had said. "Frances has worked so hard on your party, you could try to appreciate it." Of all the offenses leading up to my bar mitzvah, this was the most flagrant: that I couldn't invite my friends because Frances said so, and my parents went along. It made official what I had known from the start: not any of this bar mitzvah caper had to do with me.

When it became clear that I was no quick study in Hebrew (nor slow study), I begged Rabbi Cohen to let me perform part of the ceremony in English. Certainly not. When it came time to write a speech, I was informed that it was to go more or less like this: "I, bar mitzvah boy, humbly walk through the doorway of this rite of passage by offering displays of obsequious gratitude to all those who deny me the right to think for myself: my parents, my relatives, my teachers, my relatives' relatives, and all those locked up in Hitler's camps, whom I would betray if I spoke any words but the ones put in my mouth by the rabbi."

I did as I was told, based on a lifelong understanding that the one thing that worked with grown-ups was surrender. In any case, once I got over the initial shock, humiliation wasn't all that much of a problem for me, just another one of the numbing miseries that it was my assignment to put up with until I was old enough to bust out of this joint.

So on the day of the event, standing at the podium before an assemblage of strangers who called themselves my relatives, I stumbled in broken Hebrew, without a clue, through the traditional ceremony, a tradition that was unrecognizable by the time I had finished with it. Then came the speech I didn't write, expressing from the bottom of the rabbi's heart all my gratitude. And the job was over.

The party was held in our apartment, barely big enough with its two bedrooms for a family of five, impossibly jammed with, it seemed, thousands of strangers streaming in to celebrate Jules, whom they recognized by searching out the shortest male in the welcoming committee and shoving a present at him. What they really were celebrating was themselves— the reunion of a family I didn't know and didn't want to know.

It frustrated my mother that beyond uncles, aunts, and first cousins I remembered no one on either side of our family. My mother, who had no friends, kept in careful touch with family, had stories to recount about family, retold every story and every anecdote dozens of times. So you might think I'd remember one. But I had a delete button in my brain, and any information not directly related to comics, movies, or radio was excised to make room for the important stuff. Like why was Pat Ryan, my favorite hero, absent so long from *Terry and the Pirates,* and when was he coming back? Or what did Mimi, whose opinions held great sway over me, see in Frank Sinatra, who didn't sing nearly as well as Bing Crosby and wasn't as witty as Crosby, who was almost as funny as Bob Hope?

This was the sort of stuff I had to make room for in my brain, so how in the world could I squeeze in the Zaras and Sams and Als and Doras? But there they all were, piling through the door. And Dave and Rhoda and

Frances and little Jules, now a man, stood smiling in cramped tableau. My mother tried introducing me to the guests as they hustled by, but each introduction made me withdraw further. So she gave up, with a look that read, "We are going to discuss this later." An extra fuss was made over the Cohns as they arrived. Al was a state supreme court justice in the Bronx and a power in the Democratic Party and used to a lot of deference. He was married to the prune-faced Dora, who looked like a character out of Chester Gould's *Dick Tracy*. Dora was the sister of Alva, who was the widow of my father's wealthy brother Sol. The Cohns lived on the Grand Concourse (lots of money!) and Al, being a judge, had a chauffeured limousine that, a couple of times a year, wound its way over from the west Bronx to Stratford Avenue to deliver cartons of hand-me-downs belonging to Al's son, a straight-A student at the Horace Mann School, three years older than I and acknowledged to be brilliant and on his way to the top. This meant to me that I should steer clear of him out of fear that there might not be room for two brilliant young men in the family. Though I avoided my rival, I accepted his hand-me-downs and made occasional use of a collapsible tin water cup that bore his name in tape on the handle: Roy M. Cohn. I saved it in a box somewhere.

Of all the presents, there was actually one that meant something to me. It was from my father's brother Adolph: a wristwatch. Yes, the bar mitzvah boy's traditional watch, but this held special significance. At first sight, I imbued it with magical qualities. First of all, it was a splendid-looking, seriously grown-up Longines Wittnauer seventeen-jeweled wristwatch with a luminous dial. A watch that I had known about for years from radio commercials. From the time I was six or seven, mellifluous voices (Harry Von Zell, Don Wilson, Milton Cross) spoke glowingly over the airwaves of this wondrous instrument for keeping in touch with the world. This watch said more to me of my impending stature than a dozen bar mitzvahs. And it was from my second-favorite uncle, after Eugene, Adolph.

In this unwanted crowd of family, strangers, and near strangers who seemed to be having a perfectly good time without me, Uncle Adolph's watch stood out as the one honest representation of love to come my way that day. I withdrew with my watch into the back bedroom, the one I shared with Mimi, who in the dark one night from my bed I watched undress through half-closed eyes. At the moment of truth, the moment I'd been waiting for as she unhooked her brassiere to reveal her naked seventeen-year-old breasts, too good to be bad, I clamped my eyes shut.

Now, sprawled on that very bed where I had come this close to seeing my sister naked, I lay propped on my elbow, holding Adolph's watch in the palm of my hand. Through the door I had softly closed, the party sounded less intimidating. I stared and stared at the watch, waiting for it to rescue me, or at least make the time go faster. It didn't do either, but it was a comfort nonetheless. And I was a boy in desperate need of comfort, so who knew how long I spent on my bed in a semifetal position examining the watch.

My aunt Frances knew. She burst into the room. "What are you doing in here?" It was like a police raid.

"I'm resting," I said.

"What do you have in your hand?"

"Nothing." Feeling guilty, I held out the watch for Frances to see, this gift from her beloved brother. Surely she would think better of me for valuing it so.

Frances snatched it out of my hand. "That's your Uncle Adolph's watch. This is a very expensive watch. You must be careful to take good care of this watch. You can't treat this watch as a toy. When you wind this watch, you wind it by the stem like this. But not too hard or too fast. Gently. And that way you will have this wonderful watch for many—"

And as Frances sermonized, the stem came out between her right thumb and forefinger. She did a quick appraisal of the crime scene: watch in her left hand, stem in her right. She didn't waste another look on me. She barreled out of my room, back into the party, crying, "Look what Jules did!"

Do I need to tell you that at this celebration of my entry into manhood not a single soul, especially my parents, believed me when I said Frances broke the watch?

My memory is that the watch was sent away to be fixed. But I have no recollection of getting it back or ever wearing it. I don't mean to say that I didn't. It may be like some men in combat: you block out the worst—an undiagnosed case of post-traumatic Frances syndrome.

Bar mitzvah boy, 1942

A JEWISH MOTHER JOKE

When I was in my late thirties and a famous cartoonist and, more recently, a playwright, I could not let my mother attend my plays. They used language that would have shocked her and, even worse, I portrayed mothers onstage whom she might rightly conclude were based on her. Satiric and not all that lovable. When I was in that time where I had—or thought I had—a handle on our age, our politics, our sociology, and just about everything else that defined America's near nervous breakdown in the Cold War years, when I was riding high as the country was sinking low, my mother called me as she did (or I did) a couple of times a week. And this is what she said, almost word for word: "Sonny Boy," she began. Sonny Boy was my mother's code name for me. "I read in these magazines I get, *Ladies' Home Journal, McCall's, Cosmopolitan,* these stories of mothers and their famous sons. And the sons are always so angry at their mothers for something or other they did in their childhood. And I couldn't help wondering, Sonny Boy, is there anything I ever did to you that you resent me for?"

And there it was. My opening. She was finally, after thirty years, inviting me to tell her of the bitterness that I'd been swallowing for a lifetime. Where to begin?

Should I talk about the countless times since earliest childhood she'd been taking me aside to trash my father: that he wasn't a bad man, only a weak man, that he couldn't be relied on—but no man could be relied on—that she married him as a working woman in her early thirties with a nest egg of $5,000, and my father had borrowed, stolen, and squandered it all on failed businesses, on drunkenness, or other undescribed weaknesses that I was too young to hear about? Someday when I'm old enough. I should never grow up to be like my father (or, for that matter, a man), she told me any number of times. It was to be avoided at all costs. I shouldn't break her heart as my father had so many times, as my older sister, Mimi, was doing even as we spoke.

Should I bring that up to her at this moment when she asked me on the phone if there was anything in my past that I resented her for? Or should I talk about my puppy, Rex, given to me by my uncle Adolph, my father's brother (who gave me the bar mitzvah watch). Adolph was sweet like my father, but, unlike him, was able to keep a business going. Adolph was a barber in D.C. He had other businesses as well, investments, he had money. All my father's brothers had money. Sidney in Florida had a thriving jewelry store on Lincoln Road, Sol in New York was rich in real estate, money to burn. Even Frances, his big sister, owned a successful men's shop in Atlantic City.

But Dave, my father, lacked the family touch, couldn't make a dime or, when he did, couldn't hold on to it.

Should I mention Rex, the beagle pup, given to me when I was seven? Rex, who was my friend in a friendless world, who sat in my lap with me cross-legged on the floor worshipfully gazing up at the old Philco console as it played my favorite radio serials. Rex, who followed me, jumped all over me, licked my hands and face, Rex, who when I came home from school one day in early spring and looked for his leash in the kitchen closet and didn't find it, and called his name, "Rex! Rex!" repeatedly and Rex was nowhere in sight . . .

I found my mother bent over her drawing table, in the far corner of our living room behind the piano no one knew how to play. I asked her where Rex was. And this is what my mother told me in this Jewish mother joke: "I can't talk, can't you see I'm busy?"

But I insisted. "Just tell me where Rex is." Most of my young life, I didn't have the nerve to insist to my mother. I was no match for her. She could outtalk, outthink, and intimidate while, at one and the same time, manage to make me pity her for how much she had sacrificed and how little she was thanked for it.

I was putty in her hands, but not at this precise moment. I wanted to know where my dog had gone. And I knew she was holding out on me. Finally, after much prodding, she came out with the truth. My mother had given Rex away. To a farmer. Who had a little girl. Who would give Rex a good home in the country, better than a cramped apartment in the city. And she hadn't told me at first because she knew I'd go and make a scene. And with all that she had to do—cook, clean, make a living to see us through the Depression—with all these responsibilities she couldn't take on the extra responsibility of a dog—

I had no way of absorbing and/or making sense of her revelation.

"But I take care of Rex!" I cried.

My mother countered with her very different, entirely speculative take on the situation, which sounded perfectly plausible in her eloquent delivery. She said that, whatever my good intentions, I wouldn't have gone on taking care of Rex. I would have gotten bored or forgotten—I was, after all, a little boy—and left it for my mother to pick up the pieces (she was always picking up the pieces). She picked up the pieces for my father when he let her down six or seven times a day. She picked up the pieces for Mimi a hundred times a day.

I stood, steamrollered, by the side of her drawing table, struck dumb by her brilliant advocacy. Earlier that day she had, without warning, behind my back, given my dog away, and now she was explaining what she'd done in a defense that subtly hinted that the fault was mine: I did not take good enough care of Rex—not now perhaps, but sometime in the future—thus forcing my mother's hand. I left her no choice. As a result of my sure-to-be forgetfulness, my gross and future irresponsibility, she had to give my dog away. And in so doing, she had done nothing less than save him.

This fairy tale farmer and his daughter, they would lavish on Rex the care that I, Dave Feiffer's son (and clearly every bit as unreliable), would not. Sometime next month or next year, my mother had me convincingly fated to "fall down on the job." *Fall down on the job* was a copyrighted phrase of hers.

So here I am, many years later, living in the middle of this Jewish mother joke where she asks me: "Sonny Boy, is there anything I ever did to you that you resent me for?"

And I respond, "No, Ma."

I may be resentful, I may be bitter, I may want to murder the woman, but I don't want to wound her after all these years.

Also, I am not stupid. I didn't want to walk into the trap she had set for me. I had been in therapy on and off for eighteen years. I was not a fool, not a patsy, had found my tongue in my adult years, could even, when push came to shove, argue with her, force her to retreat—or pretend to—which was, as far as I was concerned, more than enough of a victory, especially with a past such as mine, where I had never won a fight with my mother.

But she was no fool either. She was not going to accept my "No, Ma." She carried on because she, too, was living in the middle of a Jewish mother joke: "Because you see, Sonny Boy, it was the Depression and I had to work, because your father's business failed and he couldn't keep a job, and I had to be away from home a lot, and maybe when you were little, you resented me for that."

I was not about to be suckered in. "No, Ma, I understood all that."

"Because who knew about psychology in those days?" The woman was not about to give up. "Maybe there were things I would have done different if I knew better. All these famous men hold it against their mothers. You sure you don't hold it against *me*?"

And I said, "No, Ma. I understood."

She continued to circle me. "Because with the best intentions in the world, I could have done something to hurt you and I don't want you to hide it from me after all these years."

Will she never let up? This was going to take weeks. I had important things to do. I didn't know what, but the most important was to get my mother off the phone. And, because of all my years of psychotherapy, I coolly analyzed the situation: she wasn't going to let me off the phone, even if she had to go on talking forever until I conceded her something.

So I scripted inside my head lines that let me surrender. A smidgen. In a tone meant to be offhand but affectionate, I said, "Ma, what does it matter, whatever happened, happened so many years ago and during such hard times, that I've long since forgotten and forgiven you."

I wasn't crazy about the way it came out. I held my breath. Five endless seconds went by and then my mother, in a voice dry and bitter, said, "Is that the thanks I get?"

As I lay spread out on the floor for the eight count, I thought in admiration and pride, "My God, she can still do it!" She was seventy-five.

In the *Village Voice* on December 17, 1958, I ran what I believe was the first Jewish Mother cartoon:

ONE DAY HE COMES HOME - HE SAYS - "MAMMA. I AM NOT WELL EMOTIONALLY. I NEED A PSYCHIATRIST."

SO I SEND HIM TO A PSYCHIATRIST. AFTER ALL IF YOU CAN'T HELP YOUR OWN SON, WHAT'S A MOTHER FOR?

SO ONE DAY HE COMES HOME. HE SAYS - "MAMMA, PSYCHOANALYSIS HAS TAUGHT ME THAT HOME IS A SMOTHERING INFLUENCE. I'M MOVING OUT."

SO I FIND HIM HIS OWN APARTMENT. AFTER ALL IF YOU CAN'T HELP YOUR OWN SON, WHAT'S A MOTHER FOR?

I GIVE HIM RENT MONEY. I GIVE HIM PSYCHIATRIST MONEY. I GIVE HIM A LITTLE EXTRA SO HE COULD ENJOY HIMSELF. LISTEN - WHAT WOULD I DO WITH IT? WHAT'S A MOTHER FOR?

SO ONE DAY HE CALLS UP. HE SAYS - "MAMMA, YOU ARE GIVING ME ALL THIS MONEY JUST SO I SHOULD FEEL **GUILTY!** GUILT IS A MOTHER'S WEAPON.

ALL RIGHT, WHY ARGUE? WHAT DOES IT GET YOU? SO I STOP PAYING HIS PSYCHIATRIST AND I STOP PAYING HIS RENT AND I STOP GIVING HIM ANYTHING EXTRA.

SO NOW ITS OVER A MONTH - HE'S DISPOSSESSED, HE CAN'T FIND A JOB. HIS PSYCHIATRIST IS SU'ING HIM.

BUT LISTEN - SO LONG AS HE'S HAPPY.

I took great pains in drawing this cartoon. My first pass at it made the woman look like my mother, a no-no. She would see it. She would be upset. I was after plausible deniability. So I tossed the first art and redrew it. This time I did better, or so I thought. I took it down to the *Village Voice* on a Monday and looked for it when the paper came out that Wednesday. And in my regular spot on page 4, running across the bottom of the page, there was my strip, and it was an eight-panel portrait of my mother.

How could I have screwed up so monumentally? I swear it didn't look like my mother on my drawing table after I drew it. It didn't look like my mother the next morning as I packed it in an envelope to take to the *Voice*. At the *Voice*, admiring it as I showed it off to members of the staff, it didn't bear the slightest resemblance to my mother. During all these exposures of my original art, I was proud to observe that the mother in the cartoon was a perfect stranger. Otherwise, I think I would have noticed.

But reduced on the page to almost half size, a stunning and unwelcome transformation took place. I was staring at it when the phone rang.

"Hello, Ma," I said into the phone. "I don't know what you're talking about, Ma. No . . . it doesn't at all look like you, it's not supposed to, the mother talks with a New York accent, you don't sound anything like that . . . I'm sorry you're upset but you've got to believe me. It's my friend Norton's mother. It looks exactly like *her*. I hope she doesn't see the *Voice*, I'm afraid she's going to be upset."

I've lied to my mother all my adult life and the better half of my teenage life. The choice was either lying to her or never seeing her again. I didn't think my mother's crimes against me were so serious that I should stop knowing her. And even after I learned to fight back, which took too many years, I didn't believe that continually confronting a woman who never in her life admitted she was wrong would make for a satisfactory relationship.

So I compromised, because life is made up of compromise. I withheld my thoughts, opinions, feelings, and judgments from this woman who gave me life and, beyond that, her consent to pursue my dreams, which she could have quashed in ten seconds flat had she chosen. My compromise was to never tell the truth to her about anything that I cared about.

It was exhausting. Just as I submerged myself from my entire family, most of my friends, and all of my relatives as a child, so I continued to submerge myself from my mother as an adult. But when I was a kid, it took less out of me. I had twenty-four-hours-a-day practice, so I became acclimated to hiding out as a way of life. I hid in my sleep. I hid in my dreams. I revealed myself only in comics, which were the embodiment of my dreams. I was trained (by myself) to be a marathon submerger. It didn't tire me because I didn't know any other way existed. I accepted as a given that I was to hide out underground until I was old, say, twenty-one.

But now I was well past twenty-one. I was out in the open and famous for it. I said what I thought once a week in my *Voice* strip, and what I thought was way out there. It was radical. My open aim was to overthrow the government. I saw myself as a wry, self-effacing, hard-hitting lefty. The acceptance that fame brought turned me into a talker, a wit, an actual conversationalist, well on my way to occasional eloquence. I had emerged from the underground as this humorist charmer with whom I had no previous acquaintance.

So when I finally surfaced, after all those years, a complete surprise to myself, I was, of course, thrilled. I managed to hold my own with Alfred Kazin, Dwight MacDonald, Lillian Hellman, Kenneth Tynan, Robert Lowell, Elizabeth Hardwick, Philip Rahv—intellectuals and artists with opinions no less strong than my own and a lot better informed. I was amazed that I was listened to, that I, who thought I had to be funny to be noticed, could be serious and noticed. I had opinions, evidently, that counted, though I made them up as I went along. After a few drinks, no one seemed to care.

But when I was with my mother, it was "You're wrong, Sonny Boy, you used to be sweet as sugar, who gave you this mean streak?"

So in the presence of my mother I went back to the Bronx, spiritually. Undercover again. I talked less, pretended to listen, and when I chose to speak, more likely than not, I didn't mean a word I said.

It was all about positioning myself. My guess is that I felt ill at ease from birth. My mother used to tell me what a good baby I was. But I don't believe it. I think I faked it. I believe it was my first lie. Yanked out of a comforting womb into a blindingly bright world of endless unease, where from the first moment of consciousness I was called upon to do, unwillingly, nothing less than what I'm called upon to do, still unwillingly, eighty years later: cope.

I don't like it now; I'm very sure I didn't like it then. The last thing in the world I was meant to do was cope. I was meant to have others cope for me. I was ordained to be cope-free. Waited on hand and foot. A child of privilege. Succored. Not sucked up and spit out, again and again and again.

I was meant to be adored, and I suspect I was. For about a day and a half, maybe a week. I don't know. Anyhow, it spoiled me, it set me up for my later fall, an ongoing cycle of falls.

I don't know who set me up. And I lack the funding to research this. And I shouldn't have to bother. Somebody should do the job for me. Somebody should have done it a long time ago. Dug into the scandal of my earliest childhood: how I went from being adored and spoiled rotten to, in a matter of days, perhaps minutes, a nonentity. Not slated for center stage, where I rightfully belonged, but pushed to the sidelines, largely overlooked, not ever the one picked out of the crowd, not destined for stardom, not I, never stardom. No: they cast me for best friend.

What did my father know and when did he know it? How complicit was my mother? Was it she who set me up? "Is there anything I ever did to you that you resent me for?" Was her question an encoded confession of residual guilt rising to the surface to cry out, "Sonny Boy! I was wrong!"

J'accuse!

Rhoda and Jules, 1933

DANNY

I was not a generous-hearted kid, but I acted like one in public—as much as I could, with as little cost to myself as possible. A boy in the next building, 1225 Stratford Avenue, Danny, younger even than Alice, took on great interest for me.

Danny was a blue baby. He had what they called in those days a hole in his heart. He wasn't bedridden, but he was housebound, home educated, and spoiled rotten, primarily by his mother, who was making up for the crime of bringing this deathly ill child into the world, this boy without a single friend. His parents, decent, generous working-class people, had heard of my interest in comics. Danny loved comics. He hardly ever left his bedroom, which had mountains of comics, more than I'd find in Pensky's corner candy store. Comic books were his mother's come-on to me to become Danny's friend. I could borrow any book I wanted, the world was mine, all I had to do was spend two or three hours after school several days a week and pretend that I liked Danny. I was being offered a bribe to become Danny's friend, and though I found such an offer mortifying and the comment it made on my character humiliating, I thought—what the hell—why not try it out for a while.

Danny was not predicted to live past twelve. That was a lot of comics for me to read in the four years he had left, comics I would rarely buy for myself. My dimes were not plentiful, coming mainly from delivering drugs for Kaminkowitz, our corner drugstore. So I had money to buy only the DC line: All-American, Action, Detective, as well as newspaper reprints from Popular Comics and King Comics. Danny's collection opened up a vast storehouse of additional material: the Marvel line—*The Human Torch,*

The Sub-Mariner—as well as Fiction House, with the brutal, brilliant art of Charles Biro's *Daredevil* and Jack Cole's *The Claw*. Opportunistic as I seemed to myself, how could I boot this golden opportunity?

Danny was eight at the time, small, a narrow gray face without expression, guarded blue eyes, a mop of long blond hair. He was so skinny, he made me look muscular. When Danny walked, it took his entire body pumping away to get him across the room. His arms and legs swung in and out in straight lines stiff as a gate. His breathing sounded amplified. Walking from one room to another took almost as much effort as climbing a hill.

Alone with him in his room, I felt trapped as if in a hospital ward. Virtually every move he made, everything he did, was mildly repellent to me. Here I was taking cruel advantage of this kid, and *I* felt exploited. How could I be so crazy as to think that the borrowing of comic books was enough for the self-loathing I had to endure? I couldn't and didn't hide my motives from myself, establishing a friendship that embarrassed me, working hard to please, using my talent for mimicry, mockery, wacky humor to get him laughing. And he did laugh. Nobody made Danny laugh but me. I spent endless hours with Danny in his dark ground-floor apartment, entertaining him, making up stories and funny voices to fit his small army of tin soldiers, exerting myself to such extremes of forced hilarity that I would leave this sick eight-year-old dangerously hysterical with laughter.

To laugh at me as openly and trustingly as Danny did acted on me as a form of seduction. How could I resist him? His laughter, almost against my will, moved to make us friends, real, not fake. In some ways I could see that this kid was more like me than my real friends, with whom I was just as much of a fake as I was with Danny. After a year or two of our evolving friendship, my self-loathing lifted. As I got older and smarter, I could say things to Danny that would calm him down when he went into one of his rages. His mother, Ruth, in a frenzy of slavish devotion, trying to make up for the condition that the medical world said would kill him before he was twelve, gave in to his every request, demand, outrageous outburst. Anything he needed, or said he needed, whether or not they had the money to buy it—his father Sid drove an oil delivery truck—they managed, nonetheless, to get for him. At whatever price they had to pay, financially, emotionally, argumentatively. The parents fought a lot.

Sid was a short, muscular, essentially good-natured workingman. What he saw, and could do nothing to stop, was his wife's dark and tragic need to placate and correct what was left of Danny's life. Nothing was too good for Danny, especially what Ruth saw to be the growing bond between us. In our early days I played the clown, but in three or four years—for Danny did not die—I became his mentor and role model.

At about the time he was twelve, heart surgery was developed that gave Danny a chance at some other kind of life. He did not have to remain an invalid, he was not going to die in a week or a month or a year. It was not clear how long he would live, he was not cured, but he was mobile now. He could take walks. He no longer moved his arms and legs like a cross-country skier. He could leave the house, he could go to a public school, he could take classes.

By the time I was writing plays, Danny had ambitions to be an actor. He came over to my Riverside Drive apartment every once in a while and read a part he was auditioning for in a play. I'd advise him on his lines and he said I was helpful. We weren't friends anymore. We had drifted apart in my twenties, soon after I was drafted. And now I was married, a father, settled and famous. Danny was adrift, a single young man working at junk jobs and hoping to get as lucky as his role model.

I did him small favors, the very littlest I could do, calling up a few contacts to arrange for off-Broadway auditions. But the truth was that though I thought Danny had talent and that he might develop into a good and interesting character actor, the real character that emerged in his adult years I didn't care for that much. I had done Danny so much wrong for so many years that it made me uneasy to admit I didn't like him.

At his funeral at twenty-seven, his mother in her grief accused me of filling his head with pipe dreams, as Eugene O'Neill's Hickey might have said, making him think he could act, so that he worked so hard at it, too hard, didn't take care of himself, died too soon not because he had to but because he was too ambitious, an ambition he never would have had except for me. I gave him the ambition his mother said killed him.

I didn't do it on purpose. It was the time we spent together—and the talk. I talked to Danny about what was important to me. I thought I should. It was in trade for his comic books.

RED ED

Mimi, four years older than I, preceded me to James Monroe High School. Her friends, mostly male, liked to visit our house after school and on weekends. They were talkative the way Mimi was but I found them to be wittier and more engaging. Mimi had a lot of charm but she didn't waste much of it on me. But in conversation with Emil and Woody and Willie and Sam, her charm (and theirs) was all too apparent. Charming even in regard to the Civil War in Spain (they all sided with the Loyalists and against General Franco), the coming war in Europe (they favored the Soviet Union against everyone else), labor's ongoing struggle to organize (they sided with the CIO, particularly its militant, pro-Communist wing, against the AF of L). They were vocal about civil rights and repeal of the poll tax and carried, with their school texts, copies of Richard Wright's *Native Son*. A few were active in the YCL (Young Communist League) but, whether members or not, they were equally pro-Soviet. "Fellow traveler" was the catchphrase in those years, 1938 to 1942, when Mimi was in high school and made her mark.

Mimi's crowd was fast-talking, fast-quipping, mischievous, naughty, left, meaning far left in their politics, their taste in books, art, movies, and just about everything else. When Mimi had her moment, the New York City high schools were a beehive of left-wing activity. Kids, if they were not Red, were a hottish pink. Teachers were Reds, and if not Reds, fellow travelers. Being a Communist meant a sense of commitment and mission that filled in the blanks for those who saw themselves as lost in the shuffle. In a time of Depression, anti-Semitism, racism, and a coming war, it gave them a doctrine, a dogma, *the answer*.

Thanks to the revealed truths of Marx and Lenin, Mimi and her friends were in the "vanguard." They spoke of the injustices around us and the evils that threatened us with boisterous verve, irony, and humor. History, they had learned from Marx, was on their side. Their talk was rapid-fire and wise-guy intellectual, full of self-confidence. This was her gang as she rose through the ranks from A student to girl reporter on the *Monroe Mirror,* the award-winning high school weekly, to its first-ever female editor in chief.

She was on a fast track, and I was very much in her shadow, in awe of her and her friends, who, when she brought them over to the house after school and on weekends—astonishingly!—liked to spend time with me. They liked to look at my homemade comic books—and discuss them—ask questions about my one and only area of expertise, newspaper strips and comic books.

I was enamored of them. No one that close to adulthood had ever taken me seriously or discussed my interests as if they weren't childish. And during our conversations, my level of self-deprecating smart-assery rose to meet theirs. These trenchant put-down artists, stimulating, provocative, who, because of their politics, might well lose the game but never the argument— I studied their style. Even when they were losing, they acted like winners, as if someday we would all be living in the world they advocated.

It was this style that drew me to their politics. No one of a conservative or religious bent had their nervy, cocky, turn-your-own-argument-against-you (you made my point!) swashbuckling demeanor. I wanted to be like them long before I understood what they were saying. Their style of radicalism seduced me as much as or more than its substance. Could this wry, smart-ass, wiseguy style work as my own approach? I, who didn't know how to talk back, who hadn't fashioned a language for talking back? A method, perhaps, by which I could even rebut my sister, who, when she wasn't my press agent, was my persecutor. Her temper was terrifying, her eloquence unstoppable. Was a single well-placed smart-ass comment from me likely to stop the unstoppable? I could talk myself into believing many fantasies, but not that one.

My friendships did not stand out well in comparison with Mimi's. Mimi's friends were more interesting than mine: Morty, Georgie, Dick,

Irwin, Larry, Saul, Lou were all bright and engaging. And though I liked them, I was not quite myself with them. By my early teens I had adopted a "socialized Jules" persona that conformed to the norms of expected behavior, shooting for shallowness—joking, teasing, bullshit, and bravado. Conversations were about baseball and movies and lust. Nobody said "fuck." This was the forties—and we were Jewish. But we did say, "Would you look at the pair on her?"

"What a piece of ass!"

"She's a dog."

"Arf, arf."

"I bet she fools around."

"She puts out."

"You want to do it your first time with a dog like that?"

"*Your* first time, not *my* first time."

It was social lust, different from true lust. True lust was directed at girls. Social lust was targeted at your friends in an attempt to impress them. In any case, lust was primarily a diversion. Our true passion was the New York Yankees: DiMaggio, King Kong Charlie Keller, Old Reliable Tommy Henrich, Allie Reynolds, Vic Raschi, and Fireman Joe Page. All our insider baseball knowledge was gleaned from Yankee radio announcer Mel Allen, whose comments were repeated with the urgency of breaking news. No one talked about books. Culture was generally sidelined, limited to opera talk with Irwin Jacobs. He and I played arias recorded from *La Bohème* and *Rigoletto*. My taste in opera was first formed by my mother, who, from my early childhood, tuned in to Texaco's Metropolitan Opera broadcasts on Saturday afternoons. Now my mother's influence was ceded to Irwin: a preference for Puccini (also one of my mother's favorites) and Verdi. Mozart came in a lagging third. Jussi Björling was Irwin's favorite tenor, and therefore mine. Movies were not part of culture in those days. They were not discussed other than in terms of the simplest judgments: "Wasn't that great?" "That stank!"

High school, which had been such a triumph for Mimi, was a crucible for me. In those days, kids went from elementary school to junior high, then on to high school. But Herman Ridder, the junior high to which Mimi had gone, was a trolley car ride away. I was willing to do anything to avoid a terrifying trolley ride to a far-distant place a half hour away where I had to pass through unknown, non-Jewish neighborhoods and walk two or three blocks. Who knew in which direction? I was certain to get it wrong.

But the only way to avoid that trolley car ride was to elect a language course that was not taught at Herman Ridder Junior High, a language exclusive to James Monroe, which was only a three-block walk from my house. That language was Hebrew.

Unable to learn the short Hebrew text of my bar mitzvah ceremony, I signed on for Hebrew as my language major because I was afraid of the trolley. Added to science, which I couldn't learn, and math, which I couldn't learn, and gym, which I couldn't learn, was Hebrew.

Art, English, and history were the three courses I understood. I enjoyed and looked forward to them. Every other course was an exercise in confusion, endurance, fakery, and cheating. I couldn't learn in school, couldn't listen or absorb what I was taught. Words did not come together the way they were supposed to. I struggled with elusive meanings and baffling texts and unintelligible diagrams and equations. I was stunned and blindsided, made to feel like an immigrant days off the boat. Much of what I was taught sounded like gibberish, double-talk, and the parts that weren't, that I could fathom, didn't take me far. Just as I thought I was getting somewhere, inexplicably I'd tune out. The more I tried to absorb, the more my teachers' words wafted off into a narcoleptic drone.

What I was unable to learn in class I partially made up for by studying and reading and reviewing at home. I was able to take what my teachers seemed to be saying as rudimentary lesson plans. What I was able to figure out from my notes I put to use as guidelines for my own home study. If I ignored *their* way, I might learn by my own method, which was to translate from school-speak to Jules-speak, decoding lectures into language that I thought I understood. Treating myself as just as much a stranger to these shores as my parents and grandparents. Sweating hard at decoding lessons well enough to fool my teachers and get by.

It didn't occur to me that I might have a learning disability. What I had, in my judgment, was a school disability. By gritting my teeth and slogging through to graduation (and then, by some miracle, eking out a college degree), I would turn my back on institutions of learning and become a free man. I would never be asked to pick up a textbook again. I would never again have to listen to a lecture. My high school diploma was to be my green card, my official entry into the real world, to get on with my real life, for which I knew I was better suited than for this strange and puzzling high school universe in which I pretended to be present as I tap-danced, smiling and joking, to places unknown.

I took it for granted that I would be the *Monroe Mirror*'s cartoonist. Hadn't my sister been its editor in chief? Couldn't I assume a process of natural selection? So how could I be expected to pay attention in class when the classroom wasn't my focal point? It was the *Mirror*, two floors down, that's where my thoughts were. To see my cartoons in print, reproduced in ink in a real newspaper. Not pencil drawings in a fake comic book. To pencil in a cartoon panel, then ink it in with pen, a crow-quill nib like the ones the big boys used, which, if you learned how to handle it right, gave you a thick and thin line, the kind of line a boy cartoonist had to develop if he wanted to look like the real thing. To see this cartoon in the actual newspaper instead of on my drawing board or spread out as my comic books were, all over the bedroom floor, to open to page 3 of the *Monroe Mirror*, a prizewinning, much-admired high school newspaper, and there I would be. In print.

The problem was the present editor in chief of the paper, successor to my sister Mimi, her friend. He had been to our house, I thought he liked me. He may have liked me, but . . ."You're not quite ready," he said. Friendly enough. He smiled. "Not quite ready." I left his office, burning with shame. "Not quite ready?" *You will rot in hell, you bastard, before I am quite ready to submit a cartoon to your lousy, stinking newspaper!*

That pledge I stood by until halfway through my junior year, when Monroe's star actor, the biggest of big shots, who miraculously befriended me, found me entertaining, fun to kibbitz with in the hallways, and treated me, although he was stellar and I a nonentity, as a colleague and confidant. He laughed at my jokes and, best of all, admired my cartoons. Myron

Moskowitz. The best thing he had going for him, in those middle-forties war years, was that when he was on stage and one listened to him without looking, he sounded spookily like John Garfield. And to semi-stagestruck Jewish boys in the Bronx, John Garfield was God.

Moskowitz already walked with a showbiz slouch. It was easy to see him as a star, easy to imagine him wearing his coat loosely draped over his shoulders, sleeves empty. So when he put our friendship on the line over the issue of my cartoons, I had no choice but to react. One day in a second-floor hallway when I was pretending to do my job as hall monitor, I ran into him, and after a few minutes' kibbitz, he put a hand on my shoulder. "Julie," he said, "I'm a big shot. All my friends are big shots. You can't be my friend anymore until you're a big shot. Go back to the *Monroe Mirror.*"

I went back. I couldn't put at risk my one big-shot friendship. This time there was a different editor. Or maybe after two years, I was ready. In any case, the next week and every week after, I was in the paper. Big shot.

Monroe Mirror, circa 1945

IDOL

There I was.

In his office.

Sixteen and a half and scared shitless. I couldn't believe my nerve. Will Eisner.

I had looked him up in the Manhattan directory, I, who tried never to look anything up. Just out of high school, turned down by NYU and Cooper Union, the only colleges I had applied to, I needed an interim summer job while figuring out a direction, perhaps even a plan, possibly a future. Was I too young to have a career?

Where was I going? By what means? With how much will? How little courage? How much desperation?

Thirty-seven Wall Street turned out to be where I was going. Eisner's studio was listed, to my utter disbelief, in the phone book, this larger-than-life innovator of comic book art, creator of *Espionage,* starring Black X, *Hawks of the Seas*—both childhood favorites that influenced my early attempts—and now author of *The Spirit,* a noirish eight-page feature that was the mainstay of a sixteen-page comic book supplement folded into the broadsheet-sized Sunday comics. *The Spirit* was unlike anything I or anyone else had ever seen before, and it quickly became a favorite that I followed as devotedly as I followed *Terry and the Pirates, Li'l Abner, Flash Gordon, Prince Valiant, Abbie an' Slats, Tarzan* . . .

And here I was, in his office, with a portfolio of sample art I'd brought to show him. *Will Eisner!* He was going to look at my samples. Where did I get the nerve to show him my samples?

Miles away from where I stood at the door, tucked in a corner of the darkened outer office, Eisner sat, spotlighted by a draftsman's gooseneck lamp screwed to his drawing table. He was bent over a drawing, a No. 2 sable brush in his hand, an apparition spinning magic.

Eisner, like me, was from the Bronx and had brought the Bronx with him to *The Spirit*. His art crawled with Depression-era urban imagery, his drawing dark and clotted and often ungainly. Grotesque and bulky figures fighting it out in heavyweight balletic violence, the action lifelike, despite its distortions. One felt force behind punches, the physical damage absorbed by combatants. Elevated subway tracks over slimy, puddled, scrap-strewn streets. Filth and decay and sound effects, in graphic detail. You could hear and smell the city.

He looked up from his drawing table quizzically. Quizzical was one of his frequent expressions, as if preparing himself for surprises not necessarily to his liking. It was a Bronx-Jewish expression, and Eisner presented a familiar, attractive, balding, thirtyish face to me. He seemed almost pleased by the interruption. One look at me told him that I wasn't going to take much of his time.

The sample art I showed him was of a comic book story called *Adam's Atom,* an act of collaboration penciled and inked by me and written by Dave Kaplan, the editor of the *Monroe Mirror.* It was not a happy collaboration. Kaplan was an aggressive, hawk-faced reporter-editor whose mother claimed she had connections to the publisher of a local Bronx paper that would be eager to run my cartoons if her son David wrote scripts for them. Grimly, I bit the bullet and agreed. My sister had a point about my opportunism.

I hated the idea of illustrating someone else's scripts; I didn't think of the words and pictures in comics as separate entities. My love for the medium had a lot to do with the words and pictures existing as a single unit. The best strips, it seemed to me, were written and drawn by the same artists: Milton Caniff wrote his *Terry and the Pirates,* Roy Crane wrote his *Wash Tubbs and Captain Easy,* and Eisner was the auteur, in every respect, of *The Spirit* and, for that matter, of every other comic he had drawn. And by the time I got to him, he had drawn hundreds.

I could easily identify the work of the better-known and most of the lesser-known cartoonists. My eye, from six or seven, instantly understood comics' body language: the style in which Eisner or Raymond or Hogarth or Crane or Caniff posed and executed the human figure. Eisner's men, save for his heroes, weighed heavy on the page, black, choppy folds on rumpled suits, hammerlike shoes with thick soles, heads carved from stone. Sometimes he signed his name "Rensie" (Eisner spelled backwards), sometimes it was Will Erwin. He operated under many names. Like a superhero, which he truly was to me, he liked to cloak his identity. But I was never fooled. I was Javert the boy detective, and Eisner was not going to escape my embrace.

I had fallen in love with him by six with *Muss 'Em Up,* a hard-boiled cop feature that, believe you me, didn't go in for coddling criminals. I collected everything that I could get my hands on from that point on. *Hawks of the Seas,* his swashbuckler. *Espionage,* starring Black X, his spy thriller . . . With every new comic book feature, he grew better and I grew more infatuated. I dreamed that someday I'd get to meet him, and here I was, where I was meant to be.

Eisner smiled to put me at my ease. It didn't work. He invited me over to look at the art on his table. He was inking penciled heads, some completed, others just features, no outlines. The remainder of the penciled figures and backgrounds he left untouched. So this was how it was done. "Let's have a look at what you have," he said.

I slipped him my samples. Puffing on his pipe, he went through the six pages, giving them a glance and a half. He said they stank.

Now, I understood on entering his office that my drawing was not on Eisner's level (yet) or on the level of the assistants he employed. But what Eisner couldn't possibly know and I clearly understood was (1) okay, I'm not really that good yet and (2) I am on my way to greatness.

So hearing him say my work stank took a little getting used to. I absorb bad news when I first hear it as if it doesn't matter. It's fine. Everything's fine. I'm fine, you're fine, we're all fine. I did not react to Eisner's harsh judgment. Rather, I reacted as if he hadn't said anything.

I dropped myself as the subject (a nonstarter) and engaged him on the subject of himself. I talked knowledgeably and in detail about various of his cartoons over the years. It became instantly clear that this kid who walked in anonymously was not just any run-of-the-mill, talentless job seeker. *This* talentless job seeker happened to be an expert on Will Eisner. I knew more about his career than any of the far more proficient men lettering, inking, and rendering backgrounds in the next room. To them, *The Spirit* was nothing more than a job. Eisner immediately understood that for me, on the other hand, working for him would be like entering the priesthood. How could he resist? He hired me as a groupie.

Immediately after, hired by Eisner for five half days a week with no pay, I took the subway to the Bronx, dizzy with triumph. I vividly remember what it felt like to get off the train and walk the one block to 1235 Stratford. I was exhilarated to the point of terror. This was by far the best thing that had ever happened to me. I couldn't wait to announce the news to my mother. But I was sure I wouldn't make it home. Nothing this good could happen without inspiring some awful event as payback. And now I had a dream job, I was going to be Will Eisner's assistant, hired by my hero! I had to be punished. A brick was going to fall off a roof and kill me before I had a chance to tell this great news to my mother.

The brick that fell was my mother. "Sonny Boy, let me understand, you took a job for *nothing?* What kind of job is *that?*" is what she said when I burst in with my news. "You're a wonderful boy, Sonny, and you'll have other opportunities, but you have to call him up and tell him you've thought it over and tell him politely no. The man is taking advantage of you."

My mother, direct as always, delivered her hard-earned truths no matter how much they hurt. Always trying to teach, she never failed to fail me.

This was much worse than Eisner's telling me my work stank. Outside the house, I had my defenses. I was able to rise to Eisner's put-down. I managed to use my judo to turn his insult into a job offer. But I had no defense against my mother.

Although I couldn't stand up to her, I could lie. I agreed to quit. A lie. I said I would call Eisner tomorrow. A lie. The next afternoon, when she had returned home from selling sketches to fashion design houses on Seventh Avenue, I told her that I had gone downtown to see Eisner to get a better deal or turn down the job. Faced with my firmness, Eisner caved in and offered me ten dollars a week. Not much, but it was something. Every word was untrue. "Sonny Boy, I'm very proud of you," my mother said. And, through her exhaustion, I could see that she was happy. She was happiest when she taught and I learned.

STOMACHACHE

My long siege of stomachaches began during my second year at Eisner's and hit hard and often from then on. They struck in unexpected spasms of sudden force that hung on for minutes or longer and eased with grudging slowness, as if they didn't want me to think that they were coming back. These attacks came to a mortifying end one day in 1947.

By then, Eisner had moved his studio from Wall Street to 90 West Street, overlooking the Hudson River. When I raised my head from my drawing board and looked a little to my left, out the window was a vista view of the Hudson: tugboats, double-deck car ferries, tour boats, ocean liners, including the two Cunard Queens, *Elizabeth* and *Mary,* and close upon them, so close it was surprising, the Statue of Liberty, her torch held high in a personal salute to me: "Give me your inspired but unsure, your muddled lads and lasses yearning to breathe free . . . and rich . . . and famous . . . very famous."

Her prayer was a mockery to me, crouched over my drawing table with my gut-curdling stomachaches, ramming the tilted edge of the table into my midsection to ease the pain or, if not that, to abuse it into submission.

Abe Kanegson, Eisner's lettering man, seated to my right, asked what was wrong. Abe was the left intellectual of the office, which also included Marilyn Mercer, Eisner's business assistant and secretary, and Jerry Grandinetti, Eisner's background man. I enjoyed an active and bantering relationship with my boss and the others in the studio, but I was closest to Abe, with whom I had developed a big brother–kid brother relationship. Abe played utility infielder at the office: he lettered, he inked backgrounds, he finished inking Eisner's half-finished figures. And he came from the Bronx, actually no more than four blocks away, on East 172nd Street, a block from James Monroe High School. He was five years older than I, big, burly, very hairy, a dark, wry, sardonic Russian Jew who lumbered as he walked. A strong presence but oddly, for all his impressiveness, without charisma. Maybe it was the stutter. Abe had a quick mind and wit and forceful opinions expressed in a rumbling, resonant baritone undermined by the worst stutter I had ever heard.

His sentences came out in tortured fragments, his brilliance logjammed by an unsayable *b* or *d* or *f* or *m*. I'd sit next to him at my drawing table and pretend not to notice his struggle. I had to restrain myself not to complete words for him, although I was dying to. I knew it would be an unforgivable intrusion and, in any case, what Abe had to say was often worth waiting for. So I acted as if I weren't screaming inside my head, "Finish! Finish! Finish the sentence, goddammit!"

I looked up to Abe. He was a Communist or fellow traveler (I never asked, he never told) to whom I awarded more credibility than to my sister Mimi because he didn't beat up on me. Abe didn't accuse me of being an "opportunist" or "indecisive," nor was he trying to change me into the protégé Red that was Mimi's ambition for me. My sense was that Abe was more interested in prodding/goading me into becoming a better and more serious cartoonist, the cartoonist that I liked to pretend I already was.

He nudged and wisecracked me out of my defenses, layer upon layer. He took pride, I think, in playing therapist, outsmarting me with ease and even, with his stutter, outtalking my evasive attempts to change the subject.

I was a very young nineteen—and didn't take criticism well. I had more than enough at home. Away from my mother and big sister's influence, I wanted to be free of constraints, to be myself, with high hopes of finding out who that might be. In Eisner's studio, I took license to remold myself into a brash, opinionated, and even arrogant Jules. Each day I boarded the Lexington Avenue line at Soundview Avenue, endured the forty-minute subway ride to Fulton Street, confident after two years on the job that I wasn't going to get lost. Along the way I doffed my outer guise of Bronx wimpishness. By the time I hit the office at 90 West Street, I had changed into my true but secret identity: KnowItAllMan.

KnowItAllMan didn't know why he had to have all these stomachaches, or why, at this particular moment, Abe had decided to psychoanalyze him. "You get a lot of these stomachaches," Abe stuttered maddeningly, as I pulled my drawing table hard into my stomach with the determination of a man trying to slice himself in half. Since he had come to work for Eisner about a year after I arrived, Abe had seen me through this routine a few times a week. What I resented in his casual comment was the stutter, which transformed it, somehow, into a statement fraught with meaning. As if my pain weren't enough, now I had to try to fathom what he was hinting at.

"It's psychosomatic," Abe said.

I had heard the word *psychosomatic* many times—it seemed to be in vogue—but I didn't know what it meant and it didn't occur to me to ask. God knows I felt uninformed more hours of the day than not, but I wasn't going to concede my ignorance to Abe. It wasn't that long ago that I took it for granted that I was the smartest kid on the block. But then the rest of the block went to college, and I didn't. They learned the word *psychosomatic.* Another word they learned that I didn't know the meaning of was contraceptive, both words casually dropped into conversations by boys and girls my age all the time. And while everyone else on the block understood their meaning, I was mystified. I pretended, nodding my head knowingly as the terms entered into conversation: *contraceptive, psychosomatic, contracematic, psychosoceptive* . . . I understood nothing.

I meant to find out what these words meant. Their heavy-duty significance was so apparent, you'd think I'd rush home to a dictionary. But the thought didn't occur to me. I hated looking up words, I was dictionary-challenged. I'd take note of words in novels that I didn't understand, words like *chimera.* But I almost never got around to looking them up. It took me five years to look up *chimera.* And the meaning of the word *contraceptive* became clear to me only when I started buying Trojans to hide in my wallet.

It was Abe who finally explained what *psychosomatic* meant. Doubled over my drawing table with unbearable cramps, I confessed: "I don't know what you're talking about when you say this is psychosomatic. What does that mean?"

Abe stuttered, "It m-m-m-means you hate your m-m-m-m-m-m-mother."

What?! Was the man insane? Abe, whose intellect awed me, had just stuttered the most uninformed, idiotic sentence ever spoken to me.

"That's ridiculous! I love my mother. I love my mother!!"

I rushed to her defense. I spoke of how she had suffered to bring up three children during the Depression with a father who couldn't hold a job; a mother, a career woman up to all hours of the night taking on the responsibilities that others (my father) could not handle—how could I not love my mother? To not love her would be sinful, criminal. Wasn't it my mother who gave me permission to pursue my dreams? What if she had opposed my becoming a cartoonist, as most Jewish mothers might have been expected to do during these hard times? "A *what?* A *cartoonist?!* Get that out of your head, young man! You're going to be a dentist, an accountant, a shopkeeper!" Abe was smart, certainly smarter than me, but he couldn't have been more wrong about my mother. I loved my mother. I *loved* my mother!

She could have made me go to dental school, but she didn't. I had classmates who wanted to be writers whose mothers made them go to dental school. Not mine! My father had gone to dental school. He studied to be a technician. Twice in his life. Once as a young man, a promising student, doing well, his hands broke out in an allergic reaction to the chemicals he worked with in his studies. They flaked, they blistered as if burned, they pained him. And when they didn't hurt, they itched. He applied powders and salves, but nothing worked but the passage of time. Then time ran out and so did his hope for a career in dental technology. He was forced to abandon the one thing he was good at, to go into business, the one thing he was bad at.

After the second war, now nearly sixty, he tried again, accepting a GI scholarship to dental school. This followed a very good war indeed, four years of unprecedented steady employment. He worked for the Navy Quartermaster Corps in Port Newark, New Jersey. Back to dental school he went, whizzing through, astonishing the younger students, a real gift for it, going far—until the blisters returned. The burns, the salves, the resignation from dental school, the resignation of hope.

She was our hope. My mother fed us and she clothed us. She worked and she suffered. Her shortcomings weren't her fault. I was aware of them, of course, but how could Abe or I blame her?

I explained all this. Yes, Abe, I am aware of her bossiness, her thoughtlessness, her unfairness, her insensitivity . . . But Abe had to acknowledge her torturous past and present, her rising above it all, and oh, how hard she worked! And oh, her humor in spite of it all. The little comic verses she wrote, her impromptu songs and dances . . . How dare he blame my mother? She was a life force! Larger than life! These stomachaches of mine were not "psychological." They weren't "in my head," if that's what psychosomatic meant. That was all *hooey*! No, Abe, my pain could not be blamed on some idiotic theory. It hurt too much, it was real! Abe, I loved my mother! I loved my mother! I loved my mother!

My agitation had to be evident, but Abe would not back off. He quietly and stutteringly insisted that, based on a year of confidence I had shared with him (stupidly), I was furious with my mother but my guilt would not allow me to acknowledge it. My repressed, deeply implanted, deeply evasive guilt stifled the rage I felt. It would not allow it to surface. My mother had denied me an outlet in my head for my guilt, so it went south and lodged itself in my stomach. And that's what caused my stomachaches.

Not true! Not true! Not true! Not true! Abe was driving me *insane*! Shut up with this phony psychoanalysis! Where did he learn this garbage? What was he, a doctor? Abe didn't go to college any more than I did. Anyhow, who appointed him my psychiatrist? Shut the fuck up!

But Abe would not shut up. So to shut him up, to bring our stupid argument to a conclusion, I chose to employ judo on him, employ the weakness I had so effectively used in the past as a trump card: if I couldn't get anywhere with confrontation, I'd go in the other direction, I'd pretend to surrender. "Okay, okay! I hate my mother!" I shouted.

And my stomachache went away.

"I hate my mother, I hate my mother!" I was feeling much better.

"I hate my mother, I hate her. I really do, I hate my mother!" I was growing giddy, euphoric. Abe beamed at me. How could he know? He must hate *his* mother. Then we were in this together: brothers who hated our mothers. Oh, happiness!

Jules at nineteen

ONE BASKET

At Eisner's "shop" (as he called it) I'd begun as the lowest of the low and, for most of my first year, having observed a lot and been assigned a little bit of everything and having tried and failed at most of it, I remained the lowest of the low.

But I was not unhappy. I was accepted by my fellow workers, all, like Abe, in their late twenties or early thirties, all veterans of World War II, happy to be resuming their lives, but exactly what these lives were I never found out. Aside from Abe, they were a curiously impersonal bunch, cordial but just short of friendly: a brilliantly tight penciler, John Spranger, who drew better than Eisner but not nearly as stylishly; a lettering man, Sam Rosen, short, trim, and quiet, except for an occasional wisecrack; a background man, Jerry Grandinetti, also from the Bronx, just a couple of years older, trained in high school as an architectural draftsman and therefore a whiz in all the areas in which I was incompetent.

At seventeen and eighteen, I couldn't draw a convincing chair or table or desk (it's still hard). I was hopeless at vehicles of any kind: cars, trucks, trains, planes. And don't talk to me about guns, the very staple of adventure comics, without which there are no heroes, no villains, no reasons to beat up bad guys. I drew guns as if they were made of melting butter.

Mushiness would describe the pure essence of my style at this time. Adventure comic art was programmed to look hard-edged, tough, combative. The best of this art was displayed by Eisner, Caniff, Frank Robbins in his strip *Scorchy Smith,* Jack Cole in his *Plastic Man* comic book, Joe Simon and Jack Kirby in *Captain America* and *Boy Commandos,* Irv Novick in *The Shield.*

There were others whom I admired and planned to grow up to be. But as I discovered in my first weeks in Eisner's shop, I lacked every one of the basic skills to fulfill my ambitions. My line was soft where it should be hard, my figures amoebic when they should be overpowering. The wimpishness of the inner me stripped of dreams of grandeur emerged on paper with every line I drew. My style was self-effacing, a pretend style trying to look like the cartoonists I admired—this one, that one, the other—and monumentally failing to pull it off.

Here I was, seventeen years old at the beginning of what I knew was going to be a successful career. I didn't have a single doubt. There was but one drawback: I was second-rate.

Where did it go wrong? Early on, the kids on the street salivated over my sidewalk art. At P.S. 77 and James Monroe High School I was considered nonpareil. And I still considered myself nonpareil when I didn't leak doubts that I was a fraud. I was this hardworking, never-resting combination of talent and fraud. Both seemed equally valid judgments. My ambivalence was more of a comfort than a curse. My feelings of fraudulence marched in lockstep with my talent, so that when I screwed up, as I inevitably did, I was able to blame myself and forgive myself in the blink of an eye.

At seventeen at Eisner's, leaving work each day, my tail between my legs, riding home on the subway, an ambivalent failure, I tried to quash the unwelcome perception that my golden years were behind me. What had gone wrong? At seven I was a hotshot. Don't take my word for it, I won a medal! My kindergarten teacher at P.S. 77 submitted a classroom drawing to the annual art contest for public school children sponsored by the department store John Wanamaker. It was of movie cowboy Tom Mix holding a gun (made of butter), jailing two Indians. Now this was a citywide contest—citywide! And who won first prize? Jules, that's who!

I was even better at eight and nine, and by fourteen I was making leaps and bounds. Come on, will you look at this pencil sketch I did in Max Wilkes's freshman art class?!

I was at the top of the heap. No one else in my neighborhood came close! And I was acknowledged. It was the one skill I was acknowledged

for. It meant a lot more than simply a facility for drawing pictures. It was my *calling*. Everything I needed to be to move from who I was that I couldn't tolerate was tied up in making this famous cartoonist thing work.

That's what I was trying to say to my uncle Eugene at our occasional downtown lunches when he cautioned me against putting all my eggs in one basket: "Don't put all your eggs in one basket," he'd say. And I would reply, "I only have one basket." Whether I could draw anymore or not, I was committed. If one basket wasn't enough for my one and only egg, I was done for.

The question was, if I was so good once, why was I so pitiful now? Over the years, I've wondered about it: how did I lose my talent after fourteen? And the answer I've come up with is self-mutilation.

At an early stage, I drew my own ideas, right or wrong, good or bad, and I executed them haphazardly, the only point being not the quality of the line but its presence. I penciled, I put down my substance on paper, and it was more important to have it down than to have it right. And if it wasn't right, then the next drawing was going to be right or closer to right, but anyway, who cared? I was having a ball. And since I was the one who defined the standards, for a long time there were no serious problems. In this early stage of development the conversation on paper was entirely with myself. It was ideal.

Then I reached a stage, and an age, when it wasn't enough to look like me anymore. There were masters out there who, with a little effort, I could come to look like. I became more demanding of myself. My goals shifted. The conversation stopped being only about me. It turned into a flirtation with my role model. I courted the one I loved, the cartoonist that I planned someday to equal or surpass, but not yet. The stage I was entering was where I worked my heart out not to best him but to *be* him, to make my art look exactly like his.

Unwittingly, believing with all my heart that this was progress, I began to divest myself of myself. Solipsism was replaced by self-effacement. Other, better cartoonists occupied this universe, so first I admired them, then I envied them, then I became them, then I replaced them. That was my master plan.

And as I changed from who I was to who Alex Raymond was, my work seemed to take on panache, dimension, a pretense of craft. I studied my Alex Raymond self and it was a vast improvement over my Jules Feiffer self. So I sank entirely into Raymond, except when I was being Caniff, mixed with a little Eisner, mixed with a little Roy Crane. I didn't use my betters as reference points to build a style of my own. No, I stole their drawings, line for line, fold for fold, shadow for shadow. And the more I distanced myself from what made me love being a cartoonist in the first place, the more professional I thought I was.

I had lost everything that made me choose this as a life's work, lost the energy, the quirkiness, the sense of humor. I had willingly hired myself on as a hack. And looking over my samples, which had nothing to do with who or what I was, I thought, "Jesus, I'm getting good, soon I'll be the best!"

My best was brought to its knees in Eisner's shop. There are certain basic skills that go with being a competent illustrator of adventure art: one is a knowledge of anatomy proficient enough to let you draw figures in action, hulking, muscular men chasing down and beating the crap out of one another.

I more or less knew my anatomy. In the midforties, I gave in to my mother's urgings and signed up for a drawing class at the Art Students League. I studied under a legendary teacher, Robert Beverly Hale (he later became curator of American paintings and sculpture at the Metropolitan Museum). Hale's appearance was pure Brahmin: well over six feet, he strolled the classroom in lawyerlike three-piece pinstripes, gently taking the charcoal out of my fingers to correct the drawing of a nude model I was making a mess of. By dint of his guidance I came to learn and understand the musculature of the human body.

He taught by prodding me benignly, good-naturedly, never letting me feel incompetent, as I certainly was. And somehow his Harvard Yard drawl gave comfort. If he spent so much time with me, clueing me in to perceive the obvious, then I must show promise.

So I knew how to draw the human figure, shakily but passably. But I got away with it only in pencil. I was hopeless at inking the human figure or anything else. Adventure comic inkers work in brush, finishing off a penciler's tight rendering with a thick and thin brush line that gleams on the page with a shoeshinelike sheen.

This brush line of fluidity, grace, and infinite slickness was, despite hours of practice, outside my manageable skills. My brush line didn't shine, it clunked. It wasn't thick and thin, it was splotchy and ham-handed. And I was unable to master layout. I well knew that a page of six to nine panels had to grab the reader, one panel at a time, while the design of the complete page required the look of an action movie on paper. But my layouts failed that test. Rather than move across the page dramatically, my figures hung out leadenly in their panels as if standing on a street corner, drawn by a hand held down by iron weights.

Eisner tried me on backgrounds, so that he might move Jerry Grandinetti up to figures. But here too I was hopeless, worse than with the human figure. My inking of figures, while short of proficient, had a touch of pizzazz, a hint that sometime in a distant future I might know what I was doing. But when I tried backgrounds—city street scenes, lampposts, waterfront docks with tugboats, suspension bridges, automobiles—my ineptitude was pathetic, leading one to think that I had dropped in from another century and had never seen a skyscraper, a lamppost, a bridge, an automobile . . .

At $10 a week (which I managed to work up to) Eisner could not afford to fire me. In time, I found my niche as a minimalist: half gofer, half janitor to the eight-page *Spirit* section. I ruled lines for borders, drew scalloped balloons and tails that held the dialogue, inked in shadows and silhouettes that were indicated by X marks on the page. I erased, whited out mistakes, pasted up . . . I was not unhappy.

I surveyed my tasks in the aggregate and imagined this as a journey in progress. Eventually, Eisner let me color photocopies (called silver prints) of the entire *Spirit* section. Thus, every week I was in charge of how my favorite feature appeared in syndication in a hundred newspapers: the *Newark Star-Ledger,* the *Philadelphia Record,* the *Chicago Sun-Times,* the *Detroit News,* and my local paper, the *Parkchester Review.* Every Sunday, affluent readers—at least in my terms—in Parkchester opened their Sunday papers and read the *Spirit* section, never dreaming that the dramatic display of color in the strip they were reading was the work of a boy a year out of high school, who came from the other side of the tracks in their very borough: clearly a precursor to fame.

Although I was employed as a drudge, my heart remained in fandom. Eisner had so much to say in his work, drew so brilliantly, worked in stark and vivid combinations of density, with such quickness of hand . . . a hand with which I'd clearly never compete. But I never seriously thought of competing with Eisner. I was working, almost giddily, as a total loser. My lack of qualifications didn't trouble me but rather seemed to be a basic given that dogged so many of my endeavors since earliest childhood. Really, who else flunked shop at P.S. 77?

Shop was where you learned to use the tools of carpentry to fashion handicrafts such as lamps, modest bookcases, model sailboats. I had been able to build nothing, demonstrating an almost magical gift for making the simplest task hard. My shop teacher, Mr. Margon, was convinced that I was out to make a fool of him. No kid that good at drawing pictures could be that bad with his hands in shop class. But the truth, then and now, is that I can't build anything, can fix almost nothing, don't understand how most things work, don't have a clue as to why a car moves forward when I press down on the pedal on the right. Conversely, it makes perfect sense that when I go into reverse, the logic of my shortcomings demands that I crash into whatever stands behind me.

Eisner's original black-and-white brush drawings glowed on the page. They didn't need the colors I added. The use of blacks spotted in vibrant swatches over six or eight panels had a charged electrical effect. Sitting in his studio, at my own drawing table, surrounded by pages in all stages of development, I marveled, virtually salivated, over the quality of the work that slid past me before I could totally fuck it up. It was a miracle undeterred by the staying power of my incompetence.

I was seventeen—what did I know?—but I thought this stuff was art. As Caniff's work was art, as Roy Crane's and Segar's (*Popeye*) and Frank King's (*Gasoline Alley*) and Cliff Sterrett's (*Polly and Her Pals*) and George Herriman's (*Krazy Kat*), and, just a few years later, Walt Kelly's in his monumental *Pogo*. These men, products of an old newspaper ethic, snorted when the term *artist* was applied to them, which in fact it seldom was until I and a few others of my generation started applying it. They were star players in a game made up of high-spirited drunks, carousers, and practical jokers. They identified more with Hecht and MacArthur's *Front Page* than they did with the loftiness that attended art galleries. Their definition of the work they turned out was "tomorrow's garbage." They devoted their energy, brilliance, and passion to a product that, once completed, they enjoyed demeaning. Anything less was sissyish, an offense to their manhood.

Eisner cheerfully derided my use of the term *art* in regard to his *Spirit* section. Not long out of the army, where he was stationed in Washington and edited and drew technical magazines of his own devising that served as humorous training guides for GIs, he more and more saw his future in noncomic publishing. In his early thirties, he was now in the process of redefining himself with a fishing magazine in the works, plans for a baseball magazine, and other schemes to move him at least partly away from his drawing table to a management desk.

As a result of this "maturation" process, it seemed to me that he began to lose interest in the stories he wrote. As a big fan of the prewar *Spirit*, where the stories, I thought, were as hypnotic and powerful as the art, I began to feel, a year or so into the job, disappointment in the drift of Eisner's scripts. His earliest *Spirit* adventures displayed a gift for compacting into eight short pages an abundance of character, incident, conflict, surprise twists, and happy resolution, all combined with humor, suspense, charm, and gritty realism. It was rich stuff for a boy fan, picking up a new *Spirit* section every Sunday, to find a delirious mix of O. Henry, Ring Lardner, and Guy de Maupassant infused into stories drawn with noirish RKO, Warner Brothers overtones.

But into my second year with Eisner, while I continued to find the art as exciting as ever, it seemed to me that the stories were losing their zing. Will's return from the army introduced a new density in both story and art. *The Spirit* became darker *and* funnier, wilder, and yet more serious. But by mid-1947, it wasn't what it had been. I found myself increasingly let down by Will's story writing. He was my hero, I was an idealist, I was now eighteen, so what was to stop me from bringing his loss of quality up for discussion?

This is more or less how I approached the subject: "Gee, Will, the *Spirit* stories you used to write were terrific, so much better than they are now. Why don't you go back to writing them as good as you used to?"

Why didn't he fire me? Amazingly, he said, "If you think you can do better, why don't you try your hand at one?" I asked him, "Seriously?" Whether he was telling me the truth or baiting me, I don't know, but he said yes.

Heady with excitement, I began to make notes on my first *Spirit* story. My model was the prewar Eisners. I researched, although it wasn't necessary. I knew the rhythms by heart—the slow build, the fixed camera over three or four panels that suddenly broke into dramatic crane shots, the pitter-pat back-and-forth development of plot meeting subplot, clues and coincidences coming together for the big payoff. After all, Will's art of storytelling was like no one else's in comics, and it had implanted itself in my head from the time I was eleven.

But I had a second influence: radio. I was an addict of radio drama, so much suggested so minimally, sound effects mingling with terse dialogue, movielike musical scores that heightened suspense. My favorite was the CBS drama *Suspense,* produced and directed by William Spier, who also directed *The Adventures of Sam Spade, Detective,* my second-favorite radio show, the one that got me to read Dashiell Hammett for the first time.

Using old Eisner techniques offset by settings of mood and atmosphere lifted from *Suspense,* I wrote a story about a young criminal off a Bronx-like street that could have been Stratford Avenue, robbing a candy store that could have been Pensky's. In the foreground and background, throughout the mounting bloodshed, a little girl on the sidewalk, oblivious to the action, sang street chants to a bouncing ball: "A my name is Alice and my sister's name is Alicia and we live on Alabama Street, B my name is Betty . . ."

While I had every intention of channeling Eisner, whose stories so affected me when I first came to love them seven years earlier, I managed to insert, quite without plan, significant chunks of my Bronx boyhood. This boyhood that I was so eager to leave behind so that I could move onward and upward in the world to which Eisner had opened the door. And to make good in that world, I had apparently decided that if I wasn't talented enough to be Eisner the artist, then I'd be Eisner the writer.

My goal, at this, my first attempt at writing professionally, was to become a perfect imitation of my mentor, exactly the mindset that had screwed up my cartooning. But something went awry: my cartooning side had willingly coopted itself into self-destruction; my writing side, unbeknownst to me, was made of sterner stuff. What it actually did, without letting me in on its secret, was to pretend to be Eisner while actually showing off Jules doing his Bronx sidewalk shuffle before *The Spirit*'s sizable syndicated readership.

Actually I didn't realize what I was up to until I just wrote this. Fortunately for me, Eisner didn't realize it either. He read my eight-page layout with crude sketches and dialogue and, to my complete surprise (as well as his own, I'm sure), said, "This is good, we're going to use this. Write more."

And I wrote more. And soon I was writing more of them than Will. And soon after that, I was the sole writer on almost all *The Spirit*'s stories, never meaning for it to read like anyone but Eisner but always dropping in pieces of myself.

Coming into that office as a boy cartoonist on his way, I had, from the beginning, lost my way. Looking to make up for unintentionally insulting Eisner, who had been nothing but generous to me, I had written a *Spirit* story that was really a Jules story in Eisner drag. And he ran it. And he ran all the rest, or almost all the rest, over the next three and a half years. I had graduated, without trying that hard, into ghosting *The Spirit*. And I didn't mean to do it. I had backed into it, my first experience with moving ahead by going in another direction.

I must step back from a surge of boastfulness here to modify and clarify: while I was the writer on *The Spirit,* I was by no means its auteur. That was Eisner. Every scene I conceived, no matter how it turned out, started out as if I were he. Later, when I was throwing in more and more pieces of myself, nothing went in that didn't exist comfortably with Eisner's sensibility.

He and I would first talk story. I'd do a layout of story line that was broken down into panels and dialogue. He'd okay it with changes, and I'd write in the copy. Next, I'd sketch a crude layout on sheets of bristol board that, when completed, would be the final art. Before the lettering was inked in, Will went over and revised, rewrote, and sometimes reconceived as he saw fit, seldom without discussion, sometimes even argument.

Though he could be acerbic at times, now and then sarcastic, even snide, these were minor asides that did nothing to detract from the astonishing fact that he had turned over to this eighteen-year-old who displayed more talk than talent the story line and much of the styling of this now-classic cartoon.

Gratitude can last only so long. After six months or so, I began to chafe under Will's restraints, his revision of dialogue that I thought better before his changes, his editing out the left-wing slant that I tried not so infrequently to sneak in. Underneath my compliant collaboration, hostility bloomed. Nonconfrontational as always, I restricted it to my stories and, using *The Spirit* as a stand-in for Eisner, perhaps once a month I'd write our hero, overmatched in a fight, being beaten to a pulp. It felt good.

The Spirit is © and ® Will Eisner Studios, Inc.

ED

Eisner's shop was the hub. Lunch hour was the time of the young cartoonists. The ambitious wannabes would show up at Will's, just as I had two years earlier, to display their wares in the hope of picking up some freelance work, but beyond that to connect themselves, if only briefly, to the one studio in town where one could feel an atmosphere free of cynicism and exploitation. Eisner was cheap, he took pride in it, but he didn't degrade or demean as so many editors in other comics houses seemed to enjoy doing. What you didn't get in money, you made up for in the spirit of the studio, which embodied a sense of idealism, a sense of mission. Boy cartoonists under the impression that they were going to take over the world dropped in on Eisner with their samples because it was understood that this was the place to be.

Most comic books during my time with Eisner had lost much of their appeal. Artwork had steadily improved over the neoprimitivism of the early days, but the sense of innocence and boyish wonder that inspired this cruder work of the midthirties had matured by 1948 into a corporate slickness. Proficient and soulless draftsmanship ruled the day. Joe Shuster, the cocreator of *Superman,* had been forced off his own creation, replaced by illustrators who drew better but felt less.

It was to take years for Jerry Siegel and Joe Shuster to receive proper respect (but never proper income). And as important as Will Eisner was, it was Siegel and Shuster, not Eisner, who gave us the superhero who, in one form or another, one unique attribute or another, was to seize the imagination of every generation from the midthirties to the present.

Jerry Siegel's earliest approach to a supercharacter had been in a high school fanzine run off on a mimeograph. It was called *The Reign of the Superman,* but this fellow was a villain, not a hero, sticking to time-honored tradition that presented Evil as smarter, cleverer, and stronger than Good. Good prevailed only at the last moment, through tenacity and dumb luck.

One summer night in 1934 Siegel conjured up a switcheroo: what if his superman was not a villain but a hero? In a world rife with Depression, violent crime, Fascism, and war, Siegel saw that America was in dire need of a hero with superpowers who used them to rescue, not to subjugate or destroy.

The bare bones of the origin story came to him in a rush. In a far-off galaxy, a planet called Krypton explodes. The single survivor is an infant, shot aloft in a space capsule by a scientist father. The baby Superman crash-lands in the American Midwest, where he is nurtured and raised by the kindly Kent family, who teach him the American way and inspire him to go off in cape and leotard to protect the helpless against crooks, mad scientists, natural disasters, and dictators.

The significance of all this struck close to a Bronx boy's heart. Jerry Siegel was a first-generation Jew reared in the Midwest during the burgeoning days of native American Fascism. He was witness, with the rest of us, to the rise of anti-Semitism, the radio broadcasts of Father Coughlin, the Christian Front, the America First Committee . . . Siegel was not like the blond, blue-eyed hunks who stood out from the unprepossessing Jewish kids he went to school with. Everywhere in sight of this Cleveland Jewish high school boy were Gentile jocks projecting an image of iconic Americanness. How could he not sense the difference? He might as well have come from another planet.

Superman was the ultimate assimilationist fantasy. Siegel and his illustrator partner, Joe Shuster, were not mild-mannered, bespectacled, nice Jewish boys out of choice. Their mild manners and glasses signified a nerdiness that in no way represented their inner selves. Underneath their schmucky Clark Kent facades lived Men of Steel! Or so they fantasized.

And if you're a cartoonist, a mere story line and a couple of squiggles turn fantasy into reality.

Jerry Siegel and Joe Shuster's accomplishment was to chronicle the striving Jewish boy's goyishe American dream. If that flirtatious chorus line of Lois Lanes in high school had but known what they were missing out on. Jerry and Joe, schlumpy and undersized, held more promise than the cocky Gentile jocks cruising down school hallways, their beefy arms hammerlocked around the boy cartoonists' dream girls.

Seen in this light, we can now discover Superman's true origin story. His actual place of birth was not the planet Krypton. That's a fake, a deception, a Potemkin village. In truth, Superman came down to us from the planet Poland, from Lodz maybe, possibly Crakow, maybe Vilna . . .

The commercial success of the Man of Steel opened the floodgates for an onslaught of superheroes in comic books, drawn by a new generation of kids off the street, Jewish boys out of the Bronx and Brooklyn, mostly. In newspaper strips, an older generation of Irish Catholic cartoonists held sway. The only Jewish newspaper strip artist who made a serious dent was Al Capp with his two popular strips, *Li'l Abner* and *Abbie an' Slats.*

But in comic books Siegel and Shuster with their superhero, and Eisner with his bravura off-the-page dramaturgy, encouraged a migration of young Jewish cartoonists who perceived comic books as their port of entry, an Ellis Island to the big time. Next stop, the open-ended and glamorous frontier of syndicated strips and magazine illustration. Bob Kane with *Batman,* Joe Simon and Jack Kirby with *Captain America,* Mort Meskin with *The Vigilante,* and Joe Kubert, Jerry Robinson, Alex Toth, and Irwin Hasen, inspired the admiration and envy of the next wave of young talent, who learned from these overnight Jewish boy icons the stylistic thrill of operatic overstatement, dramatically lit swashbuckling action laid out in converging chaotic panels.

This next wave, or some sizable portion of it, hung out at Eisner's shop, meeting one another for the first time, mingling, gossiping, eager to make an impression. Eisner's studio was turned into a bar without booze. Comics, with its nerve-jangling jumpiness, substituted for booze. The wisecracks, the sentimentality, the naïve excitement of being in the right place at the right time. Each young man brought back to say hello after showing Will his samples knew in his bones that he was fated to be the next success story. What none of them understood was that I was in line ahead of them.

Wally Wood, maybe a year older than I, was brought back to our office by Will, who was impressed by his samples (no threat to me, he drew backgrounds). Woody was from the Midwest. Enviably handsome, he had a squinting, tousled, mischievous charm. His squint let you know that he knew a lot more than he was saying, which was good, because he was at a loss for conversation. He seemed to be wary of speech; his prolonged silences made him formidable. While Abe and I wisecracked like smart-ass New York Jews, Woody, in no way Jewish, made sly elliptical comments that were possibly profound had we only understood what he was saying.

He shared studio space in a rundown walk-up in a Puerto Rican neighborhood in the Sixties on the Upper West Side (now Lincoln Center) with two other cartoonists and a couple of writers for comic books, already in training, with the help of beer, Chianti, and cheap rye, to make it to the top as the next generation of comic strip roustabouts. In the mid- and late forties, the first step to success for ambitious young men in the low arts was to make a mark in comic books as illustrator or writer and break into syndication with your own daily strip before you were thirty.

Cartoonists like Woody saw this as the end of the road, although some others who had the facility dreamed of moving further upscale to magazine illustration. That market was still flourishing with the *Saturday Evening Post, Collier's, Esquire, Cosmopolitan, Liberty.* A writer's ambitions, beyond comics, leaned toward breaking into the sci-fi market. And then more than a few had serious literary pretensions, becoming the next Hemingway by beginning in pulps as Dashiell Hammett did, then selling to the slicks, establishing a reputation for hard-boiled prose, then on to the real challenge, the semiautobiographical first novel. Norman Mailer had just been introduced by his publisher, Scribner's, as the next Hemingway. But why should there be only one? There might be two, three, four, any number of next Hemingways. Or Hemingway mixed with other tough guys: Hammett, Jack London, Raymond Chandler, James T. Farrell.

Woody introduced me to one of his studio mates, a lettering man named Ed McLean, who within minutes let me know that comics were not his end game, that his plan was to write the Great American Novel. Ed's heroes, besides Hemingway, were John O'Hara and James T. Farrell, whose novel *Studs Lonigan* was devoured by every pubescent city high school kid in America because of its steamy sex talk. To give a little context: this was at a time (hard to believe) when more than a few novelists had the glamour and stature of movie stars, with Hemingway the king, a near equal to Clark Gable or Gary Cooper.

Ed intended to impress me, and he did immediately. We met on my first visit to Woody's studio, a long room that deepened and darkened as your eyes failed to get used to it. Artists and writers sat like galley slaves at desks and drawing tables jammed close enough together to constitute a single piece of furniture, an intimidating world of cluttered comic pages and pounding typewriters, dingy and roach-rich. The no-frills ferocity of the place was intoxicating.

All my life I'd been drawn to good talkers—men and women like my sister Mimi who loved and needed to report on what went on in their lives from one moment to the next and were gifted with a combination of style, intelligence, and storyteller charm to make one happy to listen to their recitations, which managed to upstage and trivialize one's own sensibility. My envy of these raconteurs was palpable.

Ed was short and stocky, a big head with thin red hair, built like an Irish workingman, not a writer. But his bright blue eyes sparkled with irony and mischief and his constant half smile engaged and warned at the same time: Don't come too close. Unlike my Bronx Jewish friends, he gave off a presumption of danger—that, and he read books.

Ed was from the South Side of Chicago, Studs Lonigan territory, and like Farrell's hero and Farrell himself, he stemmed from Irish Catholic working-class roots. When we met in Woody's studio, he had been in New York for six months, on the lam from faith and family. Ed was an itinerant.

He hopped around, getting fed up with one place and moving on to another. The kind of writer he fancied himself to be was the sort whose book jackets recorded biographical information, none of it literary: bellboy, dishwasher, longshoreman, lathe operator, merchant seaman . . .

Ed called himself a communist, but with a small *c*. He expressed nothing but contempt for the Party my sister worshiped. The Communist Party wasn't radical enough for Ed; it was too theoretical for force and violence, it was too soft. Ed believed in the violent overthrow of capitalism. He lacked the patience to simply allow monopoly capital to wither away and die. He wanted to take up a club and beat it to death.

It thrilled my unquenchably equivocating psyche to befriend someone who made my sister and her comrades change before my eyes from red-hot Reds to wusses. Talking to Ed about his left-wing heroes—John Steinbeck, Theodore Dreiser, John Dos Passos, Jack London, Dashiell Hammett, the Wobblies, Big Bill Haywood, Eugene Debs, Clarence Darrow—names until then barely known to me, drove me to read and become a convert to an indigenous American radicalism that owed nothing to Mimi's Bolsheviks. Until Ed, I had never heard of Clarence Darrow or John Peter Altgeld or the Pullman strike or the Haymarket Riot or the *L.A. Times* bombing or Debs, in and out of jail, organizing, protesting, running for president, and getting more votes than anyone could have possibly dreamed. Ed introduced me to the romance of American radicalism, very different from the Soviet-inspired party and its "progressive" popular-front offshoots that I had learned about from Mimi and her lefty friends.

Though Ed and I worked in comics, Ed lettering script copy at any comic book house he could freelance at, our conversations centered not on comics or sci-fi, with writers other cartoonists liked to name-drop: Ray Bradbury, Arthur Clarke, Theodore Sturgeon. Ed preferred to talk about early Hemingway, *The Torrents of Spring,* the Nick Adams stories, writing as a way of recording truth, simply and directly, and then feeling it resonate on the page. Hemingway's alter ego, Nick Adams, a middle-class WASP from the Chicago suburb of Oak Park, Illinois, was, inexplicably, our fantasy figure. Reading "Big Two-Hearted River" made a fisherman of me. I, who could not give thought to baiting a hook without a rush of nausea.

Hemingway's way with words, or rather his way of eliminating words, made sense to a cartoonist's imagination: "Less is more." Less was, in fact, plenty. The air between words was like the silent panel in an adventure strip: it told the story by not telling, by giving over to the reader the job of filling in the writer's gaps. The reader imagines and thus becomes a collaborator with the writer in telling the story.

So for me it wasn't that much of a distance between the blank verse of "The Killers" and the blank universe of Bernard Baily's comic *The Spectre* or the deadpan bloodletting of Charles Biro's *Crime Does Not Pay* comics. Each took a spare and functional approach to his art, although neither Baily nor Biro thought what he did was art.

Ed and I could not stop talking on our daily two-hour walks through Central Park about how language in comics either did or did not do the job. And why did it, why did it not? He was as unlikely a friend as I was ever to find. An authentic vagabond. But after only a few months on the job, he announced his restlessness and promptly disappeared. Six- or eight- or twenty-page letters started arriving, fat in bulk and content, making him more present than ever. He wrote in longhand in block comic book lettering from small industrial towns in the Midwest where he had hitchhiked and got himself hired on the assembly line as a machinist, making spare automobile parts. I, who feared leaving home and couldn't drive and thought it unlikely that I would ever learn, read these precise proletarian tomes on assembling an automobile, and stark, forlorn descriptions of boardinghouse living.

Occasionally Ed wrote about women he was attracted to or dated, but not like my Bronx friends talking about girls. Ed's approach was that of his own recording secretary, simply stating the facts. Whether about a woman or a factory part, he wrote plainly yet colorfully, often wittily, with descriptions of men and women on the line, in cafeterias and bars, guiding me through the un-Bronx universe of Ohio, Michigan, and Indiana.

And then, after a few months, he was back in New York and we resumed our walks through Central Park. Ed enjoyed chatting about my contradictory qualities, my neurotic ups and downs. He spotted, appraised, and made fun of my innate cautiousness. But I found his criticism enhanced my stature. Where others seemed to make it their job to tear me down, Ed made it his to turn me into a special case, an embryonic talent to keep one's eye on. Before I was remotely capable of accomplishing anything, Ed had begun to compose my clippings.

How could we avoid becoming best friends? And when he once again vanished, I would receive these fantastic future great writer's letters that I saved and filed away by the dozens. Intimate conversations on paper. I felt honored to have his trust. His life was so different from mine, his background, his experience, his ambitions. And yet, like Hemingway's Nick Adams, I felt that the less we had in common was more. Our differences enhanced our friendship, adding a closeness that I never felt with my neighborhood friends. A lingering affection lasted between us for all the many years after we stopped seeing and mainly stopped speaking to each other.

Ed McLean, 1948

THEATER

My mother gave every impression of loving theater, but she never took us to a play. I recall going downtown with my parents to the mythic Depression movie houses—Radio City Music Hall, the Roxy, the Capitol, the Paramount—but I have no memory of this culture maven escorting us into the Shubert or the Biltmore or the Broadhurst or the Morosco. How come? Seats were cheap in those years, especially the farther up you went in the balcony, and I have no doubt that this was an experience she would have reveled in.

It seems that my mother inspired in us a love for a form we learned about entirely from secondhand sources—radio plays featuring Broadway stars (Mom's favorites being the two Helens, Hayes and Mencken); copies of *American Theatre* and *Theatre Arts,* glossy periodicals she laid out on the coffee table in the living room; and the then-named Drama section of the Sunday *New York Times.* It was my mother who introduced me to the art of Al Hirschfeld, whose wit, grace, and energy transformed every front page of the Drama section into an opening night.

My mother was knowledgeable about theater. She regularly entertained the family with songs, ditties, cute little dance steps culled from vaudeville shows and stage musicals ranging from the Gay Nineties ("I'm sorry I can't marry you today, my wife won't let me") to the 1920s ("Me and my shadow, we're walking down the avenyooo"). Through her, *I* became knowledgeable. I learned to drop playwrights' names like Maxwell Anderson, Sidney Kingsley, and Elmer Rice with almost as much familiarity as I could drop the names of Roy Crane, E. C. Segar, and Milton Caniff.

All this because of a woman who sang and danced a great game at home but never once walked her children down the aisle of a theater in the Great White Way.

My habitual response to my ignorance in this matter and others is to make up an explanation—that is, if I don't know the truth, I script it, then revise it, until I have a story line, a motive for things I don't know or don't understand, and then in the course of very little time I come to accept my story line as fact.

My mother understood the Depression to be a personal humiliation, a traumatic shift in status from up-and-coming career woman to impoverished family breadwinner. She was not a social thinker or a political thinker. If the Feiffers were poor—and when she looked around she could see that among her relatives and former friends it was we who had fallen the farthest—the blame belonged less to our national calamity than to my father and his string of business failures. His brothers and his sister managed not at all badly during the Depression. They were in real estate and the jewelry business and men's wear. All were doing well, one was rich. But Dave Feiffer had never done well. He opened and closed men's shops in New York, then New Jersey, then New York. Location did not affect his bad luck—or his acumen, which was not for business.

My mother, by nature not an uncritical admirer of men, should never have married. Men didn't really interest her, except impersonally, the ones she read about in the newspapers: artists, writers, celebrities, men of wealth, socialites . . . She had no interest in sex and not that much interest in children. But she certainly tended to us. She did her job. One of my mother's great stores of pride was that she did her job. As men did not do theirs. Men fell down on the job. Men drank. Men were weak. Men could not be trusted.

My mother married my father not out of love—I'm sure she liked him all right, he was a kind and gentle man—but because she was a nice Jewish girl and nice Jewish girls married. Nice Jewish girls may have had jobs, but they didn't have careers. Jobs were what you gave up when you married a nice Jewish man, a provider. Her family picked my father as a provider. A bad choice. Of the two, the way it turned out, my mother ended up the provider.

She was past thirty when she agreed to marry Dave Feiffer. The admonition from her mother surely went like this: "You're not getting any younger. Your sisters are all married. Also your brother. Already you're almost too old to have children. What are you doing with your life, Rhoda?" My mother was in awe of her mother, my grandmother whom I never met. She prided herself on being an obedient child. She boasted about it to us, obedience as a prime virtue. That she never got enough of it from her children was one of her many sources of sorrow.

She stood out from all the women in our Bronx neighborhood, and this was still true in her later years, long after her aspirations had dwindled into blame and bitterness. She dressed like an Upper East Side lady, not a Bronx housewife. She spoke in accentless English, in a voice that resonated class, no hint of Richmond, Virginia, or the South that she had been brought up in. Her voice alone was enough to levitate her above the nasally abrasive Bronx and European accents that were the norm for our neighborhood. She sounded superior to even her own children. To my ears she sounded like the American I wanted to be but was not. Articulation like hers you got from radio announcers: Ken Carpenter, who announced for Bing Crosby; Don Wilson, who announced for Jack Benny; Jimmy Wallington, Harry von Zell. These voices, like my mother's, resonated of belonging. What they belonged to was a club that let you in only if you had that certain sound. A sound that denoted Americanness. The way I sounded, I could never be a member. And my father? Forget it! My father spoke with the inflections of a Polish Jew. His *v*s came out as *w*s and his *w*s came out as *v*s, as in "I fought in Vorld Var Vun. I am a weteran."

The Feiffers and Davises (my mother's family) had known each other in Poland before both families migrated to the United States, the Feiffers to Yorkville in Manhattan's East Eighties, the Davises to Richmond, Virginia, where my mother was the subject of mockery and humiliation because of her immigrant mannerisms and accent.

Determination and a gift for mimicry cured her of both. By the age of fifteen, when her tailor father resettled them all in Yorkville, a block away from the Feiffers, she acted and sounded like a born and bred true-blue American. Now it was everyone around her, including her new boyfriend, Dave Feiffer, who seemed foreign.

By sixteen, my mother imagined for herself a future of fun and games and genteel bohemian living as a fashion designer. Sex and drink she saw as human frailties and had little use for. Men were kept at a courteous distance, useful as contacts, courtly as escorts. She was perky, witty, vivacious. People were drawn to her. Dave doted on her.

She thought she could control him, which had to be a primary reason for agreeing to the marriage. But control loses its appeal when your husband is deficient in feedback and strong on passivity. He couldn't hold a job or keep a business going, and, as she let out one day, walked off with $5,000 of her single-girl savings. To do what? Drink? Carouse? "The stories I could tell you, but you're not old enough."

I was never old enough. Not at thirteen, not at thirty. The dropped hints of his perfidy, plus my father's inability to mount any defense but silence, left him in a state of isolation in our household. Not much status but amiable. When I went to him with a request, he said, "Ask your mother." He was more of a presence to my sisters, but I saw him as a sweet, gentle, generally remote man reading in an armchair in the living room, little more than a tenant in the house, with opinions but no authority.

He was always reading but seldom said much about the books, beyond mentioning their titles. He loved Victor Hugo, especially *Les Misérables,* but also *The Man Who Laughed.* He thought *Les Misérables* was one of the finest novels ever written, and urged it upon me. So I avoided reading it, holding out until my midtwenties, at which age it didn't seem all that good. I confided this to my father, and he responded, "You don't know what you're talking about. You're full of hot air."

That was how he and I conversed across the years. In my teens, he turned out to be right about me. I didn't know what I was talking about or how to get out a complicated thought without the words tumbling over one another ass-backwards. My mother and sister Mimi were the talkers. I knew how to wisecrack—that was the role I played. Funny Guy. I made them laugh. I learned how from radio and movies: Fibber McGee and Jack Benny and Bob Hope and Charlie McCarthy, a ventriloquist's dummy who was funnier than I was.

But I learned fast and was narrowing the gap between Charlie and me. Except the dummy was better spoken. If it wasn't a wisecrack, I was hard put to come up with a coherent sentence. Language had not yet found roots in me. I depended on laughs.

I read, I enjoyed reading. But I started out as a slow and truculent reader. The printed word was a threat and a mockery until I was almost seven. What was the big deal about reading when there were radio serials to listen to? *Jack Armstrong, Don Winslow, Mandrake, Orphan Annie,* and, if one's taste verged toward the literary, Nila Mack's *Let's Pretend,* which dramatized fairy tales with flair and wit. When I was five and six my father worked patiently on my reading skills. He held up flash cards with simple words on them: H-O-U-S-E and B-R-E-A-D, words whose authenticity I refused to acknowledge. "Why does B-R-E-A-D have to spell bread? Who says so? Why can't D-W-P-X spell bread?" I thought I was being sold a bill of goods and I wasn't going to fall for it.

Letters on a page stared out at me as hostile gibberish. I came from a family of readers—my mother quoted Emerson, for God's sake, and Mimi read everything in sight, including the backs of cereal boxes. She even talked of becoming a writer, which meant she not only read, she spelled, which was more than I could do with B-R-E-A-D.

My father's patience had its limits. I had him stymied. So he gave up on me, a pragmatic decision that led to a lifetime habit. "I can't do a thing with that boy," he said, more times than I can count (which I couldn't do that well either).

If it hadn't been for my love of comics, I might have held out for who knows how long. The truth was that reading was the unknown and I was not good with the unknown. Adventure was not to be found in this boy's soul. Risking the unknown frightened me, and fear had me dig in my heels. I didn't seem or act frightened, just stubborn. But I was terrified. Terror was a staple of my youth. My gut response to the axiom that connects risk to growth—"You have to walk before you can run"—was "Who says I have to do either?"

My litigious front was a coverup for my certain knowledge that knowledge meant death. And it was only comics that could make me risk death. Only comics led me to recognize reading as something more than a curse, which, like sports, I was never going to be any good at.

The grim and practical truth was that comics were words *and* pictures. To understand Segar's *Popeye* or Crane's *Wash Tubbs* or Raymond's *Flash Gordon* or Foster's *Tarzan,* I had to swallow my fear and cede my principles to the grown-ups and their miserable world of rules and regulations. From my mother at the top of the pyramid to my kindergarten and first-grade teachers, I had already endured too many assaults on my fragile identity.

I wasn't meant for school. I had to be dragged off to kindergarten, and eight years later, each morning I had to drag myself off to high school, never without the same sense of dread that had been dogging me since first grade. I'm sure I must have had good days, but I remember none of them. There had to have been at least one good teacher, but if so I can't come up with a name. Yes, I can. Three or four: there was Mrs. Karow, my open-air-class teacher at P.S. 77; Max Wilkes, my high school art teacher; and Max "Sunshine" Taub, who taught me math by making jokes. But they left no mark that in any way lightened the load I carried as I made my way from 1235 Stratford Avenue to P.S. 77 three blocks away, and later, across the street, to James Monroe High School.

I hated learning. I hated doing anything anyone else's way but my own—and my way was not to do it at all. I hated the grown-up world of joyless rules and regulations, where art appreciation classes turned art into algebra, formulaic and funless, and required reading turned literature into the pleasureless pursuit of what was termed "comprehension," which meant "We don't expect you to like books. We, your teachers don't like them either. But if you don't read, you can't get a job, so we make you read writers we, ourselves, would never read a line of if we didn't have to teach you, and we resent it so much we pass on our dislike to you."

But learning to read could actually be fun if it was a comic strip.

Words were less fear-inducing, hand lettered as they were, inside scalloped balloons. Not printed in cold, heartless type that spread like an ant infestation over a page.

Comics gave me motivation. After my stubborn and principled stand that drove my father to throw down the flash cards, leave the room, leave the house, go to the bar under the El down the block, I relented. Gibberish rearranged itself into discernible patterns. And I understood them. I could place them in an order that I came to recognize as a sentence. In comics, sentences ended not with periods but with exclamation points. I was beginning to find this interesting, the business of words making sentences and how you made sense of them by way of punctuation: commas, dashes, three dots, as in "What th . . ." or "You can't get away with th . . ."

Interrupting a word in the middle, not letting it finish, in a sense abusing or overthrowing or undermining the sentence, this was of great interest to me. Not only was I becoming a reader, I was becoming a reader with an agenda. Who says it has to be done this way, when it can be done that way or another way or any way I want? Because I understand how the system works now—at age seven and a half—which means, if I have a mind to, I can redesign it.

While I projected a meek and mild exterior, Clark Kent as a boy, my interior vision cast me as Superchild: smaller and weaker than other boys my age but, if the truth were to be told, more powerful (but not a bully), more ambitious (but self-effacing), more imaginative (but operationally passive), more in charge than all the grown-ups tied together (which was exactly my plan).

Unfortunately, this plan had to be periodically revised, modified, and scaled down because of my soul-numbing, semicomatose passivity. Years later I was to recognize myself in Herb Gardner's classic cartoon of two men sunk in their chairs, feet up on a café table, and one of them saying: "Next week we've got to get organized."

Whatever my fantasies of self, they rose or fell depending on the facial expressions of my mother or a word or two from her. She was the enabler or censor of my dreams. Her praise of one of my comics pages filled me to excess. A raised eyebrow, a hooded eye, a down-turned mouth because

I wanted to finish a drawing before I dried the dishes—"Two minutes more, Ma!"

"Why are you doing this to me, Sonny Boy?" This could give me cramps.

She singled me out as her knight errant and confidant, briefing me, tirelessly, on the hardships of her working life, the broken promises, the bad faith. She lectured me on who and what I must become: a successor to one of the great men about whom she found no shortage of articles in newspapers and magazines. Every one of them self-made: Bernarr Macfadden, the body-building publisher who parachuted out of an airplane at the age of eighty; Bernard Shaw, the bitingly brilliant Irish playwright and world-renowned wit; Bernard Baruch, the elderly elder statesman who gave advice to presidents while sitting on a park bench.

Repeated mention of these names in her insistent, lesson-giving drone made me want to escape the planet, run off to sea, look away from my mother—which I was not allowed to do while she was speaking.

"Am I boring you, Sonny Boy?"

"No, Ma."

Was it any wonder that years later when I sought to create a character who represented me at my wimpiest the name I came up with was Bernard?

Our near impoverishment was her constant shame. Living hand to mouth, unlike others on either side of the family or her friends (former friends now), working girls, artists with whom she used to gab and sing songs and party—every one of them dropped as our income vanished. Our family floated on my mother's buried river of shame, which could run quietly for weeks, lulling us, only to suddenly flood over and threaten us with drowning. My mother was the river's source, and she was the dike that held it back. You could take the temperature of our household by the magnetic charges off her presence when she entered a room.

Her shame forbade her the lights of Broadway. Refinement was important to my mother. To be a lady, to look it and dress it, to carry herself with pride, dignity . . . How could she go to the theater, where even during the Depression—especially during the Depression—people dressed up, women wore their best? The ladies in the orchestra, decked out in the latest fashions, perhaps some of them designed by but not affordable to my mother, would spot Rhoda in the second balcony in her shameful frock and snicker to let her know that she didn't dress properly for the occasion.

"Heartbreak, it's heartbreak, Sonny Boy."

A fall from grace in the second balcony. It could not be tolerated.

So we didn't go to Broadway. Instead, I took myself to the Windsor Theater on Fordham Road in the west Bronx, where shows, having finished successful runs, tried out before going out on tour with their second companies, road companies.

The Windsor, a nice enough, run-down, rococo five-hundred-seat house, was built in the 1920s, a time when the Bronx was coming into its own for Jews from the Lower East Side and Yorkville with the drive and chutzpah to move to the suburbs. And the Bronx back then was—remarkably—a suburb.

But not in my time or my psyche. The Bronx was as near to being a slum as I could put up with. I didn't want to live there. Not from birth, not ever. I ranted within against the very existence of this misplaced, misbegotten birthplace where I could barely breathe, where I couldn't be me, where I couldn't stand the person who was me.

It was a mistake. I wasn't meant for these parents. I wasn't meant to be Jewish. I was Episcopalian, or whatever that church was where movie stars dressed up to go in MGM movies. Not Warner Brothers—too Irish Catholic. I couldn't identify. I was born to be one of the MGM lot and to sound like Ronald Colman or David Niven. I was born to be English.

But I was trapped where I was until twenty-one, the magic age I had picked when not only would I be old enough to vote, I would be old enough to escape. And my mother could not legally stop me.

The truth actually was that I could have escaped a hundred times in a hundred different ways. And it never dawned on me. Others, my age and younger, took the No. 6 Lexington Avenue line that stopped at the El station a block from our apartment building. Kids my age—girls!—got on the subway in groups or alone. Yes, at twelve and thirteen, alone, and traveling down to 125th Street, where they changed trains to the No. 2 or 3, which took them in two stops to Times Square. Where everything a boy who was taught to love theater by his mother and who was taught to love popular music (Glenn Miller and Tommy Dorsey and Charlie Barnet) by his big sister, *everything* I craved to be out of the Bronx for, would have been at my fingertips. All in a twenty-minute train ride.

But no! If I got on one of those trains by myself, I would get lost. Without my mother or sister or a group of friends, it would be my end. I would never be heard from again. At times when nevertheless I was tempted to face the challenge, I became dizzy with nausea.

It was safer to go to the Windsor. The Windsor I could get to by trolley car. Two trolley cars. The route was infinitely more complicated, required more walking, circling around from one trolley line to another, longer waiting. But by the time I reached my destination an hour later I was okay—because I hadn't left the Bronx. The Bronx was safe. If I stayed in the Bronx, I'd live. If I wandered into Manhattan, I'd be killed. Why? Who? What? Street gangs? A falling building? A bomb on the subway? I didn't dare ask; asking questions could kill me.

My mother never suggested I do the sensible thing and take the subway downtown into the heart of Manhattan. This was where she went virtually every day of my childhood, down to the Garment District on Seventh Avenue and Thirty-seventh Street, to sell her fashion sketches door-to-door, to designers and manufacturers at three dollars a pop. My mother was courageous in regard to herself, taking a chance on the train five days a week, but her son she watched like a hawk. "Don't!" was her watchword. Danger lurked. It was out there, everywhere, waiting for me. "Be careful, Sonny Boy." And oh, was I. More careful than if I were my own mother, carrying the baby me in my arms.

I treated myself as breakable. I must have been one of the few boys in the history of the Bronx who lived through an entire childhood without a bone fracture. I was cautious, vigilant, understood that automobiles and trucks existed to kill me. But they'd have to catch me first. I ran, not walked, across streets. Red lights, I knew, were a ploy used by drivers to put me at ease so that if I walked, not ran, in front of them (thus making myself an easy target), they would run me over.

Cars were dangerous, riding inside a car was dangerous. A car could crash and kill you. Subway trains could crash and kill you. Trolleys could crash and kill you. When these various monster modes of transit weren't plotting to run me down, they were plotting to blow me up or crush me, kill me! "Take that for your laughable hubris! Your dreams of—CRUNCH!—glory!"

A trolley car had been the cause of my sister Alice's broken leg. She had gotten off on Westchester Avenue at the Stratford Avenue stop early one evening. The tracks ran under the No. 6 Lexington Avenue El. A car, a Hudson, traveling uptown was in too much of a hurry to let Alice cross in front of it. Four steps off the trolley, she was run over. She was twelve.

Alice was rushed to Lincoln Hospital, a sick joke then, noisy, smelly, understaffed, overcrowded, overrun with cockroaches who were drawn to Alice the way cats are drawn to people who don't like them. As she lay there immobile, they swarmed over her, filling her with a fear of bugs that lasted for years.

I visited in dread and nausea, sneaking in before and after visiting hours, smuggling in food, gifts, knickknacks prepared by my mother. I traveled by trolley, the very beast that spit Alice out in front of the Hudson. I endured my baby sister's discomfort, isolation, confusion, and feelings of abandonment, told jokes in funny voices, made up stories to lift her spirits and mine in the vain hope of drowning out the all too obvious lesson of what happened to Feiffer children when they left the house to take public transportation.

Only walking was safe. I walked everywhere. It left me, I thought, in charge of my fate. I could pick the route, which was the safe street as opposed to the street where I'd surely be mugged. If I could avoid mass transit by walking a mile or more, then that's what I'd do. Walking seemed to enhance who and what I was. It made me larger than life. Not that much larger, but any additional size, weight, and illusion of manliness was accepted with surprise and gratitude.

Sitting in the back of the house, in the cheap seats of the Windsor, made me larger than life as well. Actors, a long distance away, projecting to me in the rear or in the balcony, without mikes, a skill all actors possessed at one time. Declaiming, as they stood in severe outline, brightly lit against overdressed sets of living rooms infinitely nicer than mine, or of downtrodden street scenes, which looked glamorously and enviably shabby.

Willy Loman's house in Brooklyn transplanted in two-story schematic outline to the stage of the Windsor was one of the more riveting sights of a lifetime. The stage designer—Jo Mielziner—supplied me X-ray eyes so that I could see the outside and inside of the house at the same time, observe through Willy's walls into the heart of his family. Which turned out to be my family too.

"Pop, Pop," Biff, the son, says, in this never-to-be-forgotten paraphrase from memory, "we've never told the truth for one minute in this house." The line was staggering. This assault against Biff's father . . . If only I had the courage (ridiculous!), I could have said that to my father. But unlike Biff in *Death of a Salesman,* I would have gotten nowhere. Because my father would have answered, "You're full of hot air. You don't know what you're talking about." End of confrontation, end of play.

What the Loman family taught me onstage at the Windsor was that Willy, who killed himself, wasn't half the failure my father was, and Dave Feiffer was still going semistrong, reading his Lanny Budd novels and *Les Misérables.* And I, surely, was not destined to go down the drain like Biff Loman. I was more like the neighbor's boy, Bernard (what an interesting name), who was mocked for being a nerd by Biff, the jock. But he, Bernard, went on to become a big shot, a lawyer who argued before the Supreme Court. The truth revealed! I was Bernard!

Arthur Miller rose above all other playwrights to become my hero playwright. He surpassed Clifford Odets, the founding poet of left-wing Jews on the Broadway stage. Odets had been my first love among playwrights because he seemed to write diagrammatic versions of me and mine. I picked up every play of his I could find in the library, with the single exception, oddly enough, of his most famous work, *Waiting for Lefty.* No one wrote more recognizably about poor Jewish families: *Awake and Sing!* and *Rocket to the Moon* and *Paradise Now.* I loved them then and remember little about them now. Except for Odets's voice, with its singular and unforgettable cadence, still resonating even now, years after Warner Brothers adapted it for their gangster films and dead-ended it into cliché. Warners' took Odets's benighted working-class immigrants and mobbed them up: Edward G. Robinson, Bogart, Raft, and, most particularly and brilliantly, John Garfield, who became the personification of the Odets hero as movie star.

Garfield was the first Jew to make it in Hollywood by playing an actual Jew. Edward G. Robinson and Paul Muni played Italians, sometimes Mexicans, even Frenchmen. Well, Paul Muni was a trained classical actor: he could almost get away with French. But when Garfield played anyone but a Jewish kid from the streets, his audience of Jewish kids from the streets found it laughable—and something of a betrayal. Garfield, with that Bronx Odetsian rhythm to his voice, the caustic sentences, the singsong phrases seething with the injustices done him and the rest of us. Garfield was the one Bronx Jew Hollywood allowed. Chanting in a Bronx poetry of victimization. I identified.

And then Arthur Miller came along and became something Odets never became: the playwright as movie star. No one knew what Odets looked like. No one cared. But Arthur Miller emerged after *Death of a Salesman* as the socialist glamorous fighter for peace and justice. Roughneck and victim, intellectual and common man, a writer who not only spoke for us as Odets had done but *was* us. Like John Garfield. That was the wonder of Arthur Miller: he was our Julie Garfield playing a great playwright.

FEAR

Finally, in the uncertain way one moves or does not move forward, a decision had to be reached about this fear thing. If I was afraid of everything and anything, if that turned out to be my ever-present state of mind, if fear was as much a part of my essential self as drawing cartoons or being funny, how did I alter that part of me I couldn't stand? And who gave the responsibility of doing something about this to me? I had no aptitude for taking charge. My life thus far had been ceding authority passively to others, and resenting them for it.

But what else was I to do? I was innately unqualified to take charge of myself—or anyone else. My sister Alice, for example: Only a few years earlier, when my mother would draft me to watch over and protect her, even if it was only for a half hour while she went shopping, I quaked inwardly at the perilous position she had put me in. I raged at the injustice of this imposition—to myself, of course. I didn't dare show how I felt to my mother.

Didn't the woman realize what she was getting me into? What if another kid picked on Alice and I had to defend her? I wouldn't know how to do that. What if Alice was kidnapped off the street? It could happen. She was an adorable child. Of course, I knew what my response to the kidnappers would be. It would be to charm them so that they would kidnap only Alice and not me. And whom would my mother blame for this kidnapping, which by rights she should have acknowledged was her fault in the first place for putting me in charge? She wouldn't have blamed herself; my mother never took the hit. I'd be blamed, yelled at for being helpless. But helpless was who and what I was. I couldn't take charge of myself, much less my kid sister, this albatross around my neck who insisted on exposing me to me for the miserable coward I was.

Everything at home served to remind me of my cowardice. My mother and my sister Mimi, neither of whom I could stand up to; my father, whom I couldn't stand up to even though the rest of the human race treated him with condescension; my sister Alice, to whom my mother consigned me as savior. Too much to ask! I had to get away!

My failure to cope was never off my mind except when I drew or when I read. Only under those circumstances could I escape the house while in the house. But escaping, beyond the realm of fantasy, escaping in *fact,* not fantasy, was more and more on my mind. The semicomatose state that drawing and reading put me in no longer was enough. It had become strikingly apparent that in order to go on living with myself I had to get away. From them. From myself. But stuck back in the 1940s, that pre-druggie age, without marijuana or cocaine to ease me off the premises, the conclusion set in that my only escape was to hit the road.

Under the prodding of Ed McLean, I had come across this fat tome in the library with a red, white, and blue cover: *U.S.A.* by John Dos Passos. It was *not* required reading in my school so of course I devoured it and was devoured by it. I discovered an America unknown to a first-generation Jewish boy from the Bronx. The vastness, the prairie, labor in its endless varieties and brutish romantic manifestations, the Wobblies, the vagabond life, hoboes riding rails . . . Riding the rails out West—the freedom, hopping onto a freight train. Escape!

Over by the Bronx River, a mile walk from our house, ran the tracks of the New York Central. High above the open tracks, I looked down from the refuse-laden lot that dropped beneath my feet into a narrow sixty-foot gorge, just wide enough for two sets of railroad tracks, one headed north toward freedom, the other south toward freedom. I could stand up there for hours watching trains go by, seeing myself perched perfectly to look down on these fast-moving open doors leading me out of my mother's house into Oz.

I could imagine everything about riding the rails, except a destination. Scared to take the subway alone eliminated specifics. The name and location of a place, the distance—how dare I dream of a location hundreds, thousands of miles away when I couldn't imagine myself on a seven-mile subway ride to Times Square? This fear I had was not going to be cured by naming a destination; one scary place was as good as another. And as inspired as I was by John Dos Passos, the romance of riding the rails out of the Bronx—I knew that was never going to happen. It wasn't the means of travel, it was the going, the leaving, the getaway. So, if not in a boxcar, by what other means could I escape?

A few of my left-wing friends had started to hitchhike.

It seemed safer, certainly less inviting of disaster, if three or four of us hitched together, a mix of boys and girls I had gotten to know just out of high school. We were all members of the AYD, the American Youth for Democracy, a left-wing organization I joined in high school under the sponsorship of my sister the Communist. Mimi assured me that the AYD was "Progressive," not Communist, extremely pink but not Red. In the thirties and forties these were known as Popular Front organizations, which, as far as Mimi was concerned, meant that I would now be more in line with "enlightened" political positions. I took my sister's assurances at face value and with a grain of salt, ambivalence being my only honest political position. The Cold War was in recent full swing and all arguments from Communists and anti-Communist liberals sounded persuasive to me. I swayed from one position to the other, convinced that I was being thoughtful. Mimi made it clear that she saw my wavering as gutless. Her arguments, as always, sounded convincing. Certainly they intimidated me into a half-hearted membership in the AYD, in order to prove to her that I wasn't what she openly and I, secretly, knew myself to be. But as I fell into line, I found a more personally persuasive reason to join. It was to meet girls.

The girls I met in the AYD were attractive and almost as forceful as Mimi. The boys I met—at least the one or two who became friends—were more diffident, enjoyed a good argument, and didn't mind postponing a conclusion to achieve unity. With ample amounts of wry, satiric humor, kidding as they shifted positions, they managed to be good at going along.

If you were a young lefty in New York in the mid-1940s, there were certain stylistic givens. You were understood to like folk music (the Weavers), folk dancing (the hora), Eisenstein movies at the Stanley Theater on Irving Place (*Potemkin, Alexander Nevsky*), hitchhiking on weekends to Bear Mountain (camping out).

I was partially a dissident. I loved the folk music, the Weavers in particular. But Eisenstein films bored and irritated me. *Alexander Nevsky,* a movie many of my friends claimed to adore, I saw as a plodding, heavy-handed, dumb Western. With a good score by Prokofiev. Or was it Shostakovich? Mimi liked them both, so I paid attention.

Camping, too, gave me pause. The thing was, if you went camping it was understood by all that you slept in pup tents, tiny little one-person units that you had to put up yourself, meaning setting it up with stakes in the ground so that it looked like a pup tent and not like a misconceived assemblage passing itself off as soft sculpture. And it was out there in the country, in the open, as it were, outdoors.

My fellow campers on these weekend excursions included Bob Laurie, a former classmate at James Monroe who liked art, had ambitions to paint, was committed to a not overly serious left-wing politics, and laughed a lot at my jokes—the sort of companion I could hardly improve upon.

And then there were the two girls, fellow lefties our age who must have also thought I was funny or I wouldn't have agreed to invite them. The thing about left-wing girls was that they weren't like regular girls, certainly not the ones we had known at James Monroe. They weren't girly or scary, that is flirtatious or, more to the point, intimidating. They acted more like boys than girls, which made them fun to be with, although you could never develop a real crush on one of them. They didn't walk with swinging hips or run from side to side like real girls. They were more direct and less sexy. As smart or smarter than the boys and, unlike regular girls, they didn't mind showing it. They were more earthy than regular girls, often seeming to have come right off the screen of the Stanley Theater in some Eisenstein film, to talk politics and books and to be companions to Bob and me as we hitchhiked to Bear Mountain.

Our destination in Bear Mountain was Lake Tiorati, Bob and I and our two girl companions, Doris and Paula, both short and stocky, and one of whom I was to fall in love with three years later. But how was I to know that Doris, smart, pretty, peasanty, might actually be thinking of me in the middle of the night in her neighboring pup tent? I was far too straitlaced to play with such thoughts. Here I was at eighteen, walking around with a twenty-four-hour hard-on but never losing sight of the fact that I was Rhoda Feiffer's son and therefore forbidden to make moves on a girl on Bear Mountain in the middle of the night.

Moves on girls were not what I was meant to make. Pining for girls was more like it. Walking behind the James Monroe football field on Elder Avenue on spring and summer evenings, year after year as I grew into young manhood. Spotting out of the corner of my eye boys and girls, no more than weeks, maybe days, older than I, sitting on park benches lined up outside the concrete wall that bordered the field. Row after mocking row of them, making the same moves I yearned to make but never would, never could: synchronized necking as expert as the Rockettes' routines at the Radio City Music Hall, her head tilted against his this way, his hand reaching ever closer to her breasts that way. I was content to know that I, too, would have this. But not quite yet, and not outside James Monroe, and not on Bear Mountain. It was bad timing.

Anyhow, camping wasn't about that stuff. It was not about girls or sex or even about camping. It was about how I got there, that was the point. It was about sticking out my thumb next to Bob's thumb and Doris's thumb and Paula's thumb, four left-wing kids honoring the tradition of the itinerant American—as in Dos Passos's *U.S.A.*, as in Dreiser's *American Tragedy,* as in Woody Guthrie's "So Long, It's Been Good to Know You" . . . the acting out of an American romance: hitchhiking!

We were picked up in prewar and postwar Nashes and Buicks and Studebakers and Fords on Route 9W, which we reached by walking across the George Washington Bridge. Middle-aged and older men, even an occasional woman behind the wheel. The men often the age of my father, but unlike my father these men asked me questions as if I were not there to defend, or account for, myself. These men seemed interested in me. And they weren't homosexuals, or molesters, or any of the threats to safety that my mother might conjure up. These men afforded me the opportunity, my first, to open my mouth as if I had something to say, to try out this other Jules I was waiting to become. In these cars, with these drivers who were salesmen, businessmen, laborers, I didn't sound like the Jules I knew from Stratford Avenue. I sounded like a stranger whose voice I didn't recognize. I sounded like Jules, ten years into the future in Greenwich Village, chock-full of wit and trenchant observations. I reacted to my words in awe as I heard them come out of my mouth.

So in my mind these hitchhiking trips ended up not so much as trips to go camping as trips to Dr. Frankenstein's laboratory. Each trip brought the doctor's experiment closer to realization: the creation of an unfet-tered, less fearful me. Camping had become irrelevant. Irrelevant, too, were my three friends, whose company I enjoyed but who were cast as supporting players in this movie, me in close-up in a prewar automobile, talking up a storm, making listeners of all my supporting players, most importantly the driver. Each outing was a new test, a tryout, practice to make perfect my Dr. Frankenstein's creation.

Two years later, Doris was my girlfriend and we necked. Everywhere. Maybe not on park benches outside James Monroe but just about every-where else. She had a Russian girl's sly prettiness, a twinkling eye, a teas-ing manner. I had a wild crush on her. We went to the RKO Chester and necked, the Bronx Zoo and necked, to Webster Hall to see Pete Seeger and Woody Guthrie, and on the way home on the subway, we necked. In her parents' apartment on Vyse Avenue (appropriately named), we necked . . . This girl, who no more than a year and a half earlier I had slept next to pup tent to pup tent and not a lascivious thought in my head, now made my head and other more vital parts of me quiver with passion.

Toward what end? I was no less Rhoda's son than when we hitched to Bear Mountain. Late at night, I took the trolley home, sat alone in blissful discomfort on the near-empty streetcar, walked a block home with my wounding erection, sneaked into our darkened apartment, past my sleep-ing, unknowing parents, past my sleeping baby sister (Mimi was already out of the house, organizing the workers)—and in the throes of sexual delirium fell asleep, in anticipation of nature doing for me what I was too inhibited to do for myself. In the morning my top sheet was sticky with an emission I didn't know the name for. My mother didn't have a name for it either, but that didn't stop her lecture.

I thought of Doris as my girl, and the condition I found myself in, a crush. I watchfully waited for it to develop into something more serious. I wanted us to be in love but to not rush it. I wanted to feel her up, which I had every right to do if this was love. Doris was short and solid, with round, solid breasts that I thought of day and night. I didn't actually want to screw Doris, I just wanted to squeeze her.

We talked a lot on the phone during the week, and on weekends we spent every free minute together. She was graduating from high school and applying to colleges. I was into my third year working for Will Eisner.

By this time I knew that college did not make sense for me. Having come up short on admission tests to NYU's Washington Square School of the Arts and Cooper Union, this decision was not hard for me to make. I was mortified by these rejections but in the end relieved. I disliked high school and didn't think I'd do well in college. But any girl I fell for must have a college education. I wanted a girl whom I could talk about books and movies and politics with, while feeling her up. She would need college to keep up with me because I was educating myself and was quite serious about it in a manic, eclectic, and randomly left way: taking out library books on the Industrial Revolution, the robber barons, the rise of organized labor, strikes, the suppression of dissent, the Palmer raids . . .

S elf-education was a sideline to my chief assignment, which was establishing myself as a cartoonist. By 1947 Eisner had given me, instead of the raise I asked for, my very own comic strip. It ran on the back page of the *Spirit* section. The *Spirit* section, originally sixteen pages with two accompanying features, *Lady Luck* and *Mr. Mystic,* had been downsized to eight pages. *The Spirit* took up seven pages, with page 8 reserved for a funny filler that I was allowed to create, *Clifford.* It was written from a child's point of view and drawn in a style that I hoped would look something like Walt Kelly's *Pogo.* My idea was to write and draw about the kind of kids I had grown up with, as they really were, and not as adults chose to see them—pesky, troublemaking urchins like Dennis the Menace.

I was eighteen, with the maturity of a fourteen-year-old, so this was going to take no stretch of the imagination. Drawing upon my likes, dislikes, hobbies, dreams, annoyances, and hang-ups at nine or ten years old was easy. To turn it into a nine-panel comic strip in the form of a traditional Sunday page turned out to be something I almost knew how to do, but not quite. I had an instinctive feel for the form of a Sunday comic page. I'd grown up with the Sunday supplements, studied them all, including the kids' strips from *Reg'lar Fellers* to *Nancy*. But I was unpracticed and frustratingly limited in my craft. Full of clichés that I disdained in others. It turned out to be more natural for me to write an episode of *The Spirit* than to write and draw my own comic strip.

For *The Spirit* I had guidelines to follow, Eisner's. It was entirely Eisner's creation, and almost from its beginnings he had laid out a format in terms of style, pacing, plot, and subplot that made it surprisingly simple for me to write *Spirit* episodes once I had come up with the basic plots. I took my story lines and constructed them according to Eisner's playbook: a splash-page introduction to attract the reader's immediate interest and plunge us right into the story; often enough, the use of a narrator who walks center stage and addresses the reader. Taking Eisner's lead, I came up with characters who were innocent bystanders pulled into a plot, a conspiracy, a bizarre series of coincidences that test, demoralize, all but destroy them until, on page 5, our hero, the Spirit, makes his late entry, cast in a cameo role rather than the centerpiece driving the story, which resolves itself in a traditional and violent ending, bittersweet, ironic, never entirely happy. Pure Eisner. All of this I mastered in less time than it takes the Spirit to beat up three or four bad guys.

Not ever did these stories, during the three years I wrote them, descend into hackwork. I loved writing *The Spirit*. I understood from the start what a great apprenticeship this was for the career that had to follow. But when it came to *Clifford,* my own strip, without the preset guidelines of *The Spirit,* I didn't know what I was doing or how to go about doing it.

Very little shows up in *Clifford* to predict the sort of satire I was to create for the *Village Voice* just nine years later. *Clifford* looks today like a cross between *Peanuts* (not yet in print) and *Calvin and Hobbes* (many

Back page of the *Spirit* section, June 18, 1950

years away from print). Unlike Charles Schulz's creation, which was to come along less than a year later, my little boy was as brash and self-seeking as Bill Watterson's Calvin but living in an environment markedly closer to Charlie Brown's. All three strips had the same aim: to say something deeper and truer about a kid's experience than anything that had gone before.

Now, even though I had preceded both Schulz and Watterson with my kids' strip, I was still too young and callow (and cautious) to make my point or make my mark. Both in drawing and in writing I slipped too easily into cliché. *Clifford,* viewed today, looks less like a lead-in to Charlie Brown and Calvin than like a reflexive, occasionally reflective series of prankish, noisy, predictably smart-ass gags from a young cartoonist with an attitude.

Without Eisner's guidelines I was on my own, and not up to it. Schulz and Watterson, older and more mature artists, came up with two of the great creations in comic strip history. I came up with a promising opening act for *Sick, Sick, Sick* and the *Village Voice* years that were to follow.

Doris was on her way to Berkeley, enrolled as a freshman at the University of California. And how was she getting there? She and her girlfriend Paula, also enrolled as a freshman, were hitchhiking. Her decision threw me for a loop. I thought (hoped) I was in love with Doris. Still and all, as I saw it, Doris wasn't quite in my league. I was smarter, wittier, more charming, had a better sense of humor, was better read, and had more and noisier opinions. I was the dominant one in the relationship.

But it was she who was thumbing her way to Berkeley, an act so unimaginable in my scheme of things that it toppled my sense of status and elevated Doris to the rank of goddess. I couldn't imagine myself hitching beyond Bear Mountain. Once and only once had I made it to Lake George, two hundred miles upstate. Not in my life was I going to hitchhike to California. I gave myself lots of good reasons: (1) it would break my mother's heart, (2) I had an important job writing *The Spirit* and writing and drawing *Clifford,* which now appeared in about a half dozen newspapers and, locally, in my hometown, in the *Sunday Compass.* The *Compass* was a left-wing newspaper, not quite Communist. It could have been invented for me. The *Compass* carried the column of I. F. Stone, an investigative journalist whose tough takes on Eisenhower's hard-line Cold War administration— particularly John Foster Dulles at State, his brother Allen at the CIA, and J. Edgar Hoover at the FBI—filled me with a degree of rage and joyous bile that eventually determined my career as a political cartoonist. Stone made me see government as I never had before—its deliberate lies, cover-ups, and dissembling language. Its haughtiness, smugness, and obfuscation. I worshiped at the altar of I. F. Stone. And now the hitchhiking goddess Doris, braver and stronger than I, was manipulating me to abandon my twice-a-week Stone fix and follow her out to California. Doris, how could you?

Not only that, but once she got out to Berkeley, wherever *that* was (they had perfectly good schools in the East; hadn't she heard of Columbia?), Doris started sending me letters that in a period of a month went from sweet affection to contempt. Her taunting inference was that I was a gutless coward too scared to hitch cross-country, which she, half my size but with twice my courage, had done. Her inference was indirect but emasculating. The girl of my dreams was telling me, as my mother and my sister Mimi so many times before had told me, that I had let her down. A flawless approach such as that left me no choice. How could I not turn my back on *The Spirit, Clifford,* and Izzy Stone? How could I not hitch out to Berkeley in order to walk in on her one day and yell, "Surprise!"

I was going to hitch out with Ed McLean, who not only was my best friend but had even more hitchhiking experience than the goddess Doris. If I had to go on the road, who better than Ed to go with? He was on his way to being a proletarian novelist. He already had the required résumé for his book jackets, from short-order cook to dishwasher to lathe operator. Ed would show me the ropes.

But first I had to explain to him that I wasn't going out to Berkeley solely because I had been intimidated by Doris. Doris was a secondary reason for hitchhiking west. I had given this a lot of thought and had decided that my major reason was the draft. My number was about to come up. It had looked for a while as if I'd be able to avoid the army. The Korean War was winding down, or so it seemed, or so I dreamed. The North Koreans were in full retreat, and I was saved. At which point, General Douglas MacArthur had the bright idea of driving the enemy forces right up to the Chinese border. And China was in the war. With a million men chasing MacArthur's army in mad retreat down the Korean peninsula.

Weeks away from settling the war and saving me from the draft, MacArthur had to make one of the great bungles of military history, the most important consequence of which was that I was now going into the army—which inspired a fresh rationale for hitchhiking to California. It wasn't only to see Doris: "If I'm going to die for my country, first I want to see what it looks like."

I was proud of that line. I used it on my mother, although I dared not confront her by telling her that I was hitchhiking. The story I came up with was that I was taking the bus. And then, funnily enough, once having said it, the idea seemed plausible. What if Ed and I didn't hitch? What if we went by Greyhound bus?, I suggested to Ed.

"You want Doris to know you took the bus? When she hitched?" Ed was giggling, as he was prone to do during moments when he was making me feel like a fool. He had a high-pitched derisive giggle. Not very nice, really. He had begun, some months earlier, calling me Captain Caution, a joke I saw truth but no humor in. So we agreed on a compromise: to not make me out to be a liar to my mother, we would take the bus as far as Chicago and hitchhike from there to California.

I was a little worried that I had not heard from Doris in three weeks. But my imagination reassured me. I fantasized that once I walked in her door at Berkeley, my dramatic appearance ("Surprise!") would change our lives forever. Spring was here, her semester soon over: the two of us would hitchhike back to New York, taking our sweet time about it, and why not? Two lovebirds delighting in the freedom of young adults on the road, criss-crossing the country, more or less headed east but in no hurry. Long, end-less romantic nights at cheap roadside motels. Doris and I, virgins no more.

This was a dream to give courage to a young man whose every fear had reemerged with unparalleled intensity. My one weapon against it was lust. If my lust didn't pull me through, I was a dead man. In fact, everything in me warned that by this act of brazenness, thinking that I could thumb my way across the country and survive . . . I was a dead man anyway.

Every anticipation short of lust foretold my doom. But it was too late to back out. I daren't do that to Ed, nor could I compromise my dream coupling with Doris. One thing was certain: this was to be my final act. Unless I got lucky, and my back went out. Being confined to bed for a week or two might save my life, because then it would be too late to go to California since—ha, ha—I had to hang around to be drafted.

New Tunic
Assymetric
Closing

Fashion sketches by Rhoda Davis from the 1940s

BREAKTHROUGH

My mother had an insane idea. As long as I was going west, as long as I was going to Chicago and no doubt Denver and Phoenix and Santa Fe and San Francisco and Los Angeles, as long as I was headed for these places anyway, why didn't I take along a batch of her fashion sketches, eight or ten new designs? And when I got to big midwestern, southwestern, and western cities, why couldn't I, as long as I was passing through anyway (it was hardly an inconvenience), canvass five or six or a dozen local dress manufacturers to see if they would be interested in subscribing to a New York–based "stylist" (a term my mother claimed as her invention)? It wouldn't take much of my time and it was certainly a service any good son would be happy to perform.

So there I was in Chicago at Quality Apparel, having arrived by Greyhound a day earlier. I was staying at Ed's mother's house on the South Side. The house looked like it was right out of *Studs Lonigan.* The South Side looked like it was right out of *Studs Lonigan.* Worn-down dwellings in Chicago struck me as romantic, mythic. Nothing worn down in the Bronx came close to mythic.

A little old lady at Quality Apparel sat behind a cluttered desk that was twice her size. She was as well turned out as my mother, with the same understated gift for tonier-than-thou dress. Her accent was guttural and unfamiliar to me, not German, not Polish, maybe East European. I launched into the spiel dictated to me by my mother. This was my second or third foray to find a potential subscriber to her hoped-for subscription service.

The fact that the little old lady didn't send me on my way as soon as I walked in came as a surprise, a triumph, really. I didn't look like anyone's idea of a salesman. I looked like who I was, a teenaged boy, twenty going on fifteen, awkwardly tall and underweight, unprepossessing to the point of invisibility, and dressed more like a high school kid than a businessman.

The single jacket I had brought with me on the trip west was an old, not necessarily clean gabardine top with a zippered front that, with its stuffed pockets, doubled as my suitcase.

When the little old lady went to retrieve her boss, or husband, or inker (as she termed him), I was thrilled to think that I had, through some against-type transformation, secured a foot in the door. The old lady appeared impressed by my mother's drawings. She had carefully leafed through the sketches not once but twice, then instructed me to wait as she disappeared into the back of the shop.

She brought back this man, a gnarled, thickset dwarf. He was a bulkier version of the woman, gnomish in a white shirt, tie, and open vest with a tailor's tape measure hanging from his neck. From all my unwilling childhood excursions when my mother dragged me from one fashion house to another, I recognized him as the head man, the designer.

If I managed by some inspired gift of gab to sell him my mother's sketches, this gnome might well open up the door to a brand new Rhoda Davis syndicate, a trickle and then a flood of other subscribers to follow. That was how syndication worked. I knew that from comics.

I let my imagination soar. Beginning with my mother's first sale to this dear, never-to-be-forgotten-no-matter-how-high-we-climb elf at Quality Apparel, this leprechaun out of a fairy tale was going to spin my mother's drossy sketches into gold. First a sale in Chicago, then on to St. Louis and Denver, Phoenix, San Francisco, Los Angeles . . . If syndicates made cartoonists rich, then why not my mother? Hundreds of sales, money, lots of it, debts paid, the Bronx abandoned, an apartment on Fifth Avenue—no, a mansion—a spread in *Vogue,* where my mother once interned (referred to as the little Jewess).

Rhoda Davis, elegant in an outfit of her own design, and her famous son, Jules, whose new comic strip was the fastest launch in newspaper history, caught by Eisenstaedt out dining at 21 or the Copa or El Morocco, helloed at from nearby tables by Gable and Bogie and Lauren Bacall and Lana Turner and Arthur Miller. And who stops by but Julie Garfield, who trades jokes with me about two Jewish boys escaping the Bronx.

Not only would I have made it myself, I would have paid back my mother for my years of hostility and indifference to her tales of travail, poverty, indebtedness, now coming to an end as this lovable elf thumbed through her art. He and his wife, the adorable Mrs. Elf, shared, in a tongue not Yiddish but every bit as incomprehensible to me, comments on the sketches. The old man pointed out to the old lady the position of a pocket, the flare of a jacket, the shape and seam of a sleeve. And then after intense discussion in this language not Yiddish, this gnome, whom I had mistaken for a benevolent elf, this dwarf, this shithead, said to me, "It's interesting, but we have designs for a long time like this already."

And I am instantly reminded of stories I have heard from my mother, going back to when I was six or seven, stories of designers examining her designs with an interest not in purchasing them but in stealing them.

One did not copyright a three-dollar sketch. You could not protect your ideas once they were out there to be either bought or plundered. Time after time, year after year, as she aged and I aged and World War II came and went, and high school came and went, and Korea came and I was about to be drafted, year after year, the same story—the very story now newly acted out before me. And I recall with full force the rage I now felt at my mother's humiliation. Her defeats, her desolation, her son's manifest dream of making it right, of knight errantry, of doing for her what she could not do for herself, of being the man of the house that my father wasn't.

And thus, a new Jules charged forth on a white charger, improvising with concealed but venomous irony: "So you see what my mother, Miss Davis, is trying to do here: each month she'll send you a new batch of sketches so you'll have fresh ideas for your own designs. But if you don't subscribe, the only drawings you'll ever get to see of hers are the ones you're stealing from now. You won't see next month's ideas or all the ideas after that, so you're not going to have anything more of hers to steal from."

I had never spoken like that to a grown-up, not once in my life. In a voice calm and steady, sounding reasonable, as if I were selling Ivory soap. Nonetheless, all three of us in the anteroom of Quality Apparel went into immediate shock.

"What are you saying?" one or the other or both of the old dwarfs screamed.

"I said, you're a bunch of crooks. That's okay, my mother is used to her ideas being stolen, but we'll forget about that if you subscribe."

I was talking back to the grown-ups, something neither I nor my parents had ever done. Out of sight of my rage, I was watching myself in the third person with glee. I half expected the two old farts to congratulate me. "How impressive!" "I didn't think you'd have the nerve. Have a cup of tea."

But they didn't seem to understand what a huge breakthrough this was for me. "Get out! Get out!" they screamed. Which I did, but not before I took a threatening step toward the old man, a second unprecedented act. He backpedaled in panic, which I took as the moment for my triumphal exit and curtain call. I stalked off. Floated, actually.

I ran, leaped, and bounced off downtown buildings before I caught a train back to the South Side to Ed's house. What had I done? What did it mean? It meant that I had it in me to become a better, stronger Super-Jules, leaping over tall buildings in a single bound. Leaping out of the Bronx and never having to return. I couldn't wait to report to Ed.

BREAKUP

Ed was not of a mind to believe my story. He accepted the facts but provided his own interpretation, which was not favorable to me. Rather than me being Super-Jules, I was once again supercompliant. Leaping not over tall buildings but through hoops to please my mother. Fighting her battles when she had never once fought mine. My perception of moving forward was wrong, according to Ed. I was following my mother's lead in an Oedipal dance, patterning my every step to her specifications. This breakthrough was, in Ed's judgment, nothing more than the same old eyewash, the same old Bronx boy, the same old comic book fantasies.

We had begun getting on each other's nerves on our second day in Chicago. My first impression was that Chicago was something like Ed: brash, with an in-your-face directness that was challenging, intoxicating. Ed and I roamed the streets the first day, him rat-a-tatting a wide-ranging stream-of-consciousness chatter, I reacting with opinions no less out of bounds. Ed's verbally assertive style put to shame the evenhanded, on-the-one-hand, on-the-other ambivalence that had long been my mainstay.

But now on his own turf, Ed's autodidacticism took on a nasty aspect. He had a far more serviceable memory than I. He could cite eclectic sources that I had no access to. From our first meeting in New York, our friendship had involved a degree of chiding and mockery. But in New York it was good-natured, the equivalent of towel snapping at a butt in a gym locker room. I knew Ed to be on my side, a worldly-wise coach advising me and prodding me. But here in Chicago, the prodding had turned malicious and the advice was now delivered with ill-concealed disdain.

What else was there for us to do but fight—which I both feared and wanted—or go our separate ways? We stood out on Route 66, the flat farmland laid out before us like a boxing ring, neither of us happy about what was to come next. It was clear that Ed's needling had gotten even to him. "We're getting on each other's nerves. Why don't we split up and meet in San Francisco."

A couple of minutes later he was standing alone on the highway and I was walking a half mile down. Ed had taken charge; we were not going to fight. He was not going to beat me up and lose his best friend. In any case, he had already beaten me up—a bloody nose would be redundant. He suggested that whoever got to San Francisco first should check in at the YMCA on Geary Street, and then he winked and grinned. And I, submissive to the end, shook his hand and started my solitary way down 66.

Behind me I heard Ed singing in an Okie-accented voice. A Woody Guthrie refrain: "So long, it's been good to know you." I took it as a not-too-gentle reminder that I was a boy, alone, untraveled, heading west to meet my fate.

ROAD MOVIE

Minutes later the fun began. One ride, then another, then another. I couldn't believe how natural it seemed, how easy it was. Within a half dozen rides in every sort of vehicle, from a hay truck to an old V–8 to a sleek and classy Buick, I was chauffeured across the state of Illinois, into Iowa, then Nebraska. Short hops, long monologues, lonely drivers, some talkative, some too talkative, others quiet, others reserved but friendly. A salesman confided the details of his unhappy marriage, no sex anymore. Late at night, another salesman decided he was too tired to go on, turned into a motel, and paid for both our rooms and breakfasts. Another driver pulled over when he saw that I had fallen asleep a few hours into our drive. In the morning when I awoke, I found a car blanket draped over me.

I had thumbed my way into a Frank Capra movie where threats existed only for the purposes of storytelling. I was a boy adventurer, in a wondrous land to which I didn't belong, whose storybook attractions were mapped out for me in movies and *Saturday Evening Post* illustrations and Booth Tarkington's *Penrod* stories, which I devoured at twelve and thirteen, fictional glimpses of this world that I was now seeing in person through the windows of fast-moving cars: rural and small-town America, shingled houses bordered by white picket fences and shaded by oaks and maples and sycamores and any other tree name that I could come up with because I couldn't tell one from another.

This could have been (should have been) my birthright, had I only been born in the right place in the right faith. Distant farmhouse windows lit up at night, secure and cozy. Now and then, silhouettes suggestive of happy families sitting down to dinner, comfortable give-and-take, good-

112 | *Jules Feiffer*

natured, easygoing middle-American joshing, remindful of a world I knew only from Mickey Rooney Andy Hardy movies.

I loved my country, but I didn't want to fight and die for it in Korea. I wanted to get laid in it, make love to Doris in it, a cross-country coming (of age). The erection I was seldom without throbbed with nationalist fervor. In my mind I had combined sex with the *Saturday Evening Post,* Grant Wood with making out, the Great American West with the Great American Whoopee.

In New York, illusions of power were fueled by the comics I wrote and drew. Here on the road, power moved with these caravans of cars driving me through an alien nation, half real, half movie. Epiphanies zipped by me at five-minute intervals. The ultimate epiphany was that I was not going to die. There was not going to be just retribution for my hubris in leaving my mother and the Bronx.

Occasions arose that should have killed me but, counterintuitively, didn't. Three drunk teenagers picked me up in the middle of the night somewhere in the heart of Nebraska's North Platte. I knew it was a mistake to get in their car, but I got in anyway. I didn't want to offend them. They drove furiously, careening, swerving, nearly but not quite plunging us into ditches and gorges, laughing with disbelief when, for the fourth or fifth or twentieth time, they had by a hair's breadth averted their sought-after suicides. While on a pee break in woods by the side of the road in the middle of the night, I stole away. They called me, came looking for me. No anger or hostility in the search, just eager to party. I hid on all fours in the brush, just off the road in Nowhere, Nebraska. I was racked with fear and ambivalence: I didn't want to die and I didn't want these morons to think that I looked down on them. Seconds before my guilt was going to make me rejoin them, they forgot about me and drove off.

Somewhere in Wyoming, again late at night, I got picked up and found myself seated in the back of the car with another hitchhiker. I couldn't see much in the dark, but I sensed within seconds more than I wanted to know. This kid, about my age, was twice my size and, in the glare of oncoming headlights, I could see small, deadened features on a face that had been hit and healed over with scar tissue too many times.

I knew with absolute certainty that I was about to be his victim. Whenever and wherever I got out of the car, this goon would get out with me and mug me and take my money. I didn't expect him to kill me, but his size made it clear that he could do what he wanted.

While keeping up a pretense at conversation, I kept close watch on our surroundings, determined that, when we hit a town, I would find a brightly lit, well-peopled intersection where I planned to make my getaway.

The street corner lay in a suburb of Cheyenne, one lit street in the middle of darkness, very little traffic, few houses, too many trees, any one of which I could be taken behind, beaten up, and robbed. Not what I was hoping for, but it was the best I could do.

Of course, he got out with me. I stood on the corner. He stood with me. Outside the pool of light coming from the solitary streetlamp, there was only darkness and the threat of mayhem. An Alfred Hitchcock music track boomed in my head as we spoke amiably about nothing in particular. He came up with the offer that we travel together. I found the courage to say that I did best when I traveled alone. He accepted that but didn't seem to have any plans to move on. He just stood there. Hitchcock's background music was sounding—boom-de-boom-de-boom—increasingly ominous. I was one of the Three Little Pigs and he was the wolf, licking his chops, waiting for me to lose patience and walk down the road in the dark, closer to traffic, in search of a ride. Not me. I had no intention of budging from under this one bright streetlamp, the only one in the Midwest, apparently.

He talked some more to me. One of the things he said was, "Do you have any money I can borrow?" The Hitchcock music was shrieking now. I said I had enough for one meal, I was going to have to look for a job the next day.

I could see that all of this was coming to a head. I announced that I intended to stay at this spot under this light. I would stand there as long as it took for a car to pick me up. Furthermore, I didn't think any car at this time of night was likely to pick up two riders. I suggested in a thoughtful way, as if I were trying to solve our mutual problem, that he might have a better chance for a ride if he moved a little farther down the road.

I watched while he mulled this over. He looked around, I was certain, to gauge the chances of anyone from the nearby houses coming out in response to my screams. I wasn't making it easy for him, so he must have decided the hell with it. He said, "See you," and moved on. He'd find another mark to beat up and rob. I waited for him to come back. I waited and waited, and finally a car stopped for me and my waiting was over. I hadn't gotten mugged, a fact that defied all logic. And I had learned a lesson: don't accept a ride in a car with another hitchhiker.

"JULES, WHAT ARE YOU DOING HERE?"

Ed and I hooked up in San Francisco, and it was as if nothing had gone wrong between us. He was jovial and I was more so. Whatever the problem had been, it had gone away just as pre-Freudian problems were supposed to. No discussion, no analysis, no getting to the bottom of it. We behaved like men of the old school: we didn't look back, we soldiered on. And now, we were about to get on our way to meet Doris. No advance-warning phone call—Ed's idea was that this was to be the ultimate "Surprise!" The movielike romantic idiocy behind it was irresistible. I let him overcome the Captain Caution in me.

But before Doris, he wanted to show me the town from his radical, raffish Jack London point of view—the waterfront, skid row—San Francisco as seen from a Wobbly perspective. Ed was enamored of Jack London, the early-twentieth-century tramp, seaman, and writer of men's and boys' stories. And so we toured the Embarcadero and Fisherman's Wharf and Telegraph Hill and Coit Tower, with its WPA socialist-inspired murals of heavy-muscled working-class heroes, and, if memory doesn't deceive, on the wall staring me down was Lenin. My God, what a country! I had come three thousand miles, and the first piece of West Coast art I saw featured Mimi's Communist god. Doris, whom I met in the AYD, was going to love it when I told her this. Maybe it would lead to lovemaking.

Doris's address in Berkeley was not hard to find. She lived in student housing—small one- and two-bedroom apartments with a kitchen and a bathroom—that she shared with Paula, the AYD friend she hitched west with, and one other girl, not from the Northeast. It was a three-flight walk-up, which I ran up, Ed close behind, sharing my excitement and anticipation. I had built up this moment in my head and heart. I had scripted it and shot it like a film that I played and replayed who knows how many times: the door flung open, the screech of delight, Doris throwing herself at me, clamping me in a bear hug, the glee, the promise of what was to come.

This was the final payoff for my trip west, a trip on which I would never have set foot if this girl, the obsessive object of my every thought for days now, had not goaded me into it. And she was right! This trip already gave signs of hitherto unknown resourcefulness, hitherto unsuspected courage. I stood at Doris's door, by now an experienced hitchhiker halfway to being the man I wanted to be, bursting with excitement, prepared to be in love. How could it not go wrong?

Doris and I stared at each other from opposite sides of the door, me with a shit-eating grin on my face, Ed behind me. I heard him giggle. She was not giggling, nor was she smiling. Understandable, I thought. I probably woke her up. She wore a T-shirt and panties. She looked less surprised by my appearance than nonplussed, as if she knew me from somewhere and if I gave her a couple of seconds she'd come up with a name.

Finally: "Jules, what are you doing here?" It was not the greeting that I had traveled three thousand miles to get. "I hitchhiked all the way from New York!" I said to jog her memory, hoping to encourage a more enthusiastic response. Her face was dark, clouded, not welcoming. "I wish you'd given me some warning. I'm going away for the weekend."

This *was* the weekend! This was Friday! One day after my transcontinental arrival. But Doris had plans. Was it reasonable for her to change her weekend plans, no doubt made days in advance? Her plans to go camping in Yosemite National Park, she and Paula and a boy named Wayne, who owned a car. Possibly when she came back from her weekend plans she could fit me in—say, on Monday (unless Monday was her day for washing her hair).

Who was this *Wayne*? Over all those thousands of miles, I was the boy I had fantasized her traveling with. Who was this Wayne to usurp me even if he did own a car? And why was Doris staring at me as if we had just met, and why was she talking about Wayne?

Her lack of pleasure in seeing me was so obvious that I might have been expected to scream in rage. But rage was an emotion with which I had no direct contact. Previous experiences suggested that rage numbed me. Often its timing was off, surfacing days or weeks after my reasons for it had grown moot.

Instead, I thought ruefully of Wayne, that slimy con artist who had wayned his way into my future wife's affections. I would not let him get away with this. He was not going to drive Doris and Paula to Yosemite and leave Ed and me back in Berkeley. "I've been dying to see Yosemite." I grinned, as if Doris's announcement had been not a rejection but an invitation. "Ed and I would love to go!"

"I don't think there's room in the car," Doris said.

Paula came to the door. "Hello, Jules." She looked prettier than I had remembered, prettier than Doris. Ed introduced himself; I didn't have the language for it. Paula must have liked his looks. She said, "I don't know why they can't come to Yosemite."

It became clear on the trip that the not-too-good-looking, not-talkative, not-at-all-interesting Wayne was not there to replace me. He had come as the chauffeur and seemed satisfied, perhaps flattered, that these two New York girls had chosen this particular small-town University of California sophomore to drive them wherever they wanted to go. He hardly spoke a word on the drive.

Neither did I. I stared out the window. There was much to stare at: this was northern California, more expansive in everything—hills, mountains, sky—more drama in the scenery than anything I'd seen going west. Breathtaking! But even if it hadn't been, even if there had been nothing to stare out at, even if I had been watching nature on an off day, I still would have stared out the window. Staring out the window was the only thing that kept me from jumping out the window and running all the way back to the Bronx in a sprint of woe and self-loathing the like of which I hadn't had serious contact with in a long time.

Out the window, everywhere I wasn't looking, rose the gorgeous goyische California mountain ranges soaring at impossible heights, the monumental West flexing its muscles. Every shrub, every tree, every ravine and gorge seemed to take my measure and agree with Doris that I was too pathetic to bother with.

But that dismal observation came from only one part of me. I was made up of infinite parts, and all my other parts took up arms against the presently prevailing self-loathing part. *They* insisted on seeing the bright side. Yes, there was a bright side, I just had to make it happen, take this rotten egg that hit me and turn it into a soufflé. Charm Doris back to her senses. Under the great sky, beneath the canopy of opera buffa trees, below the cascading thousand-foot falls and rainbow riotous vegetation, magic would occur. How could it not in such a setting?

Transformation! I believed that twenty-four hours from now Doris and I would be rolling around on the forest bed in each other's arms, laughing in tears over our stupid misunderstanding. This episode was a meaningless moment in the lifelong saga of Doris and Jules. We would tell stories about it to our grandchildren. She would laugh again. I would make her—being funny was my old standby. Could Wayne make her laugh?

I would be devastatingly interesting, a charmer, companion, friend. Once more, Doris and I would bond. Yosemite would be our sexual Arcadia. The majestic views gave promise of hope. That was all I needed. My spirits lifted.

Nothing worked out at Yosemite except the scenery. Mountains, trees, and waterfalls supplied the backdrop for Doris's repeated rejections, which were offered with diffidence, not a tinge of pity or regret. High on a mountaintop with God as the background artist, I said to her: "If you didn't love me anymore, why didn't you write me? I wouldn't have come!"

"I didn't know I didn't love you," she said.

"When did you find out?"

"When I opened the door and saw you."

Her exact quote, I swear. If I didn't stagger back at the statement, I should have. It was a haymaker, but only a setup for the knockout blow to follow. "Now that you've insisted on coming, please don't spoil everyone's good time."

It seems like minutes later that I was thumbing a ride to Los Angeles. Ed chose to stay behind. He was making out with Paula. Maybe Doris was making out with Wayne. How was I to know? If I had gotten it all wrong up till now, how could I be sure of anything, other than my need to make a run for it?

I AIN'T A-GONNA BE TREATED THIS-A-WAY

D izzying scenery and dashed hopes took me straight into L.A. I had made plans to stay with my aunt Alva, a tiny, birdlike woman with a falsetto voice who was the widow of Sol, my father's brother, one of the rich brothers—real estate, I think, or maybe jewelry. Maybe both. Sol, like my father, Dave, was gentle, good-humored, sweet-natured. He had been a benefactor to our family during the darkest days of the Depression. Alva was less nice. She didn't go in for spending money but nonetheless made you know that she had more than enough, certainly more than the now-and-again-impoverished Feiffers.

Two things you should know about Alva. One was that she kept the toilet seat in her bathroom glued down, the ultimate denial of men. The other thing you should know is that she had a favorite nephew who was to become famous, and it wasn't me. In my two days with Alva, she found little to approve of. She didn't like my humor, she didn't like my manners, she didn't like my politics. The politics she liked were those of the nephew she favored, Roy Cohn. Roy, at the time, was working as an assistant prosecutor on the Rosenberg case. Alva's suggestion was that I might look upon him as a role model. This led to an argument on the guilt or innocence of Julius and Ethel Rosenberg.

Now, back home in New York, if you had asked me about the Rosenberg case, I would have said, "They're probably guilty of something. But even if Julius did spy for the Russians, he didn't have access to the kind of information that was important enough to warrant a death sentence." In other words, I took my usual nuanced position.

But that was my New York opinion. In L.A., in the company of Aunt

Alva, with her glued-down toilet seat and a favorite nephew who, even before he went to work for Joe McCarthy, was making a name for himself as a hard-nosed, play-dirty, right-wing anti-Communist gun for hire, I had a second opinion. The Rosenbergs were framed and completely innocent. What choice did I have?

Alva went bananas, her falsetto crackled with indignation. How dare I take such a pro-Communist view in the light of cousin Roy's sensitive job with the Justice Department? If the FBI or his bosses found out what I thought, didn't I know what danger I could bring down on Roy, how I might injure his career?

In those dark Cold War days, guilt by relation had indeed taken its toll on a number of innocent people who lost their jobs because their loyalty was put into question. If I could do that to cousin Roy—oh, what a wonderful dream . . .

But first Aunt Alva would have to turn me in, a temptation I sought to encourage. On the very next morning, waiting for the bus to take us to Knott's Berry Farm, a tourist site for little lads and geriatrics that Alva was pleased to show me, I glanced over at a nearby newsstand and noticed copies of the *People's Daily World*, the West Coast equivalent of the *Daily Worker*, both published by the Communist Party. The *Daily Worker* was in our home on a regular basis. Mimi brought it back from party meetings. I never bought the paper myself, or its West Coast equivalent, until I happened by a newsstand in the company of Aunt Alva and considered the effect my buying a copy would have on her.

Alva's falsetto tirade was music to my ears. An octave higher and she would have shattered glass. But what completed the experience was the little old black woman standing with us at the bus stop, who, upon hearing Alva's denunciation, chimed in with her own tirade against me and all young people of whatever color who didn't follow in the Lord's path and show respect. Alva and this little old lady raving away at the injustice of the generational turnover as we waited for our bus, and I silently drinking it in with a joy I hadn't felt since Doris opened her door to me and I watched her face fall.

JOE

Hitchhiking had done for me what it was meant to, and now it was time for me to head home: one more valuable experience that I had gotten so much out of that I never had to think of repeating it.

What was now mostly on my mind was my return to New York, my date with the draft board, wangling a 4–F (unfit to serve in the armed forces of the United States because I was too cute to die), and then, on with my life, the first act of which was to move out of the Bronx.

I was twenty-one, ready to be on my own, guilt-ridden about what this would do to my mother, but certain that it was the right move if I ever wanted to grow up, if I ever wanted to get laid.

Mimi was something of a model. She had lived away from home since her college years—an apartment on Bank Street in the Village, other apartments, rooming with other young Communists, generally female, sometimes a mix. Mimi was having group sex before I had sex.

How do I know? Sometime around 2000, a former Communist room-mate of Mimi's, exotically gorgeous and sexy when she was young, sent me her novel to read. The novel was a fictionalized account of this sometime actress's affair—if one can call it that—with a young Marlon Brando. But that's not what caught my attention. It was Mimi, by some other name, and her SEX LIFE! My sister, laid by this guy and that guy and some other guy and in threesomes and I-don't-want-to-know-how-many-somes. My sister, whom I hoped to emulate and strongly disapproved of at the same time, was getting it, getting it, getting it. And I, her baby brother, was not getting it, didn't know how to go about getting it. Not a clue. Not a notion. Not a Doris.

A virgin at twenty, when by that age my bohemian Red sister had gone through God knows how many lovers.

Lover. The word *lover* was out of my league. I might, by accident, some freak of nature, get laid. Someday, not by twenty-one, twenty-two, maybe by twenty-three . . . But to have a—what was that word?—lover! *My lover and I were discussing the poetry of William Blake in bed this morning, after we did you know what.* No, not now, possibly not ever. Jeez!

Ten tiny little rides over four hours had taken me eighty miles outside L.A. to Victorville, California. Dropped off in the middle of nowhere by a local farmer. Stranded on the road. A hundred feet or so to my right lay the Mojave Desert, which at this point looked like I would have to cross on foot. Very little traffic. Few cars going east. I stood, I waited. I got hot.

A convertible the size of a football field grazed by at a speed moderate enough for me to see the driver, big, pockmarked, glowering, and his passenger, a kid my age who threw me a shit-eating grin that meant: "I'm hitching too, and *I* have a ride in this Cadillac across the desert. Ha, ha."

It was enough to move me off the spot and start me walking. No more than a half mile down the road, I spotted a gas station and, to my surprise, parked at the gas station was the outsized Cadillac convertible that had so demoralized me.

The driver was not in the car. The hitchhiker was. He was about my size and reedy, with thin brown hair, a pinched, scooped nose, and an expression that said: "If I ignore you, maybe you'll go away."

After my near mugging in Wyoming, I had made a vow never to get in a car with another hitchhiker. But this young man did not appear to present a threat, and I was stuck in the Mojave Desert, hardly in a position to be consistent.

I said, "Do you think I can get a ride with you guys?"

The young man glanced my way with a look that read: "Don't try to screw this up for me."

Before he could speak, the driver returned from the john. He was twice my size, thick eyebrows, wide nose, a scowl that suggested that whatever I wanted, the answer was no.

I wanted a ride and I said so. He said in a voice that sounded like three packs a day, "I got no place to put yiz. Where the fuck am I going to put yiz? My fuckin' wardrobe is all over the backseat and this kid here I picked up in Pasadena."

I hadn't noticed the backseat. It was a foot deep in suits, shirts, blazers, pants, all laid out neatly across the full length of the backseat.

"Where you goin'?" he asked.

"New York," I said.

"Where you from?"

"The Bronx."

He nodded. "If I could I would, but . . . ." His accent was pure Brooklyn. And I was from the Bronx. And still he wouldn't help.

"I could put the clothes on my lap," I said.

He dismissed this dumb idea with a "Waddaya gonna do?" Then he turned away, as if he could no longer stand the problem I presented, slouched into his convertible, slammed the door on me, and took off.

A hundred feet away he screeched to a halt. Not turning to look at me, he waved his left hand in the air, a "don't keep me waiting" gesture. I came running.

"Move the clothes over. I'll maybe charge yiz for the cleanin' bill."

His name was Joe Lane. He was from Brooklyn, but he wasn't ready to share with me whether or not he was returning to Brooklyn, in which case I would have made it home from the Mojave Desert in one ride. Joe was garrulous, confessional, a spurned lover (like myself). He had been with his girlfriend, a showgirl whom he had driven out to Hollywood in this very Cadillac just three months earlier, so that she could try a career in movies. Instead, she tried a new boyfriend. Joe walked in on them having sex. "I beat her up, packed up my clothes, and got outta there. Look at the size of this ring I took off her finger." He pulled a ring out of his pocket. It held an impressively vulgar, shimmering stone.

"Is it real?" the other passenger asked. His name was Rusty Frey and he was a seminary student at Wheaton College in either Iowa or Illinois— one of those *I* states.

Joe said, "I deserve something, the time I put in on her."

Joe and I, two New Yorkers from the neighborhoods, hit it off immediately in the western desert. We never stopped talking. Rusty, on the other hand, was not a responder or reactor. While making efforts to be friendly, he said little in our exchanges that could be labeled opinion. We three strangers were a sitcom before TV had sitcoms: "You got this Cadillac convertible making a cross-country trip with a Bronx Jew who's artistic, a Brooklyn Italian who's in the rackets, and an uptight Baptist farm boy from the Midwest training to be a minister. It's fraught with possibilities, like *The Fugitive*. Every week they get stuck in another town, and all hell breaks loose."

Joe Lane did not look like a Joe Lane, and from the start of our ride I half doubted everything he said, which didn't stop him. Joe was a raconteur racketeer out of the Damon Runyon school. The stories he told hinted at mob connections, no crimes spoken of, no beans spilled, nothing that could lead me to believe that Joe was crooked. Yet his manner, his style, the names dropped: Georgie Raft and Bugsy Siegel in Hollywood, Frank Costello in New York . . .

"How do you know these guys, Joe?"

"You run into people, how do I know *you*?"

"Where did you run into Frank Costello?"

"Places. You meet people the places where you meet them—the track. I'm at the track, I give you names. Mickey Cohn, Bing Crosby, Leo Durocher . . ."

Joe Lane was certainly not his name. Lanio? Lanitello? Some other variation? Joe was a mobster for sure, but low-level or mid-level. Nothing big time, I concluded. "Girls, I'm gonna introduce you. I mean, classy. Clubs I'm partners in, don't worry, they'll treat you good."

It wasn't just "girls" that Joe was hinting at on this drive through New Mexico and Arizona. Stifling desert winds peppered us with darts of sand (why didn't he put up the top?), but who cared? Joe was going to get me laid! Joe was volunteering as my connection to B girls, bar girls, bad girls. Considering the state I was in, you could wrap up a half dozen right this minute, please.

In record time Joe became my best friend. We talked politics, philosophy, movies, theater . . . "Ethel Merman, she can be trouble but she's worth it. I'll introduce you, not to screw, but she's the type if you're gonna be known, she's a good person to know."

Joe, I knew. Now that I had run into him, I didn't want to let go: the Italian father figure of my dreams. And I was his entourage. Back in New York, we'd hang out in clubs together, big-boobed blondes, statuesque, seated between us. "One more for the road, Julie?"

"Whatever you say, Joe." Joe would watch over me.

Happily cast in his shadow, I talked endlessly, using him as my on-the-road shrink.

About Doris: "She's a bitch," Joe ruled.

About Ed: "He's a jealous jerk," Joe ruled.

Rusty Frey was also a jealous jerk. Riding with these two fast-talking ethnics, he was clearly out of the loop. He limited his conversation to logistics: "How far to Wendover?" "Where do we pick up Route 192?" "Wouldn't it save us time to exit at 16?" As Joe and I amused and showed off for each other, Rusty fretted. I didn't care, I was having the time of my life. I suspected that most everything Joe told me was very likely a lie, but I admired him all the more for it. Each night we settled into motels, Rusty and I sharing a room. (Joe: "I don't share a room wit' no guys.") Each morning I expected to wake up and find Joe and his convertible gone. But he didn't go. It was Rusty who left, this boy minister who argued with Joe about God, theology, the Immaculate Conception.

Rusty: "Do you believe in the Immaculate Conception?"

Joe: "Ha!"

Rusty talked incessantly of when and where he'd take off. St. Louis seemed a possibility, even though it left him two hundred miles short of his goal. He was uncomfortable with our little family. He was the odd Protestant out. "I think you should drop me off here," he said to Joe and pointed to a spot on the map. Zanesville, Ohio.

"There's nothin' there. Fuck it, we'll find a better place." And the better places sped by. Rusty, unable to insist, didn't know how to talk his way out of Joe's car.

The more I was enamored of Joe, the more impatient I became with Rusty. Joe and Jules on the road, that was the story. Rusty was an irritating footnote. It took little effort for me to turn him into a caricature of sterile Christian faith. I switched seamlessly into an anti-Christian bigot, a born-again Jew sharing character and dimension with my Catholic brother, two standard bearers of ethnic ballsiness versus white-bred blandness.

On our fourth day out, Joe claimed he'd run out of money. He'd have to stop in the next town, Fulton, Missouri, and see how much he could raise selling the Cadillac. Unless he could borrow just enough from Rusty and me, for gas, motels, and sundries.

I was down to fourteen dollars, but I was willing, with the smallest cautionary twinge, to turn it over to Joe. Rusty denied that he had any money. But several times a day I observed him sneaking a wallet out of his pants pocket and checking its contents to make sure that Joe and I hadn't robbed him.

No matter. He had made up his mind to go, and later that day he finagled it.

We had stopped at a diner for lunch. Joe insisted on paying: "Maybe our last meal." In the middle of our meal Rusty excused himself to talk to three young people at a table across the room. He explained that one of the girls in the group was wearing a sweatshirt with the logo of a school connected to Rusty's church. Minutes later, when he returned to our table, it was to say good-bye. They had offered him a ride, and he had accepted. Were they going his way? Rusty ignored the question. They could have been going in the opposite direction and he would have gone with them.

"How much money you got?" Joe asked after I paid for the meal that he said was on him. I was down to seven dollars.

Joe thought about it: "We can make it to New York if we're careful." We were in Lansing, Michigan, when he said this.

Who cared? I had a ride that started in the Mojave Desert and it was going to take me home! A single ride of three thousand miles! We would make it on seven dollars—what was to stop us? My pal Joe was in my corner, my winning ticket to everything that I dreamed of.

Two days later, we didn't have a quarter for the toll to get us through the Holland Tunnel. I panicked. There, across the river, the towers of Manhattan teased, so near, so far. I was stuck forever on the Jersey side unless I used my last nickel to call my mother and pleaded with her to come to New Jersey with a quarter to rescue us.

Can you believe the humiliation? I was seconds away from tears when I noticed that Joe had left the stalled car waiting on line to go through the Holland Tunnel. I spotted Joe working his way down traffic, from one idling car to another, his right hand out, palm upward. He was looking for handouts. And getting them. I watched with shame (my mother's son) and glee (Joe's son) as coins and even a few dollar bills spilled out of car windows into Joe's open palm. It took only a minute or two. The line of cars began to inch toward the tunnel entrance. "Eleven bucks," Joe showed me, as he stepped back into the convertible. "You could afford a cab to the Bronx."

I didn't want to take Joe's money, but I thought I would hurt his feelings if I refused. "It's yours, I'm loaded," he said, thereby leading me to wonder once again what to believe of this man. If he was loaded, why the charade for handouts? I took the subway home wondering.

Before we parted, I wrote down my Bronx phone number, TIvoli 2–8128—after more than sixty years I still remember it—on a slip of paper for Joe. I asked him for his. He had trouble finding paper, a pen. I found paper. There was something wrong with the pen. When that problem was solved, he wrote down a nearly illegible number for me. "Is this a four or a five, Joe?"

"Lemme look. It's a four."

"And is this a two?"

"Waddaya want?"

He seemed anxious to get going.

We said our good-byes. I was certain that it was for keeps. Forget the invitations to clubs, if there were clubs. Forget the B girls, if they existed at all. I was home, back on familiar territory in a familiar stance: celibate.

I walked in on my family at dinner. I had called before I went down in the subway, so they knew Jules was home. But they didn't know how he got home. They didn't know that I didn't take the Greyhound bus. They didn't know about hitching or my breakup with Doris or my breakthrough at Quality Apparel or my fight with Ed or that I had made up my mind to refuse induction into the army. I was going to be a conscientious objector. And I was going to move out of the house and find my own apartment in Manhattan. Oh, I had so much to tell them.

Seated at the kitchen table with my mother and father and Alice two hours after arriving home, I launched into my hitchhiking revelations and the countless stories that unfolded therefrom. I left out the Doris misadventure because they hadn't been told the true purpose of my trip. I left out my fight with Ed because my mother didn't like my having friends who weren't Jewish, and I wanted to save myself from "You see, Sonny Boy, I was right about him." I held back on my story of Quality Apparel because this had been *my* adventure, and I was not about to turn it into a story about my mother's fashion business. But in florid detail, I recounted my single ride home out of the Mojave Desert with Joe Lane and Rusty Frey. Riotous laughter and shouts of "Slow down, you're going too fast!" Coming my way for the very first time was the admiration and awe that Mimi regularly encountered when telling one of her stories. It was as if my rite of passage were not in the trip but in my story of the trip.

This was what I had come home for: to be seen as different in my parents' eyes. As I concluded the story of Joe begging our way through the Holland Tunnel—more screams of laughter—the phone rang. The phone sat on a small table in the foyer between the kitchen and the living room. Alice answered and said, "It's for you, Jules."

I picked it up, wondering who could possibly know that I was home? "Hello," I said, and heard Joe on the other end: "So long as you got home all right."

I was near tears with happiness. He called! Joe was looking out for me. How could I have doubted him? "Go finish your supper, I'll call yiz next week."

When two weeks passed and I hadn't heard from him, I tried the number he had given me. There was no Joe Lane there, no Joe Lane had ever been there. I tried Brooklyn information with the name Lane, Lanio, any other imaginative embroidery of Joe's name that I could think of. I couldn't believe he had done this to me. Was this Joe's intention all along? Or was he in trouble? Was he in hiding? Was he rubbed out? I felt rubbed out.

Joe, in and out of my life in less than a week, vanished with his clubs, his B girls, his promises. I wasn't getting laid! I was without a protector.

I lacked the guts to move out. I lacked the guts to be a conscientious objector. I was going to be drafted. On Monday morning, I went back to work at Eisner's. It was as if nothing in the last month had happened.

THE SECRET OF MY SUCCESS;
OR, OVER THE CLIFF

The army made a satirist out of me. It didn't make a man of me, as promised by my sergeants and lieutenants. Manhood would have to wait another twenty years, in the aftermath of marriage, divorce, and half raising a child who believed that she was the reason I walked out.

Over the years I have been asked how I came to make certain choices. How did I know? This choice as opposed to that, this direction or that? These questions have little to do with my life as I've been led into it. Much of my life as a young man was spent ignoring or delaying choices. The choices I made were due to running out of time—or someone else's patience. Backed into a corner, a choice was made because I no longer had a choice not to. It's easier when one's choices get winnowed down from many to not so many, to a couple, to almost none.

It's a matter of personal style. I seem to be at my best backed into a corner. Having nowhere to go, I spot the one open window and jump through. Choice to me is much like Butch Cassidy and Sundance escaping a posse by jumping off a cliff. They jumped. And survived. It was the right choice. But when it's not, you're dead.

Munro was my very first satire, a cartoon narrative about a four-year-old boy who is drafted into the army by mistake and cannot get the powers that be to admit it. It was finally published in 1959 as part of the book *Passionella and Other Stories,* about seven years after I wrote it. The book became a best seller, and in 1961 *Munro* opened as an animated cartoon at the Radio City Music Hall with *Breakfast at Tiffany's.* It won an Academy Award. But prior to that heady triumph, *Munro* was rejected by every publisher in New York: Simon and Schuster, Random House, Knopf, Harper and Row, Duell, Sloan, and Pearce . . . All of the rejecting publishers admired the book. Editor after editor told me how good it was, but their problem, you see, was that they didn't know how to market it. It had the look of a children's book, but it was for adults. How could they present it to their salesmen or to bookstores if it didn't fit into a slot? It defied the established categories. If I was a name author, that would be another story. But nobody had ever heard of me, and so my satire was unpublishable.

Being good wasn't good enough. Being fresh and original was beside the point. From 1953 to 1959, *Munro* faced one rejection after another. My cartoon about a boy who didn't fit into the army didn't fit into conventional publishing. If I had been rejected by the army as successfully as *Munro* had been rejected by publishers, I might have ended up without a career.

The day I was scheduled to go down to the draft board for my physical, I went up to the roof of our apartment building and chinned myself on one of the several thin horizontal steel rods used to hang equipment. My arms were weak. Chinning three times was my limit. I had hoped that I would pull a muscle in my back. I had been suffering since fourteen with a chronic back problem—bedridden for four or five days for opening a window the wrong way with one hand while leaning over at a bad angle or for lifting a fifteen- or twenty-pound weight without properly bending and bracing. Any thoughtless move might collapse my lower back, dropping me to the floor screaming and moaning. It was exactly what I was hoping for now.

So there I was, up on the roof, chinning, contorting my six-foot, 130-pound body in order to induce that which came so easily when I didn't want it. This roof that I was trying to cripple myself on was familiar territory. In summers it was known as Tar Beach because it was where tenants of 1235 Stratford went with blankets and beach chairs and suntan lotion and baby oil and prostrated themselves in the heavy Bronx sun, which felt ten or fifteen degrees hotter than Midtown Manhattan.

Up on the roof with a 360-degree view of a landscape I couldn't wait to escape (but please, not yet!), I chinned myself, trying to force my not-nimble physique into awkward and strained positions in the hope that my weak and skinny body that couldn't throw or catch a ball, that didn't attract girls, that couldn't beat up anyone—that this loathsome, unloved body would do right by me for once and collapse into back spasm, so that I could flunk my physical and get on with my life.

Once again my body failed me. On January 19, 1951, I was drafted.

MADNESS

I went insane in the army. I was insane for two years, during which time I faked a breakdown. The breakdown was an act, the insanity was real. I didn't know I was insane. I knew I was unhappy. Distraught. Demoralized. I saw myself as a victim of a Cold War fundamentalism, mindless authority that used language as a propaganda tool, ratcheted up to Orwellian levels where up was down, in was out, and good and God were terms of war, existing under military surveillance.

Seeing all this and understanding very little, I opted for insanity. It was my way of coping in a world where, up till now, I had been expected to cope only to get along, be a good boy, and obey, more or less.

In the Bronx, the good-boy act was tolerable. I was, by nature, a good boy, so it wasn't that much of a reach even as I thought bad-boy thoughts. Besides, the bad Bronx grown-ups were, as I discovered on my first day in the service, small-bore bad guys, not setting out deliberately to do me in. The damage committed was not for lack of caring. It was for lack of insight and intelligence, which undercut their caring.

I didn't have enemies in the Bronx, no one was out to kill me. However dense and wrongheaded my parents, teachers, and other authority figures I came up against, they lived under the illusion that they meant well. You can forgive a lot of mistakes if, in the process of being beaten to a pulp, you're able to think, "At least they mean well."

They didn't mean well in the army. They meant to gut me and mount me, divest me of my Jules identity and reinvent me as an army private indistinguishable from all other army privates, no longer Jules and Gene and Rudy and Harry but a unified mass commanded to carry out orders that made no sense but army sense, without logic or reason or respect. And this platoon going by the names of Jules and Gene and Rudy and Harry was systematically robbed of its individualism, indoctrinated by lectures, taunts, insults, veiled and unveiled threats, our wills mugged into understanding that the "I" word was out of step in this man's army.

Questions asked by lowly privates, comments by lowly privates, wisecracks and differences of opinion, the weird notion of free speech, the application of—God help us!—logic were tantamount to crimes against the state, punishable by extra drill time or KP or forced marches to our final destination: unconditional surrender.

One did not question, one took orders. One accepted the army's truth, which truth stated that one's individualism must be subjugated, downsized to an insignificant cog in a war machine training to fight the Communist hordes of North Korea, but training in the long run to do battle overall with godless Communism, sworn enemies of all we believed in as our birthright. And to more effectively do so, the army abrogated our birthright in order to better fight the enemies who didn't believe in it.

By the second week of basic training at Fort Dix, I lost my power of New York speech. Wisecracks and smart-ass comments formed themselves in my head as always, but they came out garbled, syntax upended, words in the wrong order or not the words I thought I was going to say. I began to distrust what came out of my mouth. It didn't represent what I meant.

I was under ambush, self-sabotaged to a prehitchhike caricature: inarticulate, stammering, rabbit-in-the-middle-of-the-road-with-headlights-bearing-down-on-him Jules.

If I couldn't talk, I could draw.

The draft put an end to my remarkable four-year apprenticeship with Eisner. As I have joked over the years, I left Will's employ to go into the army at a slight increase in pay. I resigned as Eisner's assistant to become, unexpectedly, Private Harry Hamburg's assistant. Harry was assigned to the barracks next door. We met in company formation, where we immediately pounced on each other as kindred spirits: Jewish wise guys. Harry, as tall as I, had dark curly hair showing early signs of receding, opening on a sweet boyish face belied by a twinkle in the eye and a grin that promised mischief. Harry came from New Jersey, and his background was commercial art. He could do a lot of what I did, but he could do one thing more: hand lettering. He lettered beautifully and meticulously in expressive, showy styles that nicely launched the two of us into a partnership that got us out of basic training.

I had, from my arrival at Fort Dix, done my self-promotional best to advertise my work on *The Spirit* and *Clifford*. The *Spirit* supplement appeared on Sundays in the *Newark Star-Ledger,* available in Fort Dix PXs and day rooms. I visited as many as I could, extracting the *Spirit* section from the welter of other *Star-Ledger* supplements and displaying it with a prominence that I hoped would draw attention to the fact that there was a brilliant young cartoonist on the post. I harbored a mad hope that I could talent my way out of basic.

Basic training was what all new inductees were made to go through, but I saw mine as a special case, in that I was me and they were them. *They* probably didn't mind as much as I did the marching, the drilling, the stripping down and putting back together again our M–1 weapons, or the firing range and target shooting, or the bivouacking. Or the infiltration course, where men crawled on their bellies across frozen New Jersey landfill as noncommissioned officers shot live rounds over our heads. Bullets! *Live!* Over *my* head! No sir!

I was not about to tempt some bitter career noncom with a resentment of middle-class college-boy draftees born into privileges not open to him, whose leveler was his machine gun with live ammo, which, as I crawled on my belly across the infiltration course, might "accidentally" slip an inch, a foot, two feet. Four perfectly placed slugs between the eyes, these eyes that were meant to lift me out of the same poverty as my assassin noncom's, these eyes that, with my good right hand, were going to make me a famous cartoonist, though I came from no more privilege and had no more education than he. But does my noncom know that as he lowers his gunsight to spit out his vengeful proletarian bullets and blow me away in a case of mistaken identity? I did not appreciate the bitter irony of my situation. I had to put to use what remained of my dwindling wits to avoid the infiltration course.

A way out announced itself. Cadremen, as the noncoms who ruled our lives were called, those career army men who drilled us, marched us, inspected us, mocked and humiliated us (no special reason, just part of the game) had their own vanity and sense of company pride. They had found out, as a result of my exhaustive advance work, that I was an artist (of some kind or other), which meant that I might do them a favor. Would I be able to dress up their helmet liners (plastic lids commonly worn as headgear) by lettering on their rims in fancy script their names, rank, and company insignia?

Could I? Would I? If they were to advance me a few dollars for brushes and paints and lacquer, I'd be thrilled to emblazon their names on their helmet liners. It would be my pleasure! Except that I didn't know how to letter, on helmet liners or anything else. I asked Harry Hamburg in for a consultation. He had an idea: why waste time teaching me how to letter when he'd be more than happy to take over? We'd make it a two-man job, Harry doing the lettering, and I as the front man, the official boss of the operation. I'd handle the lacquering. Harry's only request was that I get him excused from basic training.

Work orders began to filter in: one helmet liner for a corporal, two or three corporals from other platoons, our drill sergeant, who was not going to allow corporals to parade around with their names brightening their helmet liners while he went without.

I explained to the drill sergeant that I was oversubscribed and under-manned. I couldn't handle this job alone. I knew of a Private Hamburg in the next barracks, an excellent lettering man. He could assist me, but time was the problem. If the cadremen wanted their decorated helmet liners in less than a week to show off on the parade ground, I didn't see how Private Hamburg or I could fill all of our orders, you know, with our days consumed by basic training.

Harry and I were excused from basic training—except for company formation and morning drills. Gym, I called it. Jumping up and down, hands together, feet apart. We did a minimum of drilling, and then when the punishing grind of the day kicked in, we were returned to our barracks to do our vanity helmets. We were soldier artisans glorifying the cause.

Alone, taking turns in either of our empty barracks, I processed the order forms as Harry did the heavy lifting. Corporal Ames wanted his first initial included in his inscription, his twin-chevron corporal insignia embossed in gold, and the company emblem. Sergeant Earl wanted his name in gold leaf, his sergeant stripes in white outlined in blue. Corporal Lambert, who was black and liked jazz, wanted his name in white inside the silhouette of a black top hat, with his stripes Day-Glo yellow beneath the top hat.

Harry worked away with his tiny brushes, dipping in and out of his tiny jars of color that we had been given a day pass to buy in nearby Wrightstown, which had a paint supply shop. Harry suggested that as long as we had a pass and we were in town, why didn't we take in a movie? But I was too scared, and Wrightstown didn't have any good movies. I was scared twenty-four hours a day.

I did what I could to work against it. What I was learning about fear, on a trial-and-error basis, was that instead of backing away from it, in which case you might back up all the way to the womb (*dear God, no!*), if you turned and headed right for what most scared you, it would more than likely turn out to be not that big a deal. Or you could get killed. This was not an exact science.

In the army I tended to alternately head in all directions. I did everything alternately, overscared, overimagining, overthinking. Whatever I was overthinking lost all coherence when exposed to the light of day. Part of the problem, and this is pure guesswork (I have no idea what the problem could have been to make me react so severely), was that I didn't understand, and never got to understand, the rules of the country into which I had been shanghaied. Up until I was drafted, I had found that I could survive under any circumstance, no matter how unnerving, degrading, humiliating, or demoralizing, if I could understand the unwritten rules, i.e., the code of the culture that was beating up on me. Whether it was family, school, sports, friendship, work, sex, I was accustomed to getting knocked down, picking myself up, and starting all over again (in the words of my guru, the immortal Fred Astaire).

I had grown up in the Bronx with an understanding of the code. I saw that it worked against me, but I considered that temporary, a detail. The Bronx would come around. I would somehow bring it around. Pure illusion, but what allowed for the comfort of that illusion was that I believed myself to understand the different codes. Communication was not limited to what was said. Communication might be the direct opposite of what was said. Understanding that when my mother said A, she might have actually meant it, unless she meant B or C or D, or their opposite. Whatever she meant, I learned intuitively to discern her true meaning without asking questions. Asking questions could be bad for you.

If you didn't understand, it was better to pretend and figure it out later. One did best by sliding under the radar. Though unacknowledged, the code was in place everywhere. School lived by a code, never to be brought out in the open but understood by students and teachers alike. It had to do with power and pecking orders and a system that claimed to be about education but was as much about hierarchies and indoctrination. In and out lists began in high school, but they were never part of the curriculum. Yet who didn't understand?

Getting out of school into the workplace—the real world, so-called—meant that one absorbed, and acclimated oneself to, a multiplicity of codes, not very different, just infinitely nuanced. And no one needed to have them explained. No one needed clarification. No one said, "That's not what you mean, *this* is what you mean. That's not what you're telling me to do, *this* is what you're telling me to do."

Reading between the lines was the only true approach to the text. Everybody knew how the game was played, but if you pointed that out they'd look at you as if they didn't know what you were talking about. And by understanding and accepting the code that dared not speak its name, one found a sense of place in one's surroundings. One belonged. As much of a mess as my civilian life may have been, I never doubted that it was where I belonged and where I would prosper.

But in the army I was on unknown ground. And on my discharge in two years, I felt no less estranged than on the day I was inducted. The code that my fellow draftees had little trouble falling in line with remained a confusion to me. The more I learned, the less I understood. It was this confusion that led me in more directions than I could count at the same time, but ultimately in the direction of satire, based on the theory, I suppose, that if you can't join them beat them.

They were certainly a form of satiric statement, these sleek plastic helmet liners that Harry and I concocted. To be a soldier in the army while at the same time getting oneself out of the unpleasant, you-could-get-hurt part of soldiering—why, there was a whole body of literature on that subject. Harry and I were following in the fabled tradition of Marion Hargrove, Ensign Pulver, Max Shulman's *Feather Merchants,* and, a little later on, Phil Silvers's *Sergeant Bilko.* In my own world of comics, there was Mort Walker's *Beetle Bailey.* One could go back to World War I and *The Good Soldier Schweik.* If memory serves, but it doesn't, Schweik was not a good soldier but a shameless manipulator, which would put him right down there at the bottom of the barrel with Harry and me.

Harry, who went on to have a brilliant career as a photographer and teacher and who is now retired, living in California on the outskirts of Carmel, drawing beautiful citiscapes, has faxed me this:

I had worked for Grey Advertising in the art bull pen and remembered that when a client launched a new product they gave out samples. We thought this was the route to go. We got an extra helmet liner from the supply room and lettered the supply sergeant's name on the front—using a Barnum and Bailey circus type for a little jazz—and gave it to the guy. Once he put it on and went into the mess hall, all the other noncommissioned officers asked where he got it. They came to us one at a time and Jules and I were in business. It took a week to complete all the noncommissioned officers' helmets, and then another week to paint the officers'.

That was one week—we had six weeks of basic training to go. We asked for the supply sergeant's helmet and painted a light blue stripe down the middle to designate infantry and sent him back to the mess hall. All the other helmets started coming back the next day, so another warm week was spent striping. The field first sergeant was a big black soldier who had just come back from Korea. He could read us like a three-page pamphlet. "You guys are a bunch of New York goldbricks trying to get out of training." This called for an extraordinary measure. We saw a field first sergeant's helmet from another company and it was painted bright red. We got another helmet from the supply room and sprayed it bright red with the guy's name on the front and a baby blue stripe down the middle. We sat in awe of our creation. We sneaked into his private room in the barracks and left it on his footlocker. Nothing happened until the next morning. We all fell in for the morning roll call in the dark and out walked our sergeant wearing his newest fashion. Jules and I felt the pride in seeing our firstborn. The sergeant never said thanks or anything else—he just left us alone for the rest of the training and never took his helmet off—we thought he slept in it. We still had two weeks to go. The next thing we found were decals with the Forty-seventh Infantry Regiment at the PX. We bought two for each helmet and decorated our supply sergeant's model hat. This time around, all the helmets came back at once. The officers got priority for theirs. We were running low on ideas for the last week of basic, but we did persevere. Jules found a can of high-gloss spray, and we ended the six weeks of basic by spraying all the helmets with a high sheen that made everyone look like General Patton.

Our collective memory of seven weeks of basic training was sitting around a stove in the barracks doing Art Therapy. As the Jewish philosopher would say: "It wasn't great, but it could have been worse."

Captain Green, our commanding officer, singled us out for praise. He couldn't help but notice how his officers and cadre were so impressively decked out on the parade ground. It was the talk of Fort Dix. Captain Green was a vice president of an insurance company in civilian life, called back into service from the reserves. He was husky and pleasant-looking and conducted himself with an air of just-putting-in-his-time diffidence. I might have spent two years under his command without complaint (or a subsequent career), but beneath him was a staff of second lieutenants, first sergeants, drill sergeants, and corporals whose job it was to grind us into dust and reshape us into "men."

Harry and I stood at ease on the parade ground, moments following Captain Green's flattering comments on our artwork. We were surrounded by noncoms and second and first lieutenants with their Harry-emblazoned helmet liners brightening the field, a triumph of Gothic and Olde English and P. T. Barnum. Gilded names next to ranks and attendant insignia displayed in a cornucopia of color, making of the commanding cadre and their marching, drilling troops a homoerotic musical of the military.

Carried along by the sweetness of Harry's nature and the aura of fun he brought to this game we were playing, I found his next move irresistible. Harry said to Captain Green, "Sir, Private Feiffer and I would consider it a privilege to design a very special liner for you. What would you like to see on it?"

Captain Green was not at a loss for words in describing to us the liner of his dreams. I took notes. It seemed complicated but doable until we were given our deadline. "I rely on you to have it by Saturday morning for weekly parade and review by Division Command. We expect a colonel and possibly a general up from Washington." This was Wednesday. What he was asking was impossible, but we knew we could do it. We had no choice. Our only other choice was to go back in the army.

Division Command's reviewing our weekly parade was a big deal. It meant that officers and cadre needed to look their best, and if Captain Green was setting the bar higher for Saturday's event there was nothing to be done except sharpen up all the helmet liners we had already painted. By midday they had all come back for an upgrade and retouch. Harry and I, having started out with a nice small business that we could handle, were in danger of becoming victims of our own success.

This job of not being in the army was harder labor than we imagined. All that week, preparing for Saturday's parade, we worked around the clock, delegating the touchups and lacquering of helmets to two elves we recruited and managed to get excused from duty. We reserved for ourselves the headdress of the more serious VIPs, Captain Green and his officers.

Friday night, the night before the dress parade, we ran out of lacquer. It was too late to go into Wrightstown. The stores were closed. I scoured around the paint shed and found cans of shellac. I wasn't sure how that would work. Would Harry's gilt stick or run or change color under the shellac? Can you induce shellac to dry in the eight hours we had before Captain Green was to don his helmet? If you read the small print on the can, it claimed to take twelve hours. Harry had been revising and refinishing Captain Green's helmet liner for three days. We both knew that it had to be spectacular. As the rest of us knocked out the lower-echelon headgear, we had one eye on our artist in residence taking on his white whale, Captain Green's headdress.

In 1958, in a *Village Voice* cartoon, I drew my dancer cavorting in a field of flowers, carefully inspecting each one, announcing to the world, "I am a seeker after perfection." This was Harry.

The job was done at two in the morning. The parade was at eight. Captain Green's helmet stood out among the others, lined in formation on two shelves in a back room of the barracks. It glowed in the dark. Harry, a broken man, collapsed in his bunk after his painstaking hours of labor. I bundled myself into my heavy army overcoat and a couple of scarves. With my cap pulled so far down over my face that I could barely see, I stepped outside the barracks into the fierce February wind. Gingerly, with the tips of my gloved fingers, I held Captain Green's sopping wet helmet. I rotated it in the wind slowly, in the desperate hope that the twelve-hour shellac would freeze, if not dry. I was numb with exhaustion and infinitely too stupid to figure out that wind blowing off an open field transmits an assemblage of Mother Nature's flotsam—specks, flecks, and dreck zipping through the air and zeroing in on an irresistibly sticky target.

I woke Harry up at 3:00 a.m. with the bad news. His gorgeous work of

art was splattered with the Fort Dix pox. I took full responsibility. Harry's job was to fix it. Harry did not say a word. He got out of bed. He went to his paints and brushes. He re-created line for line, color for color, the gilded letters of Captain Green's name, styled in florid Gothic, suitable for a Caesar, surrounded by company insignia aglow in red, white, and yellow and, in the very middle, his captain's bars, silvery and radiant, as if caught by moonlight.

It was now five in the morning. No time for shellac. No time for much of anything. So how were we to make this glorious but still damp artifact stand out among the two dozen or so lacquered helmet liners that had come out of our shop and that would be marching in formation across the parade ground in less than three hours?

I knew that I had more to me than being a fuckup, and now was my chance to prove it. A half hour before Captain Green's scheduled arrival for pickup, I polished Harry's creation tenderly and rigorously with three coats of Vaseline. I didn't know how long it would take for the Vaseline to be absorbed. All I needed was time for the troops to parade before the visiting brass and stun them with the radiant spectacle of Captain Green's helmet liner, making him—dare I say it?—queen for a day.

Captain Green arrived promptly in full dress regalia. He wore white gloves. I didn't want him touching the helmet with his clean white gloves. I told him that the lacquer on the helmet was not quite dry, that he should try to avoid touching it—it had the consistency of, say, Vaseline—and, with his permission, Private Hamburg and I would place it on his head now and remove it (with your permission, sir) after the parade. Captain Green was only half listening, so thrilled was he at the result of Harry's labors.

Gently, as if fitting the emperor for his new clothes, Harry and I lowered the helmet liner on Captain Green. Reflexively he lifted a gloved hand to adjust it. We shouted, "Don't!" Our captain sheepishly withdrew his hand. "He takes orders well," Harry whispered to me as Captain Green strode out, head and helmet held high.

As exhausted as we were, we were not to be excused from the march, nor did we want to be. The pageantry of our artwork dominated the field, the single ray of light, pride, and celebration in a dull, forbidding winter sky. For that moment only, it made Harry and me more than two gold-bricks from New York trying to con our way out of basic training. It made us proud to be in the United States Army. And why not? We were in command.

SOS

Talk about screwups! They were assigning me to Camp Gordon, Georgia, to begin training as a radio operator. In Korea. This was wrong! A monumental misunderstanding of who and what I was meant to be.

I had come out of Fort Dix free of basic training and the constant strategizing to avoid it, not marching, not drilling, not crawling or climbing or shooting or bayonet practicing. My kind of basic. I had graduated with high hopes. Well, midlevel hopes, which for the army was as good as it got. I was first assigned to a film unit in Astoria, Queens, a stone's throw from the Bronx, a forty-minute subway ride from Stratford Avenue. This was more like it. The Signal Corps Photo Center was a country club, a post more befitting a young man of my aspirations. All well and good, but after a mere five months something went terribly wrong. They transferred me to Georgia to train me to operate and repair radios on the front line—in other words, to be killed.

At SCPC I befriended, and hung out with, army and nonarmy types just like me. A soupçon of daytime soldiering was only part of the job: "policing" the area, circling our Steinway Street barracks from the civilian-street side, picking up cigarette butts. Primarily I was trained in the craft of adding subtitles to army training films instructing rookies in the dos and don'ts of weapon maintenance and sexual cleanliness.

I had spare time to raid the files in my sergeant's office for samples of earlier residents of this country club, World War II–vintage cartoonists who had been stationed there as I now was, Charles Addams and Sam Cobean, two *New Yorker* giants, Cobean now sadly forgotten, except in my files, where he and Addams now reside, liberated from the unknowing, uncaring Signal Corps. Given a home, safe and sound, in the file cabinet of one who appreciated their worth. Of course, I can't remember where I filed them. They have been missing for years.

The talent I met at SCPC, the connections I made. Alex Singer and Jim Harris, who were later to work with Stanley Kubrick on his early films, and introduced me to Stanley, paving the way for me to write screenplays for Stanley if only I hadn't blown it. Also stationed at SCPC were "the Juniors," the sons and nephews of the Hollywood moguls: Samuel Goldwyn Jr., Erich von Stroheim Jr., Stuart Millar, whose father was some kind of movie honcho and who had been drafted out of a production assistant job with William Wyler, director of such classic pictures as *The Best Years of Our Lives* and *The Little Foxes*.

I was on my way, until I was transferred—for no reason other than that my commanding officers couldn't figure out what I was doing there in the first place. I had no film business experience, I had never seen a Moviola or an animation camera or an editing room, I had no Hollywood patron, I wasn't a junior—who cast me in this picture?

No matter. The mistake was corrected after a giddy five months. The party over, I was shipped out to Augusta, Georgia, in the summer of 1951, a candidate in training to lay down lines of communication in advance of our troops in enemy territory. Like some comic book adventure hero that I might have created, I was being prepared for duty that included crawling through the South Korean muck and grime and grit—alone. The United States Army was behind me, some distance behind me. I was to lead them.

I saw no good reason to accept this assignment. As Vice President Dick Cheney, our fiercest Iraq war hawk, explained when asked by the press why he hadn't fought in the Vietnam War, "I had other priorities." Yes! Yes! Me too!

My desperation put me on a bus to Fort Monmouth, New Jersey. I had learned through scuttlebutt of the existence of a publications unit, the Signal Corps Publications Agency, that might just be interested in sparing a boy cartoonist from becoming a dead radio operator. Scuttlebutt was the Internet of its day, circulating rumors and useful information by phone, written notes, conversation. It was the GIs' back channel, informing us of what the army didn't want us to know.

Truth and half-truth and outright falsehood flew back and forth among GIs who wanted in on this or out of that and needed to know where to go, whom to see, how to circumvent official channels, because one learned by the end of the first week in the army that going through the chain of command to get what you wanted got you nowhere. This was the ultimate purpose of the chain of command. Appeals, petitions, letters, phone calls were stopped dead in their tracks, before they could reach the desk of an officer who might actually help you. And divert him with the inconsequential matter of your life and death.

Fort Monmouth was sandwiched between Red Bank, New Jersey, and Asbury Park, not nearly as drab-looking as Fort Dix but clearly no country club. The head of the publications unit was a man named Percy Couse, who must have been in his late forties but looked older. He was a civilian, but that didn't do me much good. He was a civilian who believed in going by the book. His presence was intimidating: thick eyebrows over squinting ice blue eyes magnified scarily through thick-lensed glasses, a deep, gravelly voice, and trimmed snow white hair that added years and gravitas. Not exactly an image to suggest hope. His manner was cordial if not helpful. Yes, he said, they could use someone of my talent on his staff, which was half civilian, half military, but no, he could not accede to my request and ask for me outright. That was not how it was done. But if my new commander at Camp Gordon was amenable to a transfer, then Mr. Couse might consider finding a place for me in his unit.

Hardly an overwhelming endorsement. Mr. Couse, at my pleading, dashed off a letter on official stationery saying that if Private Feiffer was available for transfer, the Signal Corps Publications Agency would consider him. It was the best I could do.

CAMP GORGON

My first glimpse of Camp Gordon: barren, sun-sodden grounds, so damp with humidity it made foolish my complaints of New York summers. New York was never like this. Hell was never like this. Fort Dix stood out as a vacation paradise. I realized on my arrival exactly where I was. I was in the army, God help me. Finally they had done it.

Jules was not going to take this lying down. Let others adjust, let others accept, *I* was in a rage. From my first moment of arrival, I plotted my getaway. I fondled my letter from Mr. Couse, hid it in a secret place no one would find. I thought it was my death house reprieve.

Radio repair, if that's what it was, was indecipherable to me. Talk about code—everything said to me by the sergeant instructor, laconic, soft-spoken, hard-assed, and contemptuous, sounded as if he were translating from a foreign tongue. He knew he was speaking to a room full of idiots. He didn't try to hide that. His deadpan delivery didn't help.

I was the main idiot. The other recruits, after a day or two, appeared to catch on. For these kids just a couple of years out of high school, learning how to repair a radio could be a good career opportunity. If they survived those North Koreans shooting bullets at them.

We students sat on stools, stooped over radio parts and loose wires, tinkering with tools that were meant to help but didn't. Arranged in three rows, ten repairmen trainees cubbyholed at long, wooden, scarred tables. My fellow students, generally working class and, like me, with only a high school education, seemed to master the process after a couple of days. But it eluded me. Something about "olms," which was, I think, a term of measurement, not a mantra. And then there was voltage. But isn't "voltage" also a term of measurement? So what are olms?

Everyone in the class, none of whom were a quarter as bright as I, whizzed through radio repair. This began to bother me. Everyone likes to excel, and even though I planned to flunk in the hope of not being sent to Korea, I preferred to feel clever about it, that it was my choice.

Choice or not, I was not going to be permitted the freedom to flunk. Camp Gordon had a quota of trained radio repairmen to turn out, and just as on induction day, when I was recorded to weigh 190 pounds when the scale read 130, I was going to be graduated from radio school, it didn't matter how unqualified. "No, Feiffer, them two wires, you let them touch, you're gonna fuckin' short the fuckin' system and start a fuckin' fire. Then you're gonna be fucked."

This made no sense. The Signal Corps shouldn't waste its money on the likes of me, who was bound to screw up in the field and endanger the lives of men, especially myself. I could do them so much more good if they'd only let me sit behind a drawing board.

This argument was convincing to me as I listened to it play back in my head. As I mentioned earlier, I was crazy—but the sort of crazy that led me to believe that I was the only sane person in the asylum. Which might have been fine if I hadn't acted on it and made the stupidest move of all: I went through the chain of command.

I had not been around Camp Gordon long enough to ferret out the right connection. Every post had a connection, the man behind the scenes who had the authority to cut through the red tape. The connection was an unacknowledged, ephemeral figure whom you could not get to through the chain of command, which existed solely to protect officers like him from privates like me. But once I located his hideaway, this anonymous, oh-so-protected officer—who lacked the hands-on daily contact that fostered callousness and indifference—might actually listen to me, might even be persuadable.

I understood all that, but nonetheless I panicked. I lacked the patience to search out this mysterious figure. I was crazy, going crazier by the minute. The logic of my insanity insisted that I make a request to go before our company commander.

He was Captain Something or Major Something. He cut through what I thought was my well-reasoned analysis of why I would be of more use in our nation's struggle against Communism if I fought the Korean War in Fort Monmouth, New Jersey. It took him half a second to conclude that I was a goldbricking, lying piece of New York shit.

Okay, he had his position. I had mine. Perhaps we could meet halfway . . . Apparently not. He yelled, he shouted, I was sent back to my barracks in shame and disgrace.

I went back to radio repair school not in the slightest defeated. I had goofed by going through the chain of command, but I had come out of it with a strengthened sense of mission. Here was what I had to do. I understood that I was crazy. I had to find a way for the army to understand my craziness, I had to convince them it wasn't an act. I had to raise the ante on my insanity level. I was too well behaved a nutcase, too self-effacing, too bourgeois. I had to come up with a performance that would fool the army into believing that I was, in fact, what I knew myself to be.

But this performance could not take place before I found the man outside the chain of command to go to, the officer who was out there, the fixer, the conduit, the liaison, the mystery man. He who would listen to me. And send me to Fort Monmouth. His name was Warrant Officer Hoover. Warrant officers, a rank that I don't think exists today, were, in the 1950s, liaison officers who went by the honorific title "Mister." Warrant officers played the role of shortstops, troubleshooters, problem solvers. The army knew better than anyone that its system often didn't work. It was never intended to work. Its rules and regulations were designed to keep it rolling smoothly with a deliberate mindlessness. Whether or not it worked was incidental. The important part was that it had to look as if it knew what it was doing even when it didn't know what it was doing. It couldn't afford to admit a mistake or publicly change its mind. When it changed tactics, it publicly denied that it was changing tactics. The army could not concede a point. Once you conceded a point, you undermined your credibility, you weakened your authority, or so our commanders believed. Troops would go uncertain and neurotic and resist following the orders that led them to their doom. What kind of army was it if it couldn't routinely lead men off to die?

So for a system so rigid not to back up on itself, it needed a second system working clandestinely within the official system. This unacknowledged system could bend the rules, go around the rules, ignore the rules, if it must, to right wrongs, to get things done. Warrant Officer Hoover was secluded away in an office impossible to find. He was the chosen man at Camp Gordon, the only man whose job it was to be rational. It was his job to listen, it was his job to make sense. He was a very lonely man.

He was hard to find but finally findable. In every army there is a malcontent underground. They know what everyone else knows; and what you're not supposed to know, they find out. I had come in contact with this malcontent underground. I was making such an exhibition of myself in radio repair school that I was approached as a prospective recruit, a malcontent in waiting. They found me to be ideal material.

I sat with my fellow malcontents long into the night, tossing back and forth conspiracy theories. We bandied about the names of those we knew or had heard of who had gotten transferred out of Camp Gordon by one ruse or another, who had been slated to go to FECOM (Far East Command) and had ended up in West Germany, who had managed to get a discharge because they were psycho or pseudo-psycho or were psycho on a particular day or had a breakdown or had faked a breakdown. The stories made the rounds as fables for grown-ups (not that we could be called grown-ups, but no one in the army could be called a grown-up, especially the men in charge).

I kept putting off my crack-up, but I couldn't put it off much longer. I had rehearsed in my head what was going to happen. I couldn't go stark raving insane, screaming and hopping about. I knew I couldn't pull that off. If I was going to commit myself to a crazy act, first it must be convincing to me, otherwise how would I convince my commanding officers?

My usual approach to get attention was to use self-effacement laced with humor. In keeping with what made me comfortable, it seemed to me that my only feasible move was to concoct a wry, self-effacing nervous breakdown.

It was essentially a writing and acting job, and although I was faking it, I began to wonder just how much. Was I about to act out a breakdown in order to cover up the very real wry, self-effacing breakdown that I was already in the middle of?

These two transmitter wires that aren't supposed to touch, if I put them so close together that they do touch . . . The results of all that training in radio repair that I didn't understand indicated that it would cause a short circuit. Sparks would fly, a sizzling sound, the smell of wires burning. By having these two wires, both positive charges (or were they negative?), make contact and start off a small fireworks display—that might be just the boost I needed to get me leaping off my stool and running out of radio repair class, out onto the field crying in anguish (not defiance, never defiance, it must be anguish): "I CAN'T DO THIS! I'VE TRIED! I CAN'T FIX A RADIO! I CAN'T! I CAN'T! I CAN'T! I CAN'T!"

The second lieutenant was called in by my sergeant to handle the mental case he didn't want any part of. The lieutenant called me a coward and a phony and asked me how I'd like to be transferred to Korea. I, who had broken down so much better than I expected, was now on a roll. I saw this as my moment to go for broke. Since the second lieutenant was not going to be moved by my madness, I dug deep into my movie bag of tricks. I dug up a voice quivering Jimmy Stewart–inspired Every Boy going off to fight the Japanese in World War II patriotism. Speaking from my heart, a symphony orchestra in the back of my head scoring my sincerity and love of country, "Sir," I said to my superior officer, staring him square in the eye, "I've been through basic training. I can shoot a weapon, I know the M–1. If that's where I can serve my country best, I will be happy to go. But I can't go as a radio repairman."

The lieutenant, who refused to be impressed, ordered me confined to barracks. I had another destination in mind. With legs shaky from my confrontation, I walked across the vast stretch of parade ground. The cropped grass radiated an eerie brilliance, the afterglow of turgid Augusta in August, its humidity and rainfall. A wind had whipped up. Three flagpoles spaced at wide intervals across the field flew outsized American flags in the evening dusk to the recorded blast of a Sousa march. I walked self-consciously, observing myself as an actor performing for the camera, miming a shakiness under my control onto the shakiness that wasn't.

This walk that couldn't have taken more than three minutes felt like an hour. On the other side of the field, right off a dirt path, I found Warrant Officer Hoover's office. Mr. Hoover was alone, sitting at his desk as I entered, typing out a report. I saluted. I asked if I might speak with him.

Mr. Hoover had the look of a man who was not going to make it easy for me. In his forties, tired-looking, brittle, with a pencil mustache and a face without lines or expression. He asked me who had given me the authority to approach him without an appointment. I seem to be at my best when I have everything to lose. At this point I saw myself as a CIA agent working underground, interrogated by an enemy army. It didn't matter what I said to my interrogators, as long as it wasn't the truth. "Sir, forgive my stupidity. I didn't know I needed permission, I'll go back now and see if I can get permission—"

Mr. Hoover interrupted with half a lecture, half a bawling out: I wasn't going to get anywhere in this man's army until I learned the rules and respected them. Who was I to think I was so special that I could just barge into his office without an appointment and expect a busy man like Mr. Hoover to take the time—didn't I know what the chain of command was? He explained it to me, in case I didn't know. Then, having explained the chain of command and gone on to explain why he was of a mind to kick me out, he said the magic words: "All right, soldier, as long as you're here, what's the problem?"

He was playing my script! First bawl me out, then hear me out.

The approach I took was to skip the breakdown in favor of patriotism. How could the Signal Corps waste so much money sending me through radio repair school, where I couldn't understand even the most basic rudiments, when, up in Fort Monmouth, New Jersey, in the Signal Corps Publications Agency, there was a desk waiting for me to work on much-needed training manuals, maps, charts, and graphs that were in short supply. And I could be there, within days, to supply them. Did this make sense?

Mr. Hoover listened without comment, then made it clear that it was time for me to leave. He called after me as I walked out the door, "You say you have a letter from Fort Monmouth?"

I said that I did, that I had it in my footlocker.

"See that you drop it off here tomorrow morning before 8:00 a.m."

My heart took a flying leap out of my chest. I started back across the parade ground, aquiver with excitement. *I was going to get my transfer!*

Dusk had settled. I was now halfway across the field. An amplified recording of "Taps" began to sound. The American flags were being lowered from their flagpoles. With the continuing sense of cameras rolling, spying on my every step, I came to a halt on my way back to my barracks where I was to be confined. Alone in the middle of the darkening green parade ground, I turned to face the lowering of my country's flags. I was moved. I was joyous. I had been heard. Was this a great country or what? I saluted the flags. And I said out loud, because no one was within a quarter mile to hear: "I fucked the army! I fucked the army! I fucked the army!"

Weeks later, I was still sitting on my stool in radio repair class. No one expected me to learn. I was expected to just sit. It was as if my breakdown hadn't happened. It was as if Mr. Hoover had never happened, as if time had reversed itself or was frozen, and each day began just as in the Bill Murray movie *Groundhog Day*. I waited, and that's all I did, each day, starting from scratch. Not a word about my transfer. No message from Mr. Hoover. Did I make him up? I couldn't have made him up, because my letter from Mr. Couse was no longer in my footlocker. Mr. Hoover had it.

I had taken that letter over at seven-thirty the morning after my interview, hopes high, cautiously happy. I slipped it under Mr. Hoover's locked door, his name scrawled on it. This letter from Mr. Couse from the Signal Corps Publications Agency. Without it, I couldn't prove that I was needed in New Jersey. I couldn't even prove it existed. They might deny that there was a letter. Then they wouldn't have a reason to transfer me to Fort Mon-

mouth, would just send me as a rifleman to Korea. Didn't I say to the lieutenant that I wasn't afraid to go to Korea? That I was trained in the M–1?
I thought I was clever. Stupid, fucking jerk!

Each morning I woke with a sense of doom on hold. I knew as much
about my immediate future as I knew about repairing radios. The lesson of
life was that there was no lesson. You had to take the same class over and
over in order to find out that what you didn't learn yesterday you would
not learn today. What didn't happen yesterday won't happen today.
Ciphering my way through limbo at a long table with other recruits coming
and going, promoted as radio repairmen, sent out into God knows where
to risk life and limb.

And I risked nothing but my sanity, which I'd lost long ago, marking
time at a desk with a broken radio that signaled my dwindling confidence.
I was living testament to the immutability of army logic. An embarrassment to the service—how could they give me what I wanted? It would be
a reward for my screwing up. I couldn't be rewarded for proving to them
that I was the wrong man in the wrong place and it was their fault for putting me there. If they put me where I belonged in Fort Monmouth, they
would be admitting their mistake. And even worse, they had let someone
who didn't go through the chain of command get away with it. Every other
punk who wanted out of an assignment might be inspired by my example.
You can't run an army that way. I imagined and feared that they were going
to make an example of me. I made up conversations that they were having
about me, and listened in on them: "Our best bet might be to send him to
Korea as a rifleman."

"But how can you trust someone like that to shoot at the enemy and
not our own men?"

I waited in my limbo at radio repair. The stammer I had learned in
basic training got worse. Words became one more burden to bear. Time
had extended into a vacuum, and I didn't have the words to fill it or make
it go away. And so went the month of September.

How awful it is when you think you have won and no one will recognize the fact. It was particularly hard on me because I was a coward. But I
was a stubborn coward. If they weren't going to let me win, then I was

determined not to let them win either. I had one goal, and one goal only: to sit on my stool and outlast the bastards.

And then, on October 1, 1951, my transfer to Fort Monmouth came through. Orders were cut. I was to fly to New York on October 3 and report for duty on October 4.

So there I was, at the airport in Atlanta, waiting for a plane to fly me to LaGuardia. I'd spend the night at home in the Bronx and the next day take a bus to Fort Monmouth, and all I was thinking was, "I won, where's the pleasure?" The long three-and-a-half-week wait for the transfer had taken all the joy out of my triumph. The army had both given me what I wanted and found a way to ruin it for me. Any second now I expected to hear my name called out on the airport intercom: "Private Feiffer, report immediately back to your hellhole." Instead of a sense of triumph, I felt like I was standing in the middle of a minefield.

A baseball game was in progress on a ten-inch black-and-white screen in a nearby airport bar. The Brooklyn Dodgers against the New York Giants in the final playoff for the National League pennant. Two neighborhood teams, one from Manhattan, one from Brooklyn, had made it onto Southland television. And so tense and exciting was the game that not a Southern soul was moving. Even in my punch-drunk state of mind I understood my obligation to metaphorize this moment into myth.

The Giants had come from thirteen and a half games back to draw even with the Dodgers, an amazing feat that captured the hearts and imaginations of all baseball fans except, of course, Dodger fans. I wasn't a Dodger fan; my sister Mimi was. She had to be. Jackie Robinson was a Dodger. Robinson had come out of the Negro Leagues to be the first black player to make it in the majors. The *Daily Worker,* the official newspaper of the Communist Party, had been proselytizing to get Robinson on the Dodgers years before most white-run newspapers were willing to acknowledge his existence. It was the politics of civil rights that made Mimi a Dodger fan. My fandom was apolitical, in that I didn't care about color. I cared about which team was biggest and strongest because I was smallest and weakest. Therefore I was a Yankee fan.

The Yankees were the closest thing to superheroes outside of comics.

They hit lots of home runs. I loved home runs. I, whose best effort was to hit a ground ball that slipped into the infield for a hit because of bad fielding, identified my heart and mind with the Joe DiMaggios and Charlie Kellers and Tommy Henrichs of the Yankees, the class sluggers of Major League baseball. But this was not the American League pennant race, it was the National League, and in the National League, the closest to a Yankee-style ball club was the Giants. And the Giants had a black player too, arguably more skilled than Jackie Robinson: Willie Mays. So I cast my lot with the Giants, who had come out of nowhere, thirteen and a half games back, to make a pennant race out of a walkaway. It didn't look good for the Giants, my side—but I was used to that. The Giants were behind in the last of the ninth, 4 to 2. One man out, two men on, and Bobby Thomson coming to bat. The great Brooklyn pitcher Ralph Branca had come on in relief to pitch to Thomson. Our plane, no other plane at Atlanta airport, no plane on the Eastern Seaboard was taking off until Branca pitched to Bobby Thomson and, if necessary, Willie Mays, up next.

So here was what my life had come to. On this, my day of transfer, I expected an MP to tap me on the shoulder at any second and tell me that I had to go back to radio repair school. All that remained of my tenuous ties to optimism was what Thomson was about to do at bat or, if Thomson failed to get a hit and did not bounce into a double play, Willie Mays.

You had to be there. But, of course, you weren't and I was: the shout of Russ Hodges, the Giants announcer as Bobby Thomson swung for the seats: "There's a long drive." A pause. "It's gonna be." Pause. And Russ Hodges, who had ties to my Yankee background because some years earlier he had worked with Mel Allen announcing Yankee games, shouted—no, bellowed—over a screaming crowd: "THE GIANTS WIN THE PENNANT! THE GIANTS WIN THE PENNANT! THE GIANTS WIN THE PENNANT! THE GIANTS WIN THE PENNANT!"

In the opening chapter of *Underworld,* this is how Don DeLillo writes of this: "This is how the crowd enters the game. The repeated . . . force of some abject faith, a desperate sort of will toward magic and accident."

We passengers and flight crew boarded the American Airlines flight for LaGuardia, all of us looking at one another, stunned. By pure luck, we had become part of history. We, who were not on the playing field, who were not in the Polo Grounds, had entered the game. Our collective act of will toward magic and accident—how could you not help wondering if it didn't work? The act of will that led me out of Camp Gordon onto that tarmac . . .

An hour later, our flight made a stop in Washington, D.C., to pick up and discharge passengers. Only an hour had passed, but new passengers were coming aboard and all of them seemed to be carrying copies of a *Washington Post* extra with headlines screaming, "THOMSON BEATS DODGERS. GIANTS WIN PENNANT."

So it was in print. It must be official. It happened. So other things could happen. Anything could happen. I quote a joke told me by a friend, Will Campbell of Mount Juliet, Tennessee, a town I had never heard of before my time in the south. A boy is promised by his father that a special present awaits him behind a closed door. He opens the door and what does he find but a room full of shit. And the boy says, "There has to be a pony in here somewhere."

PONY

Munro, the forty-five-page cartoon narrative that was to determine the direction of my work and my life over the next fifty years, came to me as an idea in company formation at Fort Monmouth. It, and the cartoons that followed, secured for me the reputation to do what I liked, the way I liked. It allowed me the freedom to treat my career as a series of mood swings, shuttling back and forth from relationship cartoons to political cartoons to writing plays, novels, screenplays, dancer watercolors, children's books, and this memoir. Wandering into seductive and scary neighborhoods and getting lost, just as I did in real life, circling around with no sense of where I was headed, just as in real life, until I discovered a way out and the way home.

And the way out might never have been found if I hadn't been drafted. And hated every minute of it.

But I write this as I near eighty, and I discovered long ago that age has made me stupid. It's possible that I don't know what I'm talking about. My father always said to me in argument, "You don't know what you're talking about!" It angered me, this automatic put-down, because I saw it as his way of not responding to the point I was making. And I was right. And so was my father. Many times when I was most vehement in our arguments I didn't know what I was talking about.

I make up knowledge by the same method that I make up cartoons and stories and dramatic scenes: by committing myself without any sure sense of what comes next until it comes next and keeps on coming, right or wrong. One thought or idea follows another, leading I don't know where until, moments later, it dawns on me that I know where I'm headed, and it's the right place. A half page earlier I might not have known. Once I finish the piece of work, I give it and me a break. At an appropriate time, I take it out, look it over, begin again.

The first time I worked this way, not knowing it was my method, I happened to be sitting at my desk at the Signal Corps Publications Agency, two months on the job. Bored with the routine of touching up photographs, I took out a sheet of paper and began playing with the idea of a four-year-old kid getting drafted by mistake. It was to be a cartoon in the form of a children's book. A good idea, but what happens after he's drafted? I took long walks around the post, talking out loud to myself, asking but not getting answers: "What am I doing? Where am I going?" Questions I still ask.

Munro was a departure from the stunted single-panel cartoons I had been experimenting with since early basic training. I had tried a series called *Army Types,* contorted single figures inside a panel, expressing their psychic regrets about the military. It was drawn in a clean, thick and thin brush line and looked a little like the semi-surreal *New Yorker* panels of Abner Dean, who drew full-page panels of naked men and women with one-line captions instead of dialogue. Or that's how I remember it. Dean was influenced by the inroads psychoanalysis was making into the urban consciousness. And so were we all. So I was very open to his approach and wanted to try my own variation. I had also begun to notice the more radical innovations of Saul Steinberg and William Steig.

Although I had been an admirer of *The New Yorker* since childhood, the magazine had never played a part in how I worked or thought about work. It certainly played no part in my ambitions. I was, heart and soul, a newspaper strip man, four panels daily and ten to twelve color panels on Sunday was my fancy, my dream of glory.

That dream was to join the ranks of Milton Caniff, Roy Crane, Will Eisner, Alex Raymond, Walt Kelly, Al Capp, and Crockett Johnson. If I could have turned myself into any one of them, I would have been overjoyed. But as much as I loved the work of Peter Arno, Charles Addams, Whitney Darrow, George Price, Helen Hokinson, Gluyas Williams, Alan

"Army Types," 1951

"You meet us halfway, we'll meet you halfway."

Company Formation

"I hate everything except Mozart."

Dunn, Sam Cobean, Frank Modell, and other *New Yorker* regulars, I could not imagine myself appearing in their magazine.

I had mastered the rules of the daily comic strip (or so I was convinced), its four-panel layouts, three panels acting as building blocks for a last-panel payoff. But the single-panel cartoon—whether in *The New Yorker* or *Collier's* or the *Saturday Evening Post,* or in the editorial art of Herblock and Bill Mauldin—was a mystery to me in terms of execution. I didn't know how to think in a single shot. And every time I tried, not only did I fail, but often, much too often, I didn't have an opinion on whether the cartoon was any good or not. I needed to be told. Friends like Ed McLean would have to look at my work and tell me: That's okay, not bad, needs work, stinks, no, that's really good. I couldn't tell. They all seemed—the good or the mediocre—pretty much the same to me.

And if the day came that I mastered the form, how could I ever hope to match Peter Arno's "Man in the Shower" cartoon, which happened to be on the first page of a Christmas *New Yorker* collection that Mimi gave me as a present. I must have laughed for ten minutes. I studied the cartoon, trying to understand what it was that caused this outburst. No caption, just this naked man floating upside down in a stall shower filled to the top with water, frantically pointing out the door handle to his alarmed wife standing in the bathroom door in her robe.

Why did it continue to be hysterically funny long after the surprise was over? I looked away and looked back, and broke up, and tried to get to the bottom of it. This single image was funnier than some of the great sight gags I'd seen in movies. Arno grabbed you by the shirt front and pulled you into the panel. He was all noise, virility, and charm, not a trace of the whimsy or diffidence we usually associate with the magazine. If Picasso had drawn *New Yorker* cartoons, they would have looked something like Arno's.

Gluyas Williams's cartoons in the magazine were more my style, but his drawing was tighter and better than anything I could manage. I thought that with hard work, willpower, and skillful copying, I could learn to be Williams. He, too, drew in multipanels, offering silent movie glimpses of life's minuscule moments. Working in a quiet, gentle manner, with a line light as air, he observed body language with meticulous grace: posture, hand gestures, neck, shoulder, and torso tilts, the angle of a leg; incisive, wordless essays on manners and character and class. His drawings appeared, as well, in the humor collections of Robert Benchley. Twinned together, he and Benchley seemed to me perfect exemplars of self-effacing Gentile wit, eons apart from this self-effacing Jewish boy cartoonist from the Bronx, who, if he got lucky, might someday be invited to the party.

But I was in no mood to be elegant like Williams. I was in the god-damned army. Elegance was the wrong note—I had anger to express. I found it in the savage grace of Robert Osborn's heavy brush and charcoal lines in the pages of the *New Republic, Fortune,* and the *New York Times Magazine.* Osborn's line was like an attack dog going for your throat, yet off-puttingly artful. Its artfulness gave his line a beauty that modified its grit without selling it out. Osborn as a cartoonist was able to make use of anger to fuel thought: not a bad role model.

But the three cartoonists who captured my attention most during my army time had only recently emerged into public consciousness. They were Saul Steinberg, William Steig, and André François. All three changed how we looked at cartoons and how we looked at one another. I practiced trying to be each of them.

Steinberg's line, unlike Gluyas Williams's, was angular, architectural, and barbed. Wit was present in plentitude, but not a hint of the WASP self-effacement that one found in Williams. Steinberg's line indicted. It was cultural anthropology in cartoon form, playful and judgmental and forgiving, all in one. For a while it seemed that every new Steinberg augured a breakthrough. Language was turned into line, scribbles of insight and rhetoric, single-panel monographs that were philosophical and funny and cultured and painful to look at. He was so smart that he made us feel smarter than we were just because we admired him. His work (and his mind) was not anything I would ever be able to emulate. But nonetheless he led me to try things I wouldn't have known to try before.

Saul Steinberg, from *The New Yorker*, February 12, 1955

Drawing for William Steig's *The Agony in the Kindergarten*, 1950

"Willie!"

Steig stung from the inside. He was the first cartoonist I came across who effectively translated Freud into humor. His earlier *New Yorker* cartoons—*Small Fry* and others—had not been of great interest to me. The art seemed cramped, the gags so-so. I would not have included him among the *New Yorker* notables, which, in any case, were an overcrowded field. Then in the mid-forties he started publishing books of cartoons rejected by *The New Yorker* that were revolutionary. I'm not trying for scholarship here, so I can't be sure of dates or chronology, but for *The Lonely Ones* and *The Agony in the Kindergarten* he borrowed from cubism and abstraction to present weird-looking, nerve-jangling creatures who, in poetic and hilarious one-liners, bared our inner selves. So painfully and incisively acute are these drawings that it was as if Dostoyevsky had turned cartoonist.

Seated at my desk at the Signal Corps Publications Agency, struggling to find my form with *Munro,* I had these artists in mind, all of whom I considered my masters. They were pointing the way, but their styles weren't as accessible to me as I thought they should be. My line was not nearly as precise or discerning; it was looser, okay, sloppier. So my discovery of André François, whom I came upon in *Punch,* was a godsend. François was even sloppier than I was, but he made it work.

His slapdash impressions were so crude it was hard to understand what made them stand out. It was François's sense of the moment that made me want to be him. Immediacy on paper. Drawing as if it were coming from inside the paper out, a scrawl by an invisible hand announcing itself on the page without consciousness of layout, composition, or design. Art that just happened. That's what I was after.

Munro was going to be a subversive book. Before I knew much else about it, I knew that. It was going to attack the mindset of the military in a time of war. It was going to do so not as a polemic or a scathing satire but as a funny and entertaining story. A children's story. For grown-ups. Eisner had done parodies of children's books in *The Spirit,* and I had written one of them, and that may have been where I got the idea.

I wanted to be subversive, but I wanted to get away with it. So I had to think in terms of sleight of hand. How to make it look like you're doing one

"Tell me more about yourself"

André François illustration from *The Half-Naked Knight*, 1958

thing while actually doing another. I wanted my book to be written in a childlike mode and to look childlike, almost as if a child could have drawn it. This child.

So appropriating André François seemed like a good idea. I couldn't draw *Munro* the way I would have drawn a newspaper strip. The style of *Clifford*, my back-page strip for Eisner, had been strongly influenced by *Pogo*, but Walt Kelly's appealing thick and thin, animated brush line was inappropriate for what I had set out to do. Kelly's style was not right for overthrowing the government.

I was one of three GIs newly appointed to the Publications Agency, which was civilian-run under civil service mandate. Percy Couse was supervisor in conjunction with a Colonel Somebody-or-other, a bluff, cordial man who stayed out of everyone's way while Mr. Couse ran the joint. It had been through his assent that I was able to escape radio repair—and now, with his gruff approval, I was seated at an army desk struggling to find the right voice and drawing style for my anti-army story that the Signal Corps was subsidizing.

Private Harvey Dinnerstein occupied the desk in front of mine. He was a Brooklyn boy from a left-wing family with politics similar to Mimi's, but whether Reds or not I didn't know. One didn't ask. The day we met in the agency's office, a barracks made up of two floors with an informal mix of officers and civil service civilians, we approached each other gingerly, our left-wing paranoia in play.

We were in the fall of 1951, the heyday of McCarthyism. The Red-hunting shenanigans of the junior senator from Wisconsin and his boy commandos, my cousin Roy Cohn and his partner, G. David Schine, were in the headlines, and when not in the headlines, never far from my thoughts. Joe McCarthy had turned Roy into a media star, his small, dark frame with its ever-present scowl planted next to the lumbering, intimidating senator, whispering sweet character assassination in his ear—by now a familiar sight to millions of viewers.

Roy may have been a distant cousin, but not distant enough. He and G. David were touring military bases on behalf of Senator McCarthy, checking out subversion in the military. Every McCarthy antic was amply publicized in the press. Although many editors and reporters were skeptical of the senator's charges, still they serviced him with every inch of space he desired; it sold papers and they were scared of him. Paranoia in the guise of anti-Communism had become our most thriving ideology. We had not witnessed such an epidemic since the Red Scares of the 1920s.

Paranoia was not built out of hysteria alone: the Hiss case was all over the news, an accused Soviet spy working in the upper levels of the U.S. government—and a high-class WASP, to boot. Charges and counter-charges, a trial for perjury, Hiss found guilty, leading to other investigations of Communists or their sympathizers inside the government: Harry Dexter White, Owen Lattimore, men of high repute, brought under suspicion. Loyalty oaths for all government employees to sign, pledging that they wouldn't spy for the Russians—something like that. Julius and Ethel Rosenberg, arrested as spies for the Soviets. They gave atomic secrets to the Russians. Or did they? Or was it Julius alone and not Ethel? And did the secrets amount to that much? Maybe yes, maybe no. On that basis, with a judge secretly conspiring with the prosecution, they were convicted. And executed.

The House Un-American Activities Committee were out hunting for Reds, real and imagined, among the Hollywood elite. Friends and colleagues ratting out one another. The Fifth Amendment dismissed by the press and public as a tool of Communists and their sympathizers, the First Amendment scorned as a shield for Communists who misused our constitutional freedoms to spout sedition and subversion. Were these questionable amendments to the Constitution worth keeping if they aided and abetted Communists? Was the Constitution worth keeping if Communists wrapped themselves in it, misguiding the public with pink-tinged phrases such as *peace* and *coexistence*? If Communists exploited the Constitution, maybe it was time to get rid of it so that we could better defend our freedoms.

Freedom of speech became freedom of selective speech, my speech not your speech because my speech was within the confines of acceptable debate, checked out by the network watchdogs to ensure that the point of view would not incur protests from viewers or complaints and cancellations from sponsors. No Communist need apply for TV or radio exposure, no left-wingers either—unless they were avowedly anti-Communist. No liberals whose criticism sounded disruptive. Criticism, okay, it was fine, it was the American way—but by the end of the argument, we should all be able to agree that whatever we have done wrong, we are still right. And the oversights, mistakes, and injustices we commit in the pursuit of freedom must be measured against how much better we are than they are.

If one went to American movies at the time, apart from the bursting-with-cheer musicals of the fifties, one saw invaders-from-outer-space movies, creatures from another planet, body snatchers, and weird pods hovering outside our homes, and then—God help us—they were inside our homes, they were our *children.* Our *parents!* They looked and sounded like us, but they were really Commies—oops!—Martians!

It seemed as if our response to our postwar boom, prosperity wide-ranging enough to create a new middle class, was to view our new well-gotten gains with an insistent fear that someone out there was plotting to screw us. Witness film noir, which came into vogue in the midst of our boom. Hero veterans, having fought for their country, returned to small-town U.S.A. to find it all changed: crime, corruption, cynicism, all in high-contrast black and white. A home front that had rejected them, a girlfriend who betrayed them, a best friend who had stayed home to screw our hero's girl and rob our hero blind. Hollywood was sounding a psychic cultural truth: we were living better than we ever had and feeling threatened by it.

Harvey Dinnerstein, his wife, Lois, and I spent nights at their apartment off post talking about the threat, not from the Communists but from the anti-Communists. We saw ourselves as the other, the body snatchers, the creatures from the other planet, living with our mouths shut, except within the privacy of our cabal, pretending during our day jobs in the army that we were one of them, marking time, hoping that we would get away with it. And doing everything we could on the job to not get away with it.

Harvey was a realist painter in a tradition going back to Raphael whose most recent vogue was Socialist Realism. His current subject was war, and in the apartment that he and Lois shared, there was a floor-to-ceiling canvas of multiethnic victims of war hoisted onto a giant bayonet, brilliantly drafted and painted but nonetheless reminding me of a Hugo Gellert political cartoon out of the *Daily Worker*. I was in awe of Harvey's talent but not of his larger-than-life art that so blatantly editorialized.

And during the day, our leader, Mr. Couse—or Perce, as he asked us to call him—convinced that Harvey was far too talented to waste on retouching photographs for training manuals, used him as sparingly as possible. He encouraged him to do his own art at his desk, which turned out to be remarkable little charcoal-and-wash studies of his antiwar paintings.

Perce felt that I, too, shouldn't be hobbled with army drudgery. If I completed the day's assignment early enough, I was free to spend the rest of my time, more than half a day, as it often turned out, working on *Munro*. At the height of McCarthyism, with Roy Cohn and David Schine seeking out disloyalty on army posts, Harvey Dinnerstein and I found ourselves supported by the United States Army in our dedicated and happy subversion. All because of Perce Couse.

Perce, whom initially I found to be intimidating, was behind his scowl and his growl a sweet, gentle failed magazine illustrator who joined the civil service to support his wife and children. He invited me to his home near Asbury Park for dinner with his wife, Elizabeth, his daughter, Hallie, her husband, Sam, and their son, Tom. Hallie was blond and pretty, and if she had been single, oh, would I have fallen for her. Sam, a Jew among this classic WASP family, smart, dry, funny, walked with a severe polio-induced limp. Hallie and Sam became my closest friends at Fort Monmouth and my drinking partners. They had an apartment in Asbury Park. Sam was a reporter for the *Asbury Park Press*. He would pick me up after work and drive me to their home, where we'd drink, dine, drink some more, talk, shout, laugh, and be in love with one another. Booze cured my inability to speak. After one Scotch, I stopped stammering, after two I became myself, after three I became so much better than myself that I'd write about it if I could remember any of it.

After a certain number of drinks—not that many, actually—I blacked out. Very little changed in my behavior (I was told) except I got funnier and, if I was with a girlfriend, meaner. Meanness was the only serious downside to my drinking. The blackouts worried me, but the drunkenness did not actually bother me as long as I was assured that it didn't alter my behavior to the point that I got into fights and killed anyone. Drunk or sober, I didn't think I was capable of killing anyone specific; but in general, there were masses of people I would have happily wiped out.

The Couses and I stayed friends after the army, not seeing much of one another but remaining in touch. Once a year I would rent a car and bring my family out to Asbury Park for a visit. Perce died, then Sam, suddenly and shockingly, of a heart attack, then Hallie, slowly and with extraordinary grace, of MS. Elizabeth celebrated her hundredth birthday, and I went to the party. She died a short while after.

Munro and my early struggles to learn how to do what I do, figuring out what story to tell and how to tell it, discovering that just when you think you've reached a peak, that's when you go for more, raise the ante. And just when you think you've about come to the end, that you're almost finished: Slow down, not so fast. All these facets of writing, whether for cartoons, theater, film, or children's books, I began to figure out at my desk at the Signal Corps Publications Agency.

If there was a pony to be found behind the door I opened in Fort Monmouth, its name was Couse.

"SEE THAT MAN!" said the sergeant suddenly pointing at Munro. All the new men looked.
"THAT'S A **SOLDIER!**" said the sergeant proudly. "THAT'S WHAT WE'RE GOING TO TRAIN **YOU** TO BE!"

FIFTH STREET

My mother was lying on the cot in her bedroom, which was the bed on which she took her afternoon naps, stretched out straight on her back, her eyes tightly shut, her mouth compressed into a lipless seam. In this mode she must have thought she was protected against the bad news I was about to bring her.

My mother was prescient about bad news. It had made up most of her life, robbed her of her youthful joy and exuberance, pounded out the mischief, leaving her well aware of the bitter truth it had taken the army to teach me: you get up each day and start fighting from scratch.

I had been home a month, a familiar limbo but a bad fit at twenty-four. I had aged out of the part. Each day, squirreled away in my room, hidden from my mother's inquiring eye, I scoured the classified section of the *Times* looking for an apartment.

I had found a remodeled dump in a five-floor walk-up on the Lower East Side, a few blocks from Tompkins Square. It was way east, between Avenues A and B, 521 East Fifth Street, and it cost nothing. Twenty-five dollars a month for a room and a half, which meant an alcove bedroom and a small living room with a refrigerator and a stove squeezed into a corner. I made a deposit and signed a year's lease and visited it from the Bronx every day for almost a month, buying enough kitchenware to allow me to open cans of Chef Boyardee spaghetti lunches, heat them, and eat them. I thought up and drew cartoons lying on the floor, roughs that would become sample art with which to job hunt. I took many naps on the floor, which I needed to do, since I was never not tired.

Tired but buoyant. This is what I had been dreaming about since I hitched to California. My own place! My first minute inside, with the door shut and locked against the landlord's agent, who had left a second before with a signed lease, I circled the room, giggling with surprise at my own daring. And to indelibly stamp this breakthrough moment and mark my independence, I shouted at the top of my lungs: "Fuck! Fuck! Fuck! Fuck! Fuck! Fuck! Fuck!"

I heard a pounding from the alcove wall where I intended to put the bed when I got up the nerve to buy one. An old lady's scream from the other side of the wall in a thick Ukrainian accent: "Vot do you vant from me? Vot do you vant from me? Vot do you vant from me?"

I was home.

Jules at twenty-five

Part Two

FAMOUS

THE VILLAGE

The Village, with all it signified—youth, glamour, bohemianism, exoticism, danger, promise, and pretense—was more of a temptation than I was willing to handle. Too much of a challenge, too real, too fake. The eating and drinking places (the authentic ones) for artists and writers and journalists and actors were bad enough. But it was the phonies who scared me most. The loudmouths who needed to be noticed, and boy, did I notice them, at Julius', Louis Tavern, Café Figaro, the White Horse, the Limelight, gathered in exclusionary little groups, dropping names that I had heard of but hadn't read: Kierkegaard, Camus, Sartre, Reich, Fromm, Reisman, Horney, and others. Marlon and Tennessee and Truman and Dylan (not Bob, the other one) and Norman (whom I had read) and Vance (him, too), and Anatole . . . Anatole Broyard was gossiped about as the next Norman, as Norman was the next Hemingway, unless it was Vance Bourjaily or Chandler Brossard who was the next Norman, or Harvey Swados, or . . . At this point, not yet at the starting gate, I put aside my dream of becoming famous. The name-droppers had shamed me into lower expectations: to meet and befriend better-connected young men and women who might share with me Marlon or Tennessee or Bill Inge or Gore or Anatole stories. Hearing Anatole stories from an actual friend of Anatole's would put me a rung higher on the ladder.

My army friend Jim Ellison had an amiable, sociable way about him. Jim was tall and unthreateningly handsome (leaving me just enough leeway to feel superior). His ambition was to become the next J. D. Salinger, the current rage. His *New Yorker* stories were bought up and devoured as soon as they hit the newsstands. Salinger wrote in an infectious, accessible style that invited easy imitation, and that's how Jim spent much of his first year out of the service. He rented a railroad flat on East Eleventh Street that was huge compared with my room and a half. A cavernous space, great for throwing parties. And Jim had, or seemed to have, one every week. College girls weekending from Sarah Lawrence, Vassar, and Smith, long and leggy, and oh, could they discuss Simone de Beauvoir, and oh, was I interested in what they had to say. I couldn't get close enough to hear better, my erection working overtime as I bore in. "What you're saying is so interesting. Go on, go on."

I exploded in Jim's small closet of a bathroom, shared by three apartments on the floor. Locked in, unzipped, and unleashed. It took me minutes to wipe away the evidence, grateful to have had sex at last even if it was with a bathroom wall.

The discharge in Jim's communal toilet was as seminal a moment as my discharge from the army. It doubled as my discharge from the Bronx. I had been a civilian and technically on my own for more than a month. But I was still tethered to my mother's values and judgments, with a guilt as large as my erections or my sense of futility. Why did I get my own apartment if not to have girls over? How could I have girls over if I was too guilt-ridden to masturbate, much less penetrate? All of this was clear as day but left me no less paralyzed to act without the incitement of drink. Drink provided my will and my nerve. But once I had taken the drink that provoked my will, my nerve excused itself: "Not now, I'm too sleepy." My need for sleep was more insistent than my desire. I slept more than I had since I was a baby.

I was unemployed. The army supplied a six-month lifeline to its ex-soldiers. I think it was $30 a month for six months, enough time to get one launched into the workforce unless, like me, one had no serious interest in joining the workforce.

My serious interest was in sex. And since that wasn't working out, okay then, sleep. Since sleep had to end at some point, I roused myself periodically, sat at my desk, and drew halfhearted samples, single-panel comic illustrations in black and white, wash, and limited color, in the hope of finding a job I didn't want in an art studio.

Then there was the hanging-out part. Except for Ed McLean, most of my friends were drawn from the army or postarmy period. We sat around in bars in the Village, hoping to be initiated into bohemian life, politically or sexually or any way they'd have us. We had elected to be creative types. As a result of not going to law school or medical school or business school, we weren't on that much of a fast track. Fantasy was our fast track. So there was little to keep our minds off getting laid.

Except for the fear of making a mistake. One went through the motions, day by day, night after night, that one thought of as freedom and that passed for fun. But the freedom did not include doing anything that fixed or changed or improved one's lot. What if one made a mistake? Why be a fool? Why commit?

What passed for fun—antic, falling-down, roll-on-the-floor fun—was what we did to draw our attention away from our misuse and abuse of our freedom. I spent much of my freedom behaving like a zombie, in my room staring into space for what might have been hours, making the rounds of bars where I repeated my scripted lines, acted out familiar plots, enjoyed my boredom with edgy and envy-laden comrades. What if one of us at the bar made it to the big time and left the others behind?

Hard-ons, guilt, and self-loathing played out against a raucous barroom laugh track. Carefree cocksmen wannabes grinding out a good time as we wondered why more barhopping pretty girls didn't notice how much fun we were and sashay over to meet us. Mike Stern and Terry Carmichael were handsome, charming make-out men who teamed together like a hit squad, picking up college and working girls with no effort and consummate ease. Seeing them in action made me want to become their best friend. Mike was a tall, blond graphic designer, Jewish and sweet and not particularly bright. Terry was a medium-sized, brown-skinned African American actor, smart and sly with a high-wattage smile that few Smith, Sarah Lawrence, Radcliffe, Barnard, or Bennington girls could resist. By some extraordinary stroke of luck, they let me in as their friend. As such, I found myself in an apprenticeship for my future cartoon character Bernard Mergendeiler, the luckless-with-women nebbish that I would introduce to *Village Voice* readers some three and a half years later.

Mike and Terry liked me because I was funny. They took me on as their

jester and entourage as we made the rounds of bars and coffeehouses. We listened or half listened to jazz and folk, talking our way through Miles and Mingus and the Clancy Brothers, as they gave me a tutorial on making out.

The girls they collected along the way they took home to do things that made me crazy to imagine. Before that went the buildup, the conversational foreplay, talk of movies and theater and books and where did you grow up and do you read Salinger? Mailer? The talk was a come-on to help the girl past the introductory awkward moments, past the point where we were strangers. To draw her in with high-spirited conviviality: we were so *interesting,* the most fun group of guys she had met in a long time. And the one she inevitably went home with was the one not making the jokes and most of the repartee. I was a parody of Cyrano, laying down the witty, arty, quasi-literary, semicultured soundtrack that put one Roxanne after another in the mood to get laid by Mike or Terry. My payoff was that, after the third or fourth tryst, when one or the other dumped the girl, it was I, their hanger-on, whom she sought out for counsel. What happened? she needed to know. What could be done about it? What we did about it was go to bed. And that was how I started getting laid. As a substitute. These desirable and confused young women worked their way down through something akin to a baseball farm system in reverse. They started out in the major leagues and ended up with a kid sent in as a replacement who could barely play the game. By the time Mike and Terry had finished with them, they saw themselves as second stringers with damaged self-esteem. They needed comforting from someone harmless. So we did fine.

Others might have found the position I played humiliating, but I saw it as exploiting my limitations. I would never have gotten to know these beautiful and interesting young women on my own. I lacked the sexiness, the aggressiveness, and the charm that made girls want to sleep with me, as opposed to my own special kind of charm that made them want to be my friend. The girls who succumbed to Mike and Terry never would have noticed me if I had approached them without Mike or Terry. In any case, I was much too shy to have met them on my own, to go over to a girl at a bar or a party and begin a conversation. I was incapable of beginning conversations—with men or women. If the woman I found myself with didn't pick a topic that I could respond to, there would be no conversation— or acquaintance or relationship or sex or marriage or children. Nothing would have developed in my life if it had been left for me to lead with an opening line. I lacked an opening line. Not ever had I been able to come up with one. Without an opening line, I couldn't be the one to start things off, which was one reason I had to get famous. Once you're famous, you don't need an opening line. And more often than not, the girl will know who you are. She will start off impressed. The opening line became *her* problem. Ha!

I didn't mind having to resort to fame in order for women to find me sexy. One has to deal with the material at hand. If fame was what was required for me to lure women into bed, then that was a price I was more than willing to pay.

But in the fifties I was this gawky, blond, slightly stooped, nice-enough-looking (some found me cute), boyish young man. Definitely not stud material to Vassar, Radcliffe, Barnard, Bennington, Sarah Lawrence, NYU, or, for that matter, Hunter, City, Brooklyn, or Queens College girls. So I hunkered down with Mike and Terry in coffeehouses and bars as they flipped through their well-worked-over little black address books checking for names of sexy girls who might date me.

One was a modern dancer named Jill. Terry called her from the bar we were in. Mike had dated her too. She was an NYU student, a senior.

She had a paper to write for class but we were only a few blocks away, she'd come over to say hello.

Hello, indeed. Jill stayed on and on in the bar, delighted not to be writing her paper, getting high on white wine. Terry was the one she did most of her talking to, even when she was answering my questions. I forgave her. I was willing to forgive her anything. I thought she was about the sexiest girl I had ever sat down with at the same table. She didn't say much to me, she wasn't that much of a talker, but every time she did talk, she lit up my spirits so that I had to order another drink: spirits to quench my spirits.

She was dark, regally sensuous, with heavy-lidded, daunting gray eyes under thick eyebrows set in a narrow Modigliani-ish face. Her lips stared at me like bull's-eyes. She was a little shorter than I, but her posture was so much straighter that when we got up to leave an hour later, she had to lean over to give me a good-bye peck on the cheek. And to remind me that we had a date.

Terry, the maître d' of relationships, had bounced over to me her invitation for him to accompany her to a modern-dance concert, an apparently effortless maneuver that made it seem like it wasn't a date at all—I was just filling an empty theater seat next to her.

And so began my life in dance. Not that I was that interested in dance. It was the commentary in regard to dance, the interpretation of what Jill and I were about to see, interspersed with Jill's cryptic whispers as she tried to educate me: dance's surface and hidden meanings, its symbols and metaphors, and (not that she cared to admit it) its pretensions.

It was the pretension and not the dance that drove me to draw dancers just a few years after Jill and I broke up. Increasingly, I found the differences between how people behaved and their self-serving rationales amusing—as well as irritating, sometimes enraging—and almost never endearing, except for the dances Jill escorted me to.

The dances took place in little theaters and studios in the Village in and around NYU, where Jill and her friends studied and performed. And in the way things happened in the somnolent, repressive atmosphere of the Eisenhower-McCarthy years, their leaps, falls, crawls, contortions, writhing, and high-profile anguish (emulating silent-movie acting) estab-lished the first tentative, flat-footed beachhead toward a counterculture.

Dance recitals followed certain fixed rules. The first rule was that the solo dancer or, if it was an ensemble, the lead did not dance out on stage, nor did she walk out. She trudged out, hair in a ponytail, barefoot in black leotards. She entered like a heavily shod workman slouched against the elements, stooped under the weight of the message she was burdened to deliver.

The second rule was that the little talk she gave was to be spoken in a soft, self-conscious, barely audible stammer. The third rule was that her explanation had value only if it was hard to understand.

She stood onstage, immobile, almost incoherent, letting her hands do the talking. Dancers' hands are instruments of beauty, ten fingers splayed, no two quite in unison, darting, swooping, fluttering in a hand dance that was often more impressive than the dance that followed.

Now, having set the scene, having put the dancer onstage, having described how she looked, how she moved, how her fingers moved, it seems to me that you have every right to hear a version of what she said. But while I remember all the other stuff in detail, I can't recall anything of what was said. Forty-five years of cartooning Dances to Spring and Sum-mer and Autumn (and an occasional Winter) has blotted out authentic dancer-speak from my mind.

The first "Dance to Spring," *Village Voice*, March 27, 1957

A DANCE TO SPRING

Jill was the first girl to sleep over in my first apartment in my first bed. The sex we had was not my first time, but it might as well have been. The young woman I had sex with first was a Smith girl whom I inherited from Mike and/or Terry, and she was so mad at being relegated to the likes of me that she took me to bed in order to get even. She got even in her parents' bedroom in their apartment on Central Park West.

She was taken aback by the degree of my passion, my inexperience, my clumsiness, and my gratitude, not to mention my thwarted attempt to build this episode into something more—what did we call it in those days?—oh yes, a relationship. For five minutes I thought I was in love. In another three or four minutes we both understood that neither of us had anything to say to the other. The only word spoken that night that meant what we said was *good-bye*. One of us pretended regret. She didn't bother.

It puzzled me that the girls I liked to talk to, the ones who liked to talk to me, the girls with whom I had confidences to share, books and plays and movies to critique, politics to discuss, were not the girls I wanted to go to bed with. They had become friends. Sex and friendship were counterintuitive. How could you lay a friend?

Sex was to be sought with a great-looking girl whom I wasn't that sure I liked, who wasn't sure she liked me, although the signals we exchanged were so confusing, how could we tell? Sex was with a girl with whom I didn't share much in common except for a lack of trust, which increased desire. Sex was with a girl who changed the subject just when I was in the middle of a good story, who laughed at the wrong things at the wrong times. She kept me waiting for as long as half an hour on street corners

and didn't apologize once she showed up. A girl like that—if she had good legs and great boobs—her, I could die for.

Jill and I had very little to say to each other, but it took three months to find out. So we got in a lot of sex. By our fourth date, we were going steady. I convinced myself that I was almost in love with her. In the places we hung out, we appeared to be a couple. That meant a lot to me.

Remember, this was all new. Except for movies, I had no model on which to base my behavior. I took as semigospel tips on flirtation and romance as provided by Hepburn and Tracy, Powell and Loy, Gable and Turner, gods and goddesses up on a silver screen. Instead of sex (no sex in the fifties), they had fast talk and quips. Hang around long enough with a sexy woman, kid her mercilessly, and put up with her put-downs, and by the fifth or sixth date, love happened.

Did I believe it? No, but I had no other guideposts. With Mike and Terry, I abstained from talking about sex in anything but generalities. I didn't want them to know how little I knew—and how little effort I made to learn. Finding out about sex was like looking up *chimera* in the dictionary. Theoretically it could have been done, but I loathed homework.

Further, I loathed putting my sexual ignorance on display, even if I was the only witness. I had no doubt that I was dumber about sex than most other men my age. But I didn't want to think about it. Or learn any more, except on the job. I didn't need any more excuses for self-loathing. Beating myself up was a favorite indoor sport. Alone in my apartment, I walked around for minutes shouting, "Schmuck! Asshole! Idiot! Go fuck yourself! Die, you cocksucker, die!"

This brought my Ukrainian next-door neighbor into action. She pounded the wall on her side in response to my rant. If I had my script, so did she. As I shouted at myself, "Asshole! Schmuck! Drop dead, motherfucker!" she repeated into the wall contrapuntally, "Vot do you vant from me?"

HACKWORK

When sex wasn't on my mind, I worked on cartoons. Then, too, there were my forays into the job market. Rent in the fifties was minuscule, but the landlords still expected their money on the first day of the month. I couldn't wait around to get famous, I had to look for work. I didn't like it, but there was nothing I could do about it.

I found intermittent jobs in art studios that I looked up in the classifieds or found in want ads in the *New York Times*. I was dispatched to the bull pen, assigned to illustrate spots for annual reports and come up with art ideas for slide presentations to relieve the tedium of charts and graphs. I was supposed to create decorative leisure moments for the eye, intended to be noticed but not laughed at, little spots that looked amusing but were not. The art directors at the two houses where I stayed the longest, Chartmakers and Transfilm, were in their forties, harried but affable. They would give me a subject, a size, and a notion of what was expected. I'd sit myself down in the bull pen, my drawing table surrounded by three or four other drawing tables with three or four other, more experienced illustrators doing the more grown-up jobs—charts and graphs, logos, technical drawings, diagrams. Older men, World War II veterans with families. Serious. I was hired because I wasn't serious. A moderately talented, inexperienced kid who would do what he was told.

And in the first weeks on the job, I did my best. Given a topic and sometimes a rough sketch, I designed and drew three or four pieces of finished art in pen and ink and let the art director choose among them. In the beginning, I played the good boy, but my restraint was not to last. After about a month I began to insert ideas of my own among the three or four sketches. All of the drawings but one followed my essentially humorless instructions. But in the fourth I went my own way. And it was only a matter of time before that way prevailed.

And this was how I established myself at these small art studios. The smart-assery that I had learned to suppress outside my circle, the wise-guy attitude that didn't go down well with authority, emerged in these spot drawings as clever, good-humored, just-funny-enough pokes in the eye.

I carefully restrained my zaniness to acceptable limits. I drew in a variety of styles stolen from cartoonists and illustrators I admired: the simple diagrammatic elegance of Roy Doty (whose ads were then appearing everywhere), the expressionistic power of Robert Osborn, whose line I most coveted for my own.

I was told on all of these jobs, at the time I was hired, that I was expected to *not* be unique. On the contrary, everyone who worked in the bull pen was expected to do interchangeable artwork, undistinguished and indistinguishable. I was not hired to draw attention to myself. I was cautioned repeatedly that it would be looked upon unkindly if I tried to break away from the pack. So I drew attention to myself and broke away from the pack. And the clients loved it.

A light line, a hint of wit, an appearance of cheekiness on the page—it didn't take much to make hash of the pretense that we were indistinguishable. If we were all ducks in a row, clients visiting the office began to inquire, "Which one is the funny duck?" I, alone, was singled out and introduced to clients and complimented on my sense of humor. Where did I get my ideas? they asked. And I, twenty-three or twenty-four, looking no older than seventeen, grinned, shuffled, self-effaced, and talked about the considerable help I got from my fellow artists in the bull pen, most of whom were amused, thank God, by the attention I was getting. It wasn't in their makeup to be envious of me, to see me as competition or a threat. Our context was America in the fifties, our principal ideology was conformity. My colleagues were men whose ambition it was to be ducks in a row. Their collective anonymity amounted to their dream come true. Their ambition wasn't about a career in art; it was about a bigger house, a sailboat, golf, early—very early—retirement. They saw the attention I was getting as an example of office whimsy; it offset the usual monotony that they took for granted as a condition of employment. So, rather than a threat, I was perceived as this strange and amiable nutcase, hired for comic relief, who gave them a chuckle while they did the men's work.

It was unfortunate that, once having attained the status of "privileged character," I lacked the character not to abuse my privileges. I started coming to the office late and leaving early. Larry LePeer, my boss, who supervised the entire department of which the spot artists' bull pen was merely one section, called me in for a warning. Larry was in his midforties, a pleasant, paternal adult who, from my first days at Chartmakers, had been one of my main supports. So how could I not take advantage of him?

Larry pointed out my record of latenesses, three or four times a week, scandalous, really. What reason could I possibly have for coming in so late? Was there a problem at home? Larry liked me, he had taken me under his wing, he wanted a reasonable explanation, an excuse, an apology.

Now, I liked Larry, I really did. I appreciated all that he had done for me, hiring me with little experience for the job, letting me go out on a limb with work that parted from the accepted norm. But though he may have been a nice guy, he was, nonetheless, the enemy. He was in a position of authority. My sister Mimi might not have succeeded in making a Communist out of me, but the theory of class warfare that she had programmed me for had stuck. I saw Larry on one side of the fence; I was on the other. Therefore, even though he broached the subject in the kindliest manner, I saw it as my right, practically my duty, to mislead him.

I said to him, in an explanation that I improvised as I went along, speaking in a voice that rang with sincerity (and why not—I had years of practice, standing at the bar of justice before my mother): "Larry, the reason clients like what I'm doing is I'm spending a lot of my own time at home on ideas. There is so much going on at the office, it's hard to concentrate. So I get up an hour or so early and get ideas before I come in to work. And sometimes it makes me late. Or sometimes I go home early and work on ideas. But if you want, I could do what everyone else does, and come in on time and leave on time and stop thinking up ideas, except during office hours."

God, I was good at this! I had developed this skill in my battles fought from childhood, a talent for self-serving advocacy. I could take a situation where the facts indicated that I was in the wrong and, through a measured defense, never sounding less than reasonable, manage to redefine crime into error, error into mistake, mistake into confusion, so that my misdemeanor, which seemed clear enough, was given a face-lift, a whole new look that warranted reconsideration and a second chance.

I don't know if Larry believed my explanation or not. But he clearly believed in the results that went with my hours of late arrivals and early departures. So he offered a shrug and a mumble of consent, which I read to mean: "I'm letting you get away with this for now, but don't push it." He didn't understand that it wasn't in my nature not to push it. In any case, I was allowed more or less to come and go as I pleased.

Once again, I sensed no resentment on the part of my fellow bull pen artists, who came in every morning at nine, and punched a time clock to prove it, and left at five—or after five—and punched the time clock again. I, however, marched to the hands of a different time clock. It didn't seem to piss anyone off. Maybe it was assumed that I was a dead duck, and my office mates were simply waiting to see how much longer it took to see me shot down.

Titillated by the success of my hustle, I began to wonder what I could do to shorten the hours between my late arrival and early departure. This blatant bending of the rules had a secret intent, one that I had in mind from my very first days at Chartmakers. It was to get myself fired.

I had been with the company for over six months, much of it on good behavior. After six months on art studio jobs, I began figuring out how to get fired. If I got fired sooner than that, New York State law said I would not be eligible for unemployment insurance. However, if I ratcheted up my misbehavior one infraction at a time after six months, then even the most generous and forgiving employer would have no choice but to let me go.

Unemployment insurance in New York State lasted six months. That was six months at home to do my artwork. After that, I would have to look for another six-month art studio job, maneuver myself into getting fired, and start the process all over again. This, in a sense, became my own personal National Endowment for the Arts subsidy, awarded by myself to myself at six-month intervals for a period of three years.

While my friends held down jobs they either hated or felt indifferent about, I stayed home drawing—except for one morning a week when I joined the lines of the unemployed downtown at the unemployment office and let myself be interrogated by surly functionaries sitting behind barred windows who asked: Had I looked for work last week? What sort of work? What else was I doing to find work? After this small weekly humiliation (the price I paid for my freedom from want), I took myself home and went to work (or not), or went to a bar to hang out, or, if it was July or August, went out to Fire Island, where I shared an inexpensive house with friends who worked for a living. So I had the house all to myself during the week, having to share it only on weekends, when everyone got drunk, so who cared? The down side was that one day a week I made the trek into the city to sign for my insurance check. A nuisance, but I put up with it.

Here is how I got fired from Chartmakers. Larry called me into his office on a Thursday afternoon. His demeanor was not friendly. He told me that it had been noticed for about three weeks that I had been disappearing from the office on Monday and Wednesday afternoons, leaving Chartmakers punctually at 2:45 and returning at a little after 5:00. So puzzling did my bosses find this behavior that the previous Monday they had assigned one of my friends in the office, Jeff McGrath, a fellow cartoonist, of all things, to follow me and report back.

Jeff reported back that I was going to the 3:00 p.m. film showing at the Museum of Modern Art, which changed programs Mondays and Wednesdays. Jeff had followed me there both days. Larry waited for an explanation. I thought, "What the hell, no matter what I say I'm fired." So I said, "Larry, this is really weird. I was going to come in tomorrow to quit, and now you're going to fire me, aren't you?" Larry said, "Yes."

I said, "I was going to give you two weeks' notice. Is that what you had in mind?"

Of course, that's not what he had in mind. I had been working there for six months and seen people get fired. They were called in Thursday afternoon, as I was, and told to leave on Friday. No one was ever given notice. But now I was acting so openly, in such a friendly fashion, that I had caught Larry flat-footed.

He was a decent guy. He was irritated with me, but he liked me. I could see the indecision in his eyes. If he told me he wanted me out by tomorrow, which was certainly his right, it would have undermined the good feeling between us. Possibly this was the friendliest firing Larry had ever managed. Did he really want to spoil it for a lousy extra two weeks' pay? He said without enthusiasm, "Yes, two weeks is fine. But if you want to leave earlier—"

I said that I wouldn't dream of it. We shook hands. Minutes later, I was feeling wistful. I made the rounds telling my office mates, who already knew. I liked them all, even Jeff, who spied on me. I was disappointed in him but not mad. He was too big for me to be mad at.

My fellow bull pen artists seemed both chagrined and relieved by my dismissal. In two weeks my high-wire act would be a thing of the past. How they really felt about me, I didn't know and was afraid to know. I was concerned that I might have exhausted their patience. Pretty soon their lives would be back to normal.

THE *VOICE*

The *Village Voice,* edging up on its first anniversary, occupied a crammed floor-through above a store at 22 Greenwich Avenue in the heart of the Village. Next door was Sutter's Bakery and across the street the fortresslike Women's House of Detention. A struggling newspaper, a family bakery, and a women's jailhouse lumped together like the set of a Broadway musical comedy. And I had gone there to try out for the male ingénue part.

My first visit to the *Voice* was in October of 1956. I landed there in the throes of a scheme, a desperate last shot to break into print. Nearly four years out of the army, and I had faced nothing but rejection. Not a single cartoon or illustration had been published. Not a single cartoon narrative, not the most commercially abject satire, lampoon, or spoof had made it into print. When I tried to be me, I didn't sell. When I tried to be anyone *but* me, I didn't sell. My subversive antinuke, antiwar satires had been under discussion at Simon and Schuster, Random House, Harper Brothers, Henry Holt, Crown, Atheneum, and others. Many others. Editors liked me. They admired my work. They claimed I was unpublishable.

According to these editors, it wasn't my politics—no one mentioned politics, we all shared pretty much the same politics. No one mentioned McCarthyism. No, the reason this work, passed from editor to editor's desks, evoking comment and guffaws, couldn't be published was that I was unknown. No one had heard of me. Come back, they said, when you're established. Come back when you're famous.

Without a marketable name, no publisher would go near the three cartoon narratives I was then hustling. One called *Sick, Sick, Sick,* on conformity; another called *Boom!*, on the bomb; and then my good old rejected perennial, *Munro,* who was only four years old when I first thought of drafting him into the army in late 1951. If I had allowed Munro to age normally, he would have been nine.

Friendly editors assured me that if my name had only been James Thurber or Saul Steinberg or William Steig my books would have been in bookstores. But since no one knew who I was, they couldn't afford to take a chance on me. But come back when I had more.

I came to notice that on almost every desk of these editors who admired and denied me was a copy of a new Greenwich Village weekly, the *Village Voice.* The paper was unknown to me. But not for long. I went out and bought it and then kept buying it, hoping to come up with an idea of how I might use it to change the minds of cautious editors. The *Voice* was our first alternative weekly (although no such term existed then), designed as an antidote to the staid *Villager,* a neighborhood PR sheet, today's equivalent of a pennysaver. The *Voice* boasted two big names from the beginning: Gilbert Seldes, a literary and cultural critic famous since the 1920s for his book *The Seven Lively Arts,* and Norman Mailer, our generation's successor to Ernest Hemingway, or so Norman and the rest of us assumed.

The bulk of the paper was given over to snatches of Village-related news and events, theater and movie reviews, and opinion pieces by writers who otherwise made a living by conforming to the editorial slant of the magazine or newspaper that hired them. The *Voice* attracted them by offering, for the one time in their professional lives, an outlet that let them speak as themselves, and not in the revised and edited prose styles approved by *Harper's* or the *Atlantic* or *Esquire* or the *Nation* or the *New York Times.* The tradeoff that the *Village Voice* required was this: you don't get edited and you don't get paid.

Professionals feel unprofessional when they're not paid. So it was a select few writers who came to the *Voice* in the beginning, fewer than might have been anticipated, considering the freedom they were offered. They came in dribs and drabs, a cautious bunch, hesitating until they saw the results of this strange, unprecedented experiment, freedom of the press.

I had no professional reputation to damage by working for free. No magazine or newspaper had bought anything from me in close to four years. Besides, in my first months out of the army I'd come to a decision about professionalism. I didn't want any part of it.

Before I took up working for a living, with the aim of getting fired after six months to go on unemployment, I tried making a go of it as a free-lancer. I managed to pick up a few jobs from ad agencies, and since I was being paid (not much, but something), I accepted the judgment of the people who paid me, the art director or his assistant, whoever it happened to be. And this was the procedure: I'd arrive at the studio with the layout for the assignment. Instant dissatisfaction. I'd be told how to fix it. I'd fix it. I'd be told to change what I'd fixed. I'd change it. I'd be told to fix the changes. Agonizingly, I'd move closer to, but still not quite attain, the approval of the art director. One art director actually said, while staring down at my finished art spread out on the floor, "I don't know, I get a feeling, but I just can't come." As he spoke, a hand was in his trouser pocket playing pocket pool.

I'd redraw my art over and over again, fiddle here and paste up there and white out here and there and everywhere. I'd start from scratch, try to make it better and, if not better, acceptable. Often enough, what was acceptable to them looked crappy to me. Finally, grudgingly, with the clear indication that it still wasn't right but the deadline was upon us, my sniveling illustration was bought and paid for—and by that time it was hard to remember why I wanted to be a cartoonist.

I had begun to hate the work in which I had invested my heart and soul, my hopes and dreams. Now, as I rose each day, I faced the thought of drawing with dread, the very same feeling I awoke with for most of the twelve years I went to school. Sitting at my drawing table one day, despising the blank sheet of paper on which I was expected to commit an act of hackdom, I wondered where the fun had gone. The answer was plain: it went away when I started getting paid. The conclusion I came to was obvious and instantaneous. I had to reclaim my amateur status. The *Village Voice* was my first step in that direction.

It did not impress me as a bustling, movie-style newsroom that first time I walked in. In movie newsrooms, the neophyte steps into an intimidating atmosphere of hustle. At the *Voice,* the first lack one felt was hustle, the second was intimidation. No one was trying to intimidate, manipulate, or manhandle. No one was doing much of anything that one expected to find in a newsroom, including putting out a newspaper. There weren't many signs of life. There were simply a few amiable men talking amiably—in fact, philosophically.

The conversation was led by Dan Wolf, who in his heart of hearts was a philosopher but found himself in the odd position of editing a new weekly newspaper, an area in which he had no prior experience. Dan was short and slight, with a high forehead and thin black—beginning to gray—wavy hair. His style bespoke casual formality, as he sat behind his desk in jacket and tie with his chair tilted back, his feet up on his desk, crossed at the ankles. Appealing contrasts abounded: he was avuncular *and* reserved, dismissive *and* gentle, inviting intimacies *and* offering none of his own.

The *Voice* staff, every single one of us, felt privileged to be in his company, flattered that he chose to spend time with us, although it was hard to see how else he might use his time. I never actually caught him working—say, editing copy or checking out or pitching a story. He appeared to be less an editor than a wry and bemused host of a hip journalistic salon, engaging a ceaseless flock of visitors in gossip and observations. You went to the *Voice* to turn in your copy (in my case, cartoon), but truly in the hope of chatting up Dan. Conversation with him could extend well beyond one's expectations and/or desires—and yet, when it was time to end the discussion, one couldn't help but be unpleasantly aware that a younger journalist or an aging essayist waited in the wings to replace you.

If Dan played the amiable but reclusive man of mystery, acting at times like a psychotherapist, the true therapist in our midst was our publisher, Ed Fancher, a psychologist and psychoanalyst who was Wolf's opposite in every way, big and husky, open, direct, and personable, and seemingly content to play troubleshooter for the paper and take on roles that no one else was handling, handle them, and then move on to another responsibility that needed attending to.

Jerry Tallmer, who was the first member of the staff to look my cartoons over, was associate editor, meaning that he did most of the work, because, for one thing, he knew what the work was. He was the only one of the founding staff with previous newspaper experience, having edited the college newspaper at Dartmouth. Jerry was lean and angular with sharp features and wiry brown hair. Where Dan Wolf's approach was laconic and watchful, Jerry's was intense. He was no-nonsense friendly, alive with nervous energy, every ounce of which was directed to putting out the *Voice*. His special beat was the arts, the back of the book. And in these early years of the paper, it was Jerry who was largely responsible for redefining theater coverage in the city's press.

He covered plays whose existence the *Times* seldom acknowledged, staged in small hole-in-the-wall cellar theaters or three-and-a-half-flights-up, under-the-attic-eaves theaters, with as many bridge chairs as possible squeezed together to seat whoever showed up, which turned out to be an impressively growing number.

Samuel Beckett and Jean Genet and Eugene Ionesco had made their entrances, with Edward Albee a year or so away. Jerry was one of the few, along with Robert Brustein of the *New Republic* and the English critic Kenneth Tynan, soon to be imported from the *Observer* to *The New Yorker*, who alerted us to their importance. The dailies either got them wrong or looked the other way.

Jerry's reviews brought a new tone to theater criticism. He wrote as an ardent advocate in a personal, evocative style, almost confessional in tone, with no attempt at objectivity, his writer's fingerprints everywhere.

And now he was looking through the pages of *Munro* and chuckling and laughing and passing it on to Dan Wolf, who said, "This is great stuff!" and passed it on to Ed Fancher, who also laughed, and John Wilcock, who made up the remainder of the editorial staff and wrote a popular gossip column, "The Village Square." John giggled over *Munro* as Jerry read *Sick, Sick, Sick,* my cartoon-narrative about a character so completely a conformist that he was able to transform himself physically and psychically into the several subcultures he hung out with.

They went through them all, responding not like editors but like readers, fans! "What do you want to do for us?" Jerry or Dan asked, and I was dumbfounded. I didn't have to sell them on me. "What would you like me to do?" meaning that I'd sweep floors, empty ashtrays, clean toilets . . . A collective shrug was their response. Finally Jerry said, "Whatever you bring in, we'll publish." Two thoughts immediately occurred to me: Could this be happening? And how could I fuck this up? I improvised: "I'd kind of like to serialize *Sick, Sick, Sick.* I can break it down into weekly segments like a continuity comic strip, maybe in two tiers of six to eight panels."

"Sounds good."

They didn't care what I did, and because they didn't care, I had to sell myself harder. "But maybe that will be a little too much for readers to catch on to, until they get more familiar with my work, so maybe what I should start out with—" I sensed that it was time to shut up, thank them, and leave. "Maybe in the beginning, five or six weeks of introductory strips which will be complete in themselves—and then, when they're used to what I do, I can start . . ."

By this time, I could tell that the editors and publisher of the *Village Voice* were anxious to move me out of the office so that they could get back to putting out their paper. But I couldn't shut up. I talked my way out the door, packing my wares like the salesman I was, prolonging my departure by asking about page size. They didn't care. Deadlines. They didn't care. Suggestions for subject matter. They didn't care.

I was out the door, on the street in front of 22 Greenwich Avenue, the address that was going to be my new home in print, doing the first work I cared about since Will Eisner six years earlier. It happened so fast—I hadn't been in there for more than a half hour—and now, I had a job! Not a paying job, that was made clear from the start. Who cared?

And all those book editors who rejected me, the ones who kept the *Voice* on their desk, they'd open the paper and they'd see me every week and eventually they'd *have* to say, "Isn't this the talented kid we rejected because he wasn't famous? Well, now it looks like he is. Let's give him a book."

And they'd publish my book. A best seller! And it would take me from being a little famous to more famous. All because I was appearing every week in the *Village Voice*. The entire process—the getting-famous thing—might take a year or two (certainly no longer). First I needed to establish a loyal readership, a fan base that would give me clout with publishers, who in two or three years would bring out *Sick, Sick, Sick* or *Munro* or *Boom!* This was my strategy. This was how it would happen. I had no doubts my luck had turned. I was on my way. Nothing could stop me now.

And nothing did.

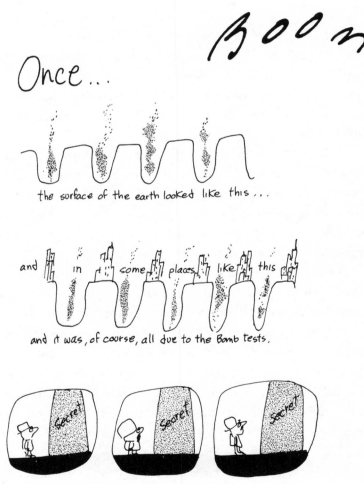

BOOM

Once...

the surface of the earth looked like this . . .

and in some places like this

and it was, of course, all due to the Bomb tests.

Almost every country had its own Bomb.

If you've got a Bomb you're supposed to test it.

Like to see if it works.

After each explosion the test areas were filled by government scientists who took readings and checked their instruments and issued a definitive statement.

"THIS TEST HAS ADDED NO APPRECIABLE AMOUNT OF RADIO ACTIVE FALLOUT TO THE ATMOSPHERE"

Naturally the more tests there were the better the Bombs got to be.

"THIS IS LAST YEAR'S BOMB. WE THOUGHT IT WAS PRETTY ULTIMATE, REMEMBER?"

"BOY, WERE WE NAIVE!"

Excerpt from *Boom!* in the *Village Voice*, October 29, 1958

ODETS IS BACK!

For a New York Jewish boy growing up in the Depression, politics was everywhere. It came over on the boat with one's parents and grandparents. It met and melded with the postwar militancy of the trade union movement. It incorporated the music, style, and swagger of midwestern and western radicalism—a bit of Woody Guthrie here, a touch of Big Bill Hayward there.

A fresh and funny acquaintance of mine, the long-forgotten comedian Milt Kamen, used to say as part of his club act: "I was brought up in Brooklyn during the Depression in what was a very political neighborhood. There was the Communist Party, the Socialist Party, the Socialist Labor Party, the Socialist Workers Party, the American Labor Party, the Progressive Party. I was twenty and had moved to Manhattan before I ever heard of the Democratic Party and the Republican Party."

HUAC, the House Un-American Activities Committee, was in town. It was holding hearings down in Foley Square at the foot of Manhattan, a courthouse view with which any *Law and Order* addict is familiar. In one of the hearing rooms on Centre Street, the brilliant young choreographer Jerome Robbins was to testify, and I went to watch.

Robbins, in the last few years, had emerged as this extraordinary crossover talent, switching between the New York City Ballet and big-time Broadway musicals, from choreographing Stravinsky to choreographing Rodgers and Hammerstein.

Officially, Broadway did not have a blacklist, but in order to go on to movies and television, actors, writers, and directors were subpoenaed to prove their loyalty and their Americanism by testifying against their friends and associates to HUAC. One could stand up to the committee, and many did, but within minutes contracts were canceled, jobs evaporated, studios fired you. Your own agent fired you. No longer were you allowed to work at the craft for which you had given your talent and established a reputation. You were instantly unemployable.

It was heartbreaking to watch Robbins go into his HUAC dance. Small, expressionless, and noncombative, he sat hunched with hands folded at the committee table. His attorney sat next to him. Across from him sat the abusive array of hack congressmen and their staffs, delighted to be the focus of all those cameras flashing away at them, their one shot at show business.

The acting chair of the committee, a raspy-voiced, somber, ministerial-looking fake, asked Robbins at the start of his sworn testimony what he did for a living. Robbins stated that he was a choreographer. The chair did not understand and could not pronounce the then-unfamiliar word. "A chori—chori—chori—what exactly is that, Mr. Robbins?" Robbins explained it was something like a dance director, described what he did, and named the shows he had choreographed, from *On the Town,* his first musical, to his current production, the Rodgers and Hammerstein Broadway hit *The King and I.*

The members of the committee seemed delighted to have this fancy new New York and, no doubt, Jewish word to play with. As each and every one took his turn questioning Robbins, he took a crack at pronouncing "choreographer." Because they were loyal Americans, and were determined to prove it on camera, no one managed to say it correctly. The point, made to the cameras filming a record for the heartland, was that loyal Americans don't need highfalutin words. No! Loyal Americans needed but one thing, fealty to God and country. Loyal Americans wrapped themselves in the flag. Disloyal Americans wrapped themselves in the Constitution.

At the conclusion of Robbins's testimony, when he had spilled all the names that had been agreed upon in order for him to go to Hollywood someday and make movies, the chair said, "Mr. Robbins, this committee would like to thank you for your patriotic testimony. And on a personal note, I would like to add that my wife and I have tickets to see *The King and I* tonight, and I know we are going to enjoy your chori—chori—chorieo—choreography that much more because of the patriotic testimony you have given this day."

And Robbins bowed his head in deference and said, "Thank you, Mr. Chairman."

Forty-five years after the fact, I wrote a play about this period and, specifically, how I was affected and changed by it. It is called *A Bad Friend.* My heroine, Rose, a teenaged girl (who is a cross-dressed version of me), has a favorite uncle, a Communist screenwriter named Morty. Morty is in from Hollywood to go to a memorial service for the blacklisted actor J. Edward Bromberg, who was a founding member of the Group Theatre.

I was at that memorial in 1953, and here is Morty's version of events, which reflects what I saw and heard:

NAOMI
    I want to hear about the Bromberg rally.
UNCLE MORTY
    Memorial.
        (NAOMI shrugs)
    Everybody was there: Howard DaSilva, Morris Carnovsky.
NAOMI
    Zero Mostel?
UNCLE MORTY
    I didn't see him.
NAOMI
    Why not, I wonder.
UNCLE MORTY
    And you know who showed up at the end and had the entire
    house standing on their feet, screaming?
NAOMI
    Who?
UNCLE MORTY
    Clifford Odets.

NAOMI

I can't believe it!

SHELLY

I thought he sold out when he went to Hollywood.

UNCLE MORTY

You thought *I* sold out.

NAOMI

You did, but that's another story.

(All laugh)

Clifford Odets? Really?

UNCLE MORTY

It was a complete surprise. He gave a speech—it could have been out of *Waiting for Lefty*—denouncing the Un-American Committee. His language soared—it was astonishing—all ad lib! . . . The way he talked about Joe Bromberg, and the Group Theatre days—the ideals they had, the kind of artist Joe was, the kind of Progressive he was—and what the Committee did to him, what the fascists put him through: how they murdered him— but not what he stood for. They couldn't murder that because they'd have to murder us all. There are too many of us, too many of us and we're not backing down, and we're not going away—I have tears in my eyes now talking about it.

At the conclusion of Odets's remarks, I was on my feet, tears in my eyes, cheering and weeping with the rest of the crowd: "Odets is back! Odets is back! Odets is back!"

It was one of those watershed moments. A turning point, with Clifford Odets's stirring and poetic defiance (and nothing I wrote was as moving as what he really said). With Odets coming out of left-wing retirement, reawakened to sing out against the plague-meisters of fear and loathing and self-loathing, hope soared. Victory was sure to be ours. I believed it. I so believed it that I, not by nature a group participant, was on my feet leading the cry of "Odets is back! Odets is back!"

And no more than a week later, Clifford Odets made an appearance before the selfsame Committee on Un-American Activities before which I had heard Jerome Robbins testify. And instead of giving them the hell I expected, he gave them names. Names of all of those he knew as Communists and suspected subversives in theater and film. Overnight, Odets swept away my hopes for a restored Frank Capra-ish America, an America rejuvenated, keyed in once more to its better instincts—all of this hope, all of this illusion demolished by Clifford Odets's friendly testimony before the House Committee on Un-American Activities.

Odets educated me. He taught me that there were no heroes, there was no one to trust. Betrayal was the watchword. Idealism was a joke that I could find nothing funny about, nothing to make cartoons of.

I could pretend it didn't happen. That's what I did with my career failures. Might it not work with my idealism failures? Lie myself into a more positive state of mind. Believing and not believing at the same time. Holding out the possibility that I was drawing the wrong lessons from this experience. I might try to put aside my anger, learn to adjust to it, along with my confusion and bitterness. *Adjust*—that new word that psychoanalysis had taught us—was supposed to be a good thing. Maybe within the context of no hope, if I kept applying myself, working out my adjustment—just maybe I could find hope.

"There must be a pony in here somewhere."

LUCKING INTO THE ZEITGEIST

From midchildhood on, I developed an interior whine that went: "Why does everything come easy to everybody else and not me?" Virtually all the other kids, certainly all the bright ones, caught on faster than I did. Or so I thought. They picked up skills and acquired facility without going through the unending string of pratfalls that regularly befell me. I missed the obvious, got stuck at the starting gate, didn't get what everybody else got, or got it more slowly. Everyone raced past me.

Other boys had no trouble catching, throwing, and hitting a baseball. I watched them scoop up grounders in the lot behind our house with ease. Why was this so impossible for me? What was the secret that everybody else knew that I wasn't let in on?

Other kids raised their hands in class because they had the answers. What I wouldn't have given to have an answer. They also raised their hands when they had a question to ask, not a show-offy question but a useful and thoughtful question. Why couldn't I ever come up with a question? In twelve years of school, I think I raised my hand a half dozen times to ask a question, and each time it was with flop sweat.

That frustration, that sense of permanent exclusion, missing out, never picked for the team, sidelined on the sidelines, nose pressed against the window . . . and what was there to do about it but yak? Yak, yak, yak. That's what my characters did—turn their pain and humiliation into talking points.

I had found my subject for the *Voice:* anxiety. Okay, self-pity.

Of all the material I'd covered in my longer, unpublished cartoon narratives (*Munro, Boom!, Sick, Sick, Sick*), individual anxiety played no part. I had bigger fish to fry, taking on the abuse of authority and the codified language that deafened debate during the Cold War. I was out to right social wrongs, so who had time for feeling sorry for myself? But the need to scale my length downward, from forty pages to eight or ten panels, led me—in a sense, forced me—to be personal. It was the limitations of space that backed me into introspection.

I thought of Dostoyevsky's Underground Man, my first experience with the unreliable narrator in fiction. What if I introduced the "I" voice to my readers in the form of eight- or ten-panel monologues—unwinding, self-serving kvetches in which my "I" character gives away more than he means to, exposes what he'd rather keep hidden. It could be comic strip psychotherapy, laugh while you wince, wince as you laugh.

The drawing style, I decided, should be direct, cartoony, animated, akin to what I so admired coming out of the UPA studios, *Gerald McBoing-Boing* and *The Nearsighted Mr. Magoo*.

The more painful the subject, the funnier it should look. So my chronic stomachaches took center stage for my first *Village Voice* cartoon in October of 1956, turning a psychosomatic problem into a metaphor. For what? Who cared? It just seemed funny.

The second strip was in another drawing style.

William Steig's collection *The Agony in the Kindergarten* was very much on my mind as I drew about my inability to play baseball. A kid who couldn't catch a ball—that was me—determined to learn—that was me—couldn't learn—me again—kidded himself that he would learn—who else but me? And didn't learn and would never learn—me again. He tried, and he failed and tried some more. Ever hopeful. Ever failing.

I adapted what I learned from Steig's Reichian-influenced *Agony* art: depictions of the inner me, drawn from the inside out. But in my case written as monologue, not the one-line captions one found in Steig. I drew this strip more illustratively than my opening cartoon, trying to ape the psychiatric Steig as if he were drawn by the more realistic and gestural Gluyas Williams.

My third strip was drawn in yet another style. And the fourth, fifth,

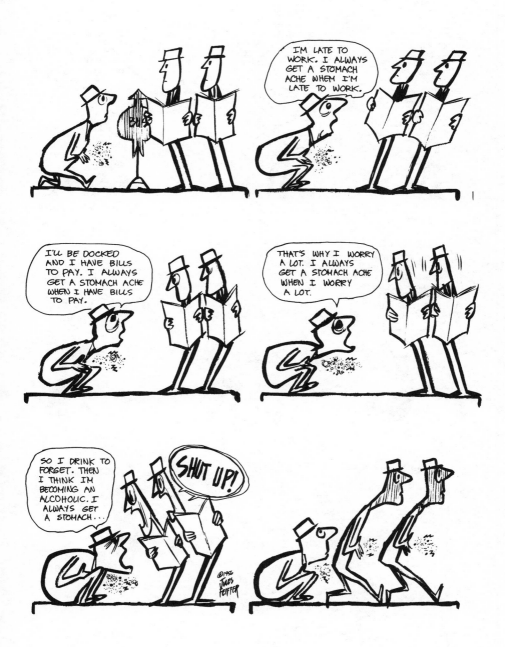

First *Village Voice* strip, October 24, 1956

Second *Village Voice* strip, October 31, 1956

sixth, etc., all in different styles. I didn't know what I was doing, but at the same time I was having a ball. My meditations on self-doubt, questioning, all those things I most disliked about myself, I now displayed giddily, almost voyeuristically.

I saw the work in print. It wasn't at all what I wanted. The gags were right, the drawing wasn't. It wasn't in my style. I didn't have a *my* style. Another week, another try, another appearance in print. I was giddy with excitement and pissed off because, at this golden moment of opportunity, I was screwing up by not being able to draw.

It didn't seem to matter. Readers were beginning to take notice. I started hearing about myself. Dan Wolf commented that his friends were commenting. Jerry Tallmer was enthusiastic. I came in with finished art on Sunday for Wednesday's paper, never questioning, simply accepting as a given that these self-pitying cartoons were finding an audience.

In general, nothing in print or on stage is more repellent than self-pity. Something about it spiritually soils, makes the reader feel unclean. Rather than feeling sorry for the person who is so blatantly feeling sorry for himself, the urge is to turn your back on him, react with contempt, disdain.

But I got lucky with my self-pity. I happened to luck into the zeitgeist, into an entire generation of the young urban educated who were looking around for where to place themselves, having found their parents' place uninhabitable.

By the late fifties, a lot was beginning to happen. Signs were everywhere, and if you belonged to my generation, you couldn't help noticing: We were the ones it was happening to. And if you belonged to the older generation, you saw little or nothing.

We were close to invisible. Locked out of the mass media but for fashion and rock 'n' roll. Locked out of politics, which was, almost without contradiction, dogma-ridden Cold War. Locked out of sex, which was smirked about but not talked about, except for the Kinsey reports, which placed the focus on statistics.

Change was in the air. Fear of change was in the air. Repression was everywhere, and it didn't come just from the government. It came, as well, from the hearts and minds of the American people. We had never had it so

Seventh *Village Voice* strip, December 5, 1956

good. So shut up! Suppress. Where there wasn't official censorship, there was the infinitely more acceptable—and popular—self-censorship. Writers were smart enough to know what they could and couldn't get away with, and they published accordingly.

We had come through a Great Depression and, more recently, two wars within a decade. It was time to bland out. Much of the fifties seemed to be about blanding out. And our reaction to blanding out. And our reaction against it. My own fifties America was one of alienation and conformity and suppression, post but not past McCarthyism. Twinned with it was another America, proud of its hail-fellow-well-met, Horatio Alger, if-you-don't-at-first-succeed, every-day-in-every-way-I'm-getting-better-and-better, power-of-positive-thinking tradition. That America was unprepared for this sudden assault from the inside, the onslaught of doubt, insecurity, neurosis. It was unarmed against the guerrilla attack on its own psyche.

Sigmund Freud, the Jew who had replaced Karl Marx (that other Jew) as the new guru, had the answer: psychoanalysis. Freudian acolytes shifted the dimensions of our self-awareness from stand-tall extroverts to round-shouldered analysands. From classic WASP stereotype to nebbishy Jewish caricature. Confused and on the defensive, WASP America, having begun to lose faith in its mythic identity, looked around and found a few funny Jews who mirrored their anxiety. They welcomed and embraced the victimized Jewish sensibility of displacement. WASP America was now feeling displaced. It chose the chosen funny people to explain them to themselves.

Jews were far more comfortable with the language of anxiety and alienation. First on the couch and later, in the clubs and my cartoons, this new, provocative sick humor (so-called), premiering in the provinces with Mort Sahl in San Francisco and catching on with me in New York and Mike and Elaine and Second City in Chicago and Lenny Bruce . . . A movement in the making, progressing from cult to midcult to mass market. The commercialization of anxiety and neurosis that would lead directly to Woody Allen, Jerry Seinfeld, and Tony Soprano, the macho capo who sees a shrink.

Who but Jews were better equipped to transcribe, and comment on, this cleft in fifties culture that marked a permanent shift in our national sensibility? It was a not-knowing-where-the-next-blow-was-coming-from shtetl approach to events, no more or less than psychic Jewish shtetl history, almost prosaic in its familiarity, now writ continentally large.

And I happened to be standing there when the door to America's crisis of identity opened. So I walked through, and once I was in the house I made it clear that I had worked too hard for this. I was not going to leave.

OUR GANG

The Lower East Side was too squalid and depressing a home for me, the Village too much of a hot spot and competitive threat. So I had moved to the other side of the river, Brooklyn Heights. From there I could see the city as I meant it to be, the New York I couldn't find while I was living in the middle of it. But if you walked the quarter-mile Promenade that frames the eastern border of the Heights, you saw the splashy movie version of the city, the soaring, breathtaking skyline that was so nice to have at a distance.

The Promenade was suspended above the mostly out-of-use waterfront, such a drop below that the Financial District across the river felt closer. It stretched along a leafy avenue of terraced and bedecked brownstones and town houses looking out on overstuffed minigardens hemmed in by stately wrought-iron fences. Its sense of place might have been lifted off a side street of old Savannah or New Orleans.

David Levine lived on Hicks Street, a couple of blocks down from where I had found an apartment on the second floor of a four-story brownstone owned and run by a retired dentist.

I had met David through my Fort Monmouth buddy Harvey Dinnerstein and his painter friend Burt Silverman. Harvey, Burt, and David, all living in Brooklyn, introduced me to other painters. I had never before hung out with painters, but here were Danny Schwartz, Herb Steinberg, Shelly Fink, Aaron Shikler, all of the realist school, most with the appropriate pinko politics to match. Their subject matter tended to be the working class at thankless labor or exhausted leisure, but David had a lighter side. He loved comics. He was delighted to learn that I had worked for Will Eisner, whom he admired. He was delighted to learn that I had grown up as a fan of Sheldon Mayer's comic book creation Scribbly, a boy cartoonist with whom we both identified.

Dave, too, had been a boy cartoonist. Now he was a heavyset, friendly-faced fellow with a good-humored, ironic manner that made him fun to be around as long as you watched yourself. He had a dry and sometimes devastating wit. He showed me a series of cartoons he was working on as greeting cards, fine-lined, cross-hatched drawings that took their lead from late-nineteenth- and early-twentieth-century English illustration. Interesting stuff but hardly an indication that within four or five years he would blossom into one of our greatest caricaturists, helping to establish, and gain fame for, the *New York Review of Books*.

Burt Silverman was a talkative, likable realist painter who taught himself how to play lefty folk songs on the guitar as a strategy to meet girls. Burt was affable even when he was pissed off. He laughed off disappointment, laughed off his own and others' failures, laughed off the sterility and seeming permanence of Cold War America. It was a survival tool: outlast the fuckers.

Norton Juster and I met while taking out the garbage. At least that's how I choose to remember it. We would have run into each other just outside Norton's barred window on the basement floor of the brownstone of my second-floor furnished room on Hicks Street. No doubt it went this way: Norton spotted a new face and made a wisecrack. I wisecracked back, and we did that for a minute or two, admiring our own and each other's wit. At the end of the contest, we introduced ourselves. I found out that Norton, though one would never guess it, was in the navy, a lieutenant stationed at a desk at the Brooklyn Navy Yard with six months to go on his enlistment. He was filling up the time he spent on duty by calling up pretty models whose pictures he had seen in newspapers and arranging to interview them for the *Navy News Service*. This was a fictional agency that Norton concocted to get himself dates, the kind of activity that, in the fifties, was dismissed as a prank but these days would doubtless get him arrested.

Norton was short and husky, with eyes that twinkled in a round face that beamed mischief. He walked and even napped as if he wore a back brace, which he didn't. Nervous energy emanated out of him. He was ever-cordial, ever-competitive, mixing whimsy, wit, and curiosity with wisecracks and put-downs. The wordplay he was to employ a few years later in *The Phantom Tollbooth* worked its way into our everyday conversations.

You had to be in training to keep up with Norton. Not a problem—everyone our age was in training. We ran in place, we joked in place, playing our games slyly to indicate they didn't mean that much. Winning was never the point, not in our present positions. The point was to score. Getting the edge on a friend once or twice in the course of a day inspired one to look forward to the next day.

Norton liked to cook. I liked to eat his cooking. And we had nonstop conversations about books, politics, and getting laid, toward which end he'd throw free-for-all garden parties. Outside his furnished basement room and a half was a small fenced-in garden, common to Brooklyn Heights town houses. Norton enjoyed preparing cold cuts and white bean salad and we split the purchase of wine and soft drinks. He'd put on some music and invite everyone he knew who might bring a pretty girl. I don't remember either of us meeting women at these parties, but they continued on a regular basis until we moved out of Hicks Street to share a duplex on State Street.

At one of the parties, we happened to meet a young couple, recent Bennington graduates and folksingers, just married. They had moved in a couple of houses down Hicks a few days earlier and crashed the first noisy party they heard going on in the neighborhood.

They entertained us with folk songs for the next hour, some of them recorded on their new album, *The Baby Sitters*, about to be released. Their recording careers got them nowhere, and their marriage broke up. The wife, Jeremy, disappeared from my life, but her husband, Alan Arkin, became a friend, a very funny Second City actor, a genius movie star, and the incisive, farcical director of two of my plays, *Little Murders* and *The White House Murder Case*.

Norton was a trained architect. Shortly after leaving the service, he applied for and received a grant from the Ford Foundation. Five thousand dollars to write a book on urban design. As it turned out, he never got around to writing the book. Instead he commenced work on a novel for children, *The Phantom Tollbooth*.

When I agreed to do the illustrations he neglected to tell me that he was writing a classic. Otherwise, I might have drawn my finished art on something more substantial than tracing paper with a survival expectancy of zilch. No more than seven or eight drawings still exist, almost all of them in bad shape.

Norton started reading me pages of *The Phantom Tollbooth* not long after we had moved to State Street, where we were joined by an English friend, Max Eckstein, a professor at Queens College and chairman of the

Milo and Tock, the watchdog, from *The Phantom Tollbooth*, 1961

comparative lit department. This being Norton's first book, he was unable to write a paragraph in his upstairs bedroom without running a flight down to my quarters to read it aloud, chuckle in admiration, and wait for me to say something and start drawing. In that manner, *The Phantom Tollbooth* began to take on shape, a case of tell and show.

Norton did all the cooking for the household and it was understood that the size and quality of the menu was dependent on the production of my art. To inspire him to excel (not in the text but in the kitchen), I did my best to appropriate the style of the early-twentieth-century English illustrator Edward Ardizzone.

Norton's gift for language and puns and his admiration, even adoration, of classic children's literature from Lewis Carroll to E. Nesbit to C. S. Lewis drove his story and his hero's toy car forward, outraging logic, turning phrases, and testing young readers in ways that, decades hence, might well not be tolerated. In the dumbed-down culture of today, Norton's wordplay can sound dangerously close to *Finnegans Wake*.

Through David and Burt, I met, and became friendly with, an older, would-be painter, an amateur who was taking lessons from my friends. A hawk-nosed, eagle-eyed fellow in his fifties who enjoyed hanging out with us, although we were from different generations and different backgrounds. He was a cheery fellow with a straightforward manner and weathered blue eyes that hinted at hard times. His name was Emil Goldfus, and he was from Canada and spoke with a light but resonant burr, a Scottish-sounding brogue.

Burt was the first to meet Emil, and he got to know him in a movie-style, meet-cute scenario. Burt painted in a sizable studio in the Overton, a downtown office building on Court Street on the edge of Brooklyn Heights. Other artists and writers found it a cheap and convenient location: David Levine painted there, and Norman Mailer had an office there where he worked on his new novel, *The Deer Park,* about Hollywood under the blacklist.

Emil entered our lives late one night by knocking on Burt's studio door as Burt was in the process of unhooking his girlfriend's brassiere. Emil announced his name from the other side of the door and asked if he could borrow a cup of turpentine. And in this comic fashion began a relationship that affected the lives of all of us.

Emil was friendly, benign, something of a burnt-out case, simpatico in a manner not unlike Dan Wolf's at the *Village Voice*. He was a semiretired photofinisher with a studio full of cameras and radio equipment. Although Emil was close to our parents' age, his lack of presence, his air of loneliness mixed with determined good cheer, led us to like him, include him, and trust him. We shared our views on everything from art and culture to politics, Reds, and Red-baiting. Emil absorbed our opinions without comment, seldom confiding his own thoughts. Not that we were interested. He was old and clearly going nowhere. We were young and our futures glowed before us with a bright light visible only to ourselves.

One look at him was enough to know that Emil was the past and we were the future. We were cocky and self-absorbed and hated to shut up. Emil's mere existence as an audience for our outrageous comments and jokes was pleasing, a kind of validation. He made up in a small way for the lack of validation that came our way in the real world.

When he was not in residence at the Overton, no one knew where Emil lived. Periodically he went off on business trips and was gone for weeks, occasionally months. Out of sight, he was out of mind. On his return, however, we were glad to see him. I watched his skills as a painter progress over the two or three years that David and Burt instructed him. He was showing a new interest and feeling for color at the time the headlines took him out of our lives and the FBI arrested him.

RED SCARE

Waiting too long on the Seventh Avenue subway platform on a hot August afternoon, I strolled over to a newsstand to see if there was anything worth looking at in the headlines. The *New York World-Telegram and Sun,* a Scripps-Howard paper, had the headline BROOKLYN ARTIST ARRESTED AS RUSSIAN SPY.

The *Telegram* was a broadsheet, so they carried the story on the front page with a banner headline and a story but no photograph. That left me to muse playfully on who among my painter friends this might be. Not Burt Silverman; there was nothing hidden about Burt, impossible to believe he had a secret life. David Levine was a possibility. David, with all his wry humor, could be reserved, at times aloof, and I sometimes found him so doctrinaire left he reminded me of Mimi. Harvey Dinnerstein was in the running, often humorlessly left, not sharing much, suspicious of other people's motives.

And then, just as my train lumbered its way into the station, a deliveryman plopped down the afternoon edition of Hearst's *New York Journal-American.* The moment played out as in a movie. The stack of newspapers in the hands of the deliveryman dumped on the newsstand, loose corner pages fluttered open like a riffled deck of cards, a tantalizing glimpse of a headline and a photograph . . . a face I knew staring up at me! And just as in an Agatha Christie murder mystery, the face was the person I least suspected. Under the banner headline RED POSING AS B'KLYN ARTIST INDICTED AS TOP SOVIET SPY was Emil Goldfus.

On the subway home, I was reacting a mile a minute, trying to fashion a reality that measured up to the unreality before my eyes. They've got to be

kidding. *Emil*? One of the more unmemorable people I had ever met, the least prepossessing. *If* he was a Red spy, what the hell was he doing hanging out with a bunch of loudmouth Brooklyn lefties? Weren't we the very people a real spy would avoid, lest he get snared in a cross-investigation?

I knew this was a crock, an FBI screwup like the Hiss case—although I had more or less come to believe in Hiss's guilt (guilty of something or other, I didn't know what). Okay, then the Rosenberg case. I had believed all along that the Rosenbergs were spies of some sort, maybe not what they were accused of—and even so, to get the death penalty for such a low-grade endeavor . . .

In Emil's case, I thought, all right, arguably he *could* be a spy. But a *master* spy, as the newspapers declared? Give me a break! Maybe a third- or fourth-grade, low-level, order-taking apparatchik, a gofer who went out for coffee for higher-up spies. The FBI was pumping this up to make it look important when it was really small potatoes. Go for the headlines, stir up the natives, beef up their budget. It was pure PR. I was not going to be hoodwinked.

I went home to Brooklyn Heights having read the *Journal* story over three times. Emil wasn't Emil, or so the indictment claimed. He was a Russian colonel named Rudolf Ivanovich Abel, or so they said. No mention was made of exactly what the charges were, but he was labeled the most important Russian spy ever caught in this country. I didn't believe it.

I walked in on Norton. At the time, he was working in an architect's office, but he was home early, napping on a couch against the wall. Norton napped on his back like a corpse, stiff as a board, eyes sealed shut against the *Journal-American* that I dropped on his chest. He blinked open his eyes, startled, and looked up to see what was happening. He took me in standing over him. He understood by my silence that I was waiting for him to look at the newspaper. He picked the paper off his chest and stared at the headline. Then he performed the most perfect triple take I have ever seen, actually the only triple take I've seen outside of movies.

Norton's triple take was a perfect metaphor for the reaction of all of us who knew Emil. It took weeks for it to become real. We, smart guys all, cocky, sure of ourselves. I, in particular, was confident of my powers of analysis and my ability to understand people. That was one of my strong points: reading between the lines, understanding the subtext. It's what I did in my cartoons.

But now I began to doubt everything. If Emil was not Emil, if Emil was a Russian whose name was Abel. And he was a spy. And I never suspected. What else out there did I have all wrong?

Were my friends actually my friends? Who were they? And what about my family? My father and mother—who might they be? I used to fantasize as a child that I had been kidnapped, that they weren't really my parents. Was I on to something? Were my sisters my sisters?

The depth of my knowingness met, and was vanquished by, the depth of my stupidity. One revelation after another mocked my belief in my perception. What I was sure I understood I misunderstood. In the Clifford Odets case, where he named names . . . I had every right to feel betrayed after his defiant speech at the Bromberg memorial. But how should I feel in Emil's case? *He* didn't betray his country. The United States wasn't his country. If he truly was a spy, then the man was only doing his job, part of which was to deceive me and my friends. What did I expect him to do, take me aside and say, "Listen, Jules, I don't want you and the others to get the wrong idea about me . . ."? What right did I have to feel angry? You can't go around telling people you're a spy!

Maybe he was innocent! Maybe we'd find out it was all a frame-up! In any case (as I insisted on telling everyone), he couldn't have been that much of a big-deal spy or he wouldn't have hung out with us.

I stuck to that opinion for a year or so after Emil's conviction as Colonel Rudolf Ivanovich Abel. And then one day I picked up the newspaper and he was in the headlines again. He'd been freed in a prisoner exchange with the Soviet Union. The Russians had been holding prisoner the most famous American spy ever captured, the U–2 pilot Francis Gary Powers, shot down over the Soviet Union in a spy plane that was designed to fly well outside Soviet missile range. Not so. The Russians turned Powers over to the United States. They traded him for Emil.

Up until that headline, I had convinced myself that if Emil was indeed a spy, he was inconsequential, a very low-level spy. Once again . . .

Oy vey!

Emil, who as it turned out was not Emil, was also not Colonel Rudolf Ivanovich Abel. He was Willie Fisher, raised in England, the son of a transplanted Russian Jew who fled the czar and returned after the revolution with his English-speaking son, who was perfect material for a spy. Not to mention a friend. All this came out years later, after Emil, I mean Abel, I mean Fisher died.

Forty-five years later my play *A Bad Friend* dealt with the confusion and consternation the Emil affair caused me and my friends. The beauty part of being a writer is that if you get it wrong in life, you can always work it out on paper.

THE MATING DANCE

S exual liberation was in the air. Hugh Hefner had begun *Playboy,* but I didn't think of it as a possible outlet for me one way or the other. The *Voice* was my single preoccupation, and on its pages I was finding my own way to sex. It wasn't the sex act itself I was interested in as subject matter, but what went on before and after: the mating dance.

Looking back on this work one can't help but wonder: What was the big deal? Now, fifty years after I introduced the mating dance into my cartoons, with the passage of time moving us out of the Age of Anxiety into the Age of Britney, Madonna, and Paris, blatant eroticism taking over the mainstream, it is impossible to parse how for more than a century sexual repression was a determining factor of our private and public lives.

Young people at play—the ironies, disappointments, and victories were years away as subject matter for film, drama, and sitcoms. The mating dance, as most of us were experiencing it, was not yet a fit subject for proper media. In New York, one discovered it in my cartoons in the *Voice.* On the West Coast, one could find it in a San Francisco cabaret called the Hungry I, where Mort Sahl, a year or so before my first appearance, walked out on stage in a crewneck sweater, carrying a rolled-up newspaper, and introduced in rambling monologue form undiscussable subjects: politics, the FBI, the Cold War, and sex.

Who had heard or read anything like it? Certainly not in the genteel pages of *The New Yorker* and certainly not in fifties movies. Marilyn Monroe titillated, and Doris Day teased, and in those days of the blacklist, no one went near politics any more than they went near honest-to-god sex.

Mort Sahl opened the discussion. If you were in his audience, you felt that this stuff was dangerous, truly underground humor. One might be arrested for listening. The things Sahl said about our sex lives, or about our president (whom no one made fun of, except for his golf), or about FBI director J. Edgar Hoover, a forbidding, iconic figure! Before Mort Sahl, no one joked about Hoover. He was beyond criticism or satire, a sainted Cold Warrior sanctified by the press, who took his publicity handouts as gospel. Hoover's image was that he had saved our shores from Communist subversion.

Only Sahl made jokes about him, a fact hard to conjure with for those whose impression of the man comes out of post–Cold War America, when he became a figure of ridicule, a closet gay scorned and mocked by comics and columnists who, were they of Sahl and my generation, would have kept their mouths shut.

But Sahl didn't. I did. I had grown a lot braver since my fear-filled predraft days, but not brave enough to take on the director of the FBI. I remained tentative about politics. A cartoon about radioactive fallout appeared in November of 1956, and then nothing political until the following March, one more in April, and one the following July.

But I couldn't shut up about sex. I saw it as my mission—relationships, meaningful or meaningless or just plain mean. It was more than enough for a starting assignment. Politics would have to wait. For now, I needed to write and draw about the young men and women I knew: how we went about conversing in code as we worked to get laid.

ALRIGHT. SO FINALLY WE DECIDED IT WAS **TOO MUCH!** WHAT WAS THE SENSE OF OUR EATING EACH OTHER'S HEARTS OUT. WE'D HAVE ONE LAST DATE AND THEN BREAK UP.

SO WE HAD OUR LAST DATE. IT WAS A BALL.

ALRIGHT. SO WE DECIDED MAYBE WE WERE **WRONG** TO BREAK UP. MAYBE WE SHOULD GIVE IT **ANOTHER** TRY. SO WE STARTED GOING OUT AGAIN.

WITHIN A WEEK THE PRESSURES WERE **INTOLER-ABLE**.

ALRIGHT. WE DECIDED WE WERE SLOWLY **DESTROYING** ONE ANOTHER.

WE'D HAVE **ONE** FINAL DATE AND THIS TIME **DEFINITELY** CALL IT QUITS. SO WE HAD OUR LAST DATE. IT WAS A BALL.

ALRIGHT. SO WE DECIDED WHY LET GO OF SOMETHING SO GOOD AND WONDERFUL WITHOUT AT LEAST **ONE** MORE EFFORT.

WITHIN THREE DAYS SHE HAD BROKEN OUT IN A RASH AND I HAD TERRIBLE MIGRAINE.

ALRIGHT. THEN WE KNEW IT WAS NO USE. WE AGREED TO HAVE **ONE** FINAL FAREWELL DATE TO CELEBRATE.

IT WAS **LOVELY**.

I CAN'T SURVIVE MUCH MORE OF THIS.

HECKLE AND JECKLE MEET MIKE AND ELAINE

For most of the first year after I started at the *Voice,* I found myself in the odd position of being modestly (and modishly) famous while remaining broke. For my first eight years on the paper, the *Voice* did not pay me a dime. So I had no choice but to continue to move from art studio to art studio seeking employment at hackwork. This changed when I went to work for Terrytoons.

Terrytoons had been a bottom-of-the-barrel hack animation studio. CBS had recently purchased it from Paul Terry, its founder. It brought Gene Deitch over from UPA (at that time the most innovative and experimental animation studio) to become its new art director. Gene's assignment was to upgrade Terrytoons into a hip, classy, stylized, but commercially hot studio, i.e., the Tiffany of animation.

I was hired with several others—Al Kouzel, Tod Dockstader, Eli Bauer—to move the studio out of the past (*Heckle and Jeckle, Mighty Mouse*) into its new and jazzy identity. To accomplish this task, we, the new blood, were thrown in with veteran animators dating back to *Popeye, Betty Boop,* and *Oswald the Rabbit,* men who had grown old in the business and were content to knock out junk just as long as they could get in their weekend game of golf. Their ambitions did not go beyond surviving the guerrilla band of arriviste hotshots brought in to replace them.

Gene was moving fast with his grand plan. He had hired Ernie Pintoff, an eccentric young animator who created a brilliant six-minute short, *Flebus,* for theatrical release. He had hired R. O. Blechman to adapt his recent cartoon novel, *The Juggler of Our Lady,* for animation and had enlisted Boris Karloff to do the narration.

Blechman drew like no one else, in captivating minimalist squiggles that Deitch presented stunningly on a panoramic movie screen. A couple of days a week, Blechman and I found ourselves sitting next to each other on a wrong-way rush hour commute to New Rochelle. We would sound each other out on the business, whom we liked, whom we didn't like, what we were going to be when we grew up. A modest man of considerable sweetness, it was surprising to find that Blechman was as dismissive as I was of the outdated but amiable hacks we had been shipped in to replace, a company of aging boys, midfifty to seventy, who were unembarrassed by and even took pleasure in their mediocrity. They could pushpin seventy-five to a hundred layouts on wall-length corkboard that showed cats and mice and ducks and pigs and elephants wreaking cartoon havoc on one another. Then, following the age-old tradition of storyboard conferences, they would mortifyingly act out in funny voices before sponsors, network honchos, and account executives what was plainly visible to anyone who could read.

A man of fifty had to bark like a dog, a man of sixty had to flap his hands and quack like a duck, a man on the verge of retirement had to jump up and down in mock excitement. All this to convey to clients what was assumed they couldn't understand without the assistance of stand-up interpreters.

And as it must to all men with an attitude, one day it came to be my turn to humiliate myself. Gene Deitch had brought me into Terrytoons in part to design a three-minute animated story to run several mornings a week on *Captain Kangaroo,* CBS's star morning children's program. Deitch's own creation for *Captain Kangaroo,* a popular series called *Tom Terrific,* was about to run its course. On the basis of my early *Voice* strips and *Clifford,* which Deitch remembered from the back page of the *Spirit* section, he thought I could design a sophisticated cartoon for kids in a UPA mode.

I went back to my *Clifford* roots and created a cartoon about a gang of street kids that I called *Easy Winners.* The title was derived from a Scott Joplin rag I happened to hear late one night on the radio. I put together a model sheet of characters and wrote and laid out a couple of episodes, one

EASY WINNERS

Arthur

distorted egg shaped head

eyes are ⅓ in on head

body is almost ½ head long

1¾ heads

3 fingers

rounded curves. no sharp edges on body

thin legs - ½ length of body

basic body shape

button nose on profile

body moves flexibly — has lots of action!

Jaunty walk - broad steps with every 3rd step being extra long - chest out. arms swing in wide arc (bending at elbow) head back, chin pressed into chest. He walks like a health enthusiast — bounces on the balls of his feet. very little body action.

of which I pushpinned to the wall. The reaction was more than I could have hoped for. Everyone at Terrytoons loved it. The new guard loved it; the old guard claimed to love it, but it was hard to tell what they really thought, other than that they wished we would all go away.

Deitch was more enthusiastic than anyone, which was not a surprise. He was happiest working at fever pitch, his energy hyped into overdrive to convince the client, through sheer exuberance, that whatever doubts he might have about the work on the wall, it was potentially a classic. Gene loved my storyboard and he anticipated the excitement of the CBS executive (on his way at this very moment) who would shortly look at and decide the fate of *Easy Winners*. My role was to do no more than thousands of hacks before me: stand and perform the storyboard before Gene and a claque of animators and layout men, along with Bill Weiss, the president of Terrytoons.

The man from CBS arrived and my heart sank. He was a tall, silver-haired, mustachioed gentleman dressed in a three-piece pinstripe who, in dress and manner, made the rest of us in the room look inconsequential. His name was Williamson, as English-sounding as his look. He outclassed us all, but Gene failed to notice. "You're going to love this!" he squealed in his high-pitched salesman's voice. One look at our distinguished visitor told me he was unlikely to love anything pushpinned to a wall in New Rochelle.

I had been through many of these storyboard sessions. I was up on the routine, but that didn't mean I was up for the job. I was years away from public speaking, deep into shyness and self-effacement. Still, I did my best to sound like the quacking, barking, oinking animators I'd seen do this many times, pumping myself up to imitate a gang of five-year-olds from the Bronx. A minute and a half in, my humiliation was intense, and what was worse, it wasn't getting me anywhere.

Behind me, Deitch and my claque had been laughing hysterically until it became clear that the unsmiling Mr. Williamson was perhaps having himself a snooze. My approach shifted from manic to wistful. The claque's laughter dwindled and died, leaving only my own strangled half laugh, half gasp.

Each time I turned from my storyboard, I noticed the room was a little emptier. My claque had decided that Mr. Williamson's side was a better one to be on than mine. They had made the only sensible choice: I didn't want to know me either.

By the time I limped to the end, only Bill Weiss, the president, and Gene, the head of the studio, remained, plus a goofily grinning threesome of loyal friends.

It was time for me to shut up and wait for Mr. Williamson's decision on *Easy Winners*. His way of presenting it stays fresh in my mind fifty years later. After an uncomfortably long pause, he said, "Well, it's a little *New Yorker*-ish."

Dead!

He had one final comment: "I mean, it's closer to Dostoyevsky than it is to Peter Pan."

As I headed home from New Rochelle that night, rage alternated with my sense of reawakened abandonment. Where had Deitch been when the time came to fight for me? I knew I had no call to be angry. *Easy Winners* was a loser. I gave them exactly what they wanted, but the they I gave it to was the wrong they.

I knew I was finished at Terrytoons, this studio where I had actually enjoyed a nine-to-five job for my one and only time since leaving the army. But it was no longer a place where my pride would allow me to work, a place where I could do quality work that also had commercial value. Seemingly, such a place did not exist.

I went home to Brooklyn Heights, where I still lived alone. I prepared myself a frozen dinner. As I was defrosting my favorite (Stouffer's Tuna Noodle Casserole) and pouring myself a therapeutic dry martini, I turned on the CBS program *Omnibus* (yes, CBS) in time to hear its host, the British journalist Alistair Cooke (a man very nearly as distinguished as Mr. Williamson), introduce a young comedy team who were making their first appearance on network TV: Mike Nichols and Elaine May.

And then this young couple I had never heard of launched into a scene that consisted of a teenage boy trying to actually screw (on television!) a teenage girl in a car.

The temperature in the room altered radically. My spirits, seconds earlier racked with rage and self-pity, yelped in joy. Could it be possible? This was *my* material, *my* humor, *my* wit, *my* wished-for-but-not-yet-attained style, acted out as if off the pages of the *Village Voice*!

But it wasn't me, it was Mike Nichols and Elaine May, and they were *better*! Better than anything I'd seen anywhere. They were doing relationships in a way that I dreamed of doing them—honestly and pitch-perfect. I didn't dare laugh, I might miss something. I couldn't afford to lose a moment because this was myself writ funnier. Observant and smart as hell. The truth I always looked for in humor, the connection to others that I always hoped to make but had such problems finding.

After this awful day at Terrytoons, I had feared the worst, that I was once again on my own, that the *Village Voice* was an aberration. But wait! Mike and Elaine were out there. And they were like me. Maybe they knew my work. I had to meet them. I had to not be alone anymore.

Jules with Eli Bauer at Terrytoons, 1957

SPOKESMAN

I had grown up dreaming of drawing my own newspaper strip in the tradition of the masters—Milton Caniff, Al Capp, Walt Kelly—of creating a stable of characters, proper Dickensian types appropriately named, who'd be caught up in situations and misadventures that lasted for months.

And in the years between the army and the *Voice,* I had tried that route. I had come up with sample strips: one named *Kermit,* about a boy genius, a musical prodigy. I submitted it to syndicates. No sale. Another called *Dopple,* about a pixyish stage Irishman who sails off the edge of the earth on a raft and finds himself in a never-never land of strange satiric creatures and nutty adventures that he and his devoted wife, Mrs. Dopple, endure. Submitted to syndicates. No sale.

A pre-Dancer Dancer named *Hemlock,* also living in a fey neverland, also submitted to syndicates, also no sale. I had met the great Crockett Johnson, the brilliant creator of the comic strip *Barnaby,* featuring a boy and his fairy godfather. It was pre-*Pogo* and easily the wittiest and most sophisticated strip of its time, or probably any time.

About a year and a half before I started at the *Voice,* desperate as ever to break into syndication, I got an offer from Johnson, who was looking for an artist to work with him on a new strip. We had met through Maurice Sendak, whom I had gotten to know during my rounds of children's book publishers in the early fifties. Maurice, very much an unknown at the time but already brilliant, introduced me to the author who gave him his first break, Ruth Krauss, with whom he did *A Hole Is to Dig,* a book that struck me then (and strikes me now) as the perfect collaboration between writer and illustrator, words and pictures becoming one.

Kermit, 1953

Dopple, 1954

And what a one. Maurice's spare, whimsical comic drawing style was the style I was about to figure out for myself if he hadn't gotten there first, mainly because he was six months older and had a head start. The way he drew was the way I wanted to draw. So I left the field of children's literature (forever, as far as I was concerned), knowing that I was never going to be able to compete with the man who drew the way I would have drawn if I weren't so busy trying to get laid that I didn't have time to develop the correct drawing style.

Ruth Krauss, a small, fey, charming ex-schoolteacher, was married to Dave (Crockett) Johnson. Dave, who was later to gain children's book immortality with *Harold and the Purple Crayon,* was well over six feet tall and built like a linebacker. Big and completely bald and pink, with open, friendly features, he reminded me of Little Orphan Annie's Daddy Warbucks brought to life. Except he wasn't a right-wing plutocrat as Warbucks was. Dave was a Rowayton, Connecticut, lefty with a house and a boat and the mildest and gentlest manner. During a weekend when he and Ruth had me up to their home, Dave made the offer to work on a strip with him.

It was the thrill of a lifetime, and what a break! A comic strip written by Crockett Johnson, how could it not sell? He came up with a boy private detective and his talking dog, potentially charming but, as things turned out, not so. It was lousy. Dave's story, my art—truly lousy. My ambition notwithstanding, it seemed that I was not meant to do a syndicated strip.

But now, a mere eighteen months later at the *Voice,* in a position to create any hero or antihero I liked, I chose to move away from a stable of recurring characters. The character I homed in on in *Sick, Sick, Sick* was the reader. I wanted to put the essence of my reader on the page—to adapt the befuddled, feckless little man of humor as conceived by the great Robert Benchley, to move him out of his genteel, benign, suburban WASP landscape. I wanted to circumcise the sucker and transplant him from the Jazz Age from whence he came to the Age of Anxiety, from Babbitry and Dale Carnegie to Sigmund Freud and characters (like my readers) so busy explaining themselves that they never shut up. I wanted to put out front the codified communication by which it seemed my entire generation lived our lives, whether it was with family, friends, sex partners, colleagues in the workplace, or simply ourselves when no one else was around to lie to.

Lincoln Steffens, the great muckraker, had taught me an unforgettable insight when I read his autobiography in my early twenties. Steffens's first job in journalism was as a cub reporter on a New York daily. He was just back from a classical European education, thought he knew everything, and after a month on the job discovered that everything he thought he knew, everything he'd been taught, was wrong. The assignment he took upon himself was to "unlearn."

Unlearn. That became my watchword. My job was to unlearn for myself and pass it on to my readers. Cut through the crap, theirs and ours, the powers that be and the powerless.

I started hearing from my readers. And this is what I didn't hear: I didn't hear "God, you're brilliant. God, you're funny. God, how do you come up with those weird ideas?" No, what I heard was: "How did you get that into print? How did they let you get away with saying that?"

Readers of my generation did not expect to see their thoughts and language and way of explaining themselves in print. On some level they believed it was illegal. Throughout the fifties they had learned to censor themselves in the company of others they didn't know well, to control their thoughts while on the job, reveal as little as possible in visits to their families. They flocked to movies, watched television, went to the theater, and read newspapers and magazines, seldom seeing themselves represented with accuracy, virtually never reading or hearing their dialogue as they themselves spoke it.

Eventually these college-educated, rising-through-the-ranks urban Americans came to take it for granted that free speech was something the establishment had, but it wasn't meant for them. First Amendment rights didn't belong to young career-minded liberals.

I came along and used the *Voice* to talk in print the way they talked in private, and it was natural, after all those years of McCarthyism and post-McCarthyism, that their first reaction was that I was engaged in some kind of criminal act.

Mad magazine, which had come along a few years before me, had, through the wit and inspiration of Harvey Kurtzman, its founder and editor, escaped serious attack by simply attacking everyone. *Mad* learned how to sidestep controversy by assaulting all sides. Taking no prisoners. The high and the mighty and the low and the lumpen, equally abused. Since everyone was offended, it was hard to take offense.

I was not a fan of *Mad.* I didn't find all sides equally ridiculous, equally vulnerable to satire. I thought it was a cop-out to not choose between haves and have-nots, bureaucrats and their functionaries, the rulers and the ruled. I believed in change, in reform, that proselytizing, education, and *unlearning* could make a difference. Eventually they could make a better world.

I was twenty-seven and I wanted to blow the cover on what was holding us back. Not politics alone—I wasn't ready for politics—but what it was that kept us passive, conformist, narcotized, running around in circles, satisfied with yak-yak-yakking ourselves into further remoteness and isolation.

"How did they let you get away with saying that?"

Clearly, I was getting away with something. But what was it? I was stunned by the feedback I was getting from readers. There I was, writing and drawing strips based on themes that did not seem all that dangerous to me. I had deliberately stayed away from politics. I wasn't trying to be subversive—that would come later. Mainly, I was trying to understand and make myself understood, to introduce myself to *Voice* readers: "Hello, this is who I am and this is what I think, and I will be doing this in front of you every Wednesday on page 4. Please say I'm good. Please like me." My ambition was narrow and specific: to get my cartoons published in order to get famous so that I would be anointed the next Thurber or Steinberg. And then I could get my books published.

The books, *Munro* and *Boom!* and *Sick, Sick, Sick* and *Passionella,* were my end game. The *Voice* was to be a means to that end. I had backed into it because I had exhausted all other possibilities. I had nowhere else to back.

And now here I was, inching self-consciously and self-effacingly into the spotlight. Aside from Mort Sahl, still generally unknown on the East Coast, I was working this avenue alone: anxiety, neurotic men and women, making out, not making out.

Fame was happening, faster than I had fantasized. This wasn't going to take the two years I had anticipated. I had met my readers and they told me that I spoke for them.

TEDSO

I was on my way to becoming a well-known angry young humorist, a midlevel star. Through the title of my *Voice* strip—*Sick, Sick, Sick*—I had helped make current the media phrase *sick humor*, which referred, misleadingly, to what was now a rising generation of young writers and comedians, from Terry Southern, Joseph Heller, and Bruce Jay Friedman in fiction to Mike Nichols and Elaine May, Shelley Berman, and Lenny Bruce in clubs.

As I never tired of pointing out (while failing dismally to change perceptions), it was not our humor that was sick, it was our society. America was sick, sick, sick! Get it? It's not us, we're the healthy ones. It's *you*!

God help me, even after you've made me famous, you still don't understand?

Six months into the *Voice* strip, a few publishers had begun to show interest, not in the work I was doing for the *Voice* but in something like it. Not quite so opinionated. It should look like satire, give every promise of being satire, except it shouldn't offend. The book should be drawn in my style, look exactly like my *Voice* strips, there was no problem with that. But what these publishers were looking for in book form was more—what was the word for it?—crap. A book written and drawn by me that was pure crap might sell very well.

I held out. I hadn't spent all those years getting beaten bloody in order to settle for so contemptible a level of compromise. With the response I was building, I was sure that some braver soul would come along who actually would want to put the work I was getting known for between covers.

It took another six months for that publisher to emerge. It was

McGraw-Hill, with almost no trade-book experience. They were known for their textbooks. And now they had decided to expand their trade-book division, and I was going to be an experimental expandee. They approached me with an offer to put the *Voice* strips between covers. The book was to be called *Sick, Sick, Sick: A Guide to Non-Conformist Living.*

I decided that in book form the strips should not be laid out as they were in the *Voice*. Instead of six or eight panels running horizontally across a double-page spread, I designed the panels to be read in the manner of traditional book texts, the first four panels on the left-hand page and finishing the strip on the page to the right. I did the mechanicals, inventing the look of the book as I rubber-cemented each panel, page by page.

In time, there were enough pasted-up panels to make a book. I designed a cover. The front matter included an introduction by a friend of my agent, a well-known humorist who was unknown to me. You didn't know I had an agent?

Well, I had an agent. He had written me on stationery that looked expensive enough, with his name, Ted Riley, engraved in discreet and elegant silvery type at the top. He wrote a dry, witty, minimalist letter that might have been composed by E. B. White, saying that he had been admiring my work, and did I have representation? The one name he mentioned as a client was Roy Doty. Doty was the hottest cartoonist around in advertising illustration. He had a fine, decorative line and used it to do a sort of doodle art that was humorously ornamental. He drew full-page ads for the *New York Times* and other publications. If I became Ted Riley's client, would he get me hired to illustrate full-page ads in the *New York Times*?

I was ready. But if I was going to do ads I wanted to design and draw them *my* way, not the ad agency's way. The beauty part of famous was that sometimes they allowed you to do that. Ten months before, when no one had heard of me, the art director would have spread my sketches on the floor, stared at them, bored, while he played pocket pool, and bloodied me with the line "I get a feeling, but I just can't come."

Now it was me who had the feeling. And the feeling was success. It was unprecedented. It signified that I had fans, was rapidly gaining influence on my way to status, on my way to big bucks.

Big Bucks. That's what this agent, Ted Riley, was hinting at. I was thirsting for some real money to go with my budding fame. The *Voice* didn't pay. The art jobs that I still had to take were a humiliation. Terrytoons was behind me. And my newly emerged ego had set its sights on *Big Bucks.*

In my heart of hearts I detested advertising. Advertising misled. Its very existence was based on misleading: to persuade the persuadable to buy what they didn't need and didn't want up to the moment they saw the ad or commercial. What better example was there of coded communication, which I had taken on as my mission to expose?

But Roy Doty did ads. Robert Osborn did ads. William Steig did ads, and other *New Yorker* cartoonists too. Where did I get off being so high and mighty? Turning up my nose at Big Bucks, the kind of money that, though paltry by today's standards, was a sure sign, back in the fifties, that one had arrived.

So I took on Ted Riley, and he talked me into the unfamiliar attitude of making money from my work. An unusual feeling, not entirely comfortable, but I can't say that I didn't like having a full-page ad in the *New York Times.* It was a Macy's ad, and then a full-page *Time* magazine ad. These were sizable illustrations, not comic strips, no dialogue. Just me showing off my art, and to my pleasure and astonishment, the ads looked pretty good. And did I mention *Big Bucks*?

Ted Riley, this drawling caricature of a Philadelphia blue blood, tall, fortyish, bald, with icy blue eyes, a hawk nose, and a jutting chin. His style dropped hints of the well-bred: prep school, Princeton or Yale, a seen-it-all-and-loved-seeing-it-all manner, casual name-dropping: Saul Steinberg, Leo Lionni (the brilliant art director of *Fortune*), Robert Osborn (my hero!). He knew, and apparently hung out with, *everybody,* and now, in his close-to-sleepy offhand manner, he was spending hours with me, on the phone, at lunch and dinner, at his home in Turtle Bay just up the block from Katharine Hepburn.

"Tedso," I called him, scarcely believing that a Jewish boy from the Bronx could establish so tight and quick a working relationship with this apparently upper-class Brahmin. What's more, I liked him. I enjoyed his talk, his literary conversations, his gossip, and his way with name-dropping.

And I liked the full-page ads in the *Times* that knocked my parents' socks off, particularly my father's, to whom the *New York Times* was the equivalent of the scrolls that came down from Mount Sinai. "I'll really believe you're famous when you have your own *comic strip* in the *Times*," he later said to me, knowing that this was never going to happen, since the *Times* doesn't run comics. He just wanted to make sure that I didn't get too big for my britches.

Ted negotiated a deal with Kenneth Tynan, newly hired by *The New Yorker* to review plays. Tynan's London paper, the *Observer,* had been publishing my *Voice* cartoons for about a year, the first paper outside the Village to run them. In the early months of my *Voice* strip, the word on me was: Great stuff, but outside the Village, no one will get it. But I now had a big following in the *Observer,* and *Sick, Sick, Sick* was a national best seller in the United States. And the next year, in the spring of 1959, the book was going to be published in London with an introduction by Kenneth Tynan. Arranged by Tedso.

Tynan was the most talked-about theater critic on either side of the Atlantic. He had reviewed John Osborne's *Look Back in Anger* with such remarkable insight that, overnight, he established Osborne's reputation as a playwright and his own as our most influential and perceptive theater critic. Months after his arrival in New York, I was in line at Town Hall on West Forty-third Street waiting to pick up tickets for the premiere performance that night of *An Evening with Mike Nichols and Elaine May,* their first full-length show and their first appearance outside nightclubs and television. I found myself standing two ticket buyers behind a man I soon recognized as Tynan. In the few months since his arrival at *The New Yorker,* he had done a number of local TV interviews, a thin, slouching, cadaverously white-faced man talking up a storm with a stylish English stammer, posing his cigarette theatrically between his third and fourth fingers.

I asked him if he was who he was and then I told him who I was, and to my delight he was pleased to meet me. He invited me to join him and a few friends for dinner after the show. The few friends turned out to be the up-and-coming literary lights of New York, all engaging, charming, funny, and—most exciting of all—fans of my strip: George Plimpton, Peter Matthiessen, Harold (Doc) Humes, Michael Arlen, Don Stewart, Nelson Aldrich, Jack Gelber, John Marquand Jr. The two women at dinner were both strikingly beautiful, one blond and perky, one dark and sexy. The blond was Sally Belfrage, a journalist whose father, Cedric, was the publisher of the fellow-traveling weekly the *National Guardian*, whom I had seen testify before HUAC on the day I went to see Jerome Robbins. Sally was charismatic and vivacious, in those years what was described as a golden girl. But it was the second beautiful woman who held my interest. Judy Sheftel. I didn't know anything about her, but I couldn't take my eyes off her face. I drank enough to counteract the shyness and reticence that made me stupid in the company of beautiful women. The booze set free my charm, wit, and literary smarts, thank God, because six weeks later Judy moved in with me.

PLAYBOY AT THE SECOND CITY

P*layboy* wrote. That is, Hugh Hefner, the editor and publisher, not known worldwide as Hef yet, not then known for living in his pajamas, not yet ready to compare himself to Gatsby. All that was in his future. And so, apparently, was I.

> Dear Mr. Feiffer:
>
> I've just finished your book *Sick, Sick, Sick* and upon that basis and a really extraordinary modern-day fairy tale that you did a few months ago for *Pageant* [*Passionella*], we are very interested in your work.
>
> I think much of what you have been doing for *The Village Voice* is exactly right for us and with even more emphasis on urban living as apart from strictly Village living, work done specifically for us could be a very exciting addition to *Playboy*. Does this thought interest you?

Well, yes and no. Who was I to look down on *Playboy*, which had emerged in the last couple of years as the hot new magazine, with Hefner already on his way to becoming a legend? I was being offered space, a monthly slot, a retainer of $500 a month whether they bought a cartoon or not.

All fine—but *Playboy*? A girlie magazine? Forgive me, I had loftier aspirations. I was appearing weekly in the *Observer*, published in London, the darling of literary intellectuals. Did I really want to go downmarket to *Playboy*? And why hadn't I heard from *The New Yorker*?

Okay, *The New Yorker* didn't solicit. You went to them, they didn't approach you. And while I admired much that was carried in *The New Yorker*, its gentility irritated the hell out of me. I worshiped quite a few of its cartoonists, but it was hard to imagine myself becoming one of them. I was too much of a rowdy for its suburban-supercilious tilt, too much Greenwich Village out of the Bronx. Too much concerned with sex and politics— neither beat covered by *The New Yorker* in its cartoons. Sex wasn't covered at all, and for politics it didn't trust cartoonists. It had *journalists*.

I could imagine Eustace Tilley, the symbolic figure who was posed snootily examining a butterfly on the cover of every anniversary issue, looking at me disapprovingly through his monocle. Of course, had *The New Yorker* called, I would have been up in their offices in a minute. But they didn't.

It wasn't as if I hadn't appeared in girlie magazines before. *Rogue* and *Rex,* two *Playboy* imitators with a hip and more Villagey bent, had run a couple of my long narrative cartoons. But these were one-shots. What Hefner was offering was a (gulp!) relationship.

Ted Riley must have written to Hefner conveying some of my doubts. I have a copy of his May 21, 1958, response to Ted:

> I don't think there's any reason for Jules entering this new associa-
> tion with anything but enthusiasm. I'm confident of its outcome
> if we approach the thing properly. He doesn't have to change his
> point of view for us. All we want him to do is bring the same sensi-
> tivity and awareness to young executive urban living. He already
> touches on some of it in many of his gags. All we need is a little
> more concern with the upper-level income guys and girls, the
> sports car set, the hi-fi addicts, the cocktail party people, the
> Madison Avenue guys. These people are not very different from
> the ones he's been placing under the microscope so far—their
> clothes are just a little neater.

I was examining Hefner through the same lorgnette that I imagined Eustace Tilley using on me. I must have resolved my doubts—funny how these things work out—in the direction of a steady paycheck. By June, there was a letter from Hefner to Ted Riley:

> Jules's first roughs are on their way back to him with a request for a finish, so we are off and running.

And in July Hefner wrote:

> I am enclosing a couple of advance copies of the August issue which introduces Jules to our readers with materials selected from The Village Voice feature. If you think his work has been well received to date, wait until you begin feeling the response of our audience to his humor. Jules's genius is as perfect for our readership as gin and tonic.

I appreciated the genius remark, but gin and tonic? In my part of town, we drank martinis.

My unaffordable loftiness was handled by Hefner with cordiality and steady reassurance. He was an amateur cartoonist himself, loved the form, and had already hired on some of the best in the business. Jack Cole, whose *Plastic Man* was one of the zaniest and best-written features in the short history of comic books, had emerged as a *Playboy* regular, reinventing himself as a sensuous watercolorist of girlie gags; Shel Silverstein, my age, was doing work that looked like no one else's and drawing it with a line that I wished was mine; Gahan Wilson had begun making appearances with his gorgeous, ghoulish art, invading Charles Addams territory while, amazingly, not reminding you of Addams.

I was taken aback by Hefner's responses to the sketches I submitted. He returned my drawings marked up with short comments in the margins, accompanied by long letters of dogged and dazzling detail. With intense scrutiny, he picked apart my work, panel by panel, prodding me to be not another *Playboy* cartoonist but a better version of the cartoonist I was already trying to be:

A couple of thoughts on copy in the middle of page five—maybe we can change *and* to *then* in the first phrase so it isn't so similar to the phrase that follows. I suggest that we change "This is all mine!" to "This is all my doing!" since that's what it really is. There is nothing really for him to possess or exclaim, "This is mine!" about. I think the growing sense of achievement and satisfaction makes the point, whereas happiness is somewhat off the point. Achievement and satisfaction might require some effort, whereas happiness could result from either activity or boredom. I'd like you to plan this as opening on a right-hand page and then going to a double-page spread—three pages in all.

This is a beaut.

My God, I was being edited by Edmund Wilson!

I started to make infrequent trips to Chicago, where I saw a bit of Hefner, who dealt with me as if I were a friend and confidant. We sat at various bars and drank (he Pepsi, me Scotch) and talked endlessly about cartoonists and show business and sexual repressiveness. Unfortunately, talk of sexual repressiveness did not lead him to set me up on dates with Playmates. I was never to get a girlfriend through my *Playboy* connection. I suspect Hefner didn't want my finer sensibility brought down by the image of him pimping for me. Fifty years later, I continue to regret his thoughtfulness.

It would be many months before I was invited to visit the Playboy Mansion. Or stay over. But on one visit to Chicago Hefner drove me, in his red James Bond convertible, to a near-empty bar on a dark side street. Over drinks, he told me that he had just bought the place. It was going to be the first Playboy Club.

The most notable of my early trips to Chicago was in the spring of 1959 to launch publication by McGraw-Hill of my second collection, *Passionella and Other Stories*. With *Sick, Sick, Sick* a best seller, I had succeeded in accomplishing what I had hoped for and plotted for years: to use my new

Superman

I USED TO BE **SUPERMAN**.

I USED TO GO RESCUING PEOPLE ALL THE HELL OVER THE PLACE. WHEREVER YOU LOOKED I WAS SAVING **SOMEBODY**.

THEN ONE DAY I PULLED THIS CHICK FROM THE RIVER. DO YOU THINK SHE **THANKED** ME? **NO!**

SHE JUST WANTED TO KNOW WHY I HAD THIS **COMPULSION** TO RESCUE.

SHE ACCUSED ME OF DOUBTING MY MASCULINITY AND HENCE MY EXHIBITIONIST TENDENCIES. SHE WANTED TO KNOW WHY I DIDN'T SPEND MORE TIME **READING**.

SHE TOOK ONE LOOK AT MY CAPE AND SAID I WAS A LATENT TRANSVESTITE, AND WHY WAS MY COSTUME SO SKIN TIGHT AND DID I RESCUE MORE **MEN** THAN **WOMEN** -

I TRIED TO TELL HER SHE SHOULDN'T JUDGE ME THE WAY SHE JUDGES **EARTH** PEOPLE. SHE JUST PATTED MY HEAD AND SMILED.

SO AFTER A LOT OF ARGUMENT BACK AND FORTH I FINALLY GOT HER TO ADMIT THAT ALTHOUGH I MIGHT NOT BE **SUPER**, I WAS A LOT BETTER THAN **AVERAGE!**

NOW I HAVE A REGULAR OFFICE JOB IN THE CITY AND A HOUSE IN THE SUBURBS. WE'RE BOTH **VERY** HAPPY.

Playboy, July 1959

celebrity to get into print my early cartoon narratives that so many editors loved and rejected. So while I led the *Passionella* volume with a redrawn version of the rags-to-riches, movie star satire that originally ran in *Pageant,* I followed it with *Munro,* appearing in print for the first time, eight years after his conception. Next came *Boom!,* my satire on nuclear testing and radioactive fallout, to which the *Voice* had devoted four full pages the previous fall. The final story, *George's Moon,* was created especially for this volume, a thirty-page introspective monologue of a man who lives alone on the moon and wants to move.

In its infinitely stunted promotional wisdom, McGraw-Hill sent me on tour with its other trade book star, the famous Washington hostess Perle Mesta, whose memoir about D.C. high life had become a best seller and the subject of an Irving Berlin hit musical, *Call Me Madam.* All that Ms. Mesta and I had in common was that the politicians she hosted at dinner, I attacked in cartoons. But there we were, this odd couple paired on two mid-April morning talk shows, one right after the other, having little of interest to say to our hosts or each other.

After the second broadcast, I retreated to my hotel room at the posh Ambassador West and hunkered down, not having a clue as to what I would do for the rest of my stay except, pathetically, call up Hefner and hope to wangle an invitation to the mansion.

The phone rang. The caller, a woman, sounding brassy and aggressive, said her name was Barbara Siegel, that she was a local publicist, and what the hell was I doing in Chicago with Perle Mesta, and what had McGraw-Hill planned for me for the rest of my stay?

The questions she asked were presumptuous from a stranger, but they were exactly the questions I was sitting in my hotel room asking myself. And my answers were unsatisfactory to both of us. Barbara Siegel asked if McGraw-Hill had set up a meeting for me with Burr Tillstrom. I responded to the name: Burr Tillstrom was the brilliant puppeteer creator of the TV series *Kukla, Fran and Ollie,* a forerunner of and inspiration for the Muppets. I told Ms. Siegel I would love to meet Burr Tillstrom.

"Has anyone set up an interview with Studs Terkel?"

Studs Terkel! I was a fan of his short-lived blacklisted TV show, *Studs'*

Place, and knew of his great reputation as a radio interviewer. "I would love to meet Studs Terkel!"

"Have you been to Second City?"

"What's that?" I asked.

"I'll be right over," Barbara Siegel said. And minutes later there she was in my forlorn luxury hotel room, an apparition not unlike the fairy godmother in *Passionella,* taking me by the hand all over town to meet and greet the people I should have been in contact with all along, but none of them had a morning show.

Barbara was dark and pretty, a raspy-voiced, gossipy intellectual. She loved books and hoped someday to own her own bookstore (which she eventually did, appropriately named Barbara's Bookstore). But now she was determined to reinvent my stay in Chicago. By nightfall on my first day, I had visited with Burr Tillstrom, a genius; become friends for life with Studs Terkel, a great man; and been introduced to Second City, the first important improvisational cabaret. Within two years Second City would become the venue for my first theatrical work and indirectly responsible for my decision five years later to become a playwright.

It's conceivable that none of this would have occurred if Barbara Siegel hadn't happened to tune in to a morning TV show and been horrified by how a *Village Voice* cartoonist she didn't know was being misunderstood.

With Barbara by my side at Second City, I became aware of what all of hip Chicago knew and few in New York had heard about. In a ninety-minute high-wire act of hit-and-miss sketches—smart, provocative, and theatrical—this band of improvisational players with its roots in the University of Chicago (beginning with Mike and Elaine and Shelley Berman) shook us up and sent us up. Its satires, inspired by audience suggestions, were political, sexual, literary, cultural, sociological . . . You name it and they made it up on the spot in front of you.

The actors played in concert like jazz musicians, setting up patterns, working off one another in counterpoint, pacing themselves with riffs, beats, and pauses. An occasional smart-as-hell monologue came from the company's bearded, shambling eccentric, Severn Darden.

Barbara Harris was in the company, as were Paul Sand and Mina Kolb and Roger Bowen and Eugene Troobnick (who doubled as assistant cartoon editor at *Playboy*). Alan Arkin, Bob Dishy, and Paul Dooley—actors who would perform in my plays in just a few short years—were soon to join them.

Beyond laughter, we in the audience responded to the show with a sense of belonging, as if we, sitting out there, were part of the show, part of a conspiracy. "I am not alone," you could sense people thinking. And the thought was growing.

PROCESS

Watching Second City and other improv groups—the Premise in New York and the Committee in San Francisco—made me aware of my own similar method of working on cartoons, to which I hadn't given much thought.

With only a topic in mind (and sometimes not even that), I would begin, as the improv groups did, with an opening line—almost any line would do. Without a conscious clue as to where I was headed, I began to riff off my opening, automatically putting words in the character's mouth, curious to see where this would take me—if anywhere.

And just as in improv a second character might decide to enter and, unexpectedly, I was writing a scene. If the second character didn't work, it was a monologue.

The words my characters spoke decided for me, by the third panel, where the cartoon was going, and by the fifth or sixth panel it was headed home.

Or it may have been headed nowhere, except into the trash, where it had lots of company.

I seldom knew in advance where this process was taking me. Any number of times over the years I'd be humming along nicely—and then I'd arrive at what should have been the last panel without a thought in my head. I didn't know how to end the thing. So I'd stash the idea in a drawer and forget it. A year or ten or twenty-five went by and, searching for something else, I'd come across the unfinished idea. Thirty seconds later the ending would announce itself. I'd draw it and send it in. Twenty-five years in the making: a comic strip.

SELLOUT

I was going to be in *The New Yorker*! What a thrill, what an irony. It wasn't that I was going to have a cartoon side by side with Arno or Darrow or Steig or Steinberg or Modell or Lorenz. It wasn't that we were now going to be colleagues, these brilliant cartoonists I admired in this magazine that I dismissed as genteel (but would have given a pint of blood to be in). My appearance was not an actual acceptance of my work by the magazine. I was, more or less, slipping in. I was doing an ad. Full-page. For Rose's Lime Juice. Something you mixed with vodka. Hey, whatever works.

Rose's Lime Juice, not *The New Yorker*, was a fan of my cartoons in the *Voice*. Through its ad agency, it had contacted Ted Riley to see if I was available, and then it sent me a nine-panel layout that tried to look and sound like one of my *Voice* strips: two characters, at a table in a bar, talking about their anxieties in imitation of my style and then relieving their stress by ordering Rose's Lime Juice in their vodka cocktails.

For the finished cartoon, I was to be paid $1,000. *Playboy* paid $500. And I would be rubbing shoulders with the *New Yorker* greats. I would have the right to call myself a *New Yorker* cartoonist. With an asterisk.

Maybe if I could get Rose's Lime Juice to let me rewrite the dialogue, it would feel a little less gamey, this use of my format to market a product. After all, I had established something of a bond between myself and my readers. They considered me a truth teller. But surely if I did a Rose's Lime Juice ad once a month, my readers wouldn't take offense just because I was using my words and pictures to sell a product. My readers also had to make a living. In a better world, where everyone had my politics and no one had to pay the rent, I wouldn't have to do ads—which, with increasing frequency, I was being commissioned to do. But not with copy, not with dialogue imitating my *Voice* cartoons. Rose's Lime Juice would have been the first.

As mentioned earlier, I didn't approve of advertising. It manipulated. It lied. Until the offers to illustrate started coming in, I was of the opinion that advertising should be outlawed. I was a civil libertarian, free speech had to be defended. But not commercial free speech. That was my position until ad agencies came after me, at which point I matured. I decided: "Big deal, who cares?" And this is where I stood when Rose's Lime Juice came to call.

Just to clarify my thoughts on this issue, let me paraphrase a section from a speech I gave five or six years later before what was called a Visual Communications Conference, sponsored by, if I remember correctly, the Art Directors Club of New York. Before my speech, I was called repeatedly by the publicist who set up the event. She said, "Don't pull any punches, our membership expects you to be irreverent." So, perhaps because *irreverent* is a word I hate in regard to my work, I wrote a speech in which I said that I knew it was popular to attack advertising these days and call for its reform, but I didn't believe that advertising could be reformed. That was like calling for the reform of the Mafia. (Is that irreverent enough?) Certain institutions were created to corrupt; advertising was one of them. Instead of trying to improve or change itself, I suggested that advertising go on doing what it was meant to do: deceive. But a federal corruption tax should be applied as a tithe against its deceptions. Tax the profits of advertising and turn the money over to the arts. Every art director who felt that he had sold out, every copywriter who had an unfinished novel in a desk drawer would thus have his guilt assuaged. Each and every sellout would mean more funding for the arts.

Few art directors found my speech amusing. I had walkouts. I would have walked out on myself if I could, so strong were the waves of hostility rising from the audience of account executives and art directors. By this time, you may guess, I was for some years out of the ad game. I had quit the business over Rose's Lime Juice.

A couple of months into the Rose's Lime Juice campaign, I found that, rather than winning new admirers, I had become the subject of debate. Herbert Mitgang of the *New York Times,* writing an otherwise splendid review of *Passionella and Other Stories,* made an offhand remark about the brilliant career that awaited me if I avoided the seduction of advertising money that was beginning to compromise my work. *Commonweal,* the liberal Catholic weekly, ran an editorial defending me against growing criticism for using my characters to sell products.

Mitgang's aside wounded me. And I was alarmed by *Commonweal's* editorial. Growing criticism? *What* growing criticism? What was the matter with these people? Just because I was on the side of truth and justice, did that mean I wasn't allowed to make a living? *Commonweal* defended me, they didn't think I was selling out. I would *never* sell out! This was one more case of the Left devouring its own!

I fell into a funk. The funk developed into a rage. I received copy for a new Rose's Lime Juice ad that the ad agency wanted me to adapt because they liked my dialogue better than their own. I stared at the copy on my drawing table, not knowing how to begin. What was I doing? Won't someone remind me?

A letter arrived postmarked Austin, Texas. Inside was one of my Rose's Lime Juice strips ripped out of *The New Yorker* with a big X scrawled across the face of it. Under the X was written in heavy marker the word *Sellout!* And it was signed "Two ex-fans."

I had a drink. I went to bed. Austin was the home of the University of Texas. This had to be the work of two students. I had meant something to them. They had looked up to me. I had disillusioned them. *Their* problem.

I called Ted Riley, who was the one responsible for getting me into all this. A diatribe of self-justification followed—yelling, whining. Ted was sympathetic as always, on my side. He said it was easy for these kids with rich parents who had never earned a dime to pass judgment. He said he would go along with any decision I made.

What did he mean by that? What did he mean by "any decision I made"? What did *I* mean? I meant for everyone to go away and stop bothering me and let me do what I wanted to do. Wasn't that the whole point of getting famous?

IT MUST BE PRE-NATAL INFLUENCE. HOW ELSE COULD I GET THIS WAY?

I GO TO BROADWAY PLAYS. EVERYBODY **ELSE** GOES TO **OFF-**BROADWAY PLAYS.

I TAKE LESSONS IN YOGI. EVERYBODY **ELSE** STUDIES **ZEN.**

FINALLY, I BUY A THREE BUTTON SUIT. SO WHAT HAPPENS? THE **ITALIAN** INFLUENCE! MY FRIENDS ALL WEAR **FOUR** BUTTON SUITS!

WHAT AM I? A **FINK** OR SOMETHING?

NOW, LOOK AT ME – DRINKING A DRY MARTINI – A BLOTTER IN AN EMPTY GLASS. HOW DRY CAN YOU GET?

EVERYBODY ELSE? HHH– THEY'RE DRINKING SOMETHING NEW AND TERRIBLY **CHIC.** I DON'T EVEN KNOW WHAT'S IN IT.

NO MATTER! I'LL PLUNGE INTO THE MAIN CURRENT OF MY TIME – **THIS INSTANT!**

WAITER – BRING ME A GIMLET!

THERE! I DID IT! BOY, WAIT'LL I TELL MY ANALYST.

JULES FEIFFER

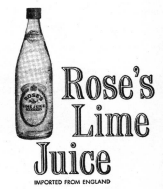

I fumed. I laid out the Rose's Lime Juice cartoons that had been published in *The New Yorker* on my drawing table. Rather nicely drawn, I thought. Typical Feiffer characters sitting in cafés, restaurants, and bars. And out of their mouths came my words written or rewritten on instructions from the client. And every word was tripe—demeaning, dissembling, and deeply distressing.

What had I done? I liked to see myself as an innocent victim but now, out of nowhere, found myself not so innocent, not by any means a victim, and caught up in a crisis of conscience over advertising. What did it say about my character that, without giving it a serious thought, I had so mindlessly sold out—the only name for it! And without a single misgiving. In these strips I had adapted, rewritten, and drawn, my cartoons endorsed with charming advocacy a product I had never tasted.

I called Ted to tell him I couldn't do it anymore. No more ads of any kind. Not ever. It was a nice chunk of money he was losing, but he didn't say a word to talk me out of it.

HERB

J ean Shepherd had a late-night radio show on WOR-AM that ran, if I remember correctly, from midnight to 5:00 a.m., during which time he talked and he talked and he talked and he talked. And once in a long while he played a record, and then he went back to talking.

His talk made a lot of sense, but it was hard to figure out why. Primarily, he cast himself as a storyteller/philosopher. In olden days he would have been called a cracker-barrel philosopher. But Jean was a different breed, a *disenfranchised* cracker-barrel philosopher with a sly and cynical urban twist.

He never touched on politics. Nostalgia was his theme. But the nostalgia was laced with recurring talk of defeat, regret, loss of innocence. What *they* did to us, what *they* took away. *They* were never identified, but his stories, political or not, took on political resonance. *They* were in, *we* were out. *They* had power. Guess who didn't.

Whispering into the mike in a purring baritone, Jean sought a oneness with his listener—one of us at a time. It was to me and me alone that he was confiding his small-town, Booth Tarkingtonish lost American childhood. His stories resounded with yearning for the good old days in that better world, albeit even *then* things went more wrong than right. Other boys won the game, wrote the prize essay, got the girl. That girl who, like Charlie Brown's redhead, didn't know you were alive. It was as if Charles Schulz, whose *Peanuts* was just taking off at the time, had a radio show and were spelling out in monologue his actual childhood.

Jean was three or four years older than I, neither ethnic nor from the Bronx. He came out of the heartland, and yet he spoke to me. He didn't speak *for* me. No talk of sex or politics or meaningless relationships. He didn't touch on urban paranoia or the Cold War. Rather his talk drew his listeners away from our daily dramas to affect us on a more mythic level where dark metaphor lived cheek by jowl with treasured innocence. We, his listeners, awake, isolated, and adrift at one or two or three in the morning, couldn't get enough. His wry, conspiratorial voice offered us a lifeline.

He didn't often do interviews, but late one night in 1954 when I still lived in my first apartment on East Fifth Street I tuned in Shepherd and he was talking to some Germanic-sounding character with an accent not unlike Sid Caesar's in one of his TV skits. The interview, clearly a put-on, had me laughing so hard that I was banging the top of my drawing table in applause.

My habit was to listen to Shepherd through the night as I worked up cartoon stories and sample art. (These were my unemployed pre-*Voice* years.) My radio sat on the windowsill next to the drawing table, and on summer nights with the window wide open my radio habit woke the neighbors, a piece of news I was made aware of the next day in the form of Ukrainian tirades.

At the end of his interview with the German guest, Shepherd revealed the put-on and introduced his guest to his listeners. He was, of all things, a cartoonist named Herb Gardner. I had seen the name. His satiric cartoons of inconsequential characters called *The Nebbishes* were displayed all around the Village on greeting cards, napkins, and coffee cups. The best of them, and the best known, showed two bulbous-shaped men sitting back in chairs, feet up on a coffee table, saying, "Next week we've got to get organized." I sensed a kindred soul. I put in a 2:00 a.m. call to WOR. Within minutes, Herb and I were chatting.

Out of that chance radio encounter began a friendship of forty-five years. Herb was no taller than I but half again wider, teddy bearish in size and appeal, with unruly black curly hair and a cherubic *punim* that many women found irresistible. He glowed with a generosity of spirit. His wit, hilarious and unstoppable, was without a trace of malice. He broke into theater first, three or four years before I did. He lent me the first draft of a play called *A Thousand Clowns,* which, to my surprise, had been optioned for Broadway. Although we had been friends for several years and been funny on so many subjects, Herb had not once suggested that he could write a play—or write at all. All he had ever shown me were his cartoons and a short story I didn't think much of. But this play was a revelation.

Most plays, even good ones, don't read well on paper. Herb's took off and never came down—smart and funny, with wonderful dialogue, incisive and witty speeches, clever but never showing off. The cleverness was organic, built into the characters, particularly Murray Burns, an out-of-work TV comedy writer who was Herb's main character.

Murray became a symbol for our time. When the movie was released at exactly the right moment in the sixties, young people, getting younger all the time in attitude, dress, music, and drugs, latched onto the film as a personal testament, seeing it three, four, half a dozen times.

But the production of the play that had opened on Broadway two years earlier—and become a hit—was a disappointment to me. It had lost a lot of the freewheeling spirit of the play Herb had given me to read. Some civilizing process had taken place. It had been Broadwayed up by the director, Fred Coe, who gave it a production the critics and audiences praised. But what I found missing was the anarchic wit and infectious charm of the original draft.

As was often the case, if I was critical of a play in previews, the critics loved it and it became a hit. The triumph of *A Thousand Clowns* was so complete and unexpected that there were friends of Herb's who couldn't stand it. Jean Shepherd, in particular. Jean was outraged. He was convinced that this was *his* play, *his* material, that Herb had stolen the character of Murray, the hero, from the persona Jean presented in his radio monologues.

Herb's and Jean's monologues had but one thing in common: they were long. But Shepherd, I suppose, couldn't stand it that this cartoonist—who was a virtual unknown, without a reputation, without a cult following—had vaulted past him to become what Jean, with all his gift of gab, was never to become: an authentic playwright. It was insult enough to end the friendship.

The movie version of *A Thousand Clowns,* which so affected its sixties audience and turned the work into legend, was successful only because Herb managed to step into a faltering production and take over the direction. He shot new scenes and fixed old ones. And in collaboration with his brilliant editor, Ralph Rosenblum, he made the movie fresher, more pointed, and better than the play, restoring the verve and audacity that I missed on Broadway.

When my own plays *Little Murders* (my first) and *Elliot Loves* (my ninth) opened to brutal notices, Herb took on the job of publicist and advocate that the paid publicists backed off from once they saw the reviews. He called my producers and tried to convince them—and, that failing, harangued them—to keep the shows running despite the fact that no one was coming.

Later, when Herb showed me his first draft of *I'm Not Rappaport,* I decided that he was the one who needed rescuing. The relationship between the black man and the white man was alarmingly stereotyped, the two characters so mismatched that I feared Herb was opening himself to attacks of racial condescension. I took a long walk to convince myself to confront my old friend with my doubts and thereby risk injuring or perhaps ending our friendship. I talked to mutual friends about what to do. And those of them who had read *Rappaport* and shared my doubts assured me, "It's pointless. You'll hurt him deeply and he'll never speak to you again."

Herb was famous for reacting to criticism with a closed-door mentality. Once he had written and rewritten and revised and revised some more, once he thought the process was completed, for him it *was.* It was plausible to imagine our friendship breaking up because I had taken on the mission of telling him his play was racially incorrect. But I couldn't allow myself to remain silent as he put on this play that I was sure was setting itself up to be clobbered.

We sat outside on the terrace of his penthouse apartment in the East Seventies on a warm spring day, and in the warmest, friendliest, most urgent fashion, I went into detail on how he was inviting disaster. And Herb, amiable throughout, said, "Really?" And "Do you think so?" And "That's so interesting."

He didn't seem at all perturbed. Not a hint of anger, not a hint that he had heard a word I said. He did not alter a line. And *I'm Not Rappaport* opened. And it was a huge success. And it won Judd Hirsch a Tony for best actor. And it won Herb a Tony for best play. And in the movie that Herb directed, Ossie Davis, as famous for his civil rights activism as he was for his acting, was clearly untroubled by what I saw as a problem. He played the part of the black man.

Before either of us got into theater, Herb and I liked to sit around doing movie star impressions for each other's amusement. We were both die-hard Warner Brothers and Frank Capra fans and could endlessly revisit old James Cagney, John Garfield, and Gary Cooper movies. Herb did a brilliant John Garfield impression. I did a pretty good Gary Cooper and a great Walter Brennan. Herb did an incomparable Sydney Greenstreet as Kasper Gutman in *The Maltese Falcon.*

Two years before Herb died, I received, by messenger, a hefty package in a brown paper bag. Inside the bag was a bulky object that weighed about five pounds, tightly wrapped in layers of newspaper and secured with masking tape. I couldn't imagine what it could be. But as I tore at the newspaper wrapping, ripping it off in strips, I began to hear a distant echo of Herb's perfectly pitched Sydney Greenstreet muttering, "The bird, Mister Spade, the bird, sir."

And as I pulled away the last strip, there it stood revealed, a perfect replica of the black bird. The Maltese Falcon. Herby's gift to me.

ALEX AND AL

Yes, I met Al Hirschfeld! I met Alex King! Al Hirschfeld you know about—or if you don't, I don't know why you'd be interested in *my* career. He is one of the greatest and certainly the most famous caricaturist of the twentieth century. And his best friend, among many best friends (because Al was a gregarious fellow and a charming, deadpan storyteller), was Alexander King, who was quite famous for a time in the fifties, having written, perhaps founded, the modern-day memoir of confessional distress. His was called *Mine Enemy Grows Older*, and what separated Alex's story from the legion of tell-alls to follow was that his was witty and erudite and somehow, despite that, became an immediate best seller.

Alex was interviewed by everyone and anyone, finally making it into media stardom as a regular on the *Jack Paar Show*, at the time *the* hot late-night talk show. Paar had an intellectually tinged bent and now and again would interview smart guests who didn't happen to be in show business. This was a generation or more before our culture was swallowed up by celebrity worship, before the media concluded that there was no business that's not show business.

Alex's appearances on Paar made him a celebrity. Every two or three weeks he'd go on to recount episodes out of his jam-packed life with wit and deft eloquence. He had been everywhere and done everything: he'd been an artist, a writer, an art director of an avant-garde magazine, a raconteur, a scholar, a bon vivant, a boulevardier. He knew everybody, and all the everybodies he knew loved him. And why not? He was a low-wattage charmer with an infectious smile and eyes that twinkled, still handsome, still curious, still knowledgeable about almost everything while holding back from showing off.

He could talk about himself for hours but was more than happy, particularly off camera, to talk of so many other things, which he did with flair. His memory was infallible. One July in the late fifties I rushed over to the house that he and his wife, Margie, were renting in Ocean Beach on Fire Island. I needed to talk to Alex about *War and Peace,* which I had just finished. Alex, of course, had read the book some fifty years earlier and still knew it by heart, going into detail about episodes that I had already pretty much forgotten.

He wasn't showing me up, he was tapping into my excitement, adding knowledge culled from all his other readings to further my interest in Tolstoy's Russia—and Tolstoy himself, about whom Alex knew more than a little.

This was the Alex one seldom saw on television, not the raconteur but the literary intellectual, and no less an enthusiast for all his erudition. His own book, *Mine Enemy Grows Older,* was a memoir of his descent into heroin addiction and consequent self-exile in a Lexington, Kentucky, drug rehab clinic. Alex was not a man who cared to be known for his suffering or, for that matter, his triumph over adversity. He would have thought that banal. But he was perfectly content for his suffering to build him an audience. He adored having an audience (*adored* was one of his most often-used words—and whatever it took, he accepted).

But once he had our attention, it wasn't tales of woe that he was selling, his or anyone else's. He was far more interested in the insanity of life (*insanity,* another favorite word). He would recount anecdotes that pointed out the madness of contemporary existence, drawing us close in a comforting circle built on our shared experiences with the insanity around us. It was as if we were sitting in front of a TV campfire, as Uncle Alex made us better by telling stories about how nuts we all were.

He was in his late fifties when we met, looking old but acting youthful, light on his feet, a light in his eyes, a smile more often than not accenting his handsome old man's face. His face showed that he had lived, but his sharp blue eyes indicated that his survival skills owed much to his canniness, humor, charm, and defiance. Humor and defiance were milk and honey to me, so I adored Alex.

We met through Ellie Friedman, like Lois Lane a beautiful girl reporter, not on the *Daily Planet* but on the *Herald Tribune,* a great, fast-disappearing newspaper. Ellie was assistant to the popular TV columnist John Crosby, who covered his beat with a wit and wry intelligence that made him stand out among regular TV critics as the smart one, a position he held all to himself until Michael Arlen began covering TV for *The New Yorker.* Ellie had called me as Crosby's assistant to ask if I would write a guest column for John, who was going on vacation. She and I made a date to talk about it, and we made another date to talk about it, and we made date after date, apparently attracted to each other while disagreeing on almost everything. I liked her enormously but the last thing I wanted was to fall in love.

Falling in and out of love seemed to have developed into a pre-programmed routine for me, a kind of blueprint that charted a course from attraction and infatuation to suffocation and we'll always be friends. My relationships lasted three months, almost to the minute. And then I would put an end to it or the girl would. (This pattern was to resolve itself a year later. In 1959 I met, and moved in with, Judy Sheftel.) But when I was still pursuing my three-month love affairs, it became a matter of pride that I be the one who would end them. Rejecting a woman was a sign of male strength. Real men didn't get rejected. They saw what was coming and acted first.

A basic drawback that prevented Ellie and me from becoming more serious about each other was that we had different faiths: she believed in Judaism, I believed in psychoanalysis. She thought psychoanalysis was a crock, and I felt the same way about religion. Analysis, on the other hand, was teaching me about my guilt, my rage, my self-loathing, my self-pity, my alienation. The complete unexpurgated package that was me. How could I not believe?

One day Ellie said, "You and Alex King will like each other." And she set up a date. The Kings had us to dinner at their apartment on Park Avenue and Ninety-fifth Street with Al and his wife, Dolly, and Paddy

Chayefsky. Alex's wife, Margie, was very pretty, blue-eyed, and oh, so young, thirty years younger than he, dressed peasant style like a folksinger, her brown hair worn in a waist-long braid. It seemed to me odd and disconcerting that this pretty young thing, whom I could easily have chased after in the Village, should be married to this relic out of my parents' generation. Or so I thought as I walked into their apartment, little dreaming that in my future lay a marriage to Jenny Allen, who was three years old the night I went to dinner at the Kings'.

Now, to be dining with Alex King, as brilliant as he was, was one thing. And to be joined by Paddy Chayefsky, who at the time was the most talked-about dramatist on television and an emerging playwright with a Broadway hit, was another thing. But to meet Al Hirschfeld, whose theatrical caricatures defined the front page of the Drama section of the *New York Times,* to have Al Hirschfeld treat me as a—dare I say it?—colleague . . . Al Hirschfeld was—well, he was self-defining, one of those rare people who not only are the best at what they do but are recognized in their lifetimes for being the best.

It's pointless to talk about the conversation that evening. I can't recall what anyone said, so overwhelmed was I to be accepted into their company as if I had a right to be there. No one, not Alex or Al or Paddy or Margie or Dolly, acted as if I didn't belong. Apparently, I was the only one at the table who knew I was a fraud.

Having passed muster at the Kings', I was invited to the Hirschfelds' for dinner. They lived in a town house a block away from the Kings. Dinner was served on the ground floor, which led out to the garden—and whom else did the Hirschfelds have for dinner that night? Well, they had Alex and Margie, of course, and an unknown young actress named Marian Seldes and the playwrights Jerry Chodorov and Ruth Goetz and the musical comedy composer Harold Rome and his wife, Florence, and Kenneth Tynan, the critic, and Marlene Dietrich.

I sat across from Dietrich at dinner and stared at Dietrich throughout dinner. She didn't notice. She had accepted an invitation to dinner with old and dear friends, little realizing that through some stupid error they would invite this kid cartoonist with the mindset of a stalker.

They all called her "Marlene." Al called her "Marlene." Dolly, who had performed with her in Berlin, called her "Marlene." Everyone around the table called her "Marlene." She was charming, she was beautiful, she was "Marlene." I didn't call her anything. I didn't speak a word to her but I was especially witty to everyone on all sides of her. Late in the evening she called across the table to Kenneth Tynan, "Ken, have you heard from Papa?"

The question came out of her mouth as if she were a Marlene Dietrich impersonator, sounding impressively like the real thing.

Ken replied in his lit-Brit stammer, "M-m-m-arlene, P-p-papa and I are n-n-n-no longer speaking."

And Marlene crooned a low "Oh no. Oh no, Ken." Her voice registered deep distress. No one at the table was aware that I was inhaling this conversation, careful not to miss a syllable. He said, "I s-s-sent P-p-papa my *N-N-ew Yorker* article on b-b-ullfighting in Spain and he wrote m-m-m-me b-back that I did-did-didn't know anything ab-b-bout b-b-b-ullfighting."

I sat there listening to this wondrous piece of theater played out at Al Hirschfeld's table for my benefit. And I thought, "This is not happening. I am making this up. Marlene and Ken Tynan talking at the table about his fight with HEMINGWAY! 'PAPA' HEMINGWAY!"

Marlene ended the discussion by shaking her no-less-beautiful-because-of-the-years head and said, "Oh no, Ken. No, no, no, Ken. We can never be mad at Papa." I heard this! "We can never be mad at Papa." *I was there! I heard this!* Little did the others at the table know of the excitement going on in my head, the pure and radiant astonishment that I had lucked into this moment. This conversation, that remark: "No, no, no, Ken. We can never be mad at Papa."

SALON

Reading Dos Passos's *U.S.A.* made a romantic of me in regard to early-twentieth-century American radicalism. I particularly admired the artists who came together to create Max Eastman's socialist magazine, *The Masses,* cartoonist agitators who were fueled by their outrage at social and economic injustice. Painters and illustrators and cartoonists turned into passionate moralists, striking out in anger, mockery, disdain, and despair made accessible through wit and scathing humor. And oh, that art! No body of subsequent newspaper or magazine cartoons rivals the illustrative talent from any single issue of *The Masses.*

A generation of mainstream cartoonists fell under their influence, not of their politics, God knows, but of their graphics. Men such as Art Young, Robert Minor, John Sloan, George Bellows, Robert Henri, and Boardman Robinson, working out of pure principle, evoked a power and sense of the moment that still blisters ninety years later. These men were my inspiration when I decided to move my *Voice* strip into political cartoons.

But enamored as I was of the political radicalism of the 1920s, I was equally enamored of the salons. Mabel Dodge, the party-throwing heiress—I couldn't get enough of her, her toney literary political soirées to which *everybody* was invited and where they discussed and argued and drank and talked about books and plays and manifestoes and drew up plans for marches and demonstrations and new radical publications and then . . . they had sex! How I wished *I* was up in Mabel's room making friends, making jokes, making out.

I had come of age in the Cold War fifties, and now, through my acquaintance with Ken Tynan, the most gregarious of critics, who mixed and mingled with anyone as long as they were famous or friends of the famous, I was inducted into the New York literary scene. Up at George Plimpton's, there were Truman Capote and Gore Vidal, the first of whom I never spoke to and the second of whom spoke one or two aphorisms at me and then took his drink elsewhere. But among the famous ones I actually got to know at Plimpton's was Bill Styron, usually lounging amiably on the couch with a drink in his hand, happily discussing the book he was currently at work on. Styron's talking about himself was oddly unnarcissistic, as if he might just as well have been talking about someone else's novel, except that was almost never the case. His wife, Rose, charged with charm and energy and beauty to boot, was a poet. But that wasn't why I got along better with her than with Bill. It was that when she and I talked Rose made the conversation about me. I found that interesting.

Plimpton's parties took place in his four-story town house in the upper seventies, off the East River. The first floor was where he published and edited his quarterly, the *Paris Review,* the second was where he had his parties, and the third was where he lived.

It was at Plimpton's that I first saw Lillian Hellman, some years before we became friends on Martha's Vineyard. She was, of course, a famous playwright, but more important to me, she was a heroine of the witch-hunt years, having defied HUAC at a highly publicized hearing where she rather elegantly told them to go to hell and, strangely, got away with it. She wasn't permitted to write another screenplay for fifteen years, but that was to be expected. Lillian's public style could be daunting, an oh-too-civilized dominatrix. I suspect she intimidated the committee. Anyhow, they didn't send her to jail.

She was the antithesis of Clifford Odets, who had named names and let me down. So I was eager to meet Lillian, sit at her feet, and praise her to the skies, and well might have done that had I not been put off by the mob of gay young men who preceded me at her feet as Lillian chain-smoked and drank, holding court in an armchair.

It was a given that the writers at Plimpton's I'd like best were the ones who went in for wisecracks, caustic exchanges, and irony. They included three playwrights: Arthur Kopit, lean, handsome, funny, and professorial;

Jack Gelber, wry, sweet-natured, and acerbically amusing when he let you in on what he really thought; and Jack Richardson, witty, darkly handsome, and dangerous-looking, called "Gentleman Jack" by his friends.

And then there were *The New Yorker*'s anonymous "Notes and Comments" writers: Tom Meehan, who was going to end up as Mel Brooks's collaborator on so many moneymaking projects you might want to kill him; Don Stewart, blond and matinee-idol handsome although he didn't seem to know it and behaved instead with amiable self-deprecating wit; and John Marquand Jr. (the son of the famous forties novelist of manners), who spoke subversively about his class in a hypnotizing upper-class drawl and after a couple of drinks didn't at all mind sharing gossip about the Kennedys, with whom he enjoyed a long acquaintance.

Bruce Jay Friedman, Joe Heller, and Philip Roth were the Jewish novelists in the group, and Terry Southern was the gravelly-voiced Texas bad boy.

Plimpton himself seemed charmingly and distantly above it all, a genial host speaking in a parody Brahmin accent and often acting like a guest at his own party. Now that I review the names, it becomes clear that George's parties were the tryouts for what was later to be the literary salon of the sixties, Elaine's.

M y girlfriend, Judy Sheftel, whom I met through Ken Tynan, had been part of this party scene for some time before I was. Sexy and beautiful, Judy had an old-fashioned, forties movie star face with eyes that shared secrets although it wasn't always clear to me what they were. This served to make her more interesting. She had lived in Paris with Elaine Dundy before Elaine married Ken, and she'd traveled around with the Tynans in Europe and the States. Since Ken and Elaine knew everyone, Judy, too, had met everyone.

By late 1959, she had moved into my apartment on Montague Terrace in Brooklyn Heights. It was a floor-through duplex in an old historic brownstone, with nineteen-foot ceilings and a baronial-sized living room, made more impressive by antiquey cream-colored walls and restored elegant moldings. Downstairs, on the garden-level floor, there was a rather gloomy bedroom, where Judy liked to spend late afternoons in bed reading novels. I worked, or tried to, upstairs at my drawing table, boxed away in a corner of the living room.

My parents, who knew as little about my life as I could get away with, didn't know Judy and I were shacking up. Living out of wedlock with a woman? My mother would have had a stroke.

Which raised a question. What if my mother called me? And Judy picked up the phone? *Yikes!* My mother called fairly frequently, my father hardly at all, except to chide me. "It's been a week since you called. Call your mother, but don't tell her I told you to."

Sooner or later there was going to be an accident. Judy would forget herself and answer my mother's call. What then? How could I lie my way out of it? Besides, it wasn't fair to keep Judy a prisoner in my home: "You can do anything, go anywhere, just don't pick up the phone."

I was waiting to get past the three-month mark with Judy to see if we'd break up. We didn't. So I solved the problem by putting in a second line, the Rhoda Feiffer line. My mother was the only one with that number, and I was the only one who answered when it rang.

Steele Commager was a Columbia classics professor and the son of the famous historian, Henry Steele Commager. Steele liked to throw parties that were more academic than Plimpton's, bringing together teachers, scholars, critics, and journalists, many of them famous, all of them talkative.

This was an older crowd than the one found at George's, and more overtly political, many of the guests coming out of a City College socialist and Trotskyite background and then having gone on to write essays and criticism for *Partisan Review,* the *New Leader,* the *New Republic,* the *Reporter,* and *Commentary.*

It was a crowd that went in for argument, so if you wandered about, drink in hand, you encountered a round robin of intellectuals happily going for each other's throats. Dwight MacDonald might be having at Murray Kempton, who ten minutes later you'd see fencing skillfully with the more easily agitated Alfred Kazin. Judy had introduced me to the

Kazins, Alfred and his sexy blond wife, Ann Birstein, also a writer, who found herself adrift in this sea of intellectuals when the person she really wanted to be was Ginger Rogers. That made it easy to become friends, because the person I wanted to be was Fred Astaire.

Argument, loud and informed, with these (mostly Jewish) intellectuals was seen by them as fun, a novel idea to me, who, going back to the days of Mimi and my mother, associated argument with retribution and death. The Kazins asked us to come to their parties early. I'd start on the martinis and they'd start on the argument so as to be in full scream just as the other guests arrived. Alfred's cheeks twitched as he argued, and his eyes went into rapid-response blinking whenever he was disagreed with.

He called me "Feiffer," I called him "Alfredo." Ann called me "Fifferman," which sounded a little like Bernard Malamud's character Fidelman. Malamud was a friend of the Kazins and became a friend of ours.

Bern taught up at Bennington, and if Philip Roth and I happened to be at Yaddo at the same time, we'd visit Malamud, a little over an hour away. He'd read to us from his latest manuscripts. Philip and I were appropriately appreciative, but mostly we were there to make jokes. When we were in each other's company, it seemed to be our mission to amuse. He was, when he chose to be, the funniest man I knew, except for Herb Gardner.

The Malamuds were good friends of the Kazins, as were Dwight and Gloria MacDonald and the *Partisan Review* crowd, William Phillips and the two Lionels, Abel and Trilling. One of my favorites of the *Partisan Review* crowd was Philip Rahv. Philip was built like a Russian bear and sounded like one. His voice came out in a low and guttural growl. Like the rest of his fellow intellectuals, he had a subject to launch into the moment he laid eyes on you. But his growl was so incoherent that much of the time I didn't understand a word he said.

One time when I ran into him on Madison Avenue soon after Susan Sontag's essay "Notes on 'Camp' " appeared in *Partisan Review*, Rahv stopped me to rant, "Susan Sontag, who is she? A literary gangster!" And just as he got interesting, he also got agitated, and the rest of what he had to say was in bear code and indecipherable.

Fred Dupee was a mild, twinkling, gentle soul, endlessly curious, certainly not someone I'd expect to see gripping hands with fellow Columbia faculty members in the spring of 1968, a cordon of middle-aged professors circling Hamilton Hall in a protective ring, fifty-, sixty-, and seventy-year-old men and women mounting a barrier against roving squads of police in an effort to dissuade them from what they most wanted to do: charge through the line and bust the heads of student strikers occupying the building.

Among these intellectuals, the one I was most delighted to see when we happened on each other was Dwight MacDonald. Dwight was tall but pretended not to be, with a pronounced stoop, his head cocked forward intently in order to rebut you more firmly. His voice was high and squeaky, reminding me of a comic actor in the Busby Berkeley *Gold Digger* musicals, Hugh Herbert. I called him "Sprightly Dwightly," and I was happy to see that during our involvement in Vietnam he was the first among the few of his generation's public intellectuals to speak out against the war. Often we shared the same platform.

Susan Stein's salon did not go in for quality-lit types or intellectuals. Susan had high-glitz showbiz parties, theater people and movie stars, which was perfectly appropriate for the daughter of Jules Stein, the founder of MCA. Susan lived in a spacious, high-ceilinged apartment in the Dakota (famous for *Rosemary's Baby* and John Lennon), cheek by jowl with Lauren Bacall and Robert Ryan, whom one often saw at her parties. Around the corner lived her sister, Jean, who entertained as much as or more than Susan. Jean's parties, however, were slanted more toward politics, with literary and showbiz types added for color. So you'd find Mailer mixing it up with Galbraith, and a Kennedy or two or three chatting with Arthur Schlesinger Jr., Kurt Vonnegut, or the Styrons.

As the daughter of Jules Stein, Susan was able to recruit the upper echelon of moviedom for her parties. On one particular spring night a few days after the Academy Awards ceremonies, who should arrive but the best picture winner, Woody Allen, who had been a no-show in Hollywood to pick up his Oscar for *Annie Hall*.

Now, I had loved *Annie Hall,* and I used to like Woody. When he started out, I'd see him perform at clubs, and after his act we'd talk and he'd flatter me and I'd flatter him. I thought he was brilliantly talented and I was under the impression that he liked me. As he moved into film with *Take the Money and Run* and *Bananas* and *Sleeper,* I became even more of a fan. I was pleased and astonished that Woody had taken the sort of humor I did, and that Mike and Elaine did, and found a way to make it palatable to a mass audience, or a masser audience than I was ever able to reach with my cartoons, plays, or movies. I found his success promising for the rest of us.

I was all for Woody—until he went shy. He didn't strike me as particularly shy when he was a struggling comic. He'd sit around in a club talking to me, and I didn't once think the poor guy was in pain. No, he seemed as much at ease as a nervous, neurotic, young Jewish genius can be. But the more he became an "auteur," the more reticent he became. His shyness, however, had an idiosyncratic twist. Woody hid away from people, as you might expect from a shy person, but he hid conspicuously, like at the head table at Elaine's.

I'd run into him there and he could barely meet my eyes. He kept barely meeting my eyes at one big party after another that he must have been attending in pain. At just about every celebrity gathering in New York, people would look over at Woody suffering with shyness within a circle of admirers.

On this particular post-Oscar night at Susan Stein's, I was headed up to her party in an elevator with Kirk Douglas and Robert Ryan and Sidney Lumet and Jay Presson Allen and her husband, Lew, and Angela Lansbury (some of these names I'm making up, but it was that kind of elevator). The last to enter the elevator were Woody and Mia Farrow, his then girlfriend. They were being stalked by paparazzi, who wouldn't let the elevator door close until they got at least one shot of Woody.

But Woody was too shy to let himself be photographed by the paparazzi, who were yelling "Just one, Woody! Drop the hat!" He had worn a big floppy hat, perfect for the occasion, and rather than try to hide behind, say, Robert Ryan, who was big and might have shielded him from all that attention, he just stood out in front with the elevator door closing, then being pushed open by paparazzi, closing and being pushed open again, his face hidden from the cameras behind his hat. Meanwhile Robert Ryan and Cyd Charisse and Gene Kelly and Fred Astaire and Clark Gable and Joan Crawford and I stood waiting patiently to go upstairs.

The scene must have played out for a minute: door closing, pushed open, closing, opened, closing, opened, as Woody held us hostage in the elevator. In the midst of this extreme awkwardness, the only words spoken were by me, standing just behind him. I snarled, "Woody, let them take your picture or get the fuck off the elevator!"

Woody dropped his hat. Flashbulbs popped. The door closed. Complete silence as we ascended to the party.

Kenneth Tynan, that man responsible, more than any other, for my knowing all these writers, intellectuals, and theater people, was leaving town, going back to London to work as Laurence Olivier's assistant at the new National Theater, which Olivier had recently been named to head. Tynan was offered the job, or so the story went, because Olivier wanted to get rid of him as a theater critic. In any case, Ken in typical style threw himself a farewell party at the Four Seasons. It was a noisy, heady mix of critics, writers, actors, and movie stars. For ten minutes I was excited to sit across a table from a drunk James Thurber, who was almost completely blind by this time and apparently deaf, too, because he reacted to not a word I said.

I remember Norman Podhoretz, the editor of *Commentary*, eyes popping out of his head, so excited was he to spot Lauren Bacall at the party. That was one of the things I liked about Norman. As oracular and stuffy as he was likely to be, there were these other occasions, quite a few, when he reverted to this Jewish kid from the Brooklyn streets, naked in his likes and dislikes, fun to be around. Norman was in the act of rescuing *Commentary* from its dreary, stifling right-wing bent (to which he would return it, in spades, just a few years later). When he took over the magazine, he brought in Norman Mailer to write for it, and Paul Goodman and Hans

Morgenthau, noted critic of the Vietnam War. He had livened up its pages considerably. Now, at Tynan's farewell party, Norman Podhoretz sighted Bacall and *he* livened up considerably.

I introduced Norman to Bacall. He was overwhelmed, and Bacall was impressed to meet an honest-to-God New York literary intellectual. An hour or so later, as I moved about the room, I happened on Bacall, deep in conversation with her friend Arlene Francis, the actress, radio host, and TV panelist. I saw Norman hovering nearby, monitoring their conversation. Being a New York intellectual, he had something to say. He interrupted. Halfway through his first sentence, Bacall shot him a Lauren Bacall glare and, with a classic growl, said: "Butt out, buster, I'm talking to one of my peers."

Norman circled the room, stopping to tell the story to everybody. "You're not going to believe this, do you know what Lauren Bacall said to me . . ." By the end of the party, the Four Seasons emptying out fast, Norman was still buttonholing anyone he could find, thrilled and making the most of his humiliation.

WHITE LIBERAL

On the one hand, there is the reasoning of the *New York Times* moderate who says that the problems are so enormous and complicated that Negro militancy is a futile irritation, and that the need is for "intelligent moderation." Thus, during the first New York school boycott, the *Times* editorialized that Negro demands, while abstractly just, would necessitate massive reforms, the funds for which could not realistically be anticipated; therefore the just demands were also foolish demands and would only antagonize white people.

Bayard Rustin

They were not called "African Americans" or "blacks" in the fifties. They were "Negroes." The term *Afro-American* was coming up on the outside, but never to become part of mainstream usage.

I saw an ad in my primary left-wing source, the *Daily Compass,* for a meeting on "The Future of Civil Rights in America." (This had to be not long after I got my apartment on Fifth Street in 1953, but how would I know? I tried to keep a journal once but nodded off after the third entry.) The event was being held at the Quaker Meeting Hall downtown in what is now the East Village. Its speaker was a man I had never heard of, who within a few years would become known all over the world as the organizer of the March on Washington, Bayard Rustin.

I was a young radical. I thought I knew what I needed to know about civil rights in America, but if there was new information I wanted to hear what it was. And then there was the possibility of meeting girls. Paramount to my interest in attending left-wing public meetings was my hope of meeting *her.* We would spot each other across a crowded room. She'd be short and stocky, because that was the only type of left-wing girl I got to meet who was attracted to me. Fine. I liked them that way, though not too stocky, just as long as they came with sizable boobs.

I would have preferred taller, movie-star-*zaftig* girls, but I was not going to find them at lefty meetings. I might find them at Ivy League mixers, but to what avail? These girls were not going to have anything to do with me, they were out of my class. I dressed wrong and looked wrong. At twenty-four, I looked less like a boyfriend than a kid brother. When I'd see myself in a mirror (a seldom deliberate choice), my reflection differed from what I hoped for. I looked like my own kid brother.

This particular meeting was sponsored by the Fellowship of Reconciliation, a nonviolent group led by the veteran organizer A. J. Muste. This group was seriously out of step with any politics that I was interested in. First of all, it was pacifist, which meant it had opposed United States entry into World War II. Many of its number, including the speaker, went to prison as conscientious objectors.

I couldn't understand how anyone could oppose a war against fascism. Still I was curious to see the speaker, a man who went to prison as a conscientious objector, a notion I had entertained when I was called up for the draft. But I lacked the courage to act on my beliefs (if they were beliefs—I may have just been chicken).

Bayard Rustin, then in his early forties, had an immediate attention-getting presence. Tall and slender, with dark West Indian good looks and eyes that shot sparks, he spoke in a clipped half-English, half-Island accent, and what he had to say I had never heard before. And it changed to this moment how I perceive race in America.

Rustin said that the issues created by the end of the Civil War were as unresolved in 1953 as they were in 1865. The inability of white America, North and South, to come to terms with its Negro citizens, a tenth of the population, was the single most important issue Americans faced.

The issue of white and black in America, he said, was more important than the bomb, the Cold War, or the witch hunts. America's future, white and black, depended on whether in the next decade we began to seriously address segregation and racism in our society. The harm we were doing by not addressing this issue was not to black America alone but to white America as well.

Whether we lived in a Jim Crow society or an integrated one defined both white and black, who, like it or not, were dependent on each other. How whites existed (or refused to exist) with blacks, worked (or refused to work) side by side with blacks, held membership in the same unions—or didn't—resided in decent housing in decent neighborhoods with decent schools or lived apart in class and race-dominated neighborhoods, good schools in one part of town, bad schools in another, ensuring a permanent division based on race and class—this would lead to a final definition of the America we were about to inherit. Little or no effort was being made to address the problem of a growing minority of undereducated, unemployed, and underemployed, predictably seething with resentment, who would eventually be driven to violence and rebellion. Urban streets would turn uncontrollable, and another great migration would begin, prompting affluent whites for their own protection to move en masse into upscale enclaves.

It wasn't the Negroes' problem that Bayard Rustin described that night, although that was the problem I had come to hear about. What I heard about instead was an impending crisis that engaged black and white equally, involved the white liberal every bit as much as it involved the white bigot. What I had not seen from my liberal do-good white perspective was that my own fate, and the fate of my children and grandchildren, was tied up in this drift toward what seemed to be an enclaved and colonized America. If we didn't act—and didn't act soon—by the end of the struggle, the U.S.A. would prove to be a myth. The F.S.A. would be the reality: the Fragmented States of America, the Fearful States of America.

Village Voice, September 5, 1963

THE WARRIOR LIBERAL

L*iberal.* It was not a bad word in the fifties and sixties, not yet the L word, not yet rejected for its scary image and succeeded by more favored terms, *middle of the road* or *moderate.* As I write this in 2008, liberals have come to favor the word *progressive,* a delicious irony if you've been around as long as I have.

When I was a boy in the forties, liberals reviled *progressive.* They thought it meant "fellow traveler." But Communism died back in 1989. Now fellow travelers had no Communists to fellow travel with. Socialism soon followed Communism into the grave. Since the Soviet Union was no longer a threat to scare voters away, it wasn't effective politics to label someone a Communist or a socialist anymore, and so it only made sense for phrase makers on the right to find a new term of fear: *liberal.*

Now, liberals had long hated Communists and Communists had long hated liberals, but no matter. In the forties and fifties, the political party that was formed in New York to combat Communist and fellow-traveling influences in city and state politics called itself the Liberal Party, but no matter.

ADA, Americans for Democratic Action, was organized back in the forties by Arthur Schlesinger Jr. and James Wechsler and other well-known anti-Communist liberals to fight the influence of Communists and fellow travelers in the Democratic Party. But no matter.

Conservatives under attack deny and retaliate, liberals under attack defend and retreat. Jimmy Wechsler, the liberal editor of the then-liberal *New York Post,* was intent on proving that his liberal anti-Communism was not to be confused with the ideology of liberals who were soft on Communism. He did not wish to compromise his paper's strong opposition to Senator Joe McCarthy, so he testified before the McCarthy committee. And just to prove that he was pure of heart, he named names. Wechsler had been a member of the YCL, the Young Communist League, when he was a student at Columbia back in the thirties. He gave McCarthy some of the names of his fellow members. He gave McCarthy the name of Murray Kempton, the *Post*'s legendary liberal columnist. As Murray noted to me with regret some years later, "Jimmy didn't know me in the YCL. The only reason he knew I was in the YCL was that long after we both quit I told him." The liberal Wechsler offered up his friend and colleague Kempton because he wanted to prove to McCarthy and company, people who couldn't have cared less, that he was an anti-Communist.

So, under attack by the Reagan right, liberals stopped calling themselves liberals and soon thereafter stopped having the politics of liberals. The purer—cleaner—term they prefer now, *progressive,* was the label used in the late forties by the left wing of the Democratic Party, fellow travelers and Communists who ran former vice president Henry Wallace for president in 1948 on the Progressive Party ticket. In life there is nothing but irony.

Isolationists who campaigned to keep America out of World War II up till minutes after Pearl Harbor were not bothered by the names liberals or Democrats called them. Call them fascists, and it didn't faze them. Call them reactionary, they didn't see it as a problem. On the right, they don't care what anyone who is not on the right calls them. They are concerned only with the opinions of people who think as they do.

Liberals, on the other hand, anguish over the opinions of people who don't like them. Liberals fret over the image stuck on them by enemies on the right. They wish to be thought well of. Often enough, being thought well of takes priority over principle. Eventually principles lose weight as principles; they are scaled back to attitudes. Almost any position can be modified in the search for agreement and agreeableness.

Called soft on Communism, liberals quieted down about witch hunts and loyalty oaths. Called eggheads, they dumbed themselves down. Displays of wit were repressed as too highbrow, humor had no place in governance. Accused of cowardice in the Cold War, liberals began appraising countries to invade.

Vietnam was a liberal war. The Republican Dwight D. Eisenhower refused to be sucked in. But Eisenhower was a general, a war hero, he didn't have to prove his manhood. John F. Kennedy, although a war hero, was unfortunately a liberal Democrat. He had to prove his manhood.

In addition, JFK had screwed up royally in his first year in office with the Bay of Pigs operation, trying to overthrow Fidel Castro's Communist government in Cuba with a gang of Cuban émigrés who couldn't shoot straight. Kennedy couldn't afford to let the Russians think that he was incompetent and inconsequential, which they might well have concluded after the Bay of Pigs. The Soviets might move on Berlin because of Kennedy's perceived weakness. Before they could make such a move, JFK moved on Vietnam. It made a Cold War sort of sense. Confronting the Soviets over Berlin could lead to World War III. But by using Vietnam as a Berlin surrogate, by substituting a small war that we thought we could handle, we could sidestep the ultimate showdown.

Vietnam, however, turned into a small war that we could not handle. And the more we could not handle it, the more men, the more ordnance, the more deadly the engagement. It undermined the administrations of three presidents and proved to be a mistake we have yet to recover from.

Yet as much of a disaster as the war proved itself to be, Kennedy could not get out and Lyndon Johnson, after him, could not get out. To cut and run was not an option for Democrats because it would make them open to attacks from the real enemy, Republicans.

But once the Republicans took power and tried escalation themselves and found, with Nixon, that it didn't work, what did they do? They cut and ran. Exactly the same thing Ronald Reagan did in Lebanon. Presidents Reagan and Jerry Ford cut and ran. But no one was going to accuse them of cowardice because Republicans were not about to attack a president of their own party. Cutting and running is criticized only when it is done by Democrats. The American electorate does not question the manhood of Republicans. They can cut and run without a downside. Not so for Democrats.

Unlike Democrats, Republicans are seen as real men. John Kerry, who fought in Vietnam, is not a real man. Dick Cheney, who shot a friend on a hunting trip and saw no reason to apologize, is a real man. It makes no difference that the Democrat is a war hero and the Republican is a draft dodger. Image is all, and real men don't apologize. Republicans own the real-man image.

But, for God's sake, George W. Bush married a librarian! His vice president married a novelist, and one of her novels is an erotic novel! And he and his wife have a daughter who's a lesbian!

If Bush and Cheney were Democrats, these affiliations would have ended their political careers. But they're not, they're Republicans. So it didn't matter that this Republican candidate, married to a bookish woman, picked for his vice president a draft dodger with a lesbian daughter and a wife who wrote erotic novels. They were given a pass. To conservative and evangelical voters, "values" are an issue only when they are the values of Democrats.

WE'VE ALL HEARD OF THE RADICAL RIGHT
AND THE RADICAL LEFT. WITH US TONIGHT
IS A SPOKESMAN OF A GROUP WHOSE
VIEWS WE'VE HEARD VERY LITTLE
ABOUT: **THE RADICAL MIDDLE**.

GOOD MORNING.
GOOD AFTERNOON.
GOOD EVENING.

WOULD YOU
DESCRIBE
THE VIEWS
OF YOUR
ORGANIZ-
ATION,
SIR?

PROBABLY. THE RADICAL MIDDLE
THINKS IT'S TIME WE TOOK THE
INITIATIVE IN WORLD AFFAIRS,
WHILE DEPLORING THE IDEA OF
CHANGE FOR
MERE CHANGE'S
SAKE.

WE OPPOSE CONCESSIONS TO THE SOVIETS.
HOWEVER, WE FAVOR NEGOTIATIONS AND
STRONGLY SUPPORT THE U.N., WHILE WE
REJECT ITS INTERFERENCE WITH OUR BASIC
INTERESTS.

WE FAVOR ARMS CONTROL AND A
CONTINUED BUILDUP, A STRONG
CIVIL RIGHTS PROGRAM WITHOUT
THE UNDUE HASTE WHICH CREATES
DEEP SCARS.

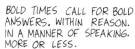

THEN, SIR,
SUMMING UP
WISE, YOU'D
SAY YOUR
PHILOSOPHY
IS — ?

BOLD TIMES CALL FOR BOLD
ANSWERS. WITHIN REASON.
IN A MANNER OF SPEAKING.
MORE OR LESS.

THANK YOU,
SIR.

ON THE
OTHER
HAND—

THE ADJUSTMENT

My first public lecture was at Sanders Auditorium at Harvard in 1961. An amateur dramatic society was putting on my first play, a one-act called *Crawling Arnold,* about a young man in his twenties whose seventyish parents have announced they're having a baby. So Arnold, their son, a thirty-five-year-old businessman, reverts to crawling. The play is about children and parents, air raid drills, fallout shelters, and black nationalism. All of that in twenty-five minutes—and why not? For five years I had been squeezing everything I knew into six to nine panels.

After the performance I was scheduled to give a talk. To an audience of over a thousand in this dark, cavernous auditorium. At *Harvard*! Just because I was famous didn't mean I knew how to speak in public. It hadn't been that many years since I learned how to speak in private. Still and all, the play had gone well. I had a script, a speech that I had written with some great lines in it. I was absolutely certain it would get a good response if only someone else would present it, someone who knew how to speak before a stadium-sized crowd of Harvard students and faculty.

I felt small. I felt insignificant. I felt that everyone in the audience, all two or three or five or six thousand of them, would know as soon as I opened my mouth that I hadn't gone to college.

"*What?*"

"You have the nerve to step on a stage at Harvard and you never went to college?"

"*What?* He never went to college?"

"What was he thinking that he never went to college?"

"*Not* thinking is more like it."

"As soon as he opens his mouth with his Bronx accent, thus revealing to us that he never went to college, let's stand and boo and walk out."

"And you know what we can shout as all fifty thousand of us exit?"

"What do we shout?"

"YOU NEVER WENT TO COLLEGE!!!"

A couple of days before Harvard, I ran into Elaine May at a party and confessed how nervous I was about my impending talk. "What do you think I should do?" I asked. And Elaine, whose work showed such a profound comic understanding of the human condition, said, "Do what I would do. Think to yourself that this entire audience is made up of fools. And you'll do fine."

I didn't think Elaine's adjustment was going to work for me. I had to find my own. And I did. Then I didn't. Then I did. Then I didn't. Dozens of adjustments were chosen and discarded.

Crawling Arnold had ended. It had gotten big laughs and thoughtful silences. And there I was backstage, in the act of being introduced. But where was my adjustment? I heard my name, followed by receptive applause. I stepped out onto the stage, suddenly knowing, at the last moment, how to make this work. I arched my back the way *he* would. I tilted my shoulders at an angle the way *he* would. I wore a small self-confident smile on my face as he, my adjustment, approached the microphone.

I moved slowly, without hurry, without nerves. I waited, grinning, for the applause to die. And one thought, one thought only, was in my head. I am Cary Grant.

Cary Grant spoke into the microphone. They listened intently. How could they not? They laughed in the right places. What do you expect, with Cary Grant's timing? Actually, I don't know how he got away with it. We don't look that much alike.

I DON'T UNDER-STAND HOW IT HAPPENED BUT WHEN I WOKE UP YESTERDAY MORNING — I **KNEW** SOMETHING HAD CHANGED!

I DIDN'T LOOK LIKE **ME** ANY-MORE!

I LOOKED LIKE CARY GRANT.

I LOOKED IN THE MIRROR AND SURE ENOUGH — THERE IT WAS — CARY GRANT.

I WALKED DOWN THE STREET AND I COULD SEE IT IN THE WAY PEOPLE STARED AT ME — CARY GRANT.

I WENT TO THE OF-FICE AND EVERYBODY SEEMED **SHY** IN MY PRESENCE. GIRLS STARTED HANGING AROUND MY DESK. **MY DESK**. THE BOSS OFFERED ME A JOB IN THE PARIS OFFICE. CARY GRANT.

I CALLED UP THE MOST BEAUTIFUL GIRL I KNEW. SHE SAID SHE HAD A DATE BUT SHE'D BREAK IT. SHE SAID SHE'D PICK UP TICKETS TO THE THEATER. CARY GRANT.

WE WENT DANCING AFTER THE THEATER. I DIDN'T EVEN KNOW I KNEW **HOW!** PEOPLE FORMED A CIRCLE AROUND US AND APPLAUDED.

I WENT HOME FLOATING. I WENT TO SLEEP DREAMING. THIS MORN-ING I WOKE UP AND KNEW SOME-THING HAD CHANGED.

BACK TO BERNARD MERGEN-DEILER.

FOR PLAIN PEOPLE THERE IS NO SUCH THING AS A PERM-ANENT CARY GRANT.

Village Voice, May 14, 1964

HALL OF FAME

In 1962 I was elected to the James Monroe High School Hall of Fame, an honor I had been plotting my response to for twenty years. One June day every year the student body, all twenty-five hundred of us, was assembled in the auditorium to fete, and be inspired by, the three honored graduates who had achieved prominence, and in some cases celebrity, in the outside world. They were doctors and judges, attorneys, business leaders, state legislators (one later indicted), and even a Metropolitan Opera star.

Their presence was supposed to prod us, the student body, into applying ourselves harder to schoolwork, goaded by the idea that someday we too might be up on that stage, the biggest stage in the world, bigger even than the famous Radio City Music Hall stage.

But the speeches these Monroe graduates gave were not inspiring; they were banal and soporific. Year after year for four years, three boring speakers, one at a time, instructed me and my peers to work hard, toe the line, don't take the easy way out, respect our teachers, listen to and learn from our elders—I put myself to sleep as I write this.

And indeed, I did doze as I heard these life-eroding homilies, first wondering, as I slipped into a semicomatose state, what had become of the kid who used to live inside the body of these corpselike grownups? There was no sign that these well-dressed, well-groomed, seriously unpersuasive adults ever had lived through childhood. Each and every one of them looked as if he had come out of the womb as he appeared that day: grave, humorless, pompous, and having nothing of interest to say.

And as I sat there, year after year after year after year, one thought occurred, awakened every spring with the advent of the Hall of Fame assembly: that someday I would be famous, someday I would be up on that stage. I would be honored. And I would not sound like these dead-on-arrival mentors. I would reveal to these kids that I was one of them and had not forgotten.

I would talk to them from the vantage point of famous cartoonist and tell them what it was like to be a kid forced to sit out there where they were sitting and listen to all this crap. I would make it clear that I was not one of the tight-lipped honorees and assembled faculty with their properly clasped hands and discreetly crossed ankles, dying by inches onstage. For the first time in the history of our high school, they would hear a graduate tell the truth.

And one spring morning in 1963, I was there. Actually up there onstage, just the way it was in my fantasy. And just as in my fantasy, my parents were there, and Mimi and Alice and my wife, Judy. I had spent most of the past week working on my acceptance speech. I was exhilarated, chomping at the bit, and scared silly. I knew what I was going to say. Was I going to get away with it?

For a very long time I had fantasized this moment. In high school I was too cowed to allow myself an adolescence. Afraid to speak out, afraid to argue, terrified of letting anyone know what I thought, I stifled my rebelliousness. I pretended that I was one of them. But now I was thirty-three, in the middle of my postponed adolescence. I was famous. I stood for something. As I perceived it, this gave me the right to run amok.

I began my speech by recalling my memory of sitting out in the assembly during these ceremonies and my puzzlement over the honorees: What had happened to the kid in them? I began to speculate. Was there a magic cutoff line that was drawn in one's psyche when time ran out on being a kid and one had to opt for grown-up, moving on from who you were and wanted to be and becoming, instead, what *they* were? Was there an unconscious decision made after a certain number of disappointments and screwups that informed you that you were getting nowhere fast, that you no longer could afford to go on missing the boat? You had to straighten up, cut out the juvenilia, stop being a smart-ass, stop responding to your elders as if they didn't know what they were talking about, even if they didn't know what they were talking about.

I said that this business of being a grown-up, a parent wasn't easy, I was not here to disparage the advice you got from teachers and parents. It was unvaryingly good advice. But it was also unvaryingly *safe* advice: don't take chances, don't risk failure, don't quit one job until you've found another better one, don't behave on impulse, don't expect too much and you won't be disappointed.

That was certainly good and responsible advice, I told them. And for anyone under thirty, if you weren't supporting a family and a couple of children, every word of it was wrong.

I began to hear cheers.

The problem with good advice, I said to the students, was that because it was good, it was *safe* advice. That's because it was coming from people who loved you and were afraid for you and wanted to protect you from disappointment and failure. But being young was all about disappointment and failure. It was about taking chances, risking everything.

What better time to risk it all than when you're young and don't have a family to support? What better time to take chances and discover, through trial and error, what works and what doesn't? What worked best for you, and not your parents or your teachers or others who wanted the best for you when their definition of the best was not yours. The applause was deafening. Shouts and cheers from young people. I looked over at my parents. They were clapping too, beaming at me.

"Uh-oh," I thought. "Here it comes." When I started out as a cartoonist, I said, I got all this good advice from my mother and father and it *was* good advice. And I followed it. And I got nowhere. I was cautious, as they suggested. I didn't take chances, as they suggested. I played it safe, as they suggested. I stayed within the rules. And then one day I decided it was time to try a different approach. Each time an opportunity arose, I thought, "What would my mother say?" And, concluding what her advice would be, I did the opposite. And that was when things began to break for me. And that was how I got to be famous enough to be elected to the James Monroe Hall of Fame.

The kids were on their feet, screaming. The sixties, as we have come to know them, were still half a decade away. Never had they heard anything like this—from a grown-up. Or in my case, a pseudo-grown-up.

And my parents? They were laughing and applauding. Tears were in their eyes, not tears of mortification because they had just been humiliated in public. These were tears of pride. Their son was *popular*, a crowd-pleaser. Who knew he could make such a good speech?

What had meant the most to them for all our young lives was that we, their children, be met with approval. And signs of approval were all over the place. Laughing, shouting, cheering. This was before the revolution, before the youth movement, when fifties conformity still held sway, before the corrupt authority of the grown-ups was replaced by the doped-up rebellion of their children.

From the stage I could see that my sisters and Judy were in a state of shock at what I had gotten away with. But Dave and Rhoda? I was their son whom this audience of students had taken to their hearts. That was all my parents cared about.

On the other hand, the principal and some members of the faculty were notably restrained. A few glared daggers at me, more couldn't look at me. But other faculty members in the audience and even on the platform were applauding. And the former principal, Henry E. Heinz, retired for some years but always showing up on this occasion, down in the audience, square-headed, tight-lipped, as rigid out of power as he was in his autocrat days, glowered at me with pure venom.

Who says you can't win them all?

"WHAT I BELIEVE" –A COMPOSITION FOR SIXTH GRADE ENGLISH.

"BE WATCHFUL — OPPORTUNITY MAY PRESENT ITSELF AT ANY MOMENT. DON'T GET **TOO** FAR AHEAD OF YOUR COMPANIONS **TOO** QUICKLY. "

" BE INDUSTRIOUS – DEVELOP A GOOD MEMORY. NEW IDEAS ARE ALWAYS IN DEMAND."

"BE MANEUVERABLE – DON'T EVER LET THEM KNOW WHAT YOU'RE THINKING. "

" BE AGREEABLE — MAKE A GOOD IMPRESSION ON OTHERS. NEW FRIENDS EQUAL NEW CONTACTS."

BE CAUTIOUS – NO ONE IS POPULAR WHEN HE'S WRONG. COVER YOURSELF ON ALL BASES. LET **OTHERS** GIVE THE FIRST OPINION. "

HOW DOES IT SOUND, DAD ?

HMMMM

I **THINK** THAT'S **ALMOST** IT. WHY NOT LEAVE IT FOR A FEW DAYS AND LET YOUR MOTHER AND ME KICK IT AROUND.

Village Voice, February 19, 1958

COLLEGE DAYS

I was drawing anti-Vietnam cartoons as early as 1963. I am quite sure I was the first cartoonist, certainly in mainstream newspapers, to attack U.S. policy in Vietnam. By the early sixties my cartoon was being syndicated in close to one hundred papers, almost every one of which I disagreed with editorially, and my cartoons reflected that. It took editors awhile, sometimes over a year, to discover that they had a viper in their nest. All that feature editors knew, and all they cared about, was that I was the new boy on the block whose cartoon appealed to college kids—the next generation of newspaper readers—whom they wanted to attract. In any case, my strip contained so much dialogue, panel by panel, that busy editors didn't know what was in it much of the time.

I had been nervous about allowing the strip to be syndicated. I loved the idea of being seen outside the Village and its environs, but I was afraid of censorship. Newspapers had a tradition of "fixing" elements in cartoons that might upset their readers. They doctored drawings and they rewrote copy. I had no intention of allowing that to happen.

Bob Hall, president of the Hall Syndicate, the most innovative (and liberal) syndicate in the business, had been wooing me for over a year. I'd go up to his Midtown office, we'd sit around. He'd lounge behind his desk, a noisy, profane, tough-talking, smart, and immensely likable salesman. Hall was a great storyteller. He knew all the cartoonists and all the old-time great reporters. Sitting with him in his office was like being down the street in Tim Costello's bar on Third Avenue. At one of our long-winded meetings, Hall became so exasperated with me and my ever-so-cautious approach to syndication that he tossed a sheet of blank stationery at me and barked, "If you're so goddamn worried about your precious goddamn integrity, write your own goddamn contract!"

So I did. Right there in his office as Hall looked on, I scrawled a deal memo that set out my terms for syndication: the usual 50–50 split, I retained ownership of copyright, and no subscribing newspaper could change a word of text. They could drop a particular strip if they objected to what I was saying, but they couldn't alter it.

Hall spent ten seconds looking over my memo, got up from his desk, and said, "It's about time, goddammit! Let's get a drink and celebrate, goddammit!"

In my syndicated cartoon, I enjoyed outraging hawk sensibilities with my opposition to the war—although I couldn't imagine why a prowar reader would bother reading me. By the time of Vietnam, I'd been in syndication since 1959. My politics should not have come as a surprise.

After an initial queasiness—a lifelong reaction that befell me every time I defied my country or my mother—I felt a measurable pride in staking out a position that no other cartoonist except for Ollie Harrington in the Communist *Daily World* had arrived at (yet). My courage and my chutzpah were solidly in place within the safe confines of the *Village Voice,* whose readers might write angry letters to the editor but couldn't get their hands on me.

But when I began accepting offers to speak at colleges, the image of myself as a fearlessly honest and lonely antiwarrior took a hit. I knew what I was going to say on campuses, and I knew that it would come as a nasty surprise to upstate and midwestern audiences who had come to hear the *Playboy* cartoonist kid around about sex.

I wasn't anxious to go out in public and talk against the war in 1965 and 1966, when most Americans still supported our efforts. It wasn't that I minded being yelled at (I rather enjoyed the idea), but I did mind some professor at some university standing up and, point by point, taking my arguments apart, making a fool of me in an area where, despite my homework, I didn't feel that qualified.

I had studied my antiwar gurus, Hans Morgenthau, I. F. Stone, Paul Goodman, and Tom Hayden, as well as Bob Scheer in *Ramparts.* In addition, I read the more balanced and therefore not nearly as useful coverage in the *New York Times*.

But stepping onto college campuses never failed to remind me—no, it haunted me—that I had not gone to college. I didn't have a degree or an education. I was lecturing students and faculty who had proof of accomplishments. Credentials. All I had was my ability to make people laugh by making points few others were making. But what did I really know?

How much did I really know about the war and how much was I making up, as I did as a kid when Mimi and I got into political arguments? Each time I took a train or flew out to give a talk, I'd move into a mode of destination panic. I wasn't invited to talk about Vietnam or civil rights or anything controversial. I was invited as a humorist. Irreverent was all right, acerbic was acceptable, but *controversial*? When I stopped being funny and started speaking my mind, audiences might rise as one and storm the stage. All my mother's caution resurfaced: "Be nice, Sonny Boy. Don't be a know-it-all. Don't get people mad at you. You can't change anything."

I was quite familiar with these panics. So, along with me on my trips, I brought my brain trust: sheafs of articles by Izzy Stone, and Morgenthau, and Goodman, and David Dellinger. Paul Goodman, in particular, focused on the morality of the war, the sheer brazenness behind our imperial policy. His high moral tone inspired a rage in me, pumped me up with the courage I needed before going on stage to shoot my mouth off and be exposed as an uninformed dolt.

I had stumbled on a formula for my college speeches: open soft with a joke or two the way you're supposed to, then devote ten minutes or so to the whys and wherefores of my work, and then, after I'd entertained them and begun to interest them, launch into a mordant but amusing rundown of the current American scene from a left perspective that they were not likely to encounter on college campuses in the early sixties.

Reactions were unpredictable. Sometimes I felt I had them in the palm of my hand, other times I lost them and sensed their discomfort and bewilderment. "Who is this madman and why doesn't he go away?" Sometimes it was both at the same time. Regardless, I would end my speech with an assault on the war, determined to impose my views in the wan hope that eventually I would see some light at the end of the tunnel.

The reactions I got seemed to have little to do with the unwelcome ideas I had to convey. My success or failure in the Vietnam part of the speech depended entirely on the opening few sentences spoken fifteen minutes earlier. A big, big laugh right at the start ensured that audiences were going to love me, no matter how seditious my later comments. If there was scattered laughter or only a titter, I was a goner.

Here's how I opened: "I have two characters who appear in my cartoons, Bernard and Huey. Bernard is innocuous, ineffectual, and in all things a loser. Huey is a make-out man, sexy, cynical, behaves badly, and women cannot resist him. The questions I get continually from my readers are, 'Are you Bernard?' and 'Who among your friends is Huey?' "

Waves of laughter, followed by applause. And after that the sober, unfunny part of my talk worked like a dream. No one stood up to dispute my facts—or on the few occasions when someone did, my response was better informed than I was and was usually greeted with approval, laughter, and applause. But only if Bernard and Huey worked. If the audience reaction to my opening gag was soft, my speech was dead in the water.

Protests against the war, even those as innocuous as mine, confused and pissed off the Johnson administration. We who were protesting and demonstrating were not playing the game as rooted in tradition. Not since World War I, when radicals and socialists opposed our entry into the war, with Eugene Debs and others going to prison for their dissent, had there been serious opposition to any of our wars once they were declared (or, as in the current fashion, undeclared).

Robert McNamara at Defense, Dean Rusk at State, and McGeorge Bundy, the national security adviser, resented and deplored outside interference in the execution of their foreign policy. We had democratically elected a government to run things, so who did we peace marchers think we were, trying to tell the experts what to do? *They*, the Pentagon, State, and the CIA, were in charge and we were fortunate to have them. They had access to information we didn't have. They had captured enemy documents. They had the domino theory, which stated that once Vietnam went Communist, Laos and Cambodia and the rest of Southeast Asia would fall, and then on to the Philippines, Hawaii, and the Red tide would soon enough wash up on the shores of Malibu and Santa Monica.

In my campus speeches I offered a view (wittily, I hoped, but only mildly satirical) on how policy is made in Washington:

It is a given that spells of paranoia periodically affect our domestic and foreign affairs. The prophets of paranoia mix and mingle with the old-boy network they went to school with—politicians, government bureaucrats, and statesmen who, as the pressure mounts, are moved to soften their "wait and see" attitude and commence a measured march to the ramparts, thus stamping the growing paranoia with "moderate" accreditation. These insiders, members of the club with their old-school institutional and foundation ties, know what's going on. They are qualified. We, who are in dissent, are not. They are experts. We are not. Consequently, our dissenting views are not to be trusted or taken seriously. To challenge the views of the club, views that with op-ed and TV talking-head exposure ascend to conventional wisdom within days, is to display a willful and dangerous ignorance in confronting the crisis at hand.

Please fill in the above with the name of the current crisis.

And when the conventional wisdom behind this month's or this year's crisis turns out to be seriously flawed or out-and-out wrong, none of its advocates, pundits, or publicists lose stature. None of them is cast out of the club, dismissed, or demoted from his government post or foundation. None is disgraced. None is asked to resign—although a few choose voluntarily to step aside to "devote more time to their families."

And few change their minds. Rather they change assignments—from high-level jobs where "mistakes were made" to new arenas where, within moments, they are just as high-level, knowledgeable, self-confident, and assertive as if mistakes had not been made. Their views are still sought and their authority is still respected. They show up on CNN, *Meet the Press*, and *Charlie Rose*. Their mistakes (and past history) have been rendered inoperative.

It was the members of the club who drew my attention as a cartoonist.

They brought screamingly to the surface everything I'd hated about authority since early childhood. The McNamara explanation—"We have access to information that you don't have"—reminded me of my mother's answer when I asked her to give me a reason for an action or decision she couldn't be bothered to explain or defend. The reason she gave that ended all discussion was "Because."

My government was, in a sense, telling me "Because." And it made me every bit as outraged as I was at eight and nine. But I was not powerless now. I was a grown-up, determined to speak out and demonstrate and write and draw cartoons and make speeches. And now the isolation was beginning to go the other way. The term *credibility gap*, which did not exist before the Vietnam years, came into use. We outsiders had managed to put the club on the defensive. "Because" no longer ended debate. It inflamed it.

Village Voice, August 4, 1966

DAVE

$\mathbf{M}$y father died watching a Yankee game. It was in the ninth inning, the Yankees behind, the bases loaded, a Yankee at bat, a hot July day in 1963 five months before the president was shot. My parents were living in a two-bedroom apartment in a high rise on Kissena Boulevard in Queens, where they had moved seven years earlier as part of the Jewish migration out of the Bronx into Queens and Long Island.

Dave had been in bad health for about a decade, in and out of the Veteran's Hospital in Queens with two heart attacks and prostate surgery. A lifetime of smoking had done him in. He breathed hard and sometimes noisily, but he walked fast, slightly bent but still with a soldier's posture.

He had two good world wars behind him. In the first, he had seen action in France, and while he himself had never spoken of the war, my mother told us that he had been a member of the company of men sent out to find the famous "lost battalion" in France's Argonne forest. This was a battalion of men that had disappeared without a trace during a firefight with the Germans. No radio contact, no hint of their fate. My father's company found them and rescued them, and more I was never to know other than that it was a feat of heroism.

World War I was the high point of his life. The rest of his life was the low point. He never, ever figured out civilian life, and while his brothers and sister did well (two of them became rich), my father couldn't keep three men's shops open. He was lousy as a shopkeeper, had no business in business.

For a while, he collected rents for a landlord named Theodore Badman. This was during the Depression, and when particular tenants couldn't come up with the monthly rent, Dave, a soft touch, paid it for them.

On Saturday mornings, my father liked to take me down to his office and let me sit at his desk, a giant old rolltop. He enjoyed bringing me to his job. It must have made him proud to show his son another world he inhabited, where my mother couldn't diminish him.

My father and I had only one safe subject to talk about: the New York Yankees. We were both fans. We talked about the Yankees from the Depression thirties into the Camelot sixties, our only conversation that was free of tension.

He was loving and sweet when he could service us, and the rest of the time he hardly said a word. Late every afternoon during my Bronx childhood and young manhood, he would prepare seeded slices of rye bread smeared with butter, topped with thinly sliced radishes, and serve them to Alice, Mimi, and me as we did our homework. He looked on, pleased with us and pleased with himself as we devoured the snack.

His life with us was nonverbal, his talk no-nonsense, getting him from point A to point B. When he'd had his say, that was it. My attempts to get a discussion going were seldom picked up on. I would make my point and he would respond, "You're full of hot air." That was it. He'd go back to his book or newspaper. This man who taught me, with infinite patience and frustration, how to recognize words off flash cards treated conversation between us as something close to an invasion of privacy.

Silence was his first language, not Polish. His life was spent translating his native silence into words that his wife and children and fellow workers and friends might understand. But when he found the opportunity to slip back into silence, he was most himself.

My mother had been criticizing my father since I was four or five, beginning with the throwaway line "Your father is a good man, but—" And the *buts* ran on for novel length.

He never spoke a word against her. His acceptance of her backstabbing, without speaking out in his own defense, without the mildest criticism of her, drove me mad with irritation. I was his advocate and couldn't stand that he refused to help his own cause.

It became my mission to prod Dave into criticism of Rhoda. One night when they still lived in the Bronx, I took him out to a bar and began pouring Scotches down him. I rottenly repeated to him some of the things she had told me about him, not at all concerned with how this might hurt him. I was interested only in advancing my scheme to get him to insult my mother.

He didn't fall for it. "She didn't mean that," he said and said again. He said, "Your mother is a wonderful woman," sticking to his story no matter how much Scotch I wasted on him.

I loved him for his sweetness, his kindness, and his gentlemanly acceptance—without a trace of self-pity—of being a victim. And a victim he was. My mother often treated him with contempt, his American Legion buddies with amiable condescension.

My father belonged to an American Legion post in Midtown Manhattan, a town house on East Thirty-ninth Street off Park Avenue. His army buddies aged into his American Legion buddies: Company E, 305th Infantry, Seventy-seventh Division, the only friendships my father maintained late in life. All were men who had done well, who were helpful to him when necessary, and who mocked him good-naturedly and habitually. It was one of his buddies, a man named Wayne Oakley, who got him a New Jersey waterfront job in the navy's Quartermaster Corps during World War II. My father was a storekeeper (once again), but in navy terms it meant that he was a civilian who kept track of requisitions, doled them out, kept inventory, and, I liked to think, maintained a stream of cheery conversation with his navy cohorts, the like of which in volubility and profanity would have been hard to believe at home.

There were few Jews among his Legion buddies. His closest friends were Mark Gropper and Manny Rosenstein. Most of his fellow legionnaires were Gentile, Republican, and unserious anti-Semites. One evening when I was in the army and on weekend pass, my father escorted me into the clubhouse dining room, which took up the parlor floor of the legionnaires' town house. He passed by table after table, introducing his soldier-boy son, on leave from basic at Fort Dix. At one table a drinking buddy genially clasped my father's hand with his two hands and yelled, "Hey, Dave, you know, there's a strong bond between the Jews and the Arabs. I guess you know who's holding the bond." He released my father's hand and both men laughed heartily. I simmered, thinking: "These ass-holes like Dave Feiffer, they really do. He's one white Jew."

"Sonny, sit down, try to not get too upset, Daddy is dead," my mother said when she called on that July afternoon.

I got a cab out to Queens. My father was stretched out on his back on the living room couch, covered from the head down with a white bed-sheet. The next-door neighbors had helped lift him from the floor where he had collapsed, and they had laid him out.

He had been in his armchair, watching the Yankee game. The door to the terrace (an actual terrace—a luxury we never imagined in the Bronx) stood open on this hot summer day. The wind was blowing in intermittent gusts. My father, who had been doing well for months after his most recent heart surgery, sat in that state of late-inning blissful anxiety that one endures for a team you love. Three men were on base. It was the bottom of the ninth, two men out, a Yankee at bat. Mel Allen, the voice of the Yan-kees since I was a baby, announced, "Here comes the pitch—"

At that precise moment, a gust of wind caught the terrace door and slammed it with the percussive blast of a gunshot—and my father's heart said, "That's it, I'm out of here!"

He was seventy-five. He was buried in a veterans cemetery out on Long Island. His Legion buddies showed up. Everyone spoke well of him. My strongest emotion seemed to fix itself on the fact that in six months Judy was scheduled to give birth to a grandchild that my father would not get to know. He adored children, particularly little children, as my mother never managed to. He especially doted on his five grandchildren: Mimi had Amy, Abby, and Jeff; Alice had Bruce and Glenn. And now my father was cheated out of meeting and playing with a child he was bound to go nuts over. My daughter Kate was born the following January, six months too late for both of them.

Dave and Rhoda, 1938

Shy Jules, Dave, and Mimi, 1930

BIRTH TRAUMA

I did not want children. I liked my nieces and nephews—what was there not to like?—but I was never tempted to have a family of my own. I knew I would make a terrible father. I had loving but awful parents who had little talent or instinct for raising children, why would I be any better? I was politely interested in the children of my friends, but no more than that. I didn't enjoy spending time with them. We had no interests to share, read different books, liked different comics and movies.

I had worked hard over many years to bury the kid I was and reinvent myself as an improved model of the flawed and fearful person my mother gave birth to: independent and successful, a famous man, gregarious (where once I was shy), a partygoer, a happy boozer, a workaplayaholic. It was the life I was meant for, the life I grew up wanting, dreamed up for me by the movies and taken by me for the real thing.

Why in my right mind would I want to take on the burden of raising a child? I was over thirty. When I spoke in therapy about my own parents, I left my sessions determined that I, the last male in the family, was morally obligated to end the line of Feiffers. *Take that, Dave and Rhoda!*

And then my bewitching, beautiful wife, who absolutely pledged to me that we would have no children—out of the question!—looked up at me in bed one night, eyes apprehensive and glowing, and said, "I have some news to tell you." She had every right to think I'd be outraged by this betrayal that she pretended was an accident. I had every right to think the same. But as the words "I'm pregnant" left her lips, my heart jumped for joy.

Who *was* I? I had spent so much time and effort willing myself into a different identity—several identities—other than the one I was saddled with at birth that the last thing I suspected was that I'd be thrilled to hear Judy tell me she was pregnant. My first narrative cartoon after *Munro,* originally called *Sick, Sick, Sick,* was about a young man, Franchot, who changes himself, over and over again, into being a member of the group he happens to be hanging out with. Had my identity become so muddled that my sense of self was that of someone I hadn't met?

For the nine months of Judy's pregnancy, I was ecstatic. And the same was true twenty years later when Jenny was carrying Halley. When my sperm count had called it a day, the last thing I thought I wanted in my sixties was to adopt a child, but I gave in to Jenny and instantly surrendered my heart to Julie.

How did it happen that one day I was indifferent to children and a few months later I went gaga over them? Not just my kids, but others as well. I grinned happily at kids on the street in their strollers. I waved, I chortled, I made funny animal noises.

I turned into a person who was content to get up in the middle of the night and walk around with a fretful or crying infant. Who, me? I was a loving, hands-on father. Who, me? I was a good father! *Me?*

Is it possible that if I'd given the army half a chance, I might have ended up loving it? But then I wouldn't have written *Munro,* nor would I have had a career. You can overdo this love thing.

What I definitely do not love is how, time and again, I discover how dismally dim I am about myself or how I really feel. This after what feels like eighty-five years of psychotherapy—plus a career that leads people to confuse the insight displayed in my work with the addled author who produced it.

Kate at her Sarah Lawrence graduation with mom Judy, 1987

Jules, Jenny, and Halley in Key West, 1992

Kate with daughter Maddy, 1999

Halley, 1996

Maddy, 2006

Little Halley and Jules, 1990

Jules and Julie, 1995

Glenn Korman, Halley, Alice, Jules, Jenny, Julie, with
friends Molly and Emma

Elizabeth Scalabrini (Beth), Julie's nanny,
and Julie, 2002

DEATH TRAUMA

A month or so prior to Kate's birth, and some months after my father's death, I was sent papers to sign by Manny Rosenstein, my father's Legion buddy, who, at my mother's request, had arranged for the interment of his remains in the Long Island National cemetery. All I had to do was put my signature on the papers, date them, and mail them back to Manny in the stamped envelope he had enclosed.

I didn't get around to it. The papers lay on the desk next to my drawing table for over two months, then three months. After the first month, Manny, this man who was doing my family a favor, called to find out what was happening. I was full of (unfelt) guilt and (un-acted-upon) gratitude. I said, "Manny, I am so sorry. I have the papers right here on my desk." (True.) "I'll sign them and get them out to you tomorrow." (Untrue.)

Another month went by, during which the only thing special in my life was not signing and mailing the interment papers.

While not signing and mailing the papers, I wrote and drew my weekly cartoon, went to lunches, cocktail parties, dinner parties, theater, movies. Somewhere during this time, Norton Juster called me and asked if I had heard the news that Kennedy had been shot. Norton didn't make it sound serious, but I knew he was dead. That was my state of mind.

His style and wit notwithstanding, I enjoyed mocking JFK in my cartoons. I was not a fan. I would have been less critical if I'd known the turn the country was about to take and how much worse everything was soon to be.

Outside of the gloom brought on by the death of the president and the fear of madness run amok brought on a week later by Ruby's shooting

Oswald, my routine continued unchanged. It was as if I had no obligations but my *Voice* cartoon. It was as if I had nothing to do but avoid signing the papers for my father's interment.

Manny kept calling. I kept telling him the papers were in the mail. I didn't sign them, but I saw them every day on the desk next to my drawing table, waiting not to be signed.

I went to therapy twice a week and sometimes I talked about my joyous reaction to Judy's pregnancy, and sometimes I talked about my guilt and bewilderment over my not signing my father's interment papers, and sometimes I talked about my sense, felt more strongly by the week, that all forms of authority were collapsing in postassassination America and that this country was on the verge of a national nervous breakdown.

By December, Judy was as big as a house, and the big house on Montague Terrace that we lived in looked like we were hiding out from the police. Mess was everywhere, even more than usual. My corner of the living room, where I maintained my studio, was a jungle. I had to search for every paper I needed—except for my father's, which I didn't need. Apparently.

The last time Manny called was early in the morning on one of the days I had therapy. Manny was a correct and courtly fellow of the old school, and on the other occasions when he'd checked in on me and I'd expressed impatience and guilt over my inability to perform this single simple task, he was constantly reassuring.

But his patience had run out. He was curt with me, clearly puzzled and angry over why I had let months go by without signing the papers. I couldn't get him off the phone fast enough. I said yes to everything. Yes, I would sign them today, yes, that minute, yes, I would put them in the envelope and rush out to the mailbox on the corner, yes, Manny, yes, just stop being mad at me, stop talking, get off the phone.

He finally did, and I went back to doing what I did best. Not signing the papers. I had three hours before I had to leave Brooklyn Heights and take the subway to Manhattan for my therapy session. All the time in the world to take care of those pesky papers. But first I had better do this, then I had better do that, then I had better rest, perhaps take a nap after all that exertion from doing this and doing that.

And then it was time to go, five minutes before I had to leave the apartment and start for the subway to go to therapy. Now I would sign those papers, sign them in a jiffy, nothing could be more simple. Jules was in charge.

The papers had been lying in the same spot on the desk I used for a side table, gathering dust for months. And now they were nowhere in sight. They were not where I had seen them that very morning—or was it yesterday morning, or the day before? I ransacked the desk to find where they were hiding. They weren't anywhere. Hundreds of other pieces of paper I had been searching for and wasn't able to find made themselves visible. But not my father's interment papers.

It was minutes before I had to leave for therapy or risk being late. I ran around the apartment in rage and panic, checking out every surface upstairs and downstairs. Nothing. Not a trace of the papers. Vanished. Gone! Poof!

I was salivating self-loathing. I fled the apartment, mortified, guilt-ridden, shamed before Manny's judgment. I imagined myself on the phone, explaining that the papers were lost—I'm sorry—that you have to start from scratch, Manny—I'm so sorry—you have to do it all over again, this task that wasn't your responsibility in the first place—I am so, so sorry—but you have to understand, Manny, your buddy Dave's son is not the kind of person you can trust with this close-to-insurmountable task of signing a paper, dating it, and sticking it in an envelope, then sealing it and taking it out to the corner mailbox to send it on its way, it's too much responsibility.

It's just one too many jobs for a cartoonist who has so much else on his mind. Did I tell you that Judy is pregnant? Did I tell you that Kennedy was shot? Did I tell you that Jack Ruby shot Oswald? It's all too much for a person of my sensitive nature and minimal organizational skills to handle. So, Manny, I leave it in your capable, grown-up hands. Do it over again from scratch, and maybe next time around I'll be in better shape to sign the papers.

On my way to the Borough Hall subway stop, I approached a parked police car on Joralemon Street. Two police officers were talking, smoking, drinking coffee, one outside the car, leaning against the front passenger door, the other in the passenger seat, his coffee cup resting on the sill of the open window.

I passed by, glaring at them out of the corners of my eyes. I shot them both dead. *Bang! Bang!* Two shots rang out in my head and the policemen fell. They were dispatched. I had dispensed justice. Vengeance was mine, sayeth whoever I happened to be at the moment.

I arrived at therapy and I told my very nice, warm, helpful therapist, Miriam Yelsky, that I had just shot two cops on the street because I couldn't find my father's interment papers. I told her that I was quitting therapy. Today was my last day.

Miriam tried to calm me down and talk me out of it, but I would not be calmed down and I would not be coaxed into acting rational when I knew that, in my case, "rational" was a hoax.

I told her that after all these years of therapy, if it was bang, bang, you're dead—now don't I feel better?—then I had no choice but to take on the job that she and I were not able to handle together. I had to learn to do it alone, I had to learn to at least assume the pretense of being grown-up.

I didn't need any more help. I needed a brain. And stamina. And I was now going to leave, go out into the world, and try to reinvent myself as a human.

I left therapy. I went home to Brooklyn Heights. I entered my apartment. The first thing I saw, lying in plain sight, where they had been all along, was my father's papers. I signed them. I mailed them. For a couple of weeks, I felt like a grown-up.

HOW DO YOU DO, MR. MERGEN-DEILER. I'M YOUR GROWN-UP.

YOU'RE MY WHAT?

SURELY YOU'VE ALWAYS WANTED A GROWN-UP? SOMEBODY WHO TAKES OVER THOSE PETTY DAY-TO-DAY AFFAIRS WHICH SO COMPLICATE ONE'S LIFE AND WHO HANDLES THEM CLEANLY AND EFFICIENTLY.

SOMEBODY WHO WILL NOT ALLOW YOUR INSURANCE TO LAPSE, YOUR RENT TO FALL OVERDUE, YOUR CAR TO BREAK DOWN. SOMEBODY WHO WILL NOT BE NERVOUS IN REGARD TO CALLING THE LAND-LORD ABOUT REPAIRS, THE GIRL FRIEND ABOUT BREAKING A DATE, THE BOSS ABOUT A NEEDED RAISE.

IN OTHER WORDS SOMEBODY WHO IS TRAINED TO DO ALL THOSE ADULT THINGS TOO MANY OF US HAVE BEEN ASKED TO DO SINCE CHILDHOOD AND STILL CAN'T QUITE MANAGE. SOMEBODY WHO IS WILLING AND HAPPY TO STAND ON YOUR OWN TWO FEET FOR YOU, TO FIGHT ALL YOUR BATTLES, TO MAKE ALL YOUR DIFFICULT DECISIONS — I.e., YOUR GROWN-UP!

YOU MEAN I WON'T EVER HAVE TO MAKE A DECISION AGAIN?

ONCE IN YOUR EMPLOY I, YOUR GROWN-UP WILL MAKE THEM ALL!

IT'S UNBELIEVABLE! IT'S WHAT I'VE DREAMED OF ALL MY LIFE! WHAT DO YOU WANT ME TO PAY YOU?

GEE, I DON'T KNOW. WHAT DO YOU THINK I'M WORTH?

Part Three

ANOTHER COUNTRY

CLOSET AMERICA

*A*n excerpt of a speech before the American Civil Liberties Union during Ronald Reagan's first term in office:

These are unfashionable times for civil libertarians. Years ago there used to be a phrase on the Left called "enlightened self-interest." Well, there's nothing enlightened about self-interest anymore. Not mine and possibly not yours. We are running scared in this land; we are scared of crime; we are scared of the unemployed; we are scared of the unemployable; we are scared of the growing underclass; we are scared of minorities that threaten to become majorities. In such a time, all-out support for civil liberties is a tricky proposition.

First of all, to believe in civil liberties you have to believe in the Constitution, but a constitution to what? If you have a constitution, you need a country to go with it. But there really isn't a country out there anymore. Looking around, it's hard to stick to the belief that America still truly exists. The ideals and faith that once unified us have largely dissipated. Our reasons for hanging together, rather than hanging separately, have fast disappeared. There used to be something out there called "the American Dream." It was our state religion; it was an umbrella ideology. Americans, having no past to sink their roots into, sank their roots into the future. Our assumption was that the future would be better, that the future would be more prosperous, there would be more work in America, there would be more dignity, there would be more equality, there would be more freedom.

From our beginning, one of the ground rules was that each generation understood that the next generation would do better, would have more opportunity, more affluence, and more equality. Well, that ground rule is no longer operative. My generation no longer believes that, and the generation of our children not only doesn't believe it, many have not even heard of it.

We look at opportunity today and see it narrowing, rather than widening. We don't see light at the end of the tunnel; we see more tunnel at the end of the tunnel, so we adjust; we acquire tunnel vision. We bury "the American Dream"; we bury optimism; we bury our sense of the future, our belief in answers, our belief in racial equality or in education or, for that matter, our belief in literacy. For if there's to be a permanent underclass, why bother to educate it? It's pointless, expensive, and potentially dangerous.

With the death of "the American Dream," we have become woefully aware that there is not one America out there anymore but 200 or 300 Americas, closet Americas, whose citizens owe a stronger allegiance to their own codes, their own systems of values, their own closet constitutions than they do to the Constitution of the United States; led to believe in the cultural and political correctness of their particular America over all other Americas, schooled first and foremost in the rules and regulations, the laws of their closet America. So fundamentalist America lives in a principality unto itself, as does corporate America, criminal America, druggy America, elderly America, blue-collar America, teenage America, middle-management America, and all the various branches of ethnic America, viewing all other Americans as active or potential enemies to defend against; therefore, acquiring codes of behavior *they* will not understand, language that is designed to confuse and mystify *them*, values that permit one to lie and cheat and bribe and steal and still feel good about oneself; because you are acting as an agent of your own America in a war against those other Americas. And we have learned that in war, in the defense of one's land, or in this case one's closet, it's ethical to lie and cheat and bribe and steal and sometimes kill.

When the New Right refers to the United States of America, it does not harken back to 1776 and Philadelphia; it really means the 1940s and Hollywood, the America of old black-and-white movies, small frame houses on shady-lane streets, white folks with white picket fences and white values—a world where Walt Disney died for our sins and the Gipper is God's messenger, a symbol of the nostalgia that these people mistake for principles, the fairy tales they mistake for history. Now they are out there contorting and distorting with old movie values and old movie magic, defining our reality, making tintypes of our hopes, turning our most creative, innovative, and ambivalent impulses into needle-point samplers. These true believers of the Right are trying to simplify us back into the Stone Age.

For years they have cried out the purity of their purpose, that they alone know the way, that liberalism was crippling us, draining us of our vital bodily fluids. . . . We are back in a debate fought over since slavery, since the Industrial Revolution, since the last Great Depression. It's the argument that stirs us awake and keeps us alive. It's reaction versus hope, freedom for some versus freedom for all. It's a continuation of the oldest game in town, the contest for the American soul.

ONCE THERE WAS A SLEEPING COUNTRY THAT HAD SPENT EIGHT YEARS UNDER A SPELL. NOBODY TALKED. NOBODY ARGUED. EVERYBODY SLEPT.

THEN ONE DAY INTO THIS COUNTRY RODE A HANDSOME YOUNG PRINCE. "IT'S TIME TO GET MOVING AGAIN," THE PRINCE DECLARED. THE COUNTRY STIRRED IN ITS SLEEP.

FOR THE FIRST TIME IN YEARS PEOPLE ACTUALLY BEGAN TO **TALK**. THEY **ARGUED**. THEY **TOOK SIDES**. "STOP TALKING SO LOUD!" THE REST OF THE COUNTRY GRUMBLED IN ITS SLEEP. "HAVE SOME CONSIDERATION FOR THE REST OF US."

BUT THE TALKING ONLY BECAME LOUDER. MORE AND MORE PEOPLE AWOKE AND, ANGRY THAT THEY HAD TO BE AWAKE, BEGAN TO **TALK**, BEGAN TO **ARGUE**, BEGAN TO **TAKE SIDES**.

THEN ONE DAY THE YOUNG PRINCE WAS KILLED— NO ONE COULD AGREE BY WHOM. EVERY SIDE ACCUSED EVERY OTHER SIDE. BUT CALMER HEADS PREVAILED.

"SEE WHAT WE HAVE COME TO WITH THIS WICKED DISSENSION." CALMER HEADS ARGUED, "LET US CLEANSE OUR SOCIETY OF THIS DIVISIVE DEBATE!"

AND THE COUNTRY, SUFFERING FROM WOUNDS AND GUILT, **CHEERED**. DEBATE HALTED. ARGUMENT DIED. AND THERE WAS NO MORE TALK IN THE LAND.

AND AS THE COUNTRY PREPARED FOR SLEEP IT HOPED NO ONE WOULD EVER ASK IT TO MOVE AGAIN—

FOR IT REALLY DID NOT WANT TO KILL ANYMORE PRINCES.

THE ASSASSINATION OF CARY GRANT

John F. Kennedy was Cary Grant in the White House. Lee Harvey Oswald shot and killed Cary Grant, and the next morning we all understood that we were living in another country. And by the end of the week, when Jack Ruby shot Oswald, surrealism was in the saddle and rode mankind.

JFK was our first movie star president. He had the glitter, the glamour, the randiness, the sexiness, the bad-boy image that moviegoers love for their larger-than-life stars. Kennedy had wit and style and a knowing slyness. He affected both men and women, making them want to play a part in the movie he starred in—and if that movie was about high times and hope replacing the blandness and conformity of Grandfather Ike, then so much the better. Who could say no to that mischievous grin? We even forgave him his failed black comedy, *The Three Stooges Go to Cuba*.

He offered himself as a symbol of change. And we were ready. And if his bad-boy pugnaciousness came perilously close to ending it all, nonetheless you had to admit, he almost got away with it. He won the missile crisis, he got Khrushchev to back down, he started the Peace Corps, he started Vietnam, he threw so many balls in the air, with so much confusion and so much spin in so many directions, that it now seems inevitable that one of them had to come down with history-changing force and blow him apart.

And with Kennedy gone, we, his audience, recognized for the first time that we were living in the wrong movie.

His movie, full of risk, made us giddy with excitement. His wild streak, couched in the language of pragmatism, kept us on our toes. Touch football, the game preferred by the Kennedy family, was the metaphor that best described his style of leadership: lots of running, dodging, fumbling, breaking free, getting nailed . . . He was youth, he was idealism, he was gone in an instant.

Our sense of shock ran in tandem with our sense of wonder at the razzle-dazzle effectiveness of the Johnson succession. If JFK was Cary Grant, LBJ invoked the spirit of FDR and the New Deal, moving on civil rights legislation with a swiftness that seemed a rebuke to his predecessor. An accidental president with no broad-based constituency, he nonetheless buttonholed, coaxed, cajoled, and convinced former Senate colleagues, deep-dyed segregationists, to support his voting rights bill.

And after his civil rights victory, he pushed through a poverty program, then ran for president in his own right, sounding like a peace candidate, and not long after that, he cynically and duplicitously escalated the war in Vietnam. After an extraordinary first year in office, he is remembered today more for Vietnam, the Chicago riots, the beginning of the belief that was to become axiomatic—that government lies—and the subsequent collapse of liberalism. On the other hand, without his civil rights legislation it is impossible to imagine that Barack Obama could have ever run for president. (Some other hand!)

LBJ's very own personal Vietnam was not the only violence confronting us. Acts of random violence, unconnected to politics, started popping up all over the place. In LBJ's own Texas, a young student, Charles Whitman, climbed to the top of a tower on the Austin campus of the University of Texas and started shooting people below.

Whitman's mass murders seemed to symbolize what was erupting in less dramatic fashion in other parts of the country. I was convinced by the end of 1964 that the Kennedy assassination was inspiring a colossal national nervous breakdown, which was going unacknowledged in our media although signs of it, large and small, were in evidence almost everywhere I looked.

One became uncomfortably aware that the U.S. was coming unglued as a nation, all forms of authority delegitimized. We were breaking into rebellion, separating ourselves into fiefdoms—emerging signs of Closet America.

As a nation we were undergoing not a change of guard or a change of values but a change of *everything*. From structure to confusion, from confusion to disillusion, from disillusion to anarchy. America was dissolving before our very eyes.

Was it a blowback from the racial wars? Was it the sexual revolution? Rock 'n' roll, early drugging, the decline and fall of official maturity? Or was it a Cold War madness brought on by twenty years of suffocation and threat and paranoia and prosperity? Had our hypocrisies become too transparently obvious for the system to go on pretending that they made sense? Were the acts of random violence breaking out helter-skelter, from the Texas tower to Charles Manson, separate but equal acts of a collective psychosis?

Was there a logic of disturbance and disenchantment at work here? The American Dream transformed into the American Killing Machine? Bitter citizens, feeling cheated and thwarted, pick up whatever weapon is at hand, in a land full of handy weapons, and cry out, in Paddy Chayefsky's immortal words from *Network*, "I'm mad as hell and I'm not going to take it anymore!"

But take it we did, and take it some more—and these outbursts, flaring incidents of violence, little murders up and down our fifty states (or was it forty-nine back then?) were indigenously American, true to how our traditions taught us to let off steam, dating from the old frontier to the New Frontier.

Had anyone written about this? Not in any of the periodicals I read. I had a vision of imminent onrushing insanity: educators no longer able to educate, leaders unable and unqualified to lead, parents unable or unqualified to establish beliefs and boundaries for their children . . . The breakdown of every form of traditional authority—why wasn't I reading about this? In *Time* and *Newsweek* and the *New York Times* or *Commentary* or *Partisan Review*?

I would have to work on this. But it was too complicated for a comic strip or a long cartoon narrative. It would have to be a novel—my second, God help me! The first, published early in 1963, the year Kennedy was shot, had been an awful experience. I had a title for this new one. *Little Murders*. I hoped it would go better.

I made copious notes, hid them away, and began writing. As I wrote I permitted myself to drift away from my theme. I found myself bogged down in writerly trivia.

Page after page of endless digression. Descriptions of nature that I had no business trying to record: what spring in Nebraska looked like, what snow in New Hampshire looked like. My readers needed to know. I needed to tell them. I needed so badly to tell them what I lacked the powers to describe that I forgot the story I meant to write. I forgot the point. Why exactly was I sitting at my desk for two years, legal-size yellow pads piling up in a file cabinet that I did not go near after locking away whatever it was that I had assigned myself to create?

I hid out in the back-room studio of our apartment on Riverside Drive, where Judy and I had moved after the birth of Kate. I was able to make up stories to tell our beautiful red-haired baby daughter at bedtime but I was getting nowhere with my own story. It took almost a year for me to admit that I was stuck. Again. Just as I'd been with my first novel three years earlier.

HARRY, THE RAT

Writing my first novel, *Harry, the Rat with Women,* had been one of the few times that I despised and resented the act of creation. Every page was a thankless effort. Even when the work was going well, I couldn't wait for this dreadful assignment I had handed myself to wind itself down, dragging myself each day to my desk to do what felt like homework.

Bogged down in the last third of the novel and hopelessly and endlessly moaning about it, I was offered a refuge. My friend Don Stewart invited me to use his father's empty house in Upper Jay in upstate New York as a hideaway to write. Don's father was the screenwriter Donald Ogden Stewart, who started out as a humorist for the original *Vanity Fair,* wrote for *The New Yorker,* and ended up in Hollywood writing famous adaptations of Philip Barry's plays *Holiday* and *The Philadelphia Story.*

Don's father was a lefty, probably a Communist, who was converted in the 1920s by his Upper East Side doorman. Old Don had been in the midst of writing a play with a working-class character. Coming from a middle-class family in Columbus, Ohio, he knew nothing about the working class. So he approached the only member of the working class he had ever met, the doorman of his apartment building, and asked for his help. His doorman lent him his copy of *Das Kapital,* and that was enough to turn Old Don Red.

Later, Don landed in Hollywood and met and married Ella Winter, the widow of my muckraking hero Lincoln Steffens. Don and Ella became mainstays of the Hollywood Left in the antifascist thirties, which of course set them up as prey for HUAC when, in the early postwar years, it went headline hunting for Reds. To avoid testifying, the Stewarts decamped for

England, where they sought sanctuary and founded a salon in Hampstead Heath, outside of London. They became the social outpost for left-wing émigrés. Sympathizers of every nationality, blacklisted or not yet blacklisted, came for Sunday lunch at the Stewarts'. Charlie Chaplin was a frequent visitor, but never while I was there.

My first visit to the famed Stewart homestead at 103 Frognal was in 1959. I was in London at the invitation of the *Observer,* which in concert with Billy Collins, the publisher of the English edition of *Sick, Sick, Sick,* was bringing me over to celebrate my book. The strip had, to my delight, created a lot of talk in London. And in London, a lot of talk means that you've arrived.

I arrived by way of the *Queen Elizabeth,* mother of all Cunard liners and straight out of a Fred and Ginger movie. And why would I travel that way? It was my fear of flying. I was terrified of flying—I did all those things on a plane you do when you know that you and you alone are responsible for keeping it in the air. When the plane banked sharply left, I leaned right so that it would regain its balance. When the plane banked right, I corrected in the opposite direction. My heart was never out of my mouth, and that was for short trips. Trips to L.A., I barely survived.

So I was not about to fly across the Atlantic. The Atlantic? Are you kidding? This vast stretch of black ocean twenty-five or thirty-five thousand feet below, flying blind at night with pilots whom I didn't know, I had never met. My boundless fear could not keep a plane in the air for the eight hours it would take to get me to London. No, I would plunge into the dark, turbulent, and murky Atlantic, gone in an instant, who would know where? Vanished without a trace, me and Amelia Earhart.

Better to go by boat. Ted Riley, my agent, was coming with me, and since he, with his high-toned prep school accent, was the most English-sounding person I knew outside of George Plimpton, he seemed like an obvious choice to accompany me. But if Ted was with me, I had to make an impression, so it was a given that we would travel first class. I bought my first tux at J. Press (fifty years later, I have a second tux). We had a farewell party in my stateroom just as Joel McCrea did in *Foreign Correspondent,* I strolled the deck with Gershwin music in my head just as

Astaire did in *Shall We Dance,* and I dined and drank and drank and dined magnificently, just as Henry Fonda and Barbara Stanwyck did in *The Lady Eve.*

I was living out my movie life. Most appropriately, our second day out, in the *Queen*'s lavish screening room, a vast theater with heavy leather armchairs spaced comfortably apart, they screened a not-as-yet-released Alfred Hitchcock film that I hadn't heard of, *North by Northwest.* Here I was, living out my Fred Astaire fantasy, and who should join us? Cary Grant.

After which, long after midnight, Ted and I, in our tuxedoes, retreated for a nightcap to the top of the top deck. Unless you climbed a smokestack, you could go no higher. We sat on bar stools in the quiet and under-attended Verandah Grill, sipping Pimm's Cups, observing another insomniac passenger looking far more elegant in black tie than we did. He was fooling around on the piano, playing Duke Ellington. And why not? He *was* Duke Ellington.

WORKING

The *Observer* had asked me if there was anyone I would particularly like to meet in London. I wrote back that if it could be arranged (and if it couldn't be, that was perfectly fine) I'd love to meet my hero, the great political cartoonist of World War II David Low. And I'd love to meet Vicky, aka Victor Weisz, another brilliant socialist cartoonist, who drew for the *Evening Standard,* and I'd love to meet Felix Topolski, the Polish émigré artist who came to London and began producing weekly illustrated journals on butcher paper, diaries scrawled in pen and illustrated in charcoal that documented his travels around the city. And, oh yes, I'd like to meet that guy who wrote *Look Back in Anger,* John Osborne.

Nigel Gosling and Terry Kilmartin, the art and literary editors of the paper, set up everything that I requested. And more. Lunch with Philip Toynbee and Gavin Young, their dashing, trench-coated foreign correspondent (who became a friend) and Anthony Sampson, their dogged and diligent and even more brilliant foreign and jack-of-all-trades correspondent, a kind of English David Halberstam.

Lunch with David Low, his wife, and his aunt: Low looked like a kindly version of his famous cartoon character Colonel Blimp. He was warm and witty and curious and everything I could have wanted in a hero, but later I couldn't remember a word he said because all my time with him I was thinking, "I can't believe I'm having lunch with David Low!"

London treated me like a rock star. It was a degree of celebrity I was yet to experience in the States. I was bowled over by the attention, the admiration, the flattery. I didn't ever want to return home to find out that this wasn't my real life.

My friend Tom Migliore, a big, bushy-haired Bronx beatnik, was in town. I had met Tom through Norton Juster. He was a builder by trade, a closet intellectual masquerading as macho working class. He was a hunk with a mouth that strung words together in jazz-riff improvisations. This was 1959, before the Beatles, before long hair, before English cool. I showed up at Chelsea and Soho parties with England's first American beatnik talking indecipherable gibberish to the English, who adored it. Tom spoke in sentence fragments, sudden stops and starts, cadenced like a bass player, a Bronx neighborhood accent (Italian vintage), stuffed with literary and political references: "You don't know," "You gotta," "You know?" "You don't wanna know."

We were a real live Bernard and Huey. Women went for Tom, literary types went for me. I had stimulating conversations, he got laid.

I took Tom to 103 Frognal to meet Donald Ogden Stewart and Ella Winter. It was at one of these gatherings that I worked up the nerve to ask Old Don the question that had been preying on my mind: "Is it true that in that great fishing scene in *The Sun Also Rises* where Jake and Bill Gorton have this long conversation—is it true that you're Bill Gorton?"

Old Don, who was known to drink, tasted his martini and paused as if to consider this question that he had to have been asked a hundred times before. In his high-pitched, Columbus, Ohio, accent, he drawled, "Well . . . that's what people say . . . but really, I was a lot funnier than that."

And now, a year later, I was in Old Don's house in Upper Jay, New York, a ramshackle, nondescript two-story barn, drab and characterless compared with Frognal, but I was thrilled to be there. Neither Judy nor I had ever learned to drive, so Don Junior drove us up to the house, shopped with us in town for groceries and booze, and drove off, cheerily leaving me to my long-delayed work. I didn't know what Judy was planning to do with her time, but I was preparing to ready myself to sit down some day that week—and write—and write—and write.

I had not touched the book for weeks. I was trapped, comfortably afloat in a sea of self-loathing. I wasn't a novelist. How did I get into writing a novel in the first place? Every sentence I wrote was an attempt to find a way of telling my story while getting around the fact that I lacked the powers of observation and description, not to mention a facility with words, that real novelists seem to be born with.

I was dealing with my deficiencies and I was bored by the effort. I was a six-to-nine-panel man who wrote the best comic strip dialogue in the business, but was I more than that? I had the ambition, but on the evidence of my paralysis, I was beginning to question whether I had the talent. Or the will.

Intent on not answering these questions, on my first morning in Upper Jay I distracted myself by attacking the Stewarts' library. It was stacked with hundreds of books, classics I was meaning to read. Now, this very moment! Political tracts documenting the history of the American Left over the last forty years, including a collection of speeches from the Waldorf Peace Conference held prior to Germany's attack on the Soviet Union. Lillian Hellman and Don Stewart had spoken out against U.S. intervention in this "phony war," as viewed by the Far Left.

I found a copy of a 1935 issue of the *Nation* magazine with an editorial condemning the passage of the Wagner Labor Act, which, for the first time, recognized the right of unions to collectively bargain. The legislation wasn't nearly strong enough, or so thought the *Nation,* which went on to editorialize that no law would be better than a weak law. I thought, "Thank God I'm a humorist. It allows me to forgive the idiocy of the Left while still considering myself one of their number."

I finally chose an anthology containing all four novels by Nathanael West. I was a great admirer of West. Perhaps an hour or so of reading his fiction would be just what I needed to set the proper mood for all the writing I was planning to do. That day, or the next, or someday very soon. I sped through *The Dream Life of Balso Snell* (new to me) and *Miss Lonely-hearts* and the first half of *The Day of the Locust,* both previously read. I was dazzled, I was sated. I had spent my entire first day reading West.

And now it was behind me, and Judy and I had dinner. I poured a Scotch or two to boost me out of my chair at the table and propel me upstairs to the cell I had chosen to confront my sadly overlooked novel. I set myself up at a small desk, with paper and fountain pens and a bottle of

Waterman's ink (I have never learned to type). And what happened next was extraordinary. Within seconds, doors that had been closed to me opened wide. All that was so muddled before suddenly cleared. I wrote five pages in an hour in longhand, went downstairs to keep afloat with a Scotch, then back upstairs for another hour to write three or four more pages, then downstairs for Scotch.

I was on a roll. Never had I written so well, not like a cartoonist uncertain of his talent, not a bit of it. Oh, the language! Oh, the grace! Oh, the wit, the style! Four hours later, drunk and euphoric, I collapsed into bed next to my long-snoozing wife. I passed out immediately and woke happy beyond memory six hours later, head throbbing with hangover but impatient to get back to my brilliant first novel. I was writing a masterpiece.

I let Judy sleep and made myself breakfast: a fried egg and a cup of coffee. Impatient to get going, I skipped upstairs to read my efforts, over which I had partied into the night. I had blacked out what I had written, my only memory being this incredible breakthrough that I had made. I might prove to be a real writer after all, almost as good as Nathanael West!

Almost as good? I *was* Nathanael West. As I read through the twenty-five or so pages I had scribbled the night before, I was dragged, disbelieving, into a state of shock, followed by dismay, followed by ironic distance, followed by hysterical laughter. I had drunkenly sideswiped myself into a case of mistaken identity. The night before, under the illusion that I was writing *Harry, the Rat with Women,* I had simply, straightforwardly, and with no awareness whatever, written my own draft of *Miss Lonelyhearts.*

Later that day, I managed to emerge from my state of satiric wonder and pull myself together long enough to come to terms with *Harry,* discarding West to find a voice that was an acceptable version of my own. The West imitation turned out to be therapeutic. The best writing in *Harry* came to me after the night I channeled Miss Lonelyhearts.

Still, I didn't think this was an experience I needed to repeat. I might be able to write a novel, but sadly I was not a novelist. I considered the novel to be the most serious and important of all art forms. If I could have been a different kind of artist, with a talent of my choice, I would have chosen novelist. But novelist had not chosen me.

UNMAKING IT

*H*arry was now finished. All in all, it was a pretty good book. I was proud of it. And the reactions were, if not celebratory, mostly positive. (My oldest friend, Ed McLean, did not like the book and expressed his dislike so gleefully that the book ended our friendship; Mike Nichols didn't like it but expressed his criticism so gracefully that I felt flattered by his rejection.)

The book even sold. I made money. *Playboy* ran it in two parts and gave me $15,000. But I didn't think this was enough reason for me to embark on a second novel.

I need to have fun at what I do. If I can't have fun, I don't see much point to doing it. It was no fun writing *Harry*. It was, to a considerable extent, fiction (good and great fiction) that taught me who I was and the person I was fated to be. Fiction evoked a tantalizing world I didn't know existed until I picked up Romain Rolland or Jack London or Ross Lockridge Jr. or James T. Farrell or Dreiser or Hemingway, Dickens, Dostoyevsky, Tolstoy . . . Fiction reinterpreted my childhood and laid out a story line for my adulthood.

Fiction was truth schematically romanticized in the form of a story that, unlike real life, was coherent. It offered clues on how to handle oneself in a confusing world outside the printed page. Fiction offered perspectives for coping. It mentored me through the self-destruction and self-loathing that came with adolescence and young manhood. Fiction upstaged my mother and father. They brought me up; fiction parented me. Fiction inspired me to invent my own story, my own fiction. The story was that I was not the person others saw me as. I was better. Guided by the novel, someday I'd prove it.

Harry, the Rat with Women sold well enough to be considered a commercial success. Over the years, there was Broadway and movie interest. Alan Menken wanted to turn it into a musical. Why I said no to the brilliant composer of *Little Shop of Horrors* and *The Little Mermaid,* I do not know. But no is what I said.

Warren Beatty talked of optioning it for a movie, but nothing happened. Sylvester Stallone tried to option it for an HBO series that he would produce. I asked to be put on as a consultant. Sly said no, so I said no.

I was in the habit of saying no to everyone, I don't know why. I still don't understand why I said no to Alan Menken. Force of habit? Earlier I had said no to Stanley Kubrick, although I was a great fan of his work. Stanley and I were both Bronx boys, I thought *The Killing* and *Paths of Glory* were fresh, original, and provocative films, and I was flattered that he flew me out to Los Angeles to talk about writing a movie for him. It was to be on the bomb, and he was going to call it *Dr. Strangelove.* But it became clear after a couple of meetings that Stanley wanted me to write *his* movie on the threat of nuclear annihilation, not mine, and Stanley's humor veered more toward *Mad* magazine. I thought I was the wrong writer for Stanley and told him so. He ended up with Terry Southern, and the rest, as we say, is history (except Terry would have said it better). *Dr. Strangelove,* of course, turned out to be a masterpiece, one of the bravest political statements in the history of American film. And I didn't write it.

There were so many things I didn't write. I didn't write a Broadway show for Mike Nichols and Steve Sondheim. Paul Sills had staged my cartoons at Second City in Chicago, and Mike had flown out to see the show. Mike was about to launch his career as a theater director and, as luck would have it, my show—or rather his spin on the Second City version of *The Explainers*—was to be his first tryout in the States. I had not been as happy as I expected to be to see my cartoons onstage. They looked uncomfortable. They looked as if they knew they belonged on paper. They felt out of place, and who did I think I was kidding? Mike had come to Chicago to see the Sills production and wanted to bring it to New York. But, in the undying tradition of show business, he intended to change most of it. Fine with me.

Mike was the smartest man in theater I knew, and although he was just starting out on a career as director, I had enormous confidence in him. Mike and Elaine as an act were so in tune with my work that I couldn't think of anyone better suited to do for me onstage what he and Elaine had done together.

Nichols's plan for the show was to get rid of the dramatized *Voice* strips and center the evening on three long pieces: *George's Moon*, adapted from a thirty-page cartoon monologue featuring Paul Sand; *Crawling Arnold,* my first play, a one-acter that I had written for the Chicago production that Paul Sills had rejected but Mike admired; and a musicalized version of my cartoon narrative *Passionella*. Mike thought he would ask Stephen Sondheim to write some songs for it.

The evening was to be produced by the low-key, soft-spoken Lewis Allen. He had found us a summer stock theater in the cow country of New Jersey, the Hunterdon Hills Playhouse. One look and I was in heaven. It was right out of Mickey and Judy renting a barn and putting on a show.

Now, this was Nichols before he was a great director, and this was Sondheim before he was a legend. And this was me, overwhelmed nonetheless by the two of them. They brought so much to the table that I, who had brought the table, began to feel that it was too flimsy a foundation to bear the weight of these two emerging stars.

Working with Mike, watching him instruct, joke, and seduce actors into performance, watching him run scenes that I thought I knew and bring to them more than I remembered writing, sharing the excitement and high spirits of the work at hand (my work!) was—yes—exhilarating and—oops—demoralizing at the same time.

As the production advanced, I retreated. I didn't belong there. I was a mere cartoonist, and these two brilliant people were propping me up. I felt like Ray Bolger's Scarecrow, not capable of standing on my own two feet. As the show ascended, I collapsed. The evening had been retitled *The World of Jules Feiffer* and, in my increasingly humble estimation, the single clinker in the creative team was he who bore its name.

Sondheim had written three lovely songs, fresh, funny, touching, and original. But any music by Sondheim in the summer of 1961 was original, by virtue of the fact that his first complete Broadway show, *A Funny Thing Happened on the Way to the Forum,* was a year into the future.

Mike's production was obviously the creation of a soon-to-be-brilliant theater director, one who hadn't quite put it all together yet or figured out how to make all that incisive rehearsal time cohere into an affecting performance. But he was then (and later) a blessing to work with, examining and reexamining every scene, lightly but firmly pushing and prodding.

Eight years later, we were to collaborate on the film *Carnal Knowledge* and, ten years after that, my play *Elliot Loves.* When Mike asked me to take a look at this young actor who had made a splash in the film *Easy Rider* for the lead in *Carnal Knowledge,* I came out of the screening thinking that my director was out of his mind. What did this Jack Nicholson, with his hip Henry Fonda stance and twangy New Jersey drawl, have to do with the young Jewish misogynist who was the centerpiece of my play and screenplay? I reported my doubts back to Nichols. His response: "Trust me, he's going to be our most important actor since Brando." I trusted him.

But ten years earlier, I didn't trust *The World of Jules Feiffer.* As Nichols and Sondheim talked enthusiastically about a New York production, I had less and less to say. This was more their show than mine, and it had my name on it. I was not ready to confront the conflicting emotions and certain humiliation of putting it on. Technically this was my work, bearing my name, but I knew that if it turned out to be a hit, it would be because of them, not me—and the fame and fat checks would, very likely, destroy me.

I told Mike and Steve that I didn't want the show to go beyond New Jersey. I wanted the last performance in Hunterdon Hills to be the last performance.

Nichols and Sondheim could not have been more gracious. They understood completely whatever lie I told them about not wanting to continue. It didn't seem to faze them at all. As the world would shortly discover, they had bigger fish to fry.

As it turned out, some five years later, Mike had another shot at *Passionella,* this time as the final act in the musical *The Apple Tree* by Jerry Bock and Sheldon Harnick. The brilliant Barbara Harris, who began her career in Chicago with Second City, was cast in the lead. It was Barbara I had wanted but did not get for the Paul Sills production. She was so extraordinary a performer that had she done the show when we first put it on in New Jersey, I have no doubt that I would have buried my anxiety and happily agreed to a Broadway production, which would have been a huge hit.

And the rest is not history.

INTO EXILE

I was reliving my *Harry, the Rat* experience. By April of 1965, I had been at work on *Little Murders* (inconsistently) for a year. I had a two-hundred-page manuscript in longhand and a dozen pages of notes. And then I stopped. I didn't know how to go on. This was my second try at a novel, the second time I found myself blocked. I distrusted that term *blocked*. I didn't believe in it. I didn't think writer's block truly existed or had to exist. On the other hand, what did I know? It could be argued that I wasn't a writer.

The times I felt most strongly that I wasn't a writer seemed to coincide with the times I was trying to write a novel. Alfred Kazin repeatedly told me to go to Yaddo. Philip Roth told me the same thing. I had to have done a lot of whining for the two of them to be that anxious to get rid of me.

But I couldn't go to Yaddo. It wasn't practical. First of all, it meant leaving my family, the wife part of which was urging me to leave: go to Yaddo, go to Europe, go to the moon, just stop this godforsaken moping from room to room. If anxiety over abandoning my family was what was keeping me home, Judy told me to forget about it. She and Kate (who was a year and a half) would be better off without me. But I knew she didn't mean it. How could they function without me? Anyhow, I couldn't leave, I had much too much to do.

For example, my *Voice* strips. Of course, I did only one a week. I supposed I could work ahead—say, three or four weeks ahead, the amount of time I expected to be in exile if I agreed to go to Yaddo, that desolate, isolated gulag to which my wife and my friends wished to see me exiled.

I thought these colonies—Yaddo and MacDowell—were for foundation bums, writers who went from one hideaway to another, leaving the world behind and producing little, when they could have committed acts more socially useful, like fighting for a nuclear freeze, demonstrating against Vietnam, marching for civil rights. Instead, they wasted away in the middle of nowhere, so-called artists one never heard of. Except I had heard of one or two of them: besides Roth and Kazin, I had heard of Robert Lowell, Elizabeth Hardwick, Ned Rorem, Hortense Calisher, and Curtis Harnack, all friends, all Yaddo-ites.

But what about the New York social scene, the dinner parties at Jason and Barbara Epstein's, where Roth and I played the class clowns, the dynamic duo brought in to lighten up an evening with Auden and Spender and the Pritchetts and the Lowells? How could I shrink from my social responsibilities?

And what about my table at Elaine's? The pre-movie-star-model-and-jet-set, early-days Elaine's, where I met two or three nights a week with Arthur Kopit and Jack Gelber and Michael Arlen and David Halberstam and Jack Richardson and Bruce Jay Friedman and Willie Morris and Buzz Farber and Sandy Vanocur, the boys' club where we ate and drank and explained everything and solved everything and I, for one, was hoping to meet, and liaison with, a woman not my wife. But nothing like that ever happened. Elaine's might have been a better pickup joint if I had been gay, except my friends, if that's what they were, were straight. So we just talked. We got us out of Vietnam, we restored relations with Cuba, we solved the assassination of JFK . . . We would have been better off getting laid.

No, I was definitely not a "foundation person." I was a single, solitary individualist, proud of my singularity. I didn't need to go to camp to write, for God's sake! Not me! I could solve my problems without running away from my family, without going into hiding. Kate would be two in a few months—how could I walk out on her?

Philip and Alfred wrote me recommendations, and I applied to Yaddo with a sense of doom. Was it really anxiety over abandoning my child that heightened my ambivalence—or was it fear that my book sucked, this novel that I had not looked at in three months? Would it be *Little Murders* that I might have to abandon once I sat down and reread it at Yaddo?

The night before I left for Yaddo, Alfred and Ann gave me a farewell party, livened up with anecdotes of miracles wrought there, writers unblocked, music composed, paintings completed, failures turned into successes. Thank you very much. I really appreciated taking on the burden of every other artist's miracle cure at this hell I was about to be consigned to.

A few days before I left, I was visited by a young man, a student at Wayne State University in Detroit who had somehow got hold of my phone number and started calling a month or so earlier, introducing himself as Richard Wishnetsky, a boy lefty disillusioned with radicalism and its various idiocies, hypocrisies, and mindlessness. He was on his way to New York for Christmas break and he wanted to meet the only two critical minds he had respect for: Hannah Arendt and me.

So he told me in three or four phone calls. How could a pseudonovelist on his way to Yaddo to expose his own fraudulence resist the flattering detour of an encounter with a bookish young nutcase who name-dropped me onto an intellectual plane with Hannah Arendt?

Young Richard, when he came by, was in no way different from what I expected: tall, slim, stooped, Jewish, Afro-Jewish hair, and with a manic intensity that despite his intelligence (which he couldn't help showing off) made me want to get rid of him as soon as possible.

He talked at me for about an hour, displaying no interest in culling knowledge from the man he ranked with Hannah Arendt. He'd sought me out, it seemed, not to hear my words of wisdom but for me to be an audience for his. His nonstop monologue, a diatribe against everyone and everything, backed me into a corner, turning me away from my own politics into an advocate for the radical middle. I tried to mollify Richard with radical-middle homilies—on the one hand this, on the other hand that— none of which gave him a moment's pause.

He was the last truth teller. Everyone else was a fraud, a liar, corrupt. Left and right were both no good, no difference between them. It was an exhausting indictment. A compulsion to ease him out of my studio, to get him the hell out of my apartment before I too was accused, drove me to divert him off politics onto culture, movies in particular. He knew nothing about film noir, he had never seen a Bogart film. Perfect!

There happened to be a Bogart festival playing around the corner at my friend Dan Talbot's theater the New Yorker. The New Yorker was the first American theater to exhibit commercial American films as if they were art house films, and on this day it was showing a double bill of *The Maltese Falcon* and *The Big Sleep,* both starring Bogart. I took young Richard around the corner, him talking all the way, me prodding him forward. I bought him a ticket and saw him through the door into the darkened theater. He was still lecturing as I waved good-bye.

The next day he called to thank me profusely for introducing him to Bogart and film noir. Film noir, indeed. The next I heard of Richard Wishnetsky was during a break in my Yaddo stay. I was on my way back to New York in a car being driven by a friend, a fellow Yaddo-ite at work on her first novel. On the car radio, we heard a news bulletin from Detroit: in the middle of a bar mitzvah ceremony a young man had denounced the rabbi as a liar and a hypocrite, taken out a gun, and shot and killed the rabbi and himself. Richard Wishnetsky. Little murders.

YADDO

Yaddo changed my life. More so than it affected Alfred Kazin or Philip Roth, who had encouraged me to go. Had Philip and Alfred never gone to Yaddo, their work would have continued as before, as it did after, Alfred writing literary essays and books, Philip writing Rothian novels. They worked faster and better at Yaddo, no distractions, but the nature of their work had been settled years before.

But if I had not gone to Yaddo in February of 1966, I rather doubt that I would ever have written a play. I might have known how to write a play—I had already shown an inclination with my one-acter, *Crawling Arnold*—but not for a moment do I think I would have achieved the discipline or the self-confidence or the unrelenting obsessiveness that came to me in a rush and with a shock of great surprise that was Yaddo's personal gift. In the fierce February cold I taught myself hard lessons as I lived in a charmless room in monastic isolation. Here I had no family to look after; *I* was looked after. I was treated as if my work was the first priority, the only priority, while at home it seemed as if it was at the bottom of the list of things I had to do for the day.

Yaddo was daunting in winter, no vegetation to soften the effect of the sentinel-like, magisterial mansion, gabled, colonnaded, and porticoed up the kazoo, a cross between Scarlett O'Hara's Tara and Charles Foster Kane's Xanadu. High-contrast grandeur holding court outside Saratoga Springs, next door to the legendary racetrack where the rich played in summer without a clue or care as to who we were. Yaddo, with its mansion and its other buildings—West House and East House, the music studio, and three or four barns for painters—was a country of its own, this institution founded by the Trask family early in the twentieth century and run since the 1920s by Elizabeth Ames, an aging, exceedingly genteel lady lioness, grand marshal of the estate, attentive warden of the inmates, our keeper, protector, and mother superior.

Elizabeth was small and gray and noticeably of another time, a character out of Willa Cather or Edith Wharton. I had been warned about her before I arrived. She could be tough, eagle-eyed, critical of how you kept your room, so look to your housekeeping. Writers were scared of her; she could be intimidating.

Jeez! These writers could not ever have been in the army. I found Elizabeth to be a pussycat—caring, sensitive to one's needs (spoken or unspoken), ever watchful over her clients, her children. She babied me. And oh, how I needed babying! I needed a mother to tuck me into bed at night, kiss me on the forehead, assure me that however hard the day went I was doing so much better than anyone could have anticipated. I needed coddling, and I was coddled. I needed the movie-style mothering that Rhoda was never much good at—Jane Darwell in *The Grapes of Wrath,* Mary Astor in *Meet Me in St. Louis,* they were good at it. I needed Mary Astor as my mother, kind, soothing, compassionate, uncritically understanding . . . Elizabeth Ames was Mary Astor, my MGM dream come true.

My room in East House was unappealing in so many ways, especially in the way it resembled an army barracks. It was a large, unadorned space on the ground floor, with a desk, two chairs, and a single bed, more a cot than a bed. Drab walls, drab wooden floor, drab furnishings, a sink in the corner, the toilet and icy cold shower across the hall. If you let the shower run for fifteen minutes, it got a little warmer, not that much. Nonetheless, I had no complaints. I was grateful.

I was grateful for everything. After my first disastrous day, if Elizabeth had asked me to camp out in a tent on the nearby frozen lakes, I would have been grateful.

My first morning at Yaddo: After a communal breakfast with the other guests (only eight of us in February), I stretched out on the bed in my room and took out the *Little Murders* manuscript. I had not read it in months. A numbing awareness, first distant and then dismal, that I was going down in flames. The grim revelation of why I had stopped work on this so-called novel. It was hopeless. It was shit. It was unsalvageable. Two years of time and effort that could have been better spent on anything else—parenting, partying . . . A complete waste, a washout, only one word to describe it: shit.

I walked to town. Now what? Saratoga, the town, was a mile away, not an easy walk in February with snow and ice patches everywhere on the road. I didn't have a car nor could I drive a car, but I had a need—to escape that room in which I was supposed to write my novel. I had a destination in mind, and I found it on Main Street, short of life and business in the windless but numbingly cold freeze: a liquor store. I bought a pint of Scotch, fit it into the pocket of my duffle coat, and walked back to my room. Now what?

It was only two days since the Kazins had thrown me a finishing-my-novel party. It would be pathetically defeatist for me to turn tail and go home. How could I return after Alfred Kazin, this leading light of the literary-critical establishment, had blessed me with his high expectations and sent me off? Running home was out of the question.

Unless I *sneaked* home. What if I didn't tell anyone, hid out in our apartment on Riverside Drive, locked in my bunker waiting for Alfred, ten years my senior, to die of old age? Buried alive, I could send out for meals. Judy, then Katie, when she's older, can leave them by the door of my studio. One or the other knocks—that's the signal—then leaves. But I ignore the knock, all knocks. Now is not the time to eat. Now is the time to figure out my next move. Change my name. Grow a beard. Drink my Scotch.

I skipped dinner that first night of my first day at Yaddo. I drained my Scotch in passive anticipation of sought-after oblivion. I stared out the window. Nothing to see. No one to look at. No one to look at me. I had self-erased. An empty writer in an empty room. I concentrated on the Scotch until it was time to fall unconscious, which I did with gratitude.

I woke before dawn with one thought in mind: "I am not that bad." I couldn't be. I might not be a novelist, but I was not stupid. I was too smart and too practical to waste two years of my life on the kind of shit I had wasted two years of my life on. There must be a reason, some good sense that I could find in this.

I dug out the original notes I had jotted down when I first had the idea for the novel. I hadn't looked at them since I began the book. It was a jolt—*oh, yeah!*—as if I had never seen them before: America on the brink of a nervous breakdown (like me, right now), the country coming unglued (like me, right now), acts of random violence breaking out in response to this climate of unacknowledged chaos. (If I wasn't so chicken, I might be close to that point.) Alfred, a photographer who believes in nothing; Patsy, his Doris Day–like savior, who is the spirit of go-getterism. Alfred believes life is shit. (Like my novel.) Accordingly, he takes pictures of shit. It is his single subject matter. So graphic, fanciful, and imaginative are his depictions of shit that he wins awards, gets a gallery exhibition, gets a *Vogue* magazine spread. This completely validates his nihilism.

Patsy is the embodiment of the American spirit, of JFK and his famous phrase "We can do *bettah*." She believes Alfred can do bettah. She will convert him. And she does. She convinces him that she is right and he is wrong, that he must fight the odds, reject the metaphor he has lived by. No, she declares, life is not shit, life is tough, but it can be beautiful—and under her guidance, it will be beautiful. For both of them.

She sells him on her rose-tinted vision. And as Alfred is ready to follow her anywhere, as they embrace to seal the bargain, a sniper from across the street gets off a shot and blows Patsy's head off. And the sixties begin.

I finished reading my notes with growing excitement. I thought, "Hey, this is good stuff! Somebody should write this!"

I had about run out of options. Okay. Think. What could be done to save this terrific idea that I had so badly screwed up? *Little Murders* was not a novel, I had proved that. It wasn't a comic strip either, or what we now call a graphic novel. It needed a more direct form, one with a sense of immediacy, confrontation . . . It didn't take much more thinking before *Little Murders* announced itself. It was a play. Whether I liked it or not. And I wasn't sure I liked it at all.

I had given up on *The World of Jules Feiffer* with Nichols and Sondheim because I concluded that dramatized cartoons did not constitute real theater. But *Little Murders* cried out that it was true theater. And that I could write it around the themes that obsessed me. And with determination and a little luck, it might be a good play.

Of course, it wouldn't run. I was a theater lover, but the theater I loved was more challenging than the plays that became hits on Broadway. I liked plays that upset me, made me think, drove me out of the theater in confusion, sometimes in anger. I liked plays that I didn't necessarily understand when I left the theater, that both pissed me off and intrigued me. Plays like *Marat/Sade* or *Ulysses in Nighttown*. If I liked a play, really liked it, it usually closed quickly. If I disliked a play enough to walk out on it after the first act, you could be sure it would win either a Tony or a Pulitzer Prize.

I understood, as I sat in my cold cell of a room, that if I actually managed to write a play that said what I wanted it to, the play of my notes that touched on the undiscussed breakdown of authority in post-assassination America—that play, by its very nature, would close in a week.

To go forward with a flop of such certainty would be an act of pure masochism. But I couldn't pack up and go home and have my friends laugh at me. Better to close in a week.

I sat down at my desk to start the first act and within an hour was having the time of my life. Within two hours, I knew that I was a playwright, that whatever its fate, this work was so much fun that it was worth any clobbering the critics were bound to hand me.

The notion of a critical clobbering began to interest me rather than daunt me. If I was going to get busted for this play, then let me outrage the critics in ways that would really get them upset. I had been lamenting for some months that my cartoons had become too popular, too readily accessible. I wanted to use theater to clear up the confusion about my subversive content. What I would demand of this play that I now passionately embarked upon was attention, controversy, and a famous failure.

The first scene opened with a conventionally wacky American family, Patsy's family. She was bringing her new boyfriend home for dinner to meet the folks. She has an amiable, ditsy Broadway mother, she has a long-suffering, ineffectual father, she has an adoring, irritating kid brother of confused sexual identity.

Into this family gathering, Patsy brings Alfred, the ultimate nihilist, a shock to their system and to the audience's, with his aggressive passivity and his choice of photographic subject matter.

There is a tradition in theater, going back to pre–World War I days, of outlaws, rebels, bad boys and girls, malcontents coming onstage, upsetting the apple cart, saying out loud what one might think but never express in public, throwing the other characters into an uproar, which amuses and titillates the audience because it knows that no matter how disastrous things may be at the end of the first act, all will be resolved happily by the end of the play.

The malcontent will come to his or her senses or get his or her come-uppance, shown up as either fool or knave. The audience will have been treated to the theater of the disposable rebel, a character who shocks just short of offending and is meted out the appropriate bourgeois punishment, that of being driven off stage in disgrace or selling out his principles and winning the forgiveness and applause of the audience.

This was the formula I wanted audiences to think I was foisting on them. And it seemed to be the play that I was actually writing, until at the end of act 2 in this three-act play, when I set up the audience for a traditional happy ending: Alfred surrenders his nihilist principles to his ever-hopeful wife. Happy ending. Not quite. Moments later Patsy is shot and killed by a sniper from a rooftop across the street. The traditional happy ending turns horrific, unpredictable, chaotic—like the times we lived in.

The play was writing itself. I began early in the morning and scribbled nonstop, page after page on legal-size yellow pads. Speech after speech, scene after scene. It was almost as if I knew what I was doing. My scenes had a shape, a thrust, a direction, whatever one calls it, whatever the technical term is for writing a scene—of which I was totally ignorant because I had never intended to write a scene. I didn't read a how-to book on writing plays, I just wrote my play as if I were in the audience watching someone else's. My education, to the extent that I had any, came from my years of theatergoing, my experience in knowing when a scene was going well, when it was building right, when it let you down, when it paid off, and when it didn't. It was as if every ticket to every show I'd bought were a form of matriculation. I worked till two or three in the morning, then up again at six. I was backing into theater as I had backed into so many other things.

The second I brought Marjorie, Patsy's mother, onstage, wheeling in the living room set for act 1 against a mad cacophony of city noises, car horns, police and ambulance sirens, construction hammers, a smog of city soot filling the air, intermittent power blackouts sending the stage into unexplained darkness—as soon as I entered the chaos of the civilization I had described in my notes, I felt a discipline and structured approach to work that was entirely unfamiliar, like waking up with a knowledge of calculus.

Broadway plays still had three acts in those days, and after I finished act 1 and knew I was on to something, I began writing reviews in my head. And what I remembered of reviews was that often, too often, the critics would tell me that while acts 1 and 2 showed great talent and excitement, there was a serious falling off of energy and inventiveness in act 3. Plays that were doing great for two acts, over and over again, seemed to come up with an act 3 problem.

I decided that the way to avoid an act 3 problem was to write the third act out of order. Instead of writing it after act 2, now that I had act 1 tucked away and more or less understood where I was going, perhaps I could avoid this problem—the falling off of act 3 that critics described—by skipping past act 2 and going on to the end of the play, as it were, with a full head of steam, at the height of my powers.

I wrote my third act, the end of my play, in three days. Now all it needed was a middle. I was in a state of dithering euphoria. The high point of act 2 was to be an emotional confrontation between Alfred and Patsy, a knockdown, drag-out fight inspired by the Biff and Willy confrontation in *Death of a Salesman,* a scene I carried with me always, a scene in which two struggling antagonists stumble upon a devastating truth. I was out to write my equivalent of this Biff/Willy scene and unearth my own truth, to grab the audience by the throat and shake, rattle, and roil them.

I finished the scene a little after midnight, exhausted but pleased. I read it over twice. It worked. I went to sleep, woke at 4:00 a.m., hopped out of bed, turned on the desk lamp, and reread the scene: it didn't work. I went back to sleep, excited. In the morning, before breakfast, I'd take another shot at it. Before and after breakfast, I did revisions on the scene. It was closer but still not right. I walked through Yaddo's piney woods, around the three small lakes frozen solid with ice. I, too, was frozen solid but didn't mind. I was happy to have a scene to revise in the first play I was writing. Yes. I was truly a playwright, not a single doubt in my mind.

Two years of writing *Harry, the Rat* and a year and a half struggling with *Little Murders,* the novel, and never once did I feel the sense of command that I now felt as a neophyte playwright. I had no doubt that my play would get written (as I continually doubted with my novels). I had no doubt that it would be good. And, oh yes, it would be panned; it would be *that* good. It didn't seem to matter to me. Reviews were beside the point. Acceptance was important to me but in some ways it, too, was beside the point.

After ten years at the *Voice,* I was beginning to feel that perhaps I was getting too much acceptance. What did it say about these cartoons that I thought were so challenging that they no longer raised much controversy? My unchallenged readers looked forward to my new strip each week as if preparing to be braced by a dry martini. Yes, that's how challenging I had become. I was cocktail chatter.

Gide or someone made a comment dear to my heart: "Do not understand me too quickly." *Little Murders* was designed to correct my having been understood too quickly.

I finished my walk around the Yaddo lakes, returned to my chilly cell, and rewrote the Alfred/Patsy confrontation scene for the fourth time, delighted to have one more chance to fix it.

I felt, as I feel in my best writing moments, as if I were a private eye on the trail, following leads, dismissing clues that were red herrings, going off now and again in the wrong direction and coming back to start all over again. I sniffed patiently away at the case, knowing the solution waited at the end of some trail that I would in my own way and at my own pace surely get to.

I had a rough first draft at the end of two weeks. I had never worked that hard or that happily in my life. I had always worked in short spurts, which was fine for six-to-nine-panel cartoons, but not when I was committed to a longer work. Yaddo, in its distance from New York, in its frigid and unrelenting isolation, in its embracing, sustaining aura (overseen by Elizabeth Ames), taught me, as if I were a child learning to walk, how to organize, how to structure work habits. Structure was foreign to me up till now; so were work habits. Obsession drove me. Once on the trail, nothing could slow me down.

I took a break, drove back to New York with my friend Nina Schneider. It was in Nina's car that I heard over the radio about the bar mitzvah murder and suicide committed by my young visitor, Richard Wishnetsky. Of course, I was horrified, but close on the heels of my horror came pinpricks of titillation. I was on to something.

I read the entire play to Judy on my first night home. Her response was, "I love it, but I don't think the third act works."

The next night, we had dinner with the Kazins and came back to our apartment for a nightcap. Alfred lounged on the couch and sipped at a Scotch. He said, "Read me your play." I had my own Scotch and sat in an armchair facing him. I said, "Alfred, I'm not a reader, and it's almost midnight." Alfred said, "Feiffer, I got you into Yaddo. Read me your play."

I went down the hall, past Kate's room, where she had long been asleep, into my studio. I retrieved the legal-size yellow pads that constituted the first draft. I returned to the living room and, very nervous indeed, began to read *Little Murders*. I was tired, I was scared, I read in a self-conscious monotone. Judy and Ann were very attentive, but Alfred was asleep in five minutes.

WHAT I DID ON MY SUMMER VACATION

Robert Brustein wanted *Little Murders* for his theater at the Yale Rep. Brustein, the theater critic for the *New Republic* and the newly appointed dean of the Yale School of Drama, was an old friend. It was Bob and his wife, Norma, who, in the late spring of 1966, introduced Judy and me to Martha's Vineyard. They invited us for a weekend, along with Philip Roth and his girlfriend, Ann Mudge. Getting to the Vineyard in those years was a nuisance, especially for a New York boy who didn't drive and had no affinity for car culture. The Brusteins drove us up from New Haven. The drive took five hours or more, at the end of which we boarded a ferry that took another forty-five minutes. By that time I had settled into an early judgment that any place that hard to get to wasn't worth it. And then we got off the ferry and it was love at first sight.

From the early fifties, I had been spending my summers on Fire Island, a long strip of sandbar particularly convenient to New Yorkers on vacation who didn't drive or didn't want to. I fit both categories, but Fire Island had its shortcomings. It was jammed, particularly on weekends, because of its easy access to the city. You had to love the ocean because that and the beach were its only attractions. I was scared of the ocean. The ocean had surf, sometimes pounding. It could slap you around, knock you into the ground. Surf had no respect for me or my family or my future. We understood each other very well, the surf and I. Surf was out to sweep me out to sea and drown me.

I was a bad swimmer, hardly a swimmer at all, twenty-five strokes and I moved a couple of feet. While I thought I was swimming, an observer would think I was standing up in the water, waving my arms.

But the Vineyard had an ocean, too, so it wasn't my dread of water that made me leave Fire Island, it was my dread of the volleyball game. Unathletic in the extreme, I nonetheless enjoyed taking part in the Ocean Beach Sunday morning volleyball games. For years they were considered not a contest but a way for both sexes to get together on weekend mornings, to meet, get acquainted, have fun. Winning was not the point, it was not competitive. It was a game for diving at the ball, missing it, and falling on your face in the sand. We inept players thought of that as a good time.

Then in the summer of '65, the good times stopped. There I was on a fine Sunday morning, playing my usual sloppy game, and I noticed something different. I was being yelled at. I was being ordered to shape up. Wall Street and Madison Avenue had discovered literary, showbiz Ocean Beach, the scene of our game. They had come to expel soft-bodied weak-kneed fun for hard-bodied kick-ass fun. Laughter was replaced by grimaces and gritted teeth.

The aim now, at all costs, was to win. *Win!* This new volleyball with its new players was a contest to crush the opposition, to incorporate the aggression and hostility of the marketplace, the worst of Madison Avenue and Wall Street pugnaciousness. The spirit of the city, which I'd left to escape, had advanced on the beach in full fury. "That was an easy shot! What the hell is wrong with you?!" Eyes bulging in rage. Fun on Sunday mornings had turned into another day at the office.

I was out of there. I said to Judy, "Either we find another place to go to next summer or we stay in New York."

As has happened so often in my life, at exactly the moment we were out of ideas for where we could spend our summer vacation, the invitation came from Bob and Norma. In the spring of the following year, 1966, we found ourselves backing into the Vineyard. When we arrived, what we found was a continent scaled to the size of an island. Within a few minutes, one traveled from Hampton beachiness to Connecticut countryside to upstate New York farmland. Romantic lakes and ponds inland, and on the ocean side, vibrant red-and-orange-and-purple clay cliffs supplementing the eye-popping grandeur of the Atlantic Ocean.

Miles of enchantment with an older crowd to appreciate it than one found on Fire Island. More literary, more elusive when it came to competitiveness, wit displayed in place of muscle. Was this ever my turf! Clusters of Plimpton-like parties for the summer residents. Bill and Rose Styron next door to Lillian Hellman next door to John and Barbara Hersey next door to the Rahvs, a few doors away from Kingman Brewster, then president of Yale, up the street from Albert and Frances Hackett, who not only wrote *The Diary of Anne Frank* for Broadway but, far more impressive to me, wrote the first *Thin Man* movie.

This was the environment that Bob and Norma Brustein invited us into, the hideaway of the fortunate few, writers, artists, academics who could take two months off in the summer, not just weekends. First we rented, then we bought. And forty years later, I remain there, in my second marriage, three generations of children grown to womanhood on Vineyard beaches. Beatific summers followed by deadline summers, interspersed with political summers and even one Vietnam summer.

In 1967, at a Styron party for Robert Kennedy, I was introduced to Lyndon Johnson's undersecretary of state, Nicholas deB. Katzenbach, who shook my hand warmly, beamed at me, and told me what a great fan of mine he was.

I was at a stage of life where I was unable to respond to flattery with a simple "Thank you." So I replied to Katzenbach, "You can't be a fan of mine. I'm against everything you stand for."

Katzenbach, a balding, pleasant-looking man, was clearly taken by surprise. "What do you mean?"

"How can you be in an administration that's fighting this war in Vietnam and say you are a fan of mine?"

Katzenbach, instead of walking off, stuck around to insist that he was as opposed to Vietnam as I was. And after a couple of minutes' conversation, accompanied by a drink or two, he had me convinced that he was a fellow dove, working from the inside, where he could get so much more done. Katzenbach, I was assured by Katzenbach, was doing all in his power to end this carnage.

The next morning I was on the phone to Brustein, Philip Roth, and John Marquand, relaying the hot news that Nick Katzenbach was one of us. Or could be. If we got a group together one weekend when my new friend Nick took time off from the war, maybe, just maybe, we could convince him what a great move toward peace it would be if he resigned from the government as a matter of conscience. It seemed to me that this was possible. Katzenbach had become famous in the Kennedy Justice Department as a civil rights advocate, a man of conscience. Why not Vietnam?

If we found a soft spot in Katzenbach, if we talked him into leaving the government, denouncing the war that he hated as much as I did (he told me so himself), who knew who else might resign? A covey of doves hiding out in the State Department? In the Pentagon? The Feiffer Domino Theory of Resignations.

In the midst of feverish phone calls and late-night conspiring, I happened to turn on the TV one morning, no more than a week after meeting Nick, and—my God! there he was, standing before Senator William Fulbright's Senate Foreign Relations Committee, raising his hand to take the oath. My new pal, Nicholas deB. Katzenbach, testifying nauseatingly in support of the Tonkin Gulf Resolution, which gave total war powers to the administration, a full-scale endorsement of open-ended escalation. Say it ain't so, Nick!

Talk about a betrayal of friendship. My buddy Nick, whom I was going to get to quit because he hated the war, appearing as the government's personal advocate for the war's escalation.

What to do? I called a meeting. Some of us (me) wanted to picket Nick's Vineyard home. Secretary of Defense McNamara also had a summer home on the island. I suggested that we picket him too. They can't screw around with me!

Except for myself and one or two others, the idea of picketing McNamara and Katzenbach, in shorts and flip-flops, in front of their summer houses drew more wisecracks than support.

We came to the not-surprising decision that, as writers, our best form of protest was a full-page ad in the *Vineyard Gazette,* the island's *New York Times*–like newspaper. Roth volunteered to write a first draft. It was gussied up by Brustein, with a final edit by John Marquand. John drew on his better-informed prep school sensibility to retrofit the language into a coded assault certain to offend all those in the Pentagon or State who had attended Ivy League schools—that is, the entire crew.

The ad caused a rift in the liberal island community. Some, like King-man Brewster, the president of Yale, argued that the Vineyard was a sanc-tuary. Problems and differences should be deferred as one boarded the ferry at Wood's Hole. We, the ad's organizers, had violated basic Vineyard rules and ethics. Our act was nearly as offensive as the war itself.

Among the signers of the ad—an open letter to Katzenbach—the name that created the biggest stir was that of the venerable and widely respected editor and publisher of the *Vineyard Gazette,* Henry Beetle Hough, a beloved nineteenth-centuryish Vineyard elder of dignity and rec-titude who, when first approached about placing the ad, instead of turning it down, as we feared, asked deferentially, "Would you very much mind if I added my name?"

We created our share of noise, stories in the *Times,* the *Washington Post, Time,* and *Newsweek.* Predictably the ad was dismissed as "frivolous" and "unserious." Among those Vineyarders appalled at our behavior, our action was branded "that *Village Voice* ad," although I had not written a word of it.

FIRST MISTAKE

The Feiffers and the Brusteins had been friends since the late fifties. Norma Brustein was blond, sexy, and chatty. She spoke in the high-pitched squeal of a showgirl a few years out of the chorus. She reminded me of Judy Holliday in *Born Yesterday*. Norma's sexiness and near parody of a voice hid the fact that she was smart, quick-witted, and perceptive, and had a great sense of humor, meaning she laughed at my jokes.

She and Bob were a theatrical-looking couple. He was tall and handsome and spoke in an oracular radio-actor's baritone, which he employed with a friendly but forceful style as he commented on contemporary theater, culture, and politics.

Being a humorist and satirist, I took a lighter, funnier tone, even when I agreed with Bob. But Bob was a critic and an academic. He spoke with a solemnity that resonated gloom. One came away from a conversation with him thinking, "It's over! We are all going to die!" But because of the high intellectual content invoked in describing our ineluctable downward spiral, one felt better informed, even cheery about it.

The doom I wrote into *Little Murders* played very well into Brustein's vision. This was going to be a cinch, a production at the Yale Rep, possibly with Walter Matthau playing Alfred, the lead (he demurred, didn't understand a word of the play). Possibly Mike Nichols directing (he was sent the play, didn't respond, and I didn't speak to him for two years). Okay, we would do our time at Yale, get the necessary attention, build momentum, then move into a Broadway or off-Broadway house. Sounded like a plan.

At least, that was my view of the production. Brustein had another. He was, somewhat sniffily, I thought, opposed to using the Yale Rep as a tryout house for Broadway. He had no intention of allowing his nonprofit theater to become a feeder house for commercial theater.

Bob was not commercial. Nor was I, God knows. I was as opposed to commercial theater as he was. But what did that have to do with my first play, subversive as hell, having the chance to open in a Broadway house and, possibly, make it as a hit?

It wasn't likely. The odds were against it. But as I explained to Brustein after a good deal of pained and strained discussion, I didn't write *Little Murders* to have it run for six weeks in New Haven. New York was where I wanted it to be. On Broadway in front of the audience it was about. Brustein, along with his academic loftiness, has an inherent sweetness. He expressed with resonant gravity his disappointment in what he was convinced was this dumb move I was about to make. Nonetheless, he wished me luck. Our friendship was not affected. The play moved on, and as I had once predicted (but forgot), it opened and closed on Broadway in a week.

LITTLE MURDERS

A Comedy

by

JULES FEIFFER

1st draft
2-66

Robert Lantz
Literary Agency
111 West 57th Street
New York, N.Y. 10019
PLaza 7-5076

ACT I

No curtain. The stage is bare.
(For about 15 minutes before the start of the play there has been, at 7-minute intervals, the sound of a helicopter. It hovers about for a minute, and then fades.)

MARJORIE
(Offstage)
Oh My Good Heavens!
(Rushes on, a small, energetic woman in her fifties. SHE carries a shopping bag)
Kenny! Are you here? Ken-nee!
(Out of breath, puts bag on floor, holds chest)
That boy is never here when I --

(Offstage sound of toilet flush. KENNY enters, tucking shirt in pants, reading McCalls. A listless young man in his early twenties)

You picked a fine time to read, young man.

KENNY
(Oblivious. Reading)
In a minute, Mom.

MARJORIE
(Shakes head, rushes off)
Don't dawdle, Kenny. I need your help!
(Rushes on sliding long dinner table)
They'll be here any minute, Kenny!
(Rushes off L. Rushes on R. pushing row of 5 chairs. Rushes off R., rushes on L. sliding end table with a lit lamp standing on it. Rushes off L. Rushes on R. with 2nd end table, lit lamp. Rushes off R. Rushes on L. pushing couch to which is attached the living and dining room back wall, complete with hung pictures and a large draped window out of which we see the many lit windows of the apartment building across the street.

FLOP

Elliott Gould flew up to the Vineyard to talk to me about playing Alfred. Alexander H. Cohen, the producer, had suggested Elliott, whom I had seen in Jerome Weidman's Broadway musical *I Can Get It for You Wholesale.*

That was the show that, according to legend, was stolen by Barbra Streisand. But not the night I saw it. I liked Elliott, I didn't like Barbra. He was big and goofy-looking and had a relaxed, shambling charm. His naturalness onstage instantly engaged me. On the other hand, Streisand's over-the-top salesmanship grated on me.

The night *Little Murders* opened on Broadway, by which time Barbra Streisand had become *Barbra,* she showed up wearing a foot-high pillbox hat, perhaps to correct anyone who might want to look at her husband onstage instead of the real star. Her high hat blocked the view of whoever was sitting behind her. Too bad it wasn't a critic.

I got lost on my way to pick up Elliott at Katama airport, the small private airfield just outside of Edgartown on the Vineyard. By this time I had a driver's license, but it didn't mean I could drive well or find my way around in a car. To this day I am capable of getting lost when I leave my driveway, so you'd think I'd have taken precautions to be on time when I was to pick up an actor who was coming all the way from New York to talk to me about starring in my first play. You'd think I'd have taken pains to get to the airport early instead of fifteen minutes late. When I drove up, Elliott was perched on a wooden fence that bordered the airport, the kind of fence that pens in horses. Elliott, in jeans and a light suede jacket, sitting on the top slat in the manner of an ordinary guy. Who guessed that in a couple of years he would be a big movie star?

I drove him to our rented house in Chilmark, just off the ocean, where we spent the rest of the day into the evening talking about our production because, by then, both of us took for granted that the part was his.

Recently in a downtown new-glitz restaurant, I ran into David Steinberg, the director and comedian who, as a young actor, originated the role of Kenny, the kid brother in *Little Murders*. A booth away, I was hailed by Oliver Platt, the actor who was one of the stars of *Elliot Loves,* the play that drove me out of the theater for ten years, swearing that I would never return. Both plays, twenty-three years apart, had scripts that pleased me and casts I admired. Both were critical flops. One of them deserved to be, the other not. The one that deserved to be was *Little Murders.*

With my lack of experience, I didn't realize that *Little Murders* required a director with the ingenuity to figure out how to stage a piece that required something apart from a conventional Broadway approach. Someone like Mike Nichols or Alan Arkin, with a background in improvisation. But Mike didn't like the play, and Alan was busy becoming a movie star, not yet ready to direct. (Two years later he would do a stunning revival of *Little Murders* off-Broadway.) I had offered the play to Gene Saks, a wonderful actor who had taken up directing Neil Simon comedies. Gene was as confused by the play as Walter Matthau.

I had knowingly written a play not meant for the usual Broadway presentation, then, perversely, gone after a commercial comedy director who had the good sense to turn me down. So I switched my sights to regional theater, hoping for—I don't know what—something experimental. Directors are groomed for the theater that exists at the moment, and I was not writing for that theater. I was writing for a theater that was informed by improvisational cabaret and absurdism. Directors trained in putting on more conventional comedies—the works of F. Hugh Herbert or Norman Krasna or the best of them all, Neil Simon—were confounded by my script. It was chaotic, scattershot, three acts different in tone from one another, not by any definition a well-made play as the species was defined. If I'd known how to write a well-made play, I might have tried my hand at it. As it was, I just put down everything that came to mind: fast-breaking scenes, long set-piece monologues, killing off my heroine, the only likable person on stage, in the middle of the play. I can well imagine Broadway directors reading this and thinking, "What the fuck?"

I had found my regional theater director in Philadelphia, where he had just had great success with an absurdist comedy by Saul Bellow. I chose a director (whose name I will keep to myself) who was brilliant in his analysis of the play, perceptive about our goals, articulate and nuanced in expressing himself, exuberant in regard to the scope, promise, and ambition of the production. He was also genial, charming, intelligent—and he didn't have a clue as to how to direct *Little Murders*. With all his gung-ho attitude and love for the script, he was completely flummoxed. He blocked a scene only to change the blocking the next day and the day after that and the day after that. Scenes did not grow; they were changed, and changed again. Weeks into rehearsal, the actors did not know where they were going onstage or why. All the director's good ideas were topped the next day by better ones. He was every bit as excited about today's ideas as he was about yesterday's and the ones he'd had the day before.

Actors approached me with suggestions for line changes, which a stronger director would not have tolerated. In the spirit of collaboration, he gave in to them. So did I. If an actor said he couldn't do a certain speech, I rewrote it, subverting my cadences for his or hers. What the actors seemed to have most trouble with were my quick shifts within the body of a scene, so I tried to smooth out the scenes, tamp them down. To please the performers, I sold out the play.

This is what one did in collaboration, I thought. I was a cartoonist, spent my entire career working alone. What did I know from collaboration? I had no experience in team sports or playing with others. My one experience in playing with others was within my family, where I hid my thoughts and modified my behavior to make for smoother sailing. That may have gotten me through a family alive, but shucking off the authority of a playwright in order to revert to the role of middle child was not my best move.

We opened at the Wilbur Theater in Boston to bad reviews, which were not entirely deserved. The critics were right to be unhappy with the production, but they were even less happy with what the play had to say.

Critics are uncomfortable with the unfamiliar, particularly when it comes to ideas. They prefer not to deal with ideas in a play. They are likely to say, "This is a play that *purports* to be about ideas, but it is merely pretentious." *Little Murders*, however, was so little regarded in Boston that it wasn't even labeled "pretentious."

Critics mean little to a play, except life and death. The audience that I cared about—or that portion who didn't walk out as soon as they heard the word *shit* for the first time in a theater—responded with enthusiasm. This Boston tryout was way too slow, way too long, deeply in need of revisions and cuts and so much else—and even so, a sizable percentage of the audiences understood that for the first time they were seeing a brash, satiric comment on the post-JFK sixties. And this excited them in the way my early *Voice* cartoons excited readers. At long last, they were seeing a play that was trying to address what we all felt had gone wrong but almost no one was talking about.

I had been told many times that real theater was not at all as it was portrayed in movies. But after the Boston tryout of *Little Murders,* I began to look on all those backstage musicals I'd seen over the years as documentaries. Stuck in my room at the Ritz-Carlton Hotel doing late-night rewrites after every performance—elevator operators taking me up to my room, gossiping about what they'd heard about the show; a bellman with a play script he wanted me to read; down the hall Betty Comden and Adolph Green, authors of *The Band Wagon* and *Singin' in the Rain* in the midst of rehearsing their new show, *On the Twentieth Century*. Al Capp called and wanted me to appear on his local TV talk show.

I said no to Al. I hadn't looked at a newspaper in about a month. I didn't want to go unprepared into a political debate with Al, who had moved to the right since his liberal youth and was presently a passionate supporter of the war and a hyperbolic critic of the peace movement. Besides, I had to revise the detective scene at the beginning of act 3, a parody murder mystery that went on far too long and wasn't funny. Everything was going wrong, and I was having a ball because it felt like the movies.

Locked in my room overlooking the Public Gardens, rewriting and sipping Scotch, answering phone calls I warned myself to ignore, arguing with Alex Cohen over how many *shit*s to cut without disemboweling the play even further, taking one call, then another from Al Capp's daughter, then his producer, then Al himself, who, after all, had been my hero when I was a kid, not only for *Li'l Abner* but for creating just about the best-told story strip of all, *Abbie an' Slats*. Al promised we wouldn't talk politics. "You love comics, I love comics, we'll only talk comics."

I put Al on hold for a bellman delivering a 1:00 a.m. snack. Before he would leave, he had to tell me a joke that he thought would go great in my show. I got rid of the bellman, got rid of Al by saying yes, had a great idea for the detective scene that I'd put in the next night. Then I fell into bed thinking, "I'm trapped inside a backstage musical."

The new detective scene worked, the Al Capp show didn't. I showed up and was held offstage as Al introduced me by reading a commentary off a prompter about a New York Town Hall meeting of some months back sponsored by Artists and Intellectuals Against the War in Vietnam. In Al's version, as all these anti-Americans went up to the microphones and spouted their Hate America speeches, it became too much for a poor, solitary policeman, a security guard in the back of the house. He interrupted the denunciations of our great country by singing, in top voice from the rear of the house, "God Bless America." The audience of peaceniks and anti-Americans booed. They booed this patriotic police officer, and they booed "God Bless America," can you imagine? Without skipping a beat, Al said, "And now I want to introduce my good friend, the great cartoonist Jules Feiffer."

I stood backstage in a fury, not at Al but at myself. I'd set myself up, I'd got what I deserved. I thought of walking off, out of the studio. But that would leave Al with the last word. I couldn't allow that to happen. I walked out onstage grinning stupidly, goofily shook Al's hand, and said, "Al, I was one of those anti-Americans—" Oh, my God, I had lost my voice! I had become a soprano. I could have been doing an impression of Mickey Mouse. Rage had throttled my vocal chords, no one was going to be able to hear my response to this jerk except dogs watching TV who respond to high-pitched whistles.

Gradually my voice came to its senses and I was able to confront Al with the fact that I was one of the organizers of the event he had just slandered. He chortled. "I thought you might be." He had planned this ambush from the beginning!

He and I went on to engage in a full-throated, thoroughly unpleasant exchange. I batted back one ad hominem digression after another. Al's response was to guffaw (his way of expressing aggression) and launch another pointless assault. We didn't get to talk about comics, we didn't get to plug my play. We wrangled to a draw, and I walked off at the end of my segment without saying good-bye or shaking hands.

Al and I ran into each other just one time more. A year later, flying in from a campaign trip on behalf of Eugene McCarthy in his antiwar bid for the presidency, I passed Al going in the opposite direction at LaGuardia Airport. He shouted after me as I fled, "You know your problem, Feiffer? You're a self-hating Jew!"

M y producer, Alex Cohen, had been trying to fire my director for weeks. And I wouldn't let him. Then I woke up one morning and thought, "What do I owe my loyalty to, my play or this man who's ruining it?" I called Robby Lantz, my agent, and told him to tell Alex to dump the director. Robby said, "Alex has shown the play to Elia Kazan and he's willing to come in and take over."

What?

So much of my political sensibility had been shaped by the blacklist, the warfare that took place between those who named names and those who stood up to the House Un-American Activities Committee. I liked to fantasize the day I would be called before the committee and asked if I was a Communist. And to name names. In my fantasy, I testify, "Yes, Mr. Chairman, I was a member of the Communist Party. And you, sir, were the head of my cell."

Elia Kazan was the most famous director in American theater. And now he was winning awards for his movies. I despised everything he represented. Not only had he named names before the committee, he took out a full-page ad in *Variety* and the *New York Times* in the early years of the blacklist, when his standing up against HUAC might have done something to turn the tides, and he boasted about his sellout, defending the decency and the morality in his betrayal of friends and colleagues.

I told Robby over the phone, "Kazan is what this play is all about. How could I think of letting him come in to direct it?"

Fifty years later, I have no idea what I meant by that remark. My play was not about the witch hunts or the blacklist or naming names. In 2001 I was to write that play, *A Bad Friend*. Trying to reconstruct my thoughts after all these years, the best I can come up with is that perhaps I considered even a discussion of the pros and cons of a Kazan takeover as an act of monumental hypocrisy, a sellout of the highest order. To allow near my play the weasel who aided and abetted, then promptly promoted the atmosphere of fear and demoralization in our arts and culture would make my production a mockery.

I called Alex Cohen and told him that I would rather *Little Murders* close in Boston than have Kazan come in and make it a hit (which, in any case, I doubted he'd be able to do; he was not noted for his comic flair).

My last act in Boston, after packing to fly to New York for a week of previews and then our opening, was to fire my director. Alex Cohen, who had been pushing me hardest on this, made himself unavailable for the job. No one else was willing to do it. Everyone liked the director. He was a sweet fellow, he was an enthusiast, he was brilliant, he had ruined my play. (I helped him ruin it, but I couldn't fire myself, although that might have been a possibility before all those years of therapy.)

The director and I met in my room at the Ritz-Carlton. He refused to believe I was firing him. I had to say it two, then three, then four times. The words didn't form a concept that he could understand. "What if I can't convince him," I wondered. "What if he leaves here refusing to acknowledge that he's fired?" It was a reminder to me of how he directed. Once he was fixed on an approach, it couldn't be modified, altered, or dislodged.

He stuck out his arms and started flailing his hands at me. "You're cutting off my hands. How can you cut off my hands?"

Instead of sympathy, I felt anger. He had yet to admit, he *refused* to admit, that he had screwed up, that the production was in serious trouble, that the actors were confused by his inept blocking, or that entrances and exits had become traffic jams. He couldn't see his failure. He could see only his hands flailing at me like sausages in a high wind. "You're cutting off my hands!"

"Not a moment too soon," I thought.

LITTLE WONDERS

*L*ittle Murders opened on a Tuesday in April of 1967. It closed on Saturday. In those days, the New York critics still came to review plays on opening night. Walter Kerr was there for the *Herald Tribune,* his wife, Jean, seated next to him. I knew the Kerrs through Al and Dolly Hirschfeld, and liked them, although I couldn't imagine Walter thinking well of my play. I sat a row behind and a little to the side and kept my eye on him, curious to see the effect that bad word I was introducing to Broadway would have the first time he heard it.

A third of the way into the first act, Alfred explains to Patsy's family what he does for a living. In a long, rambling monologue, he describes his career in photography and his disdain for the success he's achieved. Carol, Patsy's father, Marjorie, her mother, and Kenny, her brother, are in attendance.

MARJORIE: You must be extremely talented.
ALFRED (more to himself than to family): I got sick of it! Where the hell are standards? That's what I kept asking myself. Those people will take anything! If I gave them a picture of shit, they'd give me an award for it!

A surprised laugh from the audience.

MARJORIE: Language, young man!
ALFRED: Mm? So that's what I do now.
CAROL (hesitantly): What?
ALFRED: Take pictures of shit.

This time the laugh built and didn't stop for what seemed like twenty seconds. Walter Kerr threw back his head and let out a sustained bark.

MARJORIE: Language! Language! This is *my* table!
ALFRED: I don't mean to offend you, Mrs. Newquist. I've been
    shooting shit for a year now [big laugh], and I've already won a
    half dozen awards [smaller laugh].
MARJORIE (slowly thaws): Awards?
ALFRED: And *Harper's Bazaar* wants me to do its spring issue.

The audience went nuts, as did Walter Kerr. The laugh must have gone on for thirty seconds. It was the high point of my evening.

A week earlier the English director John Dexter had been brought in by Alex Cohen to save us. Dexter had become well known in the States for directing Peter Shaffer's plays in London and New York. He was a smart, no-nonsense, efficient craftsman. But he had only a week to get his work done, and much of that week was spent being a traffic cop. Cleaning up entrances and exits so that the actors stopped tripping over one another. There was little time to work on character, so John simply speeded up the pace of the show. Without cutting a line, he shortened the play by fifteen minutes. And as he cleaned up and paced and polished, the play I wrote (and did so much to undermine) began to emerge as what I thought it was during my euphoria at Yaddo.

By now most of the company was punch drunk, but not Elliott. He was a rock throughout the previews, solidly supportive, giving his every ounce of oddball charm and deadpan intensity to my passive, listless antihero. You couldn't take your eyes off him.

The other actors delivered wildly uneven performances. Too much had happened in Boston and beyond. They'd been told too many things by too many authorities and, to add to their confusion, we were now home in New York and their friends in the business came back after each preview to give them their notes—what they better do onstage to dissociate themselves from this turkey so their careers would not suffer.

I knew we were doomed. The lack of suspense eased my anxieties. At least I wouldn't be on tenterhooks opening night. I had told my mother that she couldn't come to the opening, that the play's language would upset and offend her. In fact, she shouldn't come to the play at all. I would write other plays that she could see. She didn't argue; she must have sensed something. That something was the prospect of watching herself portrayed onstage by Ruth White, who looked a little like her and got laughs with lines taken right out of Rhoda's mouth. She would have thought she was being held up to ridicule. She would have had a point.

Accidents happen. At our very last preview, the night before our opening, the theater was sold out. It was filled with theater people. I remember Lanford Wilson and Jon Voight, among others. And it was at this performance, for the first and last time, that the play and the production came together. The actors fed off the audience, and the audience was inside the play, onstage with the performers, rocking the house with laughs, followed immediately by intense and resonant silences. The play that night was pure and happy subversion, with the audience behaving as co-conspirators.

Seconds after the final curtain, a mob of people rushed up to congratulate me. I felt relieved and grateful to the point of tears and, at the same time, more sorry for myself than ever in a lifetime of feeling serially sorry for myself. I knew how great and compelling the performance I had just witnessed was. And I knew there was no way that this cast could repeat it the next night. And the next night was our opening.

Opening night was the disaster I expected. For most of the last act, I hid out in a bar down the block. I returned to the Broadhurst in time to see a dismayed and irritable audience leaving. I stood on the sidewalk across the street from the theater feeling like Tom Sawyer watching his own funeral. Then, an unexpected moment of uplift: Leonard Lyons, the popular Broadway gossip columnist for the *New York Post,* a dapper little man who was sweet and likable, and often as not got his stories wrong, rushed up to me, his face livid. He screamed, "How dare you use language like that on the second night of Passover?!"

My response to Leonard was to give him a bear hug. I said, "Leonard, thank you. You've rescued my evening."

I left the not-much-of-a-party at Sardi's to go upstairs to the ad agency and monitor the bad reviews filtering in, none worse than that of the *New York Times*. Herb Gardner came along as my spin doctor and bodyguard. Each time we were shown a bad review, Herb scanned it with a copy editor's eye. He never failed to find a line buried somewhere toward the bottom of the pan. "That could be a quote!" he'd announce cheerily to the demoralized few still in attendance.

Judy and I quit the death watch at about one thirty in the morning. I said that I had to go to Elaine's. The joint was locked when we stepped out of the cab at Second and Eighty-eighth Street. I saw signs of life inside the darkened interior. I knocked on the door. Elaine Kaufman came to the door and opened it. She led us inside without a word, turned on a couple of lights, went behind the bar for a bottle of champagne, and we proceeded to celebrate my first flop.

Late the next day, Sam Zolotow called. "Okay, Mr. Big Shot Cartoonist, you wrote a play that's a flop. Now what?" Sam was a theater reporter for the *New York Times*. He ran its "News of the Rialto" column. I liked Sam because he sounded exactly like the actor Sam Levene, who played Nathan Detroit in the original production of *Guys and Dolls*.

On paper, his remark sounds harsh and hostile, but he didn't mean it that way, nor did I take it that way. It was simply Broadway wise-guy banter, and I chose to go along with it. My response to him was, "Sam, I'm just going to keep bringing it back until you guys get it right."

A month later, *Little Murders* went into rehearsal in London. It was the first American play produced by the Royal Shakespeare Company. Our director, Christopher Morahan, came out of BBC TV dramas. In contrast to everything that had gone wrong on Broadway, Chris, in his dry, witty, at times self-effacing, at times Jules-effacing manner, found the key to the play, or at least the English production of it. *Little Murders* was resuscitated a mere two months after the New York critics left it for dead.

Chris Morahan went back to the original script that I had sent him, preferring it over the changes I had made to "fix" it and accommodate my Broadway cast. "Why don't we just wait for now and put in the changes as we need them?" he said at our initial meeting. As it turned out, the changes never went in. Chris gave the show a cohesiveness, a pace and vitality that it never came near having in New York. And with that, the point of the play became clear as it never had on Broadway, except for our last preview.

The English love America-bashing, particularly when an American does it on an English stage. So *Little Murders* won prizes, and this critic-bashed American was grateful. If that's all it took . . .

But there was a problem with the production, a sizable one: I wasn't allowed to use the word *shit*. In 1967 Britain still had its Lord Chamberlain's Office. This was the official censor whose mission it was to keep obscene language off the London stage. Jeremy Brooks, the literary manager of the Royal Shakespeare Company, had made an appointment for the two of us to meet with the lord chamberlain in his Downing Street headquarters to argue our case. Jeremy, friendly, charming, urbane, and a great supporter of the play, thought our chances were nonexistent. But I didn't think a lost cause was a good enough reason to give up the only chance I might ever have of going up against the lord chamberlain.

We met the great man and his aide, two cordial, spiffily dressed, exceedingly correct Englishmen. One was assigned the good-cop role, the other played the bad cop. The argument I had come up with in defense of the word *shit* was that Alfred, the nihilist, the bad boy, the cynic who believed in nothing, was the only character to use foul language in the play. This was a deliberate ploy on my part to show the audience that this otherwise attractive rebel was a representative of all the wrong, anti-authoritarian values, the values that were dragging down both British and American society. If Alfred was not permitted to say "shit," audiences might well miss my point and mistake my antihero for a hero. They might, God help us, identify with the fellow, which would be a misreading of the play and would pervert its message.

I feared (I said) that if the lord chamberlain deprived us of *shit*, he would deprive the audience of the signal that would allow them to understand the play correctly. The cultural decay that Alfred's taking pictures of shit signified might be mistaken for a healthy critique of society, which was the last thing I wanted to suggest. Take away *shit*, I said to the lord chamberlain, and you take the audience down the wrong path, from which it might never return.

As Jeremy and I left the lord chamberlain's headquarters, he looked at me in consternation. "Jules, have I completely misunderstood your play?"

I couldn't stop laughing. "Jeremy, it was an improvisation! I made the whole thing up!" I had convinced Jeremy. He shook his head, puzzled and a little pleased. "I didn't think we had a chance when we went in there. Now I think it's fifty-fifty."

We lost. However, they did allow us to substitute *dog crap* for *shit,* a word I found infinitely more vulgar. But that's the English for you—no ear for language.

The success of the play in Britain reawakened the innate snobbery of American producers. Since *Little Murders* had come up with an English seal of approval, it might be worth taking a second look at it in New York. Ted Mann and Paul Libin ran the Circle in the Square, then located on Bleecker Street, downtown in the Village. They presented the play to Alan Arkin to direct. Alan said he was interested. Since we had met as near neighbors in Brooklyn Heights, I had come to know and admire Alan as a Second City performer. He was smart, intuitive, and very funny, and with his cabaret experience I thought he was the right choice to bring the play back. It was what I had been waiting for. It had taken a year and a half, and now *Little Murders* was coming back to New York.

I decided that the play would be best served if I had nothing to do with the production. I had made so many mistakes with the Broadway version— the wrong producer, the wrong director, some inept casting, and stupefyingly wrong cuts and script changes. It was very clear that my best bet to save my play in its off-Broadway revival was to stay away from it. In addition, however tough and defiant the stance I maintained in public, I knew I could not take a second failure. If I allowed myself to get too involved with Alan's production and that too failed, it would break my heart. I doubted if I had the bravado to come back to the theater after that. I instructed Ted Mann to tell the director: "You can cast anyone you like, do anything you like. And under no circumstances do I want to be consulted."

Alan didn't consult me. And I thought his casting was way off. Linda

Lavin, who was too short and entirely the wrong look, was cast as Patsy; Elizabeth Wilson, who was to be Marjorie, the mother, was too tall, not at all like my mother; Vincent Gardenia, whom Alan cast as the father, Carol, didn't remind me of my father in looks or demeanor. He was clearly miscast.

Fortunately for me, I understood that I was miscast as playwright in regard to choosing actors for the show. Everyone Alan cast, including Jon Korkes as Kenny, the brother, and Andrew Duncan as Lieutenant Practice, was fresh, funny, and exhilaratingly good.

Village Voice, December 29, 1966

RIOT

Alan's production of *Little Murders* went on in the spring of 1969. It followed the upheaval of 1968: student strikes and demonstrations, police repression and violence, the march on the Pentagon and countless other marches, student occupations of college and university buildings, police riots in Chicago brought on by the Democratic Convention, the assassination of Martin Luther King Jr. and Robert Kennedy . . . The lesson hammered home in 1968 was that we were living in another country.

I was at the Democratic Convention as a Eugene McCarthy delegate, but the spirit and momentum of McCarthy's antiwar campaign had palled considerably. Inside the convention hall, hanging around caucuses in order to affirm or oppose motions made pointless by the action in the streets, I found the rituals demoralizing. Much of my time was spent in the streets with the protesters, meeting and greeting friends and strangers, an amiable, high-spirited mob on its way to getting gassed and assaulted. Late afternoons I hung out in the Hilton Hotel bar, a favorite convention drinking spot, with Chicago legend Studs Terkel, his journalist friend Jim Cameron of the London *Evening Standard,* and Bill Styron. We drank martinis in the bar, which faced out on Michigan Avenue with a picture window of CinemaScope dimension that provided us a view of the police in the process of committing mayhem. Pissed off by the rebellious long-haired, druggy kids who had taken over their turf, the police began to section off marchers, corralling them into an increasingly narrow perimeter butting up against the Hilton's picture window, the very one we were staring out of with martinis in hand. With the protesters boxed in, the police began pounding them with nightsticks, all of this witnessed by us from the vantage point of our bar stools.

Within moments, there was no longer a picture window for us to stare out of. The demonstrators had been beaten against, and then through, the plate glass. They lay sprawled on the floor inside the bar, cops bent over them continuing to work them over with nightsticks. Finally they were dragged through shards of glass back into the streets to be arrested. Delegates and media looked down at the violence everywhere at our feet. So stunned by the brutality, so sickened by the injustice, so helpless to do anything about it in this purportedly free society, what was left to do but finish our drinks.

I took my outrage out on Hefner. I was staying at the Playboy Mansion during the convention. Every night after the bloodletting, there was a party. Delegates, politicians, media, and celebrities recovered among the Playmates. Hef didn't have the vaguest clue what was happening on the streets. After the Hilton bar assault, I angrily insisted that he leave the house, which he was loath to do, and see what was really going on, as opposed to what he was watching on his closed-circuit color TV. I guilt-tripped him into letting me lead a delegation—Hef and friends—out into Lincoln Park, where even now, hours after the police assaults, the scent of tear gas was still strong. I wanted the editor and publisher of *Playboy* to see our shame firsthand.

By the time we were out on the streets, the day's violence had ended; everything looked calm, quiet, unthreatening. This adventure might even turn out to be fun. There were about ten or twelve of us, including Hef's resident guru, the columnist and historian Max Lerner. The rest of us were either Democratic Party honchos from various delegations or a mix of media types, including Art Buchwald, the humorist. We were taking a shortcut through an alley when suddenly both ends were blocked by police cars with flashing lights. We couldn't go forward, we couldn't go back. The cops herded us in, apparently unmoved by the fact that we weren't long-haired hippies. Hefner tried to explain who he was: *Hef!* Chicago's own! A local boy who made good; whose magazine they kept stashed in their police lockers. But these were Mayor Daley's thugs in Mayor Daley's town in the worst of times in the 1960s. Hef was shoved against a wall by a police officer who then slapped him hard on the butt with his nightstick. A historic butt thwack: the sound of Hugh Hefner being radicalized.

I don't claim that I am the man responsible for radicalizing Hefner. That distinction belongs to an unidentified Chicago policeman. But I can and do boast that I was responsible for getting him out of the house. One thing may not have led to the other, but the next move Hef made was to a more reclusive gated and electronically protected mansion in Holmby Hills, California. No Chicago cops in California.

My candidate for president, Gene McCarthy, did not behave well in Chicago. He displayed little interest in his young supporters who were getting pounded by Daley's cops in Lincoln and Grant parks. Walking through Lincoln Park one afternoon, I ran into Jerry Rubin and Abbie Hoffman, star movement revolutionaries who were instrumental in conceiving, planning, and organizing the protests. Jerry, who was hairy and diminutive and boyishly cute, proudly showed off his security to me as if this were proof that he was a true VIP. "This is Phil, my bodyguard. He's a Hell's Angel." Phil was twice the size of both of us, a hirsute biker in leather boots, menacing in size and demeanor.

Jerry grinned from ear to ear, proud to have a bodyguard. One day you're a nobody demonstrating for the legalization of drugs and against the war in Vietnam, and the next day the revolution has recognized your prominence and assigned you protection. America!

A year and a half later, when I was back in Chicago doing a book of drawings at the conspiracy trial of Jerry and Abbie, Dave Dellinger, Bobby Seale, Rennie Davis, Tom Hayden, John Froines, and Lee Weiner, whom should I see up on the witness stand, testifying for the prosecution? Jerry Rubin's bodyguard, Phil, clean-shaven, wearing a blue suit and tie. He was testifying against Jerry. He was an undercover cop. America!

MY CANDIDATE

Gene McCarthy, whose worst and most revealing moments came during the Chicago convention, had had his best and quirkiest moment three months earlier in an Oregon hotel room where I happened to be a day before that state's presidential primary.

I had flown off the Vineyard with Bill Styron at the behest of the McCarthy campaign to make speeches in Salem and Portland. After McCarthy's final rally, at which Robert Lowell and Styron and I spoke, we were invited back, with Jason Epstein, to McCarthy's hotel suite. Drinks were handed out, and the antiwar candidate and the antiwar poet sat around for over an hour genially trying to stump each other with the opening and closing lines of poems.

Lowell, with his robust good looks and flowing white hair, had a demeanor that was casual, intense, and intimate. He was nearly as tall as McCarthy, and far more charismatic. Cal, as his friends called him, loved to drink, talk, and conversationally quote poetry. In a mesmerizing gesture, he would extend his arm to full length, hand out, palm up, and, as if it was an offering, recite obscure lines to McCarthy, who, diffidently, without missing a beat, finished the poem. McCarthy then tossed his own four or five lines back, which Cal completed. An amiable exhibition, not unlike a tennis match, with two pros at the top of their game thoroughly enjoying themselves but much too aristocratic to let it show.

A little after midnight the phone rang. An aide to McCarthy announced, "Scotty Reston's downstairs. He wants to come up and interview you." Now, James Reston was the star columnist of the *New York Times*, an opinion maker, a consensus builder. A friendly column from Reston might take McCarthy's campaign several giant steps down the road. The important California primary against Bobby Kennedy was only a month away.

McCarthy reflected for only a moment, and then, as Cal and the rest of us stared in wonder at our serenely remote antiwar candidate, he said with an air of dismissal, "Oh, just tell him I'm asleep." Then he returned to the more serious contest with Lowell.

Jules and Gene, 1968

THE COMEBACK KID

In its first incarnation, admirers described *Little Murders* as "prescient," meaning that I had dramatized what was not yet clear to most of my audience—notably theater critics.

The respected reviewer of the *Boston Globe* was hardly alone when he said that he couldn't make sense of the play or figure out what point it was making (if, indeed, it had a point) or recognize the world it was describing. It certainly wasn't any world the Boston critics recognized.

That was in March of 1967. By 1969, the world of *Little Murders* was too recognizable. After the King and Kennedy assassinations and the attempt on George Wallace's life, after one escalation after another in Vietnam, after Kent State, after the blowing up of college campuses, after thousands demonstrated in the streets, after the rapid trajectory of the Left from explosion to implosion, the point of my play was self-evident—and Alan Arkin's production at the Circle in the Square was ready to take off.

Arkin had done with the play what it needed all along, but only after he had shown me did I understand. I had assumed that the style of the piece was rooted essentially in the conventions of sketch comedy, such as Second City's.

That was how it played in London, and it went well. But Alan staged it as all-out, over-the-top farce, with many improvisational moments that took me by surprise. No lines were changed or altered but he added actions and reactions, bits of improvised business and familiar family banality that slipped back and forth between competitiveness and chaos. Arkin informed the audience that what it was watching was an entirely credible family seen through a distorted lens. Eye exchanges, interactions, a half turn this way or that—viewers sat there astonished. They were watching their own families, and what they were seeing was insanity. A wildly exaggerated but true, oh so true drama.

And the truth staged farcically allowed the audience to stay with the play as the comedy darkened. Violence erupted offstage, then on, Patsy shot to death and the Newquist family descending into urban paranoia. At play's end, our antihero, Alfred, surrenders nihilism for cool. He is in tune with his times: a happier, more idealistic mass murderer.

The style Arkin found permitted the audience to go with the play without recoiling from what it said. It connected its events to our specific moment in history, but the grim realities were viewed through an ironic prism that allowed audiences to feel the thrill of truth diluted with that other thrill, of pure theatrical invention. Alan's staging skillfully whistled us past the graveyard of sixties America.

As the play took off, so did I. At dawn the next day, having been informed by my producers that the early reviews looked good, before seeing a copy of the *New York Times,* I fled with Judy and three-year-old Kate on a flight to Jamaica. I was out to make the point that commercial success in the theater was less important to me than a tropical holiday with family and friends.

John and Sue Marquand had rented a rather large beach house on a spit of land in the Caribbean called Salt Cay. The Styrons and Bob and Norma Brustein and their son, Danny, were already down there. On our arrival, I announced that I was there to have a good time and had no interest in how things were going in New York. I would learn all I needed to know in good time, but I had no intention of becoming a hostage to my notices from the theater critics. I was not going to invest the power to affect my thoughts or emotions in the sort of people I wouldn't have to my house for dinner.

I was surprised and pleased to see—as if it were some kind of omen— that on our bedroom wall hung a beautiful original editorial cartoon in color. It was drawn by the early-twentieth-century *Chicago Tribune* cartoonist John McCutcheon. McCutcheon was one of the most famous cartoonists of his time, a prairie conservative glorifying the rural values that had begun to fade even in his time. Politically, we couldn't have differed more. But I felt a kinship to that cartoon on our wall.

Whatever fate befell my play at the Circle in the Square, I would remain, first and foremost, a cartoonist. I had no desire to use theater to upgrade me from status-free cartoonist to lofty playwright. Since the early success of the *Voice* strip, I had periodically found myself cornered by literary types at Plimpton and Tynan parties who would start, "I love that thing you do, that column—"

"My comic strip?"

"No, no! It's not at all a comic strip, it's so much more."

"It's a cartoon."

"No, no, no! It's an essay, it's a little play, that's what it is, it's a play on paper!"

Intellectuals could not admit that the work they attached significance to was a mere comic strip. It was degrading for them to admire a work in so unserious a form. So to permit themselves to appreciate me, they social-worked me into a profession they respected: hence, I was redefined into playwright.

So, okay, I wrote a *real* play. To me, it had different rules and different rhythms and developed in an entirely different way from my strip. But two years earlier, when *Little Murders* had its original opening on Broadway, one of the complaints from almost every critic was: "This isn't a play, it's a Feiffer cartoon!" Writing a flop play was how I came to be validated as a cartoonist. That's not what I had in mind.

No one flatters you when they refer to you as a cartoonist, even a great cartoonist. An ordinary screenwriter occupies a higher status than a great cartoonist. Illustrators, who aren't expected to come up with their own ideas, enjoy a higher status. I know too many colleagues who are flattered, who are pleased when they are labeled illustrators instead of cartoonists. I'm offended. I know what it means. It means that I'm not good enough.

I once chaired an evening of cartoonists at the Society for Ethical Culture on the Upper West Side of Manhattan. On the panel with me were Lee Lorenz, at the time the cartoon editor of *The New Yorker*, and George Booth and Ed Koren, two of the best *New Yorker* cartoonists of that time.

Along with them on the panel were David Levine and Edward Sorel, the two most trenchant political caricaturists of the late twentieth century. All of us were more than happy to be labeled cartoonists.

But our audience of fans wasn't all that happy. These were people who loved our work or they wouldn't have been there. But their comments, every now and again, reeked of doubts about our legitimacy. Toward the end of the evening, a woman in the balcony asked, "You men are all so gifted at what you do, have you ever thought of expanding into something more profound? Like directing film?"

I laughed, an instinctive reaction that has plagued me my entire life: Things I can't stand I react to as if I find them funny. I said, "Here in a nutshell is the cartoonists' curse. Even our fans condescend to us."

McCutcheon's picture on the wall at Salt Cay provided comfort for a day or two. John and Sue and our other friends were good company—the Marquands always were. I loved to track the meandering Marquand mind as he told a story or made an observation. He never ended up where you thought he was going, but wherever he went it was worth the trip. And no better drinking companion existed than Styron in the right mood.

But I was miserable. I was living a lie. I was not indifferent to my fate in New York. I thought by this time someone would have called to read me my reviews. But there was no telephone service on our little island.

I invented an excuse to go to the mainland. The women thought that was a great idea—they could shop. I had no interest in shopping. I wanted a long-distance phone line. But by now it was the weekend. I found my phone line but no one was around to take my calls. No one to tell me if I was a hit.

I had worked myself into a parody of my own self-righteousness. Too above the battle to care about reviews? Fine. Years will pass before I find out.

After three technically glorious, fun-filled days at Salt Cay, every minute of which was mired in anxiety and frustration, I said good-bye to my wife and child and dear friends. I flew back to New York to read what Clive Barnes in the *New York Times* had to say.

THE CRITIC ON THE MORNING PAPER SAID OF MY FIRST PLAY "INEPT." THE CRITIC ON THE AFTERNOON PAPER SAID: "DRIVEL."

BOTH REVIEWS TOTALLY MISUNDER-STOOD THE PLAY.

THE CRITIC ON THE MORNING PAPER SAID OF MY SECOND PLAY: "PRETENTIOUS." THE CRITIC ON THE AFTER-NOON PAPER SAID: "ABHOR-RENT."

BOTH REVIEWS TOTALLY MISUNDERSTOOD THE PLAY.

THE CRITIC ON THE MORNING PAPER SAID OF MY THIRD PLAY. "A SMASH HIT!" THE CRITIC ON THE AFTER-NOON PAPER SAID: "A TRIUMPH!"

BOTH REVIEWS TOTALLY MISUNDERSTOOD THE PLAY.

THEY ARE NOW MIS-UNDERSTANDING TO MY ADVANTAGE.

IN THE ARTS THAT'S KNOWN AS SUCCESS.

Village Voice, November 14, 1976

PRO BONO PLAYWRIGHT

*L*ittle Murders was a hit. The critics got it. They loved the production, they loved—but not uncritically—the play. They responded positively enough to give us a two-year run down at the Circle, to give me a steady, not great, but not measly royalty for a two-year period, the one and only time I have made money out of the theater.

This, my first flop play, became a hit. All my other flop plays remained flops. *Knock Knock* started out as a hit, then it moved from off-Broadway to Broadway and into the flop category. *The White House Murder Case* was a hit, rave reviews for this political satire on cover-ups in the Oval Office in regard to a future war in Brazil. Then Nixon and Kissinger started a real war in Cambodia and my imagination seemed too close to reality. Overnight, audiences shunned us, and *White House* closed in a month.

Grown Ups got great reviews, but it was about an acrimonious Jewish family that didn't kiss and make up in the end. Audiences in the eighties— and Jews made up much of the Broadway audience in the eighties—didn't mind a fighting Jewish family, but they needed a happy resolution. Other- wise, it came too uncomfortably close to their own lives. But in *Grown Ups,* matters only got worse. The play closed after a short run. I realized, too late, that I should have made it about an Irish family or, perhaps, set it in Cape Town, not on the Upper West Side. I might have had a hit.

Elliot Loves got incredible reactions from preview audiences, but guess what? The critics, most notably Frank Rich of the *New York Times,* he who had raved about *Grown Ups,* hated it. It closed in a month.

Rightly or wrongly, I was convinced that there was an audience for my plays. They were very good plays, but ticket prices prevented audiences from going to the theater without the prior approval of critics. I had no doubt that if there had been comic strip critics back in the fifties, I would have been drummed out of the *Village Voice* in a couple of weeks. I was convinced that if *Carnal Knowledge,* the play, had been done by Mike Nichols on Broadway and it was every bit as good as the film, it would have been panned. And would have closed immediately. I was convinced that I had a following. What I didn't have was a theater-critic following. Worn out by rejection and stymied as to how to get to audiences without the approval of critics, I swore off playwriting. I had aged out of the rage that used to fuel my defiance. I didn't want to fight. I wanted approval. I wanted love.

So I showed them. I quit the theater forever. Forever lasted ten years. But in the meantime, I backed into children's books.

Jules at fifty

THE JEWISH MOTHER CABAL

I anger Jewish mothers by the way I talk about my mother. I have read chapters of this memoir to JCC (Jewish Community Center) audiences here and there, and the Jewish mothers in my audience, almost all a generation or more younger than I, say that I'm wrong about my mother, that I misrepresent her.

They say this with absolute conviction about a woman they have never met. "She couldn't have been as bad as you claim," they say. "Look how you turned out. Did you turn out so bad?"

Now, the section I read to these JCC groups is from the early part of this book, the part where I come home from school and find that my mother has given away my dog, Rex. Without telling me. And these women are unaffected by that—no, I'm wrong, they're not unaffected. They take my mother's side. "She must have had her reasons," they tell me.

Remember, this is a woman they have never met. Me, they have met. But of the two of us, when it comes time to choose up sides, to identify with one of us or the other, they decide for this total stranger, dead many years, when an hour earlier I was saying hello to them, shaking hands, sharing a glass of wine with some of them, pretending to be personable.

And none of it counted. Their first loyalty was to the Jewish Mother Cabal. If you think *cabal* is too strong a word, call it what you will: a sorority, a club, a conspiracy that spans centuries, secretive, communicating with nods, grimaces, shrugs, heightened stares that speak volumes, and, of course, tightly pursed lips, that dagger in the heart.

They do good, this cabal. They take pride in doing good, and so does that other group with which they have so much in common, the Masons.

But they also wield influence far beyond their number, again like the Masons. And when one of them is criticized, turned into a figure of ridicule or, worse, contempt, they go on the offensive. They attack.

Because if I am allowed to talk about my mother with such disrespect, what ghastly door does that open for *their* children to kick down? What will they, having been swayed by my bad example, confess about their mothers? Ungrateful wretches! Someday they'll find out. Someday they'll be sorry.

"You will never know the sacrifices I made for you." That is the line from which all opposition shrivels in shame.

My mother, who dies in this chapter, started out with so much talent, intellect, wit, charm, prettiness, vivacity, humor, grace . . . What could stop her? What did stop her? Others, millions of others, went through hard times and survived the Depression. But it crushed and embittered my mother. It implanted in her first the courage and fortitude to save our family and afterwards the rage and bitterness that ruined her life. I don't know why. Was it that she could not recover from the humiliation of being the breadwinner when it was then understood by the Jewish girl in her, by the Southern girl in her, by the culture at large that this was supposed to be the man's job?

And her reward? Her children mourned the father who let them down and scorned the mother who kept them afloat.

I said to Mimi once, over drinks at my apartment, "You know, we both think of ourselves as rebels, but we were really obedient children. Ma raised me to be a success and I am, and she raised you to be a failure and you are."

Mimi threw her glass at me—and why not? Then, after screaming insults for a while, she went home. She called the next morning to say, "You know, I can't get what you said out of my head, and I think you may be right."

My mother was a strong woman who never sat still and never stopped complaining about her health. "My stomach, it gives me so much trouble, the doctors say it's upside down. My head, too much thinking, I have to think all the time to come up with new designs. My temples press in on me, it feels like my head is being crushed."

Walking on the street with her was pure torture. She was the slowest walker alive. I, who could barely swim, could swim faster than my mother walked. Her slow walk, I was convinced, was not the result of bad health, it was an exercise of control. By forcing me, a loping adolescent, to walk at a snail's pace, she was asserting who wore the pants in the family, although she never wore a pair of pants in her life.

Just about every action of hers seemed connected to establishing proof of her authority. She was a control freak whose control did her no good at all. She controlled nothing. Her children gave way to her to make her less unhappy (and in the hope of getting her to leave us alone), but behind her back we did exactly as we pleased. And she knew that we did.

Her authority was in name only; it was the image of authority without substance. She was a micromanager who managed ineptly. She expected her authority to be either ignored or disobeyed. Acts of defiance by others made up her life. Endless letdowns, betrayals (as she saw them), weakness on the part of men who left her holding the bag.

After my father's death, now in actual failing health, she lived in Queens alone, insisting, when she visited the city to see her grandchildren, on taking the subway. Over and over I offered to pay her cab fare. "A waste of good money," she said, and then complained about the hardship of the hour-long subway ride, the dirt, the heat, the difficulty of getting up and down stairs.

And I would say, "Ma, take a cab next time. I can afford it." To which she had one set response: "Spend the money on your family."

She was disappointed over so much, bitter over so much: the dutiful but undevoted care she received from her children, the indifference bordering on disrespect from her grandchildren, who tried not to show (but they did show) that they dreaded her visits. She preferred them to line up like an army of little courtiers to pay her obeisance, to submit to her as she had submitted to her parents and grandparents. She related to Amy and Abby and Glenn and Bruce and my Kate through lectures and intimidation. She loved them, but she saw it as her job as grandmother to teach and advise, knowing that her own children were not up to the job. And that just added to her bitterness over the raw deal she had been handed in life.

She could get no respect. The older and sicker she got, the more unwanted she felt. And the more alienated. We took care of her without caring for her, and that made itself perfectly clear. It drove her inward and downward.

She was short of breath; she had been short of breath for years. "I can't breathe—" she'd say. And sit herself down in the nearest chair and wait, we all waited, as she caught her breath. "My flushes—" Her flushes came upon her regularly, most often in response to disagreement, when she wasn't getting her way. Her flushes prevented her from breathing. We sat watching her as she waited out her flushes. Our breathing was affected by her not breathing. When hers resumed, our breathing went back to normal. Our emotions dangled from hers, as if on a string.

Her shortness of breath became more and more serious. She was hospitalized. Booth Memorial Hospital in Queens. We talked about what was to be done with her when she got out of the hospital. My mother could no longer take care of herself. She could not go back to her apartment and live alone. Someone had to live with her. Someone had to be there to take care of her.

Mimi and Alice and I discussed the situation, out of concern not for my mother's needs but for ours. None of us wanted to take her in. None of us wanted the responsibility, to have to deal with the care that would not be enough, the tending to her that would be met with reproach, the effort at keeping her alive that would undo our families.

My mother, in good health or bad, was in charge of the temperature in the room. None of us could tolerate the idea of her in control of our households, of our helplessly standing by as she raised or lowered the temperature. We picked out a nursing home. On the day that I was getting ready to move her, the message came that she had died.

It was her breath. I believe she was driven to hold it. "I'll show you, I'll hold my breath till I die." She did show us. "I'll die and then you'll be sorry!" She died. We weren't sorry.

The news of her death came through a voice mail on my answering machine. It was a doctor with an Indian accent. He gave his name on the machine and then said, "I am sorry to inform you that your mother, Rhoda Feiffer, is deceased. Will you please call me to inform me what to do with the remains." And then, on the machine, he left a referral telephone number. Dignity, which was so important to her, eluded her to the end.

It was a hard life that she never stopped making everyone pay for. But when we were kids she sang show tunes and danced comic dances. And on the subway downtown to sell her sketches, she observed everything around her, made notes on a pad of paper, and wrote comic verse that commented on her home life:

I'm sittin' here wishin'
The electrician would stop drilling the walls and would leave,
The rain of plaster
Is like a disaster,
I tremor in each sleeve.
If only it weren't
That we needed strong current
The house would be tidy and quiet,
But now we're upset
And the end is not yet
On his own home
The landlord should try it.

NO SENSE OF DIRECTION; OR, HOW TO GET FROM *CARNAL KNOWLEDGE* TO *BARK, GEORGE*

M y life as a father began in middle age (thirty-five) with Kate, Judy's daughter, succeeded twenty years later by Halley (I was fifty-five), and, ten years later, Julie. By then I was sixty-five and married for over a decade to Jenny, the second and final Mrs. Feiffer.

Throughout my attenuated production of daughters, I (and they) got into the habit of expecting Dad to tell them bedtime stories. Julie, being the last, was the toughest, not willing to accept your run-of-the-mill Red Riding Hood or your Three Pigs and Bears. Julie appointed me her Scheherazade. Three hundred or so nights a year, my assignment was to make up a story for Julie (repeats were not acceptable). So every night I had to mint her a new story. She slept in her bedroom in a two-tier bunk bed, and since she took the top, I stretched out on the lower bunk to tell my story. One night without a clue as to what I was getting into (I never had a clue), I began: "George's mother said, 'Bark, George.' George was a dog, but George went, 'Meow.' 'No, George,' said George's mother. 'Cats go meow. Dogs go arf.'"

Word for word, as it appears in the published text, I made up the story. As I ad-libbed *Bark, George* (or as it ad-libbed itself), the thought struck, "Oh, my God! This is a book!"

But I faced a dilemma. My bedtime stories for Julie not only put her to sleep, they put me to sleep. Seconds after I finished telling a story, I dozed off, sometimes before Julie. When I awoke, always twenty minutes later, I had no memory of the story I had just told. Nor did Julie. We were bedtime story amnesiacs. So it was clear to me that *Bark, George* would never see itself between covers if I allowed myself to fall asleep after I finished telling it.

As soon as I came out with the last line of the story, with George's surprise word to his mother (see book), I forced myself, groggily, out of Julie's lower bunk, already halfway into my stupor. I staggered to my studio next door. Semicomatose, I scribbled down a half page of notes and prayed that they were legible, and in a language I could recognize, and would make sense when I awoke from my nap. After writing down a short list of key words and phrases, "Mother," "Meow," "Quack," "Oink," "Moo," "Vet," "Hello!" I staggered back to the lower bunk in Julie's room. I collapsed. Twenty minutes later when I awoke, I didn't remember a word. But I had my notes, I had my book, published a year later, the most successful thus far of my ten books for children.

I started writing children's books only because I was mad at Ed Sorel. Ed is the brilliant and celebrated cartoonist, caricaturist, illustrator, muralist, writer, bon vivant, and grouch-about-town. He and David Levine are the cartoonists I admire and envy most in this world. If I could draw like anyone else, I would draw like Ed.

Ed had an idea for a children's book. He had been writing and drawing his own for some years now, but this one he wanted to illustrate, not write. He asked me if I would write it for him. I loved the idea he told me, I loved the idea of working with Ed; as far as I could see, this combination was a natural, a no-brainer. Ed's idea was about a kid living in the Bronx in the early 1940s, ten years old and on his way on the subway to a violin lesson. The kid gets off at the wrong stop and discovers—remarkably—that he is not in the Bronx anymore but in a Hollywood black-and-white version of Manhattan. In fact, in Movie City, that *other* glittering, glamorous Gotham, where Depression kids like Ed and me liked to imagine ourselves in residence.

Ed was after a story that gave him reason to draw lavish old-time-metropolis movie sites and landscapes, formidable movie palaces that we entered with a veneration we never gave to synagogues. He was dying to draw the interior of Loew's Paradise in the Bronx, the Roxy, Radio City

Music Hall . . . architectural dreamscapes that merged Versailles with the Taj Mahal. He was dying to caricature the great old stars whose names still made our pulses beat faster.

Fifty years later it was still possible to summon pure and radiant memories of giant silver screens in darkened theaters, to feel the excitement and contentment of Movie World taking over, the ultimate romantic vision for kids like Ed and me, before sex changed everything and brought us down to earth faster than a speeding bullet.

The magic pull of movies started when I was about five and, as I write this, I am eighty and I'm no less in its thrall. When Mike Nichols was shooting my screenplay for *Carnal Knowledge* in Vancouver in the fall of 1969, I found myself in a constant state of dithery wonder. A one-line description in a script transformed into a college campus. Amherst College. (In Vancouver!) Snow falling on a mild day in mid-October. Jonathan and Sandy, my two heroes, were trekking outdoors through made-for-movies snowdrifts, breathing actual white clouds of vapor in the manufactured atmosphere, a bare nine months after I wrote, "Exterior Amherst Campus. Jonathan and Sandy on their way to class in the snow." I stood behind the camera witnessing, with the kind of pleasure you cannot believe, fake snow falling. I made it happen! I wrote one sentence in a script, and without that sentence, no snow. This very adult, dark, and controversial movie inspired in me, as I watched the cameras roll, a magical, childlike glee.

Carnal Knowledge came into existence as a play, written at Yaddo at the same time that Philip Roth was in residence working on *Portnoy's Complaint*. When my first draft was finished, I sent it to Mike Nichols. The next morning he called. "I want to do it. But I don't think it's a play. It's a movie."

"Can we get away with the language on film?" I asked him.

Mike, whose recent film *The Graduate* had taken the world by storm, was the hottest director in Hollywood. He said, "We can do anything we want."

"Give me thirty seconds to think it over," I said. And then, after five seconds, "Okay."

The summer before production began, Mike instructed Jack Nicholson (Jonathan) and Art Garfunkel (his best friend, Sandy) to start hanging out with each other. He wanted a natural camaraderie on-screen that reflected an authentic relationship between these two horny young men as we observe their sexual journey over thirty years, from romanticism to rejection to disillusion to cynicism to misogyny.

This was my toughest piece of work since *Little Murders,* a play about sex in my time as I had lived and observed it in and around the Village and its environs. We were in the early years of the women's movement and a rising tide of feminism. I chose this moment to dramatize the little-noted or understood fact that too many heterosexual men liked sex but didn't like women. Men liked the parts you could play with in a woman: breasts, ass, vagina, soft and pliant, inviting and scary flesh . . . Men liked every part of a woman except the part that talked. The uninhibited yackety-yack that men endured in order to bed a woman down. And then the conversation after. What men wanted to avoid at all costs was the discussion over what now, what next? A relationship? Commitment? Permanence?

Women, comfortable with conversation, came up against men who talked primarily to make a point, *their* point. About themselves, jobs, sports. Men used talk to flatter, tease, seduce, and cajole a woman into bed, but they were at a loss afterwards. Conversation following coitus was an irritant and a bore.

Before marriage and domesticity, men occupied center stage. They were good at talking while their women listened: "How interesting, go on, dear." After marriage and the children and the house and the dinner parties with other couples with other children, the women moved onto center stage. Domesticity was not natural male turf. The men, off balance, were now the ones who found themselves saying, "Yes, dear, go on."

Men longed for relief, time off, dreamed of those golden years of irresponsibility when they did the talking and the women's role was, "Yes, dear, go on." Men had little left to say to women they lived with. On occasional boys' nights out, they had more to say, a lot to catch up on, too much to drink, and then one might get lucky and meet another woman. The luck lay in the fact that afterwards he never had to see her again.

This was the journey I took with *Carnal Knowledge,* two men descending that sexual slope from the innocent lust of young manhood to the muddled misogyny of middle age.

My first choice for director had been not Mike Nichols but Alan Arkin. After Mike had failed to respond to my *Little Murders* script, I began cutting him at parties. He looked anxiously uncomfortable around me. And why shouldn't he? He had behaved inexcusably. We were friends. He had not liked *Harry, the Rat with Women* and told me so, and I wasn't at all angry. But to not respond to *Little Murders* because— I was never to know a reason. All I could think was that he didn't like the play and felt awkward about disappointing me. Maybe he thought that by not saying anything he was saving my feelings. I thought he was saving his own.

After almost two years of not a word exchanged between us, I was invited to one of the later screenings of his new film, *The Graduate,* about which I had heard nothing. I attended the screening, hoping to hate the movie. I wanted a flop for Mike and what I saw instead—and I knew it from the first shot onward—was a revolutionary breakthrough in American cinema, a kind of Nicholsian blending of French New Wave (particularly Truffaut) with Mike and Elaine's sensibility—but better than anything they had done. It was deep, incisive, and honest and, at the same time, romantic, telling tough truths encased inside a movie gloss, an effective piece of sleight of hand. I was blown away.

I went home and immediately wrote Mike a fan letter. I gushed. My grudge seemed trivial compared with his extraordinary achievement. Within minutes, it seemed, he sent me a graceful acknowledgment by messenger. Our breach was healed. When Arkin's revival of *Little Murders* opened at the Circle in the Square a year later, Mike was there and rushed over at the end to hug me and say, "I didn't get it! I just didn't get it!"

But it was Arkin who didn't get *Carnal Knowledge* when I offered him the script. He thought it was too dark; he wanted a more upbeat play. Later he was to direct *The White House Murder Case,* darker and more nastily cynical about our nation's leaders and their wartime lies than my cartoons. He gave it a fast, farcical, hilarious production that softened not a blow. But *Carnal Knowledge,* which was about men and women, was too dark for him. Politics, yes; sex, no.

Working with Nichols on adapting my play into a screenplay was like a tutorial on writing and editing. Mike made me go through the script, line by line, defending virtually every word spoken by every character. "Why does he do this?" "Why does she say that?" "What does this mean?" "This is very funny, but I'm not sure it belongs in the script. Why does it?"

At times I felt like a witness undergoing cross-examination. I had to keep my story straight, avoid contradictions, make up on the spot reasons for inconsistencies so that they sounded plausible enough. I had to sound as if I'd given thought to the questions Mike was raising when, in more cases than not, his questions—sharp, pointed, penetrating—took me by surprise. I was adrift in my own dopiness and managed (just) to make it to shore by way of improvisation and wit.

I lied my way through my tutorial. I had not given enough thought to my characters, so I invented answers for Mike on the spot. And in the act of acrobatic improvisation, I came to understand the questions that had to be asked and answered. I learned how to study, to prepare—and most important, I learned how to be teacher and student to my own work. Not for a minute did I think Mike was trying to put me on the spot. His tutorial was as much for him as for me. He was trying to learn everything he could about the characters he was responsible for bringing to life on-screen.

Each night, after the day's shoot, we'd watch the dailies and discuss what was right and what wasn't. The night before we were to shoot the Jonathan/Bobbie fight, in which Jonathan (Jack) goes berserk because Bobbie (Ann-Margret) wants to get married, Mike called me into his office. We sat over glasses of wine. He said he didn't think he could shoot the scene. Too ugly. Jonathan's behavior was too repellent for an audience to stomach. They would recoil from his character and never get back into the movie. The danger was that we could lose the entire picture over that one scene.

Now, the scene he was talking about was perhaps my favorite piece of writing in the movie. I believed it to be essential, but I didn't say a word to Mike, I didn't argue with him, I didn't defend my scene. I let him talk. We had now worked together for many months. I had seen the level of integrity he brought to my script. I concluded that no argument of mine was likely to change his mind, that it might do the opposite, harden his position. I thought that if anyone could bring him down from his case of nerves, the fear that he was going too far out on a limb, it wasn't me. It was Mike himself. And I was convinced that he was up to the job. It wasn't conceivable for him to do the high level of work already in the can and then sell the film out.

We broke for dinner. Mike drove us to a restaurant and talked more, going into every aspect of Jonathan's character and every reaction of Bobbie's. He talked about all of the things that could go wrong with the film if we shot the scene. He thought about what we could replace the scene with, what might fill the hole, what might work, what might not work.

Then, as we pulled into the parking lot of a Chinese restaurant, Mike looked at me and said, "No, I guess we have to shoot it . . . because that's what would happen."

I had told myself all along that this was the decision he was bound to arrive at. But a moment after he said it I realized how shaken I was, how scared I'd been.

The scene as written had so many levels for Nicholson to act that it was hard for me to imagine how he would approach it and what he would finally make of it. Jonathan, in his attempt to circle around the threat of marriage, is defensive, enraged, contemptuous, and bullying. The scene is brutal but funny, stacked with ironic overtones that were, I thought, self-evident on paper but that I couldn't imagine coming through in the heat of performance. And this was acceptable to me. If Jack got half of everything I put into that scene, I would be more than satisfied.

Jack got everything. And he got it on the first take. Staggered by the level of performance, I approached my director. "What did you tell him?" I asked Mike. He grinned at me. "Nothing. I told him absolutely nothing. He came up with it all himself."

If there was any question that Nicholson was on his way to becoming "Jack," the superstar with shades, it was answered when the director Bob

Rafelson flew up to Vancouver to screen for us a rough cut of his recently assembled film, *Five Easy Pieces*. The entire *Carnal Knowledge* company sat there loving the film and, more than that, awed by Jack's performance. "Trust me," I remembered Mike telling me a year earlier, "he's going to be our most important actor since Brando."

Later in the week, I asked Jack and Arty Garfunkel to join me at a party Robert Altman was giving. Altman, who for some years had been an Elaine's drinking buddy, was shooting his new film, *McCabe and Mrs. Miller*, up the hill a couple of miles away. His stars were Warren Beatty and Julie Christie. Two films by two great directors that turned out to be classics, shot at the same time within a mile or two of each other. Go figure.

Jack, Arty, and I stood outside in the hall observing the mob scene in Altman's living room. Altman loved partying and parties loved Altman. Jack had but one focus and that was on Warren Beatty, who stood in the corner of the room holding court. They had not yet met, I was about to introduce them, but Jack felt at a disadvantage. "He's the right height for a movie star. I'm too short for a movie star."

Carnal Knowledge turned out to be everything I hoped it would be and more. Some nine months later, after the Directors Guild screening in Hollywood, Mike and I stood outside the screening room in Westwood during the reception, engaged in the official meet and greet. The great Hollywood director William Wyler shook our hands warmly and said to both of us, "Uncompromising." The great director John Frankenheimer shook our hands warmly and said, "It was like open-heart surgery."

I leaned over to Mike and whispered, "We're dead."

The film was all I could have hoped, a critical success, an audience success, and controversial in a way that left me self-satisfied. It was assaulted by some women writers as sexist and exalted by other women writers as the first film conceived by men to show what we're really like: creeps.

Hollywood hated the movie. It was too raw, too revealing, it stuck in their craw. The only Academy nomination it was to receive was for Ann-Margret, one of Hollywood's own. She deserved her nomination. But so did Nichols, who didn't get one, so did Nicholson, who didn't get one. So did I, also left out.

Mike Nichols and Jules at Mike's stable in Connecticut, 1970

Jack Nicholson, Art Garfunkel, cinematographer Giuseppe Rotunno, and Mike Nichols shooting *Carnal Knowledge*, Vancouver, Columbia, 1970

I was shunned by Hollywood for ten years after *Carnal Knowledge,* not a single offer, blacklisted, it seemed, because of my piece of "open-heart surgery." And then one morning Robert Evans, the producer, called and asked me if I would consider writing a screenplay for his movie version of *Popeye.* It was to be a musical.

Now, although I loved *Popeye* and I had loved movie musicals since early childhood, I was once again prepared to look a gift horse in the mouth. I asked Evans, "Which *Popeye* do you have in mind, Max Fleischer's (the animated cartoon) or E. C. Segar's (the newspaper strip)?" I expected Evans to give me the wrong answer and I would politely decline. But Evans, producer of *Chinatown, Love Story, The Godfather,* and *The Godfather: Part II,* well knew how to deal with an unemployed, self-sabotaging screenwriter whom no one was after. He replied, "I want to do any *Popeye* you want."

Popeye was one of the earliest cartoon characters I drew as a kid. One drawing after another of Popeye beating up bad guys or getting beaten up by bad guys. Sheer heaven for a seven-year-old cartoonist. Now, for my first effort at writing for children, I was being asked to write my own version of Popeye. About five years before Evans's call, I had picked up a Nostalgia Press edition of the 1936 *Popeye*s, the daily strips as created, written, and drawn by E. C. Segar, the genius who gave us the immortal sailor.

Here is an extract from what I later wrote about the sailor in the Fantagraphics anthology *Popeye: I Yam What I Yam:*

> In Popeye's world everyone (but our hero) was cheerfully corrupt, giddily greedy, amoral, immoral, without a sign of compassion or conscience—in other words, a farcical cartoon version of Depression-age America. . . . No strip has more contradictions, a noisy tenement of clashing impulses: gentleness meets with nastiness; courtesy meets violence; greed, loutishness, and brutishness knock heads with kindness, righteousness, and moral vigor. Brute strength, used by all sides, is so run-of-the-mill, it is like steak and fries. And fistfights are uncommonly good-natured. Popeye . . . in Segar's vision, was a flawed common man as Walt Whitman might

have imagined him, Frank Capra directed him, and Samuel Beckett, mixed with Eugene Ionesco, hired to write his dialogue.

Evans's first choice to play Popeye was his good friend Dustin Hoffman. I wrote a first-draft treatment loosely based on the 1936 *Popeye* strips, trying to fuse Segar's anarchy and nonsense with a relationship story built around Popeye, Olive Oyl, and Popeye's papa, Poopdeck Pappy. Evans and his producer, my friend Richard Sylbert, the production designer of *Carnal Knowledge,* liked my basic approach but wanted changes. We met at Evans's house, around the corner from the Beverly Hills Hotel, and I made copious notes, went home, and wrote a new treatment. Evans liked it; so did Sylbert. Evans wanted changes. I wrote a third treatment. Evans liked a lot of it but wanted a fourth treatment, more changes.

I went back to New York to think the situation through. I spent a day or two devising a plan, then writing a script in my head as to how I would present it to Evans. I called Evans in Hollywood. I told him that I didn't think it was a good idea for me to write additional treatments. I was not going to be able to produce this great treatment in the sky that would answer his questions or satisfy his doubts. *Popeye* was going to rise and fall on characterization, which meant taking these overly familiar comic strips and animated cartoon characters and transforming them into film reality. I said that nothing was going to please him until I showed him the interaction on paper of Popeye and Olive Oyl. Actual scenes with dialogue. Only then would he know—and I know—whether I was the man for the job, and possibly whether this was an idea worth pursuing. I asked him to advance me $10,000 to write fifty pages of script. He agreed immediately.

I wrote the fifty pages and sent them on to Evans and Sylbert. I found that it was a relief to get away from my own cartoon characters. My work for much of the past year had lost interest to me. I had begun recycling old strips, redrawing them as if they were new. And the new strips too often read to me like Feiffer imitations. I had entered the age of self-parody, so it felt good to write from inside the sensibility (or what I hoped to be the sensibility) of another cartoonist, one I venerated.

Working on *Popeye* took me away from who I was (*boring!*) and channeled me into who Segar was. But when I began work on the script, I found that I couldn't make the transformation of Segar's characters come alive in screenplay form. Popeye and Olive Oyl remained stuck on the comic page, refusing to budge out of the place they called home. The model I had in mind for them was Hepburn and Tracy as they were in Garson Kanin's film *Pat and Mike.* So knowing the story I wanted to tell, I abandoned the cartoon characters Popeye and Olive Oyl for Pat and Mike types whom I called Sam and Minnie. By this means I hoped to escape the intimidating presence of Segar as I tried to honor him. With Sam and Minnie as my beard, my two leads took on life. They began to act and interact, and within a day or two I was able to discard their false identities, riff on Segar's style of humor, and watch my hero and heroine go through their paces.

Evans loved the fifty pages. He sent them to Dustin Hoffman. He loved the fifty pages. As I was walking from the Beverly Hills Hotel to Evans's house, Dustin drove up in his Mercedes convertible and offered me a ride. We had known each other since I had seen him as an unknown off-Broadway actor give an amazing performance fifteen years earlier in Ronald Ribman's play *The Journey of the Fifth Horse.* As we drove to Evans's house, he gushed over my script. Not since *The Graduate* had he seen a script this promising. It reminded him of Beckett, it reminded him of Kafka. On and on he went, and when we got to Evans's house, Evans and Dick Sylbert joined in the praise.

I floated back to New York, finished the first draft, sent it on to Evans and Sylbert. They loved it as much as the earlier pages, sent it on to Dustin, who asked for a new writer. He demanded that I be fired.

Evans could not find out from Dustin what he thought was wrong with the script. He urged me to intervene. Dustin was now in New York, staying at the Carlyle Hotel. "Talk to Dustin," Evans told me. "You're the only one who can save the project." I was flattered, also stupid enough to believe him. I went to see Dustin, who could not have been more friendly, more pleasant, more voluble, more intelligent, open to discussion on any subject—theater, film, books, politics, anything but my script.

I urged, I cajoled. He would not bite. Nary a word out of him on *Pop-*

eye. We ended up in a screaming match. In my rage, I picked up a script that happened to be lying on the coffee table in the sitting room of the suite where we met. I screamed, "You make me jump through hoops to find out why you won't do my beautiful screenplay, and instead you're going to do this piece of crap?" The piece-of-crap script I was waving in my hand was *Kramer vs. Kramer,* which was to win the Oscar for best picture along with an Oscar for Dustin for best actor.

If Evans had agreed to fire me he could have held on to Dustin. All he had to do was hire the writer of Dustin's choice. Dustin Hoffman was a big movie star. His name had the power to move a picture forward. Most producers, most studios would have fired me the minute the star made known his demands. Instead, Bob Evans, Dustin's good friend, said, "Dustin, I'm the producer of this film, you're the star, Jules is the writer. If you want to be connected to this film, that's the way it's going to be." This is not done in Hollywood.

Moved as I was by Evans's decision to stick by me, I soon realized that without a star we had no financing and no movie. *Popeye* was dead, going nowhere. About nine months later, with me back to self-parody in my weekly strip, Evans called from Hollywood. "Jules, have you seen *Mork and Mindy?*" I immediately understood: Robin Williams, the frenetic and magnetic star of this new TV series, was going to be our Popeye.

The list of directors who said no to *Popeye,* or whom Evans insanely gave me veto power to say no to, included Hal Ashby, Louis Malle, and Jerry Lewis. And just when we had run out of choices, Robert Altman said he wanted to make the film. He said he loved the script, wouldn't change a word. I laughed when Evans reported this to me. I was a friend of Altman's and a fan. As a fan, I knew what was coming.

Now, I loved Altman's work. His films were wildly uneven, but virtually any frame told you that he was pure artist, meaning that he'd throw out my script first thing. Altman didn't believe in scripts except as a necessary evil to get films financed. He didn't much believe in words, he didn't care if you heard the dialogue or not. And he didn't believe in story. But I could imagine no one better to give credibility to Segar's outlandish creations on-screen.

In Altman's repertory company of actors, he had Shelley Duvall, who seemed to me to be the perfect Olive Oyl. I could think of no one better to play Popeye's sweetie, and Altman had discovered her. But Shelley had done something on their last movie to offend him. Bob didn't want her. He made offers to every actress in Hollywood who was not Shelley Duvall: Lily Tomlin, then Goldie Hawn, then God knows who. It was embarrassing. When none of his preferences, which were getting sillier by the minute, were interested, Altman grudgingly accepted Shelley, who gave the best performance in the movie.

The film was shot on the island of Malta, for no reason other than that Altman preferred locations in terms of their distance from the studio brass. If he could have rationalized a shoot on the moon, that's where we would have shot *Popeye*. Malta is a rock. It has little indigenous wood. The script called for Popeye to come ashore in the shantytown of Sweethaven, a ramshackle village of vari-angled, weather-beaten, cartoony dwellings made of wood.

Tons of wood were imported from Canada and the western United States to construct our shantytown. Under the guidance of production designer (and Sweethaven's architect) Wolf Kroeger, it emerged as half village, half roller coaster, not a right angle in sight. Nor did Wolf build it like your usual movie set. This was a real town, no backdrops. One might live in it, bed oneself down if one didn't mind sleeping on a slant. Late at night, after occasional fights with Altman, I would walk down the hill from the motel the cast and crew were staying in and visit the set. I climbed rickety, narrow steps to look out over cramped and deliciously exotic dwellings. High over Sweethaven, I perched myself on porches and decks as substantial as matchsticks that could collapse under me at any moment. What did I care? I was depressed.

Three weeks before I had left for Malta, my girlfriend of six years, Susie Crile, had broken the news that she was opting to be my ex-girlfriend. Susie was a painter. We had met and come together at Yaddo two years after my marriage to Judy had ended. And now, at fifty-one, I was decoupled, a situation I saw little possibility of changing for the rest of my life. That gave me motivation to climb to the top of this fake town without regard to treacherous decks and look down on this wondrous fantasy creation. I was contented, living inside this cartoon I had written, to know, as I knew at seven, that I was happier in comics than in life.

Altman and I had been fighting. I had come to understand that my script was primarily his beard, the cover story that got him financing for the real movie he intended to shoot, the one he was busily improvising on the set, sandwiched between mandatory scenes he was under contract to shoot from my script. This other movie featured the townspeople of Sweethaven, most of them hired as extras, little suspecting that they were going to figure prominently in this second, parallel movie that Altman planned to make while he was shooting *Popeye*. Included among the extras was a company of free-form clowns from San Francisco calling themselves the Pickles Family Circus, featuring Bill Irwin. Altman choreographed madcap stunt improvisations, funny or not so. (He didn't make a distinction.) His plan—if he had a plan—might have been to liven up this script he had signed on for, and was thus obligated to shoot, by inserting scenes that were more to his liking.

Whether Altman seriously intended to kidnap my movie and turn it into a circus act, I can't say. He was an elusive character, rumpled and charm-laden, a twinkling teddy bear who was happy making mischief. When Robert Evans saw the first rough assembly of the film, he went bananas. "It's a mess! It's got no story, it's practically got no Popeye, it's incoherent!" he stammered in the first of several panicky calls from Hollywood to New York.

I assured Evans that Altman, despite the rough cut, had shot most of my script, he had just chosen to bury it, but I didn't think he had burned the footage. I was sure that Evans could dig it up and make Altman restore it to create some semblance of continuity.

I was not privy to Evans's next confrontation with Altman, whether or not they argued or if Altman, having screened his preferred cut (nearly giving his producer a heart attack), affably retreated and agreed to include the story of Popeye in the movie *Popeye*.

Harry Nilsson had written a charming and altogether lovely score that Altman downgraded as he did my script, burying Harry's songs amid dopey bits of business. Evans pressured Altman, and the songs made a comeback. Not everywhere they should have, but enough to make an impression, particularly in the "Sweet Sweethaven" number and—one of the few quiet moments in the film—Shelley Duvall's poignant love song, "He Needs Me."

Robin's great musical moment, on the other hand, was trashed. Harry and I planned a "Singin' in the Rain" breakout number. This was Popeye's big credo song: "I Yam What I Yam." But Altman shot it perversely, with Popeye obscured almost entirely by dancing extras. At the very moment he growls out his defiant song, he is all but offstaged by a phalanx of leaping, twirling, cavorting clowns. The star relegated to a supporting role in Altman's circus. It was as if Gene Kelly's "Singin' in the Rain" number were shot with the camera focused on the puddles.

Evans and Altman eventually cobbled together a final cut that was an odd, engaging, and eccentrically charming film with astonishingly convincing cartoon characters brought so completely to life that one forgot they were cartoons. Half my script never made it to the screen, but what Altman had abandoned in story, he made up for in imagery. The film had (and still has) a glorious look and a sweet nature. The studio thought otherwise, as did the critics. Nonetheless, *Popeye* made money despite Paramount's halfhearted efforts to sabotage it. The studio hated Altman, and didn't much like Evans, and kept under wraps the fact that it was a hit. I didn't find that it had gone into profit until almost ten years later, when I started receiving royalties.

After the film was screened in Chicago, I received a call from a woman who introduced herself as the daughter of E. C. Segar. "I heard you in a couple of interviews saying how you were going to write this film as a testimonial to my father and not do the Max Fleischer animated *Popeye*. And I've heard people say that before and they didn't mean it, so I didn't think you meant it. But I just came from a screening and I want to thank you. It is my father's *Popeye* and this means so much to me."

I hung up and wept.

P*opeye* was my first work for children. My second was for Shelley Duvall's series for Showtime, *Faerie Tale Theatre*. She asked me to write a script for *Puss in Boots*.

It was ten years after *Popeye* that Ed Sorel asked me to write his picture book about old movies. How could I resist? I took two cracks at a story line. Ed, who does not suffer fools gladly, dismissed both versions, not very kindly. I slunk off to Martha's Vineyard for the summer. During the last two weeks of August, I came up with an idea far simpler than anything I had shown him before. I wrote feverishly for ten days, then as soon as I got back to the city I called Ed. I yelled over the phone, "I've got the story. I think it's good!"

There was a long pause at the other end, and at last Ed said, "Um—I guess I should have told you. I decided to write it myself."

Subdued rage. Really well hidden. "When did you decide this?" I asked, feigning calm.

"About two weeks ago," Ed said. In other words, just when I had begun work.

I snarled into the phone, "That's when you should have called me." I hung up on Ed. He called back in ten seconds, stammering apologies. "You do the book. I'll give it up. I won't do it. It's yours!"

His apologies didn't make a dent. "No, it's your idea," I said. "You do your kid's book, I'll do my kid's book. My book will be better than your book."

And so it was spite that decided my unlikely late-life conversion to writing and illustrating children's books. And I owe it all to Ed Sorel. Spite works!

I sat down the next day to write something reminiscent of Ed's idea but different. It wasn't going to be a kid who liked movies but a kid who liked—what did he like? What else did I adore as a kid besides movies? Well, there was old-time radio, but I couldn't see young readers of today, immersed in electronics and technology that I will never understand, displaying an interest in my interest in old-time radio. But comics, what about comics? A boy who loved comics! *Yes!* A book about me as a kid and my love for comics—oops, I wrote that book in 1965, *The Great Comic Book Heroes*. It reinvented the comics career of Will Eisner and helped create a new generation of superhero readers. I wasn't about to do that again. Nor did I want to. No, there had to be something in regard to comics that I could turn into a kid's book . . . Duh! *A boy who drew comics!*

This was not to be an autobiographical novel about a Bronx boy living in the Depression forties. Too close to my own past, too close to Ed Sorel's book. I wanted this to be about me—but as a *fictional* boy cartoonist. I created Jimmy Jibbett. Jimmy thought like me and drew like me when I was ten and a half, but he didn't live in the Bronx. He lived in Upper Montclair, New Jersey, and he lived not in the forties but now, *right now*. Jimmy didn't have two sisters named Mimi and Alice, no way! He had two sisters named Lisi and Susu. And he didn't have Dave and Rhoda as parents. Other than Jimmy's mother's being a fashion designer who told endlessly boring stories in the vain hope of educating her son, his parents were a complete creation.

From the time I began work on the book, I was in love. The same euphoria I felt in writing my plays, I felt in writing my first novel for children. The uncertainty and self-consciousness that plagued the writing of *Harry, the Rat with Women* did not once surface. I wrote steadily every day for four months, half the time not knowing where I was going but curious to find out—and pleasantly surprised when I got there. By the time I finished the novel, it had become clear that I was not writing a one shot. I had stumbled backwards into my next future.

I was sixty-two. The strip was treading water, theater had beaten me to a frazzle, and what I required was a major new obsession.

I decided not to offer *The Man in the Ceiling,* as I called the book, to my agent. Robby Lantz knew nothing about children's books or the children's book market. I knew only a little more. But I was a friend of Maurice Sendak. I called Maurice and told him what I had done. I asked him, "What now?" There was only one man in the business to go to, Maurice said. He gave me the name and phone number of his editor. A half hour later Michael di Capua called, introduced himself, and said, "Maurice says you have a book for me. Can I send a messenger?"

Late the next afternoon, just twenty-four hours after the manuscript was sent to HarperCollins by messenger, Michael was on the phone again. He opened with, "I've been waiting twenty-five years for this book."

The manuscript seemed to be in pretty good shape, it wouldn't need much revision, Michael assured me. We made a date to go over it and four days later, after a two-hour session in his office, I went home and rewrote almost everything.

The tutorial I got from Michael di Capua in our two-hour session was the equivalent of what I learned about screenplays from Mike Nichols in his tutorial on *Carnal Knowledge*. From that point on, I understood the form and what it demanded, the questions that I needed to ask myself before I considered a first draft complete.

A second novel followed on the heels of *The Man in the Ceiling*. This one, *A Barrel of Laughs, a Vale of Tears,* was a fractured fairy tale. And following that, in quick succession, came a series of picture books for young readers where the illustrations dominated and I found myself struggling to learn how to use color as if I knew what I was doing.

In the usual way, I had backed into what became one of the most rewarding and easily the most sentiment-laden career move of my life, creating picture books for young readers that were inspired by the Sunday comics supplements of my childhood: reinventing, for my own purposes, the line, the layouts, the colors, all led by the text—words and pictures— the very form that seduced me at six and seven and eight and led me, first as an aging and then as an old man, back to my masters to learn my craft.

Final illustration from *I Lost My Bear*, 1998

ALICE

Alice, my mother's third child, was a mistake. Rhoda did not want more children. Why should she? After two tries, she got her son, the Jewish prince she desired, in the gender she disapproved of. And four years later, in her forties, she became pregnant with Alice. It's a less risky age today, much riskier then.

One day in the early sixties, at the V.A. hospital in the Bronx, after a visit with my father, who was recovering from his heart attack, Alice, my mother, and I were leaving. As we stood waiting for an elevator, my mother, to whom any male dressed in white was a figure of authority even if he turned out to be a porter, started chatting up a man in white who, for all I knew, might have been a pizza deliveryman. She said, "That's my daughter over there, a wonderful woman. She raises two children, she teaches in school, she never stops. But three times a week she drives all the way in from Long Island to drive me from Queens, no less, up here to the Bronx for a visit to my husband in the veterans hospital. And she has never once complained about the inconvenience. Can you imagine? And just think, before she was born I tried to abort her."

Alice and I stared at each other, text messaging "What the fuck?" with our eyes. My mother, who had hundreds of secrets we weren't old enough to be told, had revealed to a complete stranger (because he wore white) a mind-boggling secret, stated so casually that if the two of us weren't standing there, witness to what the other heard, we might not have believed our ears.

I shook my head at Alice and glared. The glare meant: "Do not, under any circumstances, respond. We will talk about this the second we escape from this maniac."

Her confession to the man in white explained a lot. Family photos from childhood documenting day trips, outings, family vacations were a puzzle to my sisters and me. There would be the three of us in drugstore-developed snapshots: caught in Central Park, the Bronx Zoo, up in Wappinger Falls at a two-week summer bungalow rental. Pictures of the three siblings posing with my mother, my father, assorted animals, dogs, a horse, a goat. And my mother fastidiously labeled, on the bottom of each picture or on the back, the subjects of the photograph. Repeatedly you might read, Jules, Mimi, Ma, Dad, goat, dog, horse, but year after year, picture after picture, the name seldom inscribed—the name aborted—was Alice's.

But it was not that simple. My mother loved Alice. When she was an infant, my mother dubbed her "Lovey" because of her cuddly adorableness. She paid her as much attention and related as many anecdotes about her as she did about Mimi and me. She boasted about her gift for affection, her love for children, her babysitting skills at ten and eleven, boasted later about her daughter the college graduate, the social worker, the history teacher. "Can you imagine? How does she keep so much in her head? Doesn't it give you a headache, Alice, all that thinking?"

At those times when she remembered her, she was proud of her youngest child. She doted to the extent she could (which was hardly at all) on Alice's sons, Bruce and Glenn. The adult Alice was someone she took pride in, a successful teacher and mother, the only one of her children who was a college graduate; this Alice was a recognizable and certifiable entity. But the child Alice, named after Lewis Carroll's immortal creation, stared out at us from early photographs with nothing for a mother to show off about. She was not a cartoonist like her big brother or a talented writer like her bigger sister. This may have left my mother nonplussed, challenged as to what to do with a child without artistic talent. What do you say about such an Alice? Not that much. Maybe it's better to disappear her down a rabbit hole.

Because she was the child my mother overlooked, Alice grew up the least neurotic, married Hal, a musician and social worker from the other side of Stratford Avenue, the 1100 block, across the trolley tracks. They moved to East Meadow, Long Island, and then into a beautiful large home in Huntington. Alice taught American history for twenty years in the Island Trees district under the sway of a McCarthyite superintendent of schools whom my sister agitated against as a union activist.

Presently she is reminisced about on Web sites set up by former students as the teacher who meant the most to them and understood and addressed their problems when no one else bothered to try. Mrs. Korman. Thirty and forty years later, they chat online about my baby sister.

A good thing my mother let her live.

Lovey, 1939

MIMI

Mimi's death was her triumph. Her final act, an embracing, love-filled, bedridden departure before an awestruck family. We were free at last to be with her without having our heads handed to us. She stage-managed her death as she never could her life, telling stories and jokes, exuding cheer. The innate personal magnetism, free now of the explosive temper that, on too many occasions, drove us away. Her death was orchestrated by her as performance art: death as a healer, death as love, death as victory over oneself.

Not only was all forgiven, all was transforming and transcendent. Over the months when her emphysema (which had disabled her for years) reached its final stages, becoming what might, for others, be a death watch, under Mimi's direction it turned into a show. A tribute to the extraordinary courage that evolved out of rebellion, Stalinism, bad behavior, self-destruction, booze, cigarettes, drugs . . . In the memorable words of Don Marquis's Mehitabel the cat, "Wotthehell, wotthehell, there's a dance in the old dame yet!"

At the end, Mimi rose to heights she never managed during a life that tricked her out of most everything she considered her due. She had never made an effort to work in journalism or to fulfill her earliest ambition and write fiction. She never became a teacher, though she could have become one (and been beloved like Alice); she didn't exploit her ample gifts or extraordinary charm to mark out a career that would have rewarded her, in reality, with the power and influence she imagined for herself. "I should have run for mayor!" she regularly announced, often drunk and under the influence.

Her life was bravado without backbone, her death was courage without grief, a refusal of grief, a celebration of herself as she most wanted to be: the center of attention, an example to us all.

Her doctor took me aside moments after her death: "Your sister was an inspiration to me."

I write this twenty-one years after her death. Mimi died at sixty-two, and I am now eighty. She was my older sister. Imagine.

Mimi, 1942

VOICELESS

The *Voice* had changed. By 1998, it was more of a lifestyle paper, not a writer's paper. It had drifted into a smug and nasty pop-funk-gay-crypto-counterculture paper. Its old-guard politicos, Nat Hentoff (the Rabbi) and Wayne Barrett (the Muckraker), were, as ever, holding up their end. But the paper resisted reading, certainly from my generation of *Voice* readers, and, in fact, I knew few people who referred to it or admitted to reading it. Including me.

"You're still great," I'd be assured by friends and others who hadn't read me in five years.

The *Voice* had been sold and resold and, along the way, traded in its soul for attitude. I had wanted out for some years now, but the question was, Where would I go? Who would have me? Where would my living come from?

After my first eight years on the paper without making a dime, I had gone into Dan Wolf's office and demanded that he start paying me. The *Voice* had begun paying some of its contributors about a year earlier, but not me. Nonetheless, Dan looked at me astonished. My request clearly made no sense to him. "But you're a mandarin!" he told me. It was my opinion that mandarins shouldn't be penalized. As a mandarin, I should get paid like everyone else.

Pay me they did. Grudgingly. And over the years, with the raises that were built into collective bargaining contracts negotiated with District 65, the *Voice*'s union, I became, out of longevity, the *Voice*'s highest-paid contributor. For one cartoon a week, I was making $75,000 a year. It wasn't irrational to wonder what other newspaper would offer that kind of money.

As I was aging, the *Voice* was youthening up. I understood that and had been concerned for some time that they might consider getting rid of me. So I had begun to do some looking around. I would have switched if I could have found someone who wanted me for the money the *Voice* was paying. My friend Pete Hamill was now the editor of the *Daily News*. Pete said the *News* would love to hire me but they couldn't afford what the *Voice* paid. *Newsday* said the same thing. So did the *New York Observer.*

With my friends Judith Goldman and Davis Weinstock I talked over the idea of publishing my own subscription-driven biweekly four-page broadsheet, an overambitious endeavor for a man approaching seventy. I would expand into new features, serial strips, caricature, reportage, essays. It would quadruple the work I now did. The idea was pure fantasy, the production figures far too daunting. While I found the *Voice* in its present incarnation an embarrassment, I could find no other publication interested enough in my cartoon to pay me $75,000 a year.

So I stuck around for Don Forst, the *Voice*'s new editor, the latest in a string of new editors, to call and take me to lunch. Always a bad sign. Forst was an old newspaper hand, a former editor of *Newsday,* a wry, charming, and agreeable fellow. Forst had been brought in to cut costs. I was one of the costs he and publisher David Schneiderman had decided to cut.

But in the act of firing me Forst came on as my fan. "We love your cartoon, I want to keep you in the paper, but I can hire two reporters for the money I'll save cutting you off staff. I'd like to buy you in syndication, and that way you can go on appearing."

It took me over an hour to process my way through Forst's fawning and flattery, then to realize that the deal he was offering was a 75 percent pay cut. This charming fellow had made me an offer I was meant to refuse.

I was sixty-nine, with a wife and two children to support. Eight years earlier I had fired myself from the theater. *Elliot Loves,* a play about relationships and the near-impossible struggle that two attractive and likable people must go through to not give up on each other, was, I thought, my best play. But it was brutally panned by the critics and ran less than a month. It was a Mike Nichols production, beautifully staged (Mike at the top of his game), so it was one of the few times that the reviews came as a shock. The feedback had been incredible. Preview audiences at the Promenade, a wonderful theater just a block from my apartment, were talking Hit, Hit, Hit!

John Guare, who had his own play in previews at Lincoln Center, came to a preview and between acts sought me out to rave. The cast was led by three remarkable young actors who, in a few years, everyone would know: Christine Baranski, Oliver Platt, and David Hyde Pierce. I felt sorry for my friend John. I knew that the critics were unlikely to approve of two plays opening within a week of each other. Bad critical form. They were honor bound to destroy one, just to keep their hands in. From the reactions we were getting on *Elliot Loves,* it seemed certain to be poor John's play, *Six Degrees of Separation,* that would suffer.

As I write this nineteen years later, *Six Degrees* is still running somewhere, everywhere, and *Elliot Loves,* a play that night after night thrilled me as I stood in the back of the house, has vanished into ignominy and shame. It took me ten years to get over it. Actually, I got past it, not over it.

Following the death blows by Frank Rich and company, I swore I was through with theater. I would no longer indulge myself as a pro bono playwright. I had mouths to feed. I had pride to feed. Never again!

The children's books started coming out as my alternative to theater. For the next decade new picture books and novels were published every twelve to eighteen months. I surprised myself by backing into this new obsession, so full of unexpected rewards. The books made money! (I never made money in theater.) They were well reviewed! ('Nuff said.) Critics liked them, readers liked them, I loved writing and drawing them! No suffering, no anguish, no rejection. How can one call this an art form?

The very nature of this new work released a playfulness, a silliness in approach that I had never tried out on my audiences before. Silliness and playfulness are not the way you write and draw about civil rights and Vietnam and the duplicity of our leaders. They were a side of myself that readers of my cartoons and books had seldom seen. Theatergoers could point to only two of my plays, *The White House Murder Case* and *Knock Knock,* as examples of unrestrained wackiness. But wackiness was now to be my job description.

For more than thirty years, I had labored, on and off, to overthrow the government. And in ways I had never intended, liberal government had been overthrown. And what we got instead was considerably worse. And seemingly popular. It was time to reappraise my agenda, if not my politics, to put politics behind me, switch sights, and opt for a little fun.

The *Voice* strips still gave me pleasure but after forty years were little more than a weekly twitch. A couple or three days before deadline, I had to come up with an idea, stop whatever else I was doing, and start scrambling. My professional life, for as long as I can remember, has maintained itself as a system of avoidances. Whatever I am supposed to be doing, I write or draw something else. I finish or run out of patience on the work at hand, so I segue into career choice number two or three. After exhausting my patience with two and/or three, I begin the cycle all over again. Eventually, in no particular order, everything I am obliged to do is finished.

It took me a full day to acknowledge the anger and resentment that came in the aftermath of my lunch with Don Forst. The editor of the *Voice* had been so amiable, so convivial, so admiring, that getting fired seemed like a secondary byproduct of an otherwise good time. I felt almost caddish when I called him the next day and asked for a settlement. I had in my forty-two years at the *Voice* brought more attention to the paper than any other contributor. I had received more honors than any other contributor—a Pulitzer, a George Polk award, the Newspaper Guild Page One award—so many awards but no settlement. I asked that my health coverage be extended for ten years (hoping to settle for five). I was given six months, until the end of the year.

Nor did it matter what else I asked. By the end of a couple of phone calls (none with publisher Schneiderman, whom I had thought of as a friend; no contact at all), it had become clear that mine was a no-fault dismissal. For *Voice* management, the sooner that I was disappeared, the better.

I called my friend David Halberstam and gave him the news. David, whose outrage was something to witness as long as you were not on the receiving end, called Joe Lelyveld, then the executive editor of the *Times*.

Lelyveld assigned a reporter and the next day, page 1 of the Metro section ran a feature story about my dismissal. It was not the objective reporting that the *New York Times* is noted for. In the story, I was presented as Jimmy Stewart; the *Voice* was Satan. At Halberstam's further suggestion, the *Times* commissioned me to draw a cartoon on my firing. This, too, was not objective: in this case, I was Bob Cratchit, the *Voice* was Scrooge.

My friend David made two other calls, one to Graydon Carter, the editor of *Vanity Fair*, whom he got to put me on as a contributing editor at $2,500 a month. The other call was to Howell Raines, then editorial page editor of the *Times*.

The next day Howell Raines called me in for a chat. We met in his office surrounded by framed front pages of the *New York Times* from the past hundred years: the *Titanic* sinking, World War I declared, the stock market collapse in 1929, Pearl Harbor, the A-bomb . . . rather impressive, but none of them about me.

Howell's approach was leisurely, dry, and deferential. It was couched in the courtly good manners natural to his Southern upbringing—mild condescension masked by outrageous flattery. Fine with me. Don Forst's flattery was a mask for hostility and contempt. I preferred Howell's way of handling me. "I know that we may not be what you're used to or go as far as you might like, but if you're willing to take a chance on us, we'd like you to contribute a page of op-art to the *Times* on a regular basis, say once a month, for a fee of one thousand dollars whether we print it or not."

Not to be believed! Four days after the *Voice* fired me, the *New York Times* was offering to put me on staff as its one and only resident cartoonist.

Years earlier, when I was a boy, the *Times* ran an innocuous and deliberately forgettable Sunday strip in the Week in Review section. But never, not ever, had they put a cartoonist on a par with their op-ed columnists. I was being offered unprecedented freedom in a newspaper that, for all its history, was too haughty to run comic strips, so much so that my father, at the height of my early success, enjoyed putting me in my place by saying, "I won't believe you're really famous until they print you in the *New York Times*." That remark had become family lore. Alice, remembering my father's barbed jest, choked up when I told her my news.

I was reborn. The *Times* ran me at a third of a page, then a half page. In the following year they ran me in two columns down the entire length of a page. This was exposure to die for! And I was being talked about again, responded to as I had not been since my early years at the *Voice*.

Within three months I had made back the $75,000 a year that I had lost with the *Village Voice*. In addition to my work for the *New York Times* and *Vanity Fair*, I was appointed at $35,000 to a Senior Fellowship at Columbia University's National Arts Journalism Program. It was headed by my friend Michael Janeway, former editor of the *Boston Globe*, and later dean of Northwestern's Medill School of Journalism. My duties for the semester were to meet twice a week with students of Columbia's Graduate School of Journalism and instruct them in the business of fame and failure.

I was pitied, I was a victim, I was in clover. Had Schneiderman and Forst offered me a reasonable settlement and continued my health care for five years, it would have effectively ended my career. By behaving like jerks, they gave me a new lease on life: new offers, new self-confidence. Who could have dreamed that by the simple act of being themselves, they would so profoundly bless my life.

Roger Rosenblatt called. Roger was an old friend who did everything in journalism and did it with extraordinary flair and grace. Later, he would go on to write satiric and hilarious plays and, in his spare time, two hyster-ically funny novels. In typical Roger manner, wherein he acts gruff, thus thinking that no one will take him for a softy, he said, "I only want to know one thing. What's your health insurance situation?"

"At the end of the year, I don't have any," I told him.

"Now you do," said Roger. "I'm starting an MFA writing program at Southampton College and you're going to teach out here."

I was grateful. I was confused. "Teach what?"

"Anything you want," snapped Roger.

"How often?"

"Once a week. We can thrash out the details later. Will you stop both-ering me?"

"When do I start?"

"Anytime you want to start. Why are you asking me these idiotic questions?"

"This year?"

"This year, next year, any year you like," Roger said.

"What about the insurance?"

"As soon as you say yes, the insurance starts."

"Even if I don't teach for a year?"

"Yes," Roger said.

"Roger," I said. "You know I didn't go to college."

"Obviously you're overqualified." He sounded as if his patience was wearing thin. I didn't want him mad at me. I said yes.

THE PROFESSOR OF I DON'T KNOW WHERE I'M GOING WITH THIS BUT LET'S FIND OUT

Roger's offer to teach at Southampton College (now Stony Brook Southampton) backed me into one of the joys of my working life. My class is called "Humor and Truth." During the spring semester I teach every Wednesday for three hours. I jitney out to Southampton, reading or rereading student papers, making notes, and deciding, on the basis of what I've read in their papers or that morning's *New York Times,* the theme of the class for that day.

The class is extempore, driven purely by instinct. As much as I try to prepare a day or two before, the class doesn't begin to take shape until I take the walk from the Times Square subway station to Fortieth Street and Third Avenue, where I pick up the jitney for the hour-and-three-quarter bus ride to Southampton. By the time the bus arrives, I have plotted my context, an overview from which most of my comments will derive.

The students are local, but they have been everywhere and done everything: from bartending to massage therapy to teaching preschool to litigating lawsuits to copyediting at the *New York Times* to writing sports for *Newsday* to, God help me, modern dance.

The size of the class has varied over the years, from as many as seventeen students to as few as ten. For my get-acquainted assignment, I ask them to write 1,500 to 2,000 words (they always write longer) in the first person on an injustice done to them. They are to write the story lightly, in a humorous mode. Then they are to go at it a second time, also in the first person, but this go-round it will be a table-pounding rant.

The second assignment, a week later, is to revisit the same event but in the voice and from the perspective of the other party, justifying with humor and rant *that* position.

I see it as my job, week after week, to throw them curveballs, to force them to write in voices that don't come naturally or easily. I encourage them to try what they don't know how to do, take risks, and not worry. And definitely not to think of writing pieces to please the professor. Playing it safe is the only way to go wrong. Each semester I start off with this statement: "My class is un-American. I give you license to fail."

They have license, as well, to speak openly in class, commenting on one another's papers, one another's comments, my comments. Often (sadly, too often) my students will pick up on things I've missed. In too many ways, they can be more astute than the professor who thought he had figured everything out on the jitney.

I cover my ass with infinite charm. I am funny but not a jokester. I am the professor but not the center of attention. The students' work is the center of attention. The class is solely about work, and I talk to my students, repeatedly, about how they must separate their egos from the work under consideration.

Judgment of their work is not a judgment on them or their worth. I warn them that if they turn the built-in problems of an assignment into a statement of their own inadequacy, they will have sprung a trap on themselves that trades the difficulties of process for the more seductive diversions of self-examination.

I prod them to experiment with voices distinct from their own. In the course of the semester, they will write essays, monologues, observations from a variety of angles and in changing voices. At the end of the semester, they write a one-act play.

I urge them to work, if they can manage it, with a sense of play. Writing, I insist, is a form of play. It is serious fun. As far as I'm concerned, if it doesn't end up as fun, why bother? The job of a writer is too hard, too full of disappointment and failure, too calculated for rejection. If it can't be fun, not all the success in the world is worth it.

Village Voice, March 5, 1978

BEDTIME FOR MEMOIR

I backed into fatherhood with all the reluctance of a man who knows what he thinks but not what he wants. I thought I wanted privacy when what I wanted was children interrupting my work. I thought I wanted independence when what I wanted was responsibility. I thought I feared commitment, but I pursued it. I thought I needed peace and quiet when all along it was confusion that I needed. I needed whatever it took for a shy boy to grow into socialized manhood. So in order to pull myself out of boyhood into manhood, I needed children, the ultimate test, those carriers of chaos.

Whatever one's plans, children screw them up. Whatever one's routine, they upend it. Whatever one's deadline—children are death to deadlines. They play Russian roulette with schedules. Ever the contrarian, I found myself far happier ensnared in the muddle of child rearing and child survival than without.

You must realize by now that, for me, *happiness* is a term of ambivalence. It's entangled with so many other feelings, among them rage. For example, Kate Feiffer on the Vineyard back in the early seventies. It is ten in the evening, Kate is nine, she is upstairs in bed (finally). I am a single parent, having walked out on my marriage two years earlier. I have driven Kate to horseback riding lessons at Pond View Farm, I have driven her to the library and the playground a block up from the library. She likes the airport playground better, so I drive her there, only ten minutes away, near the great little diner that specializes in malteds and frappes. I drive her home and we go next door to Seth Pond, where all three of my children swam almost every day of every summer into their teens. I pan-broiled her a hamburger, which she liked, accompanied by vegetables, which she ignored. I played a game of Aggravation with her, which I loved, especially when I knew I could beat her and didn't. Then I put her to bed.

It was *my* time now. Out on our screened porch, reclining on the glider that is a major part of my summer happiness, relaxing for the first time that day, smoking a Monte Cristo smuggled in from Cuba, looking out at the first stars and the rising moon, a half-empty glass of Scotch in my hand, a fresh one soon promised. Kate's day is done and I am relieved, also exhausted, but pleasantly so.

A call from upstairs. "Daddy!"

"What is it, honey?" She is supposed to be asleep.

"Come up here!" shouts my darling daughter.

"Go to sleep, honey!" She *was* asleep when I left her.

"I need you!"

"I'm resting!"

"Daddy, I need you! Please come up here!"

"No, you come down here!"

"It's important!"

"If it's so important, come down and tell me!"

"I can't, I'm in bed!"

Now, if you replay this scene with essentially the same dialogue repeated with minor variations for five or ten minutes, what an outsider would perceive might be a congenial, amusing family moment reminiscent of that old TV series *The Waltons*. Sweet, homespun Americana.

But that would be on the surface. Inside my head resounded a frenzied Bernard Herrmann score from a Hitchcock thriller: boom dum-de-dum, boom boom crash mangle kazam tear limb from limb zap boom dum-de-kaboom!

The contrast between what lay on the surface—this sweet, banal encounter between long-suffering father and persistent but adorable daughter—and what was buried in the subtext: an urge to run up there, scream, yell, jump up and down in fury. But instead of pounding my beloved daughter, I'd pound the walls of her bedroom with my fists. "Take that, you wall! And that! How do you like that one, wall? Plenty more where that came from!" That moment went into my play *Grown Ups.* It got laughs of recognition (humor, the great accommodator).

Fifteen years later, Halley Feiffer at four interrupts me at work in my studio. She wants something or needs something or has lost something. I have learned not to be irritated or impatient with these interruptions. I myself interrupt my work, to do absolutely nothing, more times in the course of a day than any of my children. But in response to interruptions, I have developed a strategy, my Creative Defense Initiative (CDI). It is a child-interruption device that I have metaphorically installed in my head. It is a pause button that I activate the moment I am waylaid by a child while in the middle of writing a scene, drawing an illustration, or trying to finish this memoir.

I push the pause button. I deal with the child. It can take up to a quarter of an hour. Once she is pacified, satisfied, deflected, detoured, slickly maneuvered by this old hand at fathering to wander off down a path where her soon-to-be abandonment is agreeable to both of us, I return to my desk, deactivate the pause button, finish the drawing, the scene, or this sentence.

My life is like a comic strip: short breaks between panels, the briefest of breaks. Each break comes from a child stepping between me and my process. I am so used to it, I hardly ever scream anymore.

Katie, Halley, and Julie have all sat in my lap at my drawing table, playing comic strip in exactly the same way I play it alone for real. I'd compose a first panel, draw it, and write in the dialogue. My daughter would come up with a second panel and either draw it herself or dictate the scene and the dialogue she imagined. I took it from there and wrote and drew a third panel, she did the next panel, and so on and on until we had finished the page or the story.

Part of the fun was stumping each other, coming up with ideas for the next panel that defied follow-up—the introduction of monsters, dinosaurs, impending disasters that could only lead to hopeless conclusions—and yet we managed always to maneuver ourselves out of our own traps into usable, if not plausible, endings.

My daily routine for my second children's novel, *A Barrel of Laughs, a Vale of Tears,* came out of this game with my children. I started work in the morning, writing all day until I put my hero, Prince Roger, into a situation from which he could not possibly escape. And then I quit for the day and resumed the next morning, having overnight devised a way out for myself and Roger. This took me through another day of writing until nightfall, a new trap set, no solution in sight until the following morning.

The inspiration my children represent in terms of my present line of work is so overarching that I often mean to ask my accountant if I can deduct them as a business expense. Following three-and-a-half-year-old Halley around our West End Avenue apartment, I can't help but notice the absence of even the vaguest linear process. No action necessarily connects to what proceeds or follows it. A stuffed bear exists for the purpose of seating her Barbie on its lap until it becomes more interesting to pull a leg off the Barbie and try to fit it onto another Barbie as a third leg, and then both Barbies are forsaken for a toy freight train car on which it might be possible to seat one of the Barbies but not the stuffed bear, so a wrestling match ensues between child and bear to teach one or the other to sit properly on the freight car.

Bear and toy freight car are abandoned for blocks that are made into a tunnel that Barbie hides in, challenging me to find her. I find her too quickly, which is my mistake. The price I am made to pay is to dig out more blocks from under Halley's bed in order for her to build a better tunnel, an idea which is soon abandoned in favor of a skyscraper of blocks (forget the tunnel), ascending in a single wavering row headed for the ceiling.

My insane desire to scream "No, no!" to my child, to advise her to complete one task before starting another, led me straight to my earliest picture book, *I Lost My Bear,* in which a blond little girl (Halley) loses her favorite stuffed bear and while anxiously searching for it completely forgets what she's looking for because there are so many distractions that compete for her attention.

On a family holiday in the Dominican Republic, I watched Maddy, my two-year-old granddaughter (Kate's child), at the shallow end of the swimming pool instruct her father, Chris, on how to hold and assist her as she made him over into an edifice and before my eyes composed an instructional manual on how to climb your father from his feet to his shoulders. "That's a book!" I said to myself at my end of the pool.

A year later, when I showed the first color proofs of *The Daddy Mountain* to my family at the dinner table, nine-year-old Julie became very silent (no reaction at all), then looked at me wounded and accusing, and quietly said, "You did a book about her before you did a book about me."

I was staggered in the way one is when one thinks one is the bearer of glad tidings and discovers—not so fast!—it's the opposite. Jenny reacted first: "Julie, that was a mistake, Daddy is very sorry, and his next book is going to be about you." I was six months into this memoir. What a relief to have to write about something else. The next day, I opened a discussion on the subject. "Julie, my next book is going to be about you, but I don't have any ideas. Do you have an idea?" Julie did not pause for a moment. "How about a girl with a zoo in her room?"

This from a child who was the owner of two hamsters, three fish, a turtle, a hermit crab, and two cats, Timmy and Jessie. Timmy and Jessie had preceded Julie into our lives. They were given to Halley as birthday presents. Halley's interest in cats didn't last long, no more than a year or two, and then the cats—Jessie, black with white markings, and Timmy, a brown tabby—had to wait till Julie came along to receive their proper due. Julie adores animals. She talked of becoming a vet, and she talked about the animals her friends had for pets, mostly their dogs, big dogs, little dogs, how much fun they were, how much she wanted a dog. I did my best to avoid the subject.

"How about a girl with a zoo in her room?"

It was a perfect subject for a kid's book. And the idea came out of Julie's phrasing. If she had said, "How about a girl who loves animals?" I wouldn't have had the hook to hang a book on. If she had said, "How about a girl who wants a dog and her father won't buy her one?" the self-laceration involved would be too problematic to turn into a book. But . . . a girl with a zoo in her room?

A Room with a Zoo! With a title like that, the story poured out. It was Julie's voice that I channeled onto the page—and every member of our family, all of us, appears in fictionalized episodes (some almost true) that make up this book I was guilt-tripped into writing and that I'm as proud of as anything I have ever done.

My children backed me into this joyously accidental career, which has reintroduced me to the Sunday supplements of my youth. I have volumes of them, going back over fifty years. When it comes time to illustrate a new story, I think, "Which master will I steal from now?" Winsor McCay (*Little Nemo*)? Frank King (*Gasoline Alley*)? Percy Crosby (*Skippy*)? Cliff Sterrett (*Polly and Her Pals*)? I browse through my comics collection, grateful to my children for inspiring my move from satirist to children's book author, taking me back to the best part of boyhood—on the floor on all fours. I followed the funnies, never suspecting that they would lead me down this crooked, uncharted, barely navigable trail. Good thing I don't have a sense of direction. I might have given up.

Sidewalk poster for New-York Historical Society retrospective, 2003

AND IN CONCLUSION

Jenny asked not to be in this book, so mostly she's not. But her presence is everywhere—like Conan Doyle's dog that didn't bark.

Her influence on me has been remarkable since the minute we met, which was by way of a phone call from New York to Martha's Vineyard in August of 1980, when she introduced herself as Jenny Allen, a reporter for *Life* magazine. She wanted to come up and interview me for an article timed for the release of the movie *Popeye*.

I made a joke about this being a mistake, screenwriters did not get interviewed. But despite my banter and her banter, her voice came through on the phone as vital, funny, sexy, and so female that, then and there, a crush developed, put on hold until I was able to get my first look at her, which took place ten days later when she flew to the Vineyard during a rainstorm and was delivered by taxi soaking wet to my door.

Instantly, I fell in love.

She altered my mind in so many ways, most importantly about having more children. Without Halley and Julie, my life would be unimaginable. Without Jenny, my life would be nonexistent. So I apologize to my readers that you haven't met her in this book.

If she had been included, you would have found that she is brilliant and entertaining and writes like a dream. Her essays are serious, amusing, and unpredictable. She performs stand-up comedy on a personal level that's both intimate and full of laughs—and without telling a single joke. She does an evening-length performance piece about her life and her family that's moving and hilarious. Her humor embraces audiences in a hands-on, unsentimental way. And audiences return the favor. They love her.

We have done one book together, *The Long Chalkboard and Other Stories,* three urban fables that she wrote and that I laid out and illustrated.

That seems to be much of what I do these days: I work in the company store.

Kate, my eldest, now writes picture books for children that are like no one else's, charming, witty, and infectious—and fictively autobiographical. Her first, *Double Pink,* was about Maddy, my granddaughter, who is also the protagonist of my own book *The Daddy Mountain.* Not bad for a kid who wasn't yet seven.

Kate's second book, *Henry the Dog with No Tail,* is about her Australian shepherd, Henry, and his envy of dogs who have a tail while Henry does not. Our second book together was *Which Puppy?* about a contest among dogs (and other animals) to pick a puppy for the Obamas. I am about to start work on our third book together, *My Side of the Car.* In the meantime, Kate has turned out five other books with other illustrators. And she's written and directed an hour-long documentary called *Matzo and Mistletoe,* a personal essay about being raised a nominal Jew by a family so secular that they forgot to inform her of her Jewishness until she was six years old. Can you believe such people exist?

Halley, twenty years younger than Kate and my first child with Jenny, is an actor (*actress* seems to have fallen out of usage). She is also a playwright and, when opportunities arise, a theater director. She is brilliant, but I shouldn't have to tell you that, because if you're bothering to read this book you may already know a little something about my family. She has been featured in several films, among them *The Squid and the Whale, Margot at the Wedding, The Messenger, Fighting Fish,* and *Gentlemen Broncos.* Off-Broadway she's appeared in Eric Bogosian's *SubUrbia, Election Day, None of the Above, Some Americans Abroad,* and *Still Life.* Her father takes it for granted that someday she's going to be a star and make a pile of money and retire him from having to write more memoirs.

Julie is ten years younger than Halley and came about as a result of Halley's announcement when she was eight that she was tired of being an only child. So we went out and adopted Julie, whom we found through an adoption agency in Texas.

I held her in the palms of my hands when she was a week old. Everything she has now—her beauty, her intelligence, her wit, her strong humor—all of it was there looking up at me from the palms of my hands. As good as I imagined her then, the reality is better.

Julie is the one whom I denied a dog until she was old enough to take care of it by herself. I had lived too long and had spent too much time with dogs to want to deal with another one now that I was in my seventies. So here I am, at eighty, about to walk Lily, an adorable one-eyed Chihuahua mixed breed whom three times a day I take to Riverside Park. Yes, I gripe about it but always have a good time. (Lily coexists with Daisy, who came into our household as a kitten whom Lily adopted. Daisy acts as if Lily is her mother. Lily does not discourage the notion.)

I walk Lily, as I said, three times a day, something I swore I would not do. Much of what I do is what I swore I would not do. That is the best part of my life.

Once I believed that if you saw that the glass was half empty, you did your best to fill it, in the hope and understanding that you would not be alone in this effort. Now I believe that if the glass is half empty, more of us than not will do our best to keep it that way. I grumble about this. I grumble about what this country has turned into in the twenty-first century. This is not my century. I am a fogey. And I am proud. I enjoy my dotage. The current year is my favorite year until next year, which I am determined to enjoy even more.

I don't enjoy our politics (which are an embarrassment), or our media (which are our shame), or what I see us becoming. Whatever I see and can't stand I hope is a sign of age, not acuity . . .

S top the presses!

Since I wrote the above in the winter of 2008, we've had an impossible election and Barack Obama is president. The first president I've been smitten with since 1932! I have renewed my citizenship (spiritually revoked four years earlier). Now I am an American again. I am proud. I am riding a pony. I think of my children, and grandchildren to come, and my heart swells. I drink from a half-empty glass of water, but with growing optimism. Never has water tasted so good. Never has the day loomed so bright. Yes, I know everything can go wrong. I know that my hopes can crash and burn, as they have so often in the past. But I have rediscovered illusion. Once I have illusion back, it can carry me far. My pony breaks into a gallop. I stare at my glass in wonder. No matter how fast I go or how much I drink, it doesn't lose any water. My glass is half full.

April 2009

LAST PANELS

The end.

The book is over! Now you know everything.

Well— close to everything.

Some things I just didn't get around to.

Or left out on purpose.

Now this is my cartoon voice which is different from my writers' voice...

Or maybe you don't think so.

This book was supposed to be mainly about my work life—

O.K, I've got a lot of personal stuff in here—

But mostly in how it relates to my work life.

At least, I hope so.

Have you noticed my cartoon voice is more ambivalent than my writers voice?

Some stuff I left out on purpose, like I said.

Susie Crile...

He made what was hard look easy.

And that's been a model to me my whole working life.

Now the great thing about being a cartoonist—

is that you can draw yourself as anyone you like.

So excuse me —

As I finish my dance.

ACKNOWLEDGMENTS

Howard Kaminsky nudged me into this memoir and, before I had a word written, got Nan Talese involved, thereby wrenching me out of my comfortable existence as cartoonist, playwright, and children's book author and illustrator.

Overnight I found myself transformed into an overcommitted, over-anxious memoirist who thought and thought, and remembered next to nothing. However, memory returned. Narrative and structure followed, aided, as always, by my longtime friend and editor Michael di Capua who knows what I'm trying to say and tells me when I've failed to say it. Painlessly.

And after Michael did his job, Nan Talese and Ronit Feldman did more of the same. Thank you all for helping. Thank you all for leaving me alone, finally.

And to my old friend Harry Hamburg who over half a century ago rescued me from basic training and has come to my rescue again by putting down reminiscences so bizarre that, without Harry's witness, I wouldn't blame you for thinking I made them up.

And to Dana Wyles, my typist of many years, who had to transcribe my audio-tape dictation from my handwritten manuscript (I never learned to type)—and, on those occasions when she couldn't make out what I was saying, invariably improved my language.

Onward to my children and grandchild whose presence is a daily reminder that I have a wonderful life, although I take pains in this book not to show it.

And to Jenny who got sick, got better, created a brilliant performance piece out of her illness, and, through her courage and example, permitted us all to breathe normally again and return to our labors—of which this book is one part.

ILLUSTRATION CREDITS

Page 166, top: Saul Steinberg, *Untitled* (detail), 1954–55. Ink on paper. Originally published in *The New Yorker*, February 12, 1955. © The Saul Steinberg Foundation/Artists Rights Society (ARS), New York.

Page 166, bottom: © 1950 William Steig.

Page 168: André François illustration from *The Half-Naked Knight*, 1958. © Artists Rights Society (ARS), New York/ADAGP, Paris.

Page 223: "Illustration" by Jules Feiffer, copyright © 1961 by Jules Feiffer. Copyright renewed 1989 by Jules Feiffer, from *The Phantom Tollbooth* by Norton Juster, illustrated by Jules Feiffer. Used by permission of Random House Children's Books, a division of Random House, Inc.

Page 314, top left: © Roddy McDowall

Page 314, top right: © Meg Handler

Page 390: © John Olson

Page 404, both photos: © Mary Ellen Mark

A NOTE ABOUT THE AUTHOR

Jules Feiffer's Pulitzer-winning comic strip ran for forty-two years in the *Village Voice* and one hundred other papers. His cartoons have been collected into nineteen books and have appeared in the *New York Times*, the (London) *Observer,* *The New Yorker, Esquire, Playboy,* and the *Nation.* He is the author of a wide range of additional creative work, including the Obie Award–winning play *Little Murders,* the screenplay for *Carnal Knowledge,* and the Oscar-winning short animation *Munro.* Other works include the plays *Knock Knock* (a Tony Award nominee) and *Grown Ups*; the novels *Harry, the Rat with Women* and *Ackroyd*; the screenplays *Popeye* and *I Want to Go Home* (winner of the best screenplay award at the Venice Film Festival); the children's books *The Man in the Ceiling, Bark,* and *George;* and the illustrations for *The Phantom Tollbooth* and *Which Puppy?* by his daughter Kate, and *Some Things Are Scary* by Florence Parry Heide. Feiffer is a professor at Stony Brook Southampton. Previously he taught at the Yale School of Drama, Northwestern University, and Dartmouth College. He has been a senior fellow in Columbia University's National Arts Journalism Program. Feiffer is a member of the Dramatists Guild Council and has been elected to the American Academy of Arts and Letters.